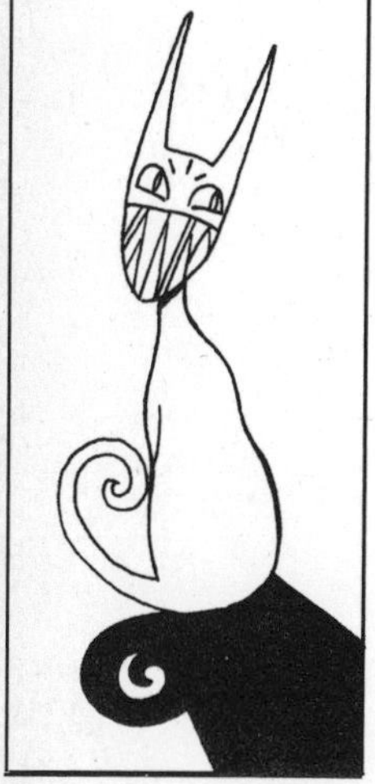

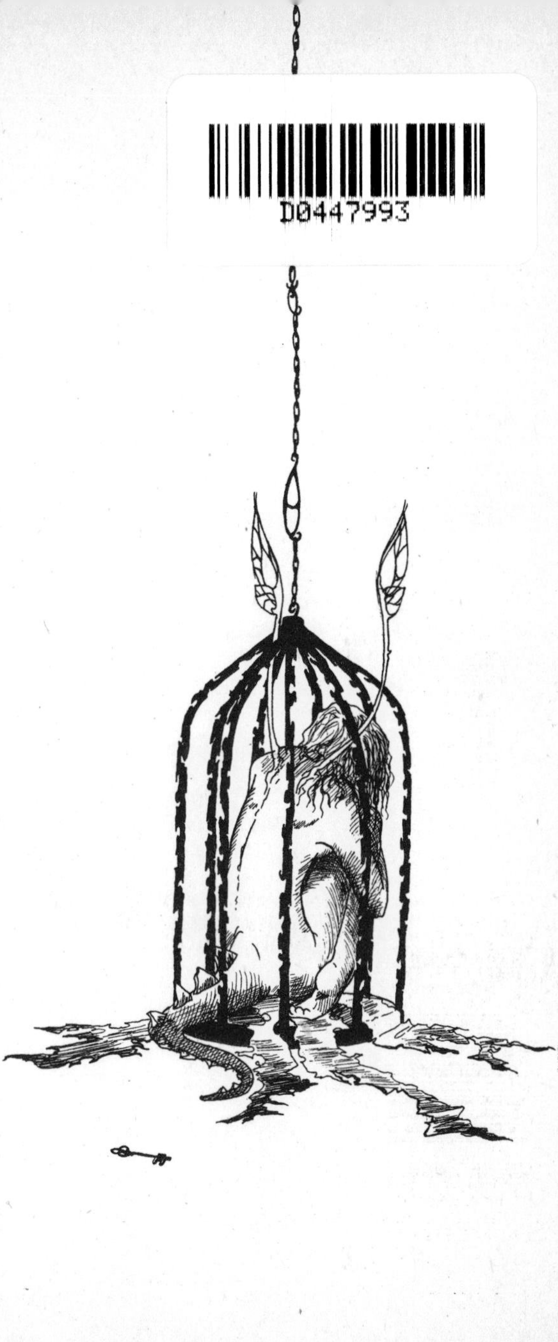

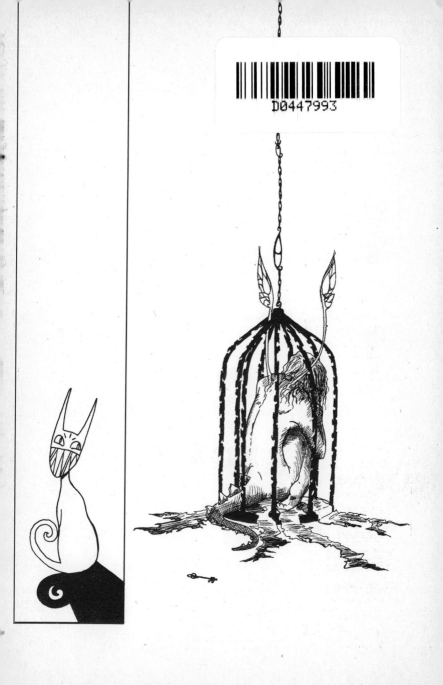

Bizenghast Volume 2
Created by M. Alice LeGrow

Development Editors - Jodi Bryson & Aaron Suhr
Layout and Lettering - Rob Steen
Toning - Catarina Sarmento
Production Artist - Erika Terriquez
Cover Artist - M. Alice LeGrow
Cover Design - Al-Insan Lashley

Editor - Lillian Diaz-Przybyl
Digital Imaging Manager - Chris Buford
Managing Editor - Lindsey Johnson
VP of Production - Ron Klamert
Publisher - Mike Kiley
Editor-in-Chief - Rob Tokar
President and C.O.O. - John Parker
C.E.O. and Chief Creative Officer - Stuart Levy

A **TOKYOPOP** Manga

TOKYOPOP Inc.
5900 Wilshire Blvd. Suite 2000
Los Angeles, CA 90036

E-mail: info@TOKYOPOP.com
Come visit us online at www.TOKYOPOP.com

ISBN: 1-59532-744-4
First TOKYOPOP printing: June 2006
10 9 8 7 6 5 4 3 2 1
Printed in the USA

Volume 2

By M. Alice LeGrow

HAMBURG // LONDON // LOS ANGELES // TOKYO

Bizenghast

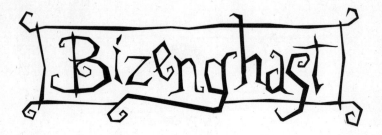

Contents

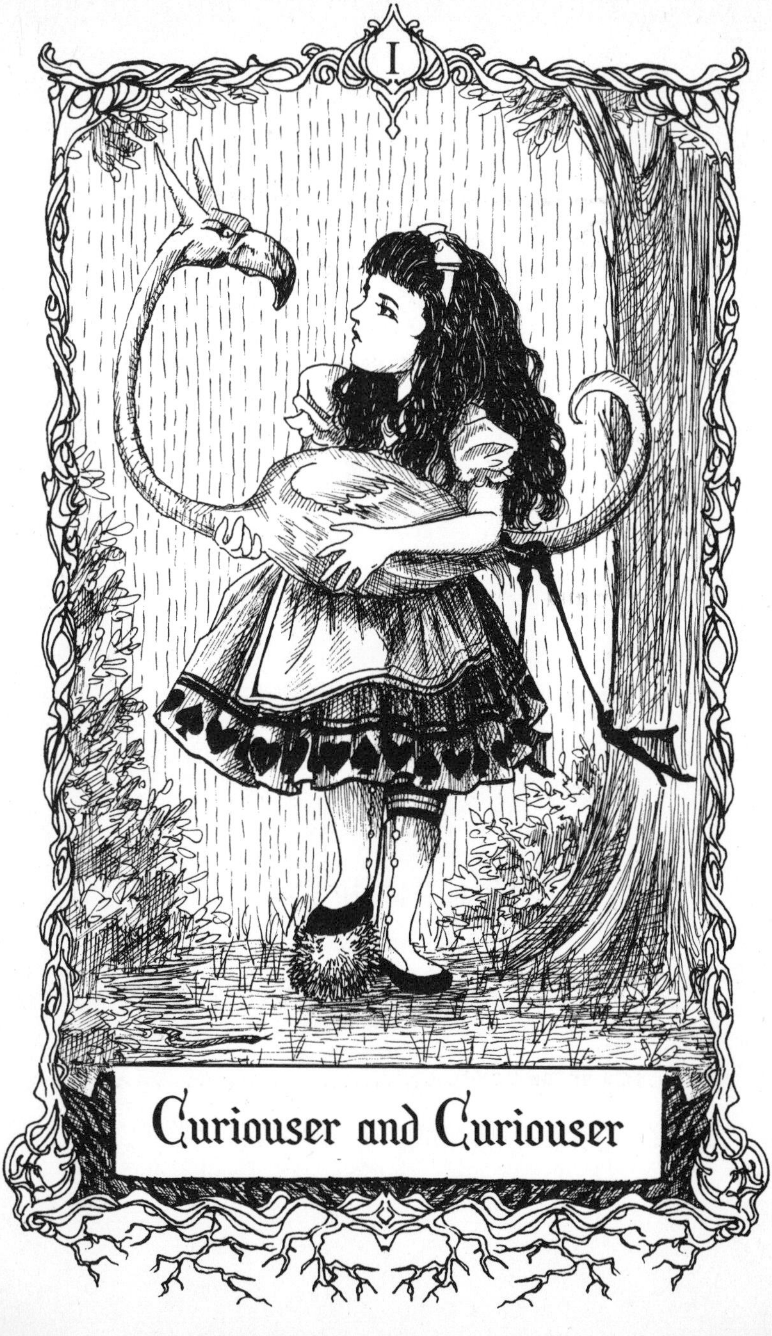
I
Curiouser and Curiouser

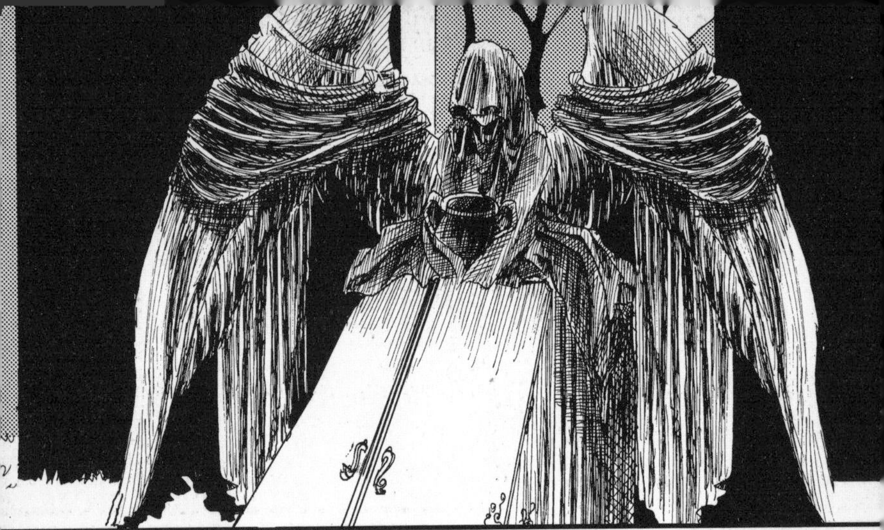

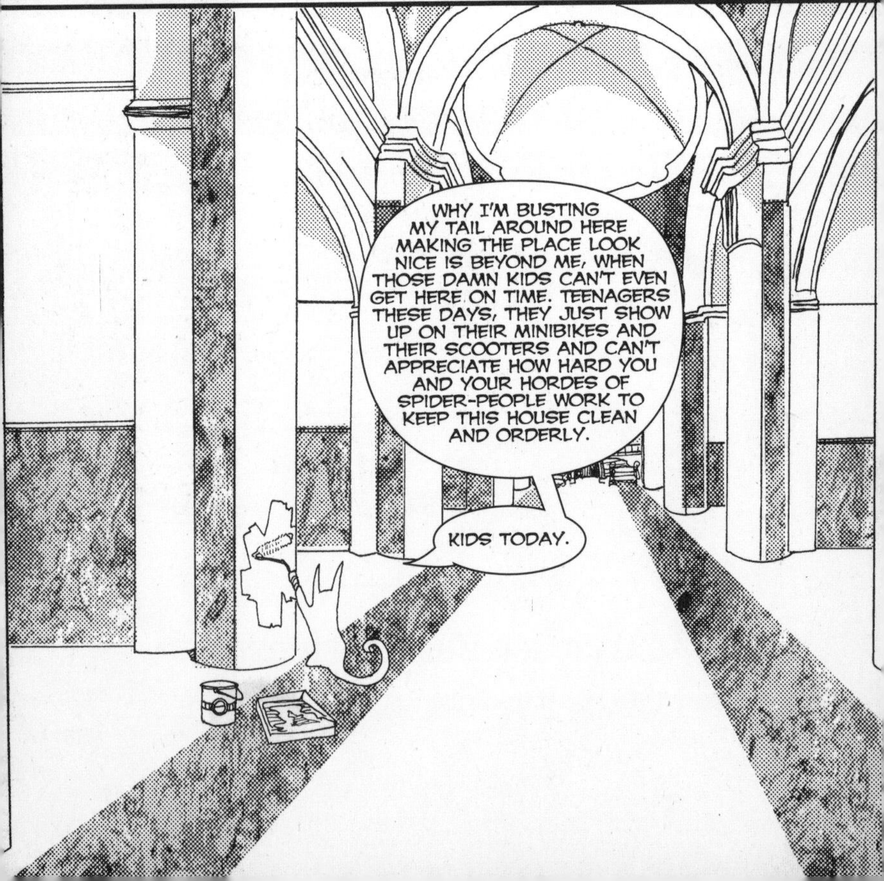
WHY I'M BUSTING MY TAIL AROUND HERE MAKING THE PLACE LOOK NICE IS BEYOND ME, WHEN THOSE DAMN KIDS CAN'T EVEN GET HERE ON TIME. TEENAGERS THESE DAYS, THEY JUST SHOW UP ON THEIR MINIBIKES AND THEIR SCOOTERS AND CAN'T APPRECIATE HOW HARD YOU AND YOUR HORDES OF SPIDER-PEOPLE WORK TO KEEP THIS HOUSE CLEAN AND ORDERLY.
KIDS TODAY.

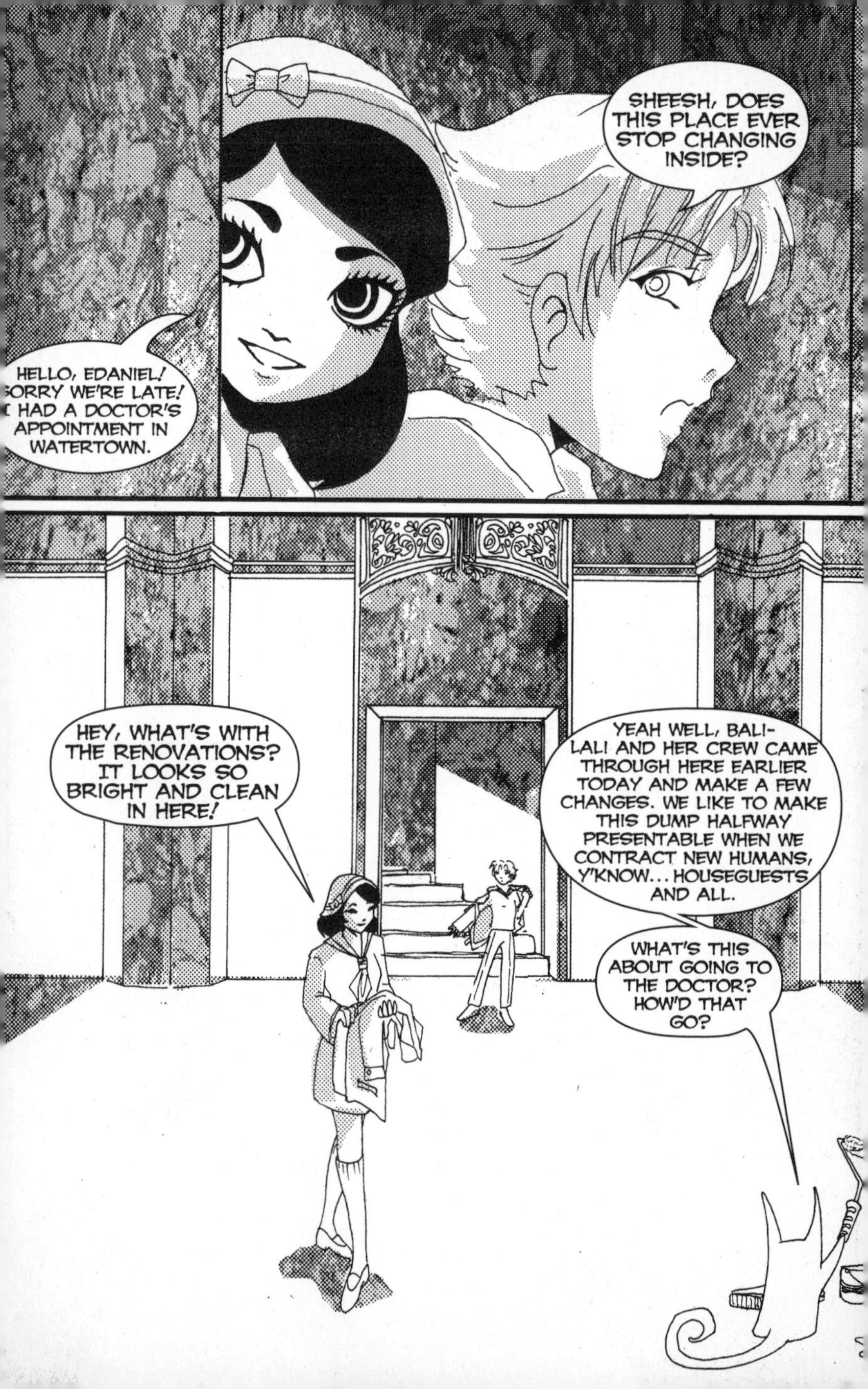
HELLO, EDANIEL! SORRY WE'RE LATE! I HAD A DOCTOR'S APPOINTMENT IN WATERTOWN.
SHEESH, DOES THIS PLACE EVER STOP CHANGING INSIDE?
HEY, WHAT'S WITH THE RENOVATIONS? IT LOOKS SO BRIGHT AND CLEAN IN HERE!
YEAH WELL, BALI-LALI AND HER CREW CAME THROUGH HERE EARLIER TODAY AND MAKE A FEW CHANGES. WE LIKE TO MAKE THIS DUMP HALFWAY PRESENTABLE WHEN WE CONTRACT NEW HUMANS, Y'KNOW... HOUSEGUESTS AND ALL.
WHAT'S THIS ABOUT GOING TO THE DOCTOR? HOW'D THAT GO?

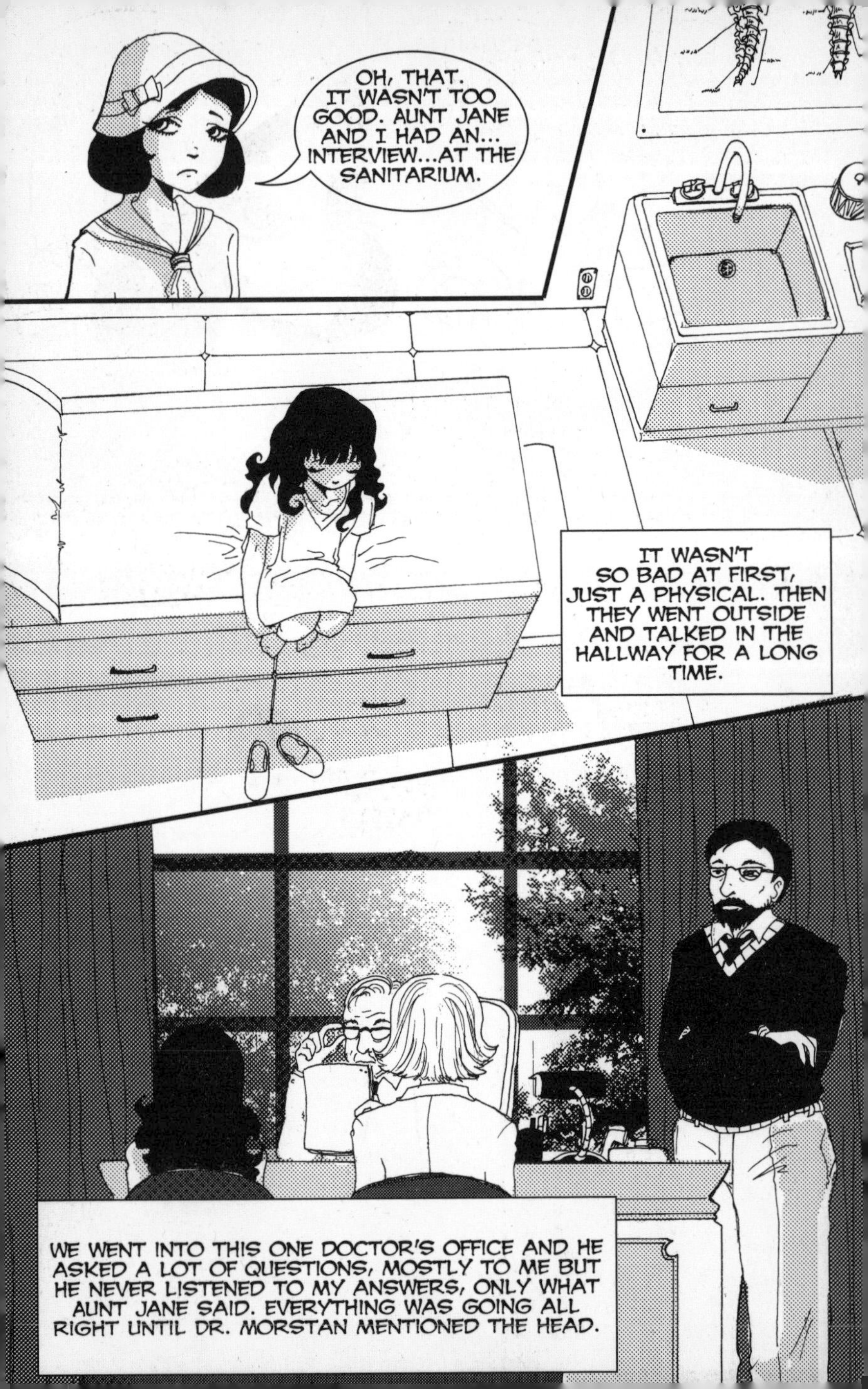
OH, THAT. IT WASN'T TOO GOOD. AUNT JANE AND I HAD AN... INTERVIEW...AT THE SANITARIUM.
IT WASN'T SO BAD AT FIRST, JUST A PHYSICAL. THEN THEY WENT OUTSIDE AND TALKED IN THE HALLWAY FOR A LONG TIME.
WE WENT INTO THIS ONE DOCTOR'S OFFICE AND HE ASKED A LOT OF QUESTIONS, MOSTLY TO ME BUT HE NEVER LISTENED TO MY ANSWERS, ONLY WHAT AUNT JANE SAID. EVERYTHING WAS GOING ALL RIGHT UNTIL DR. MORSTAN MENTIONED THE HEAD.

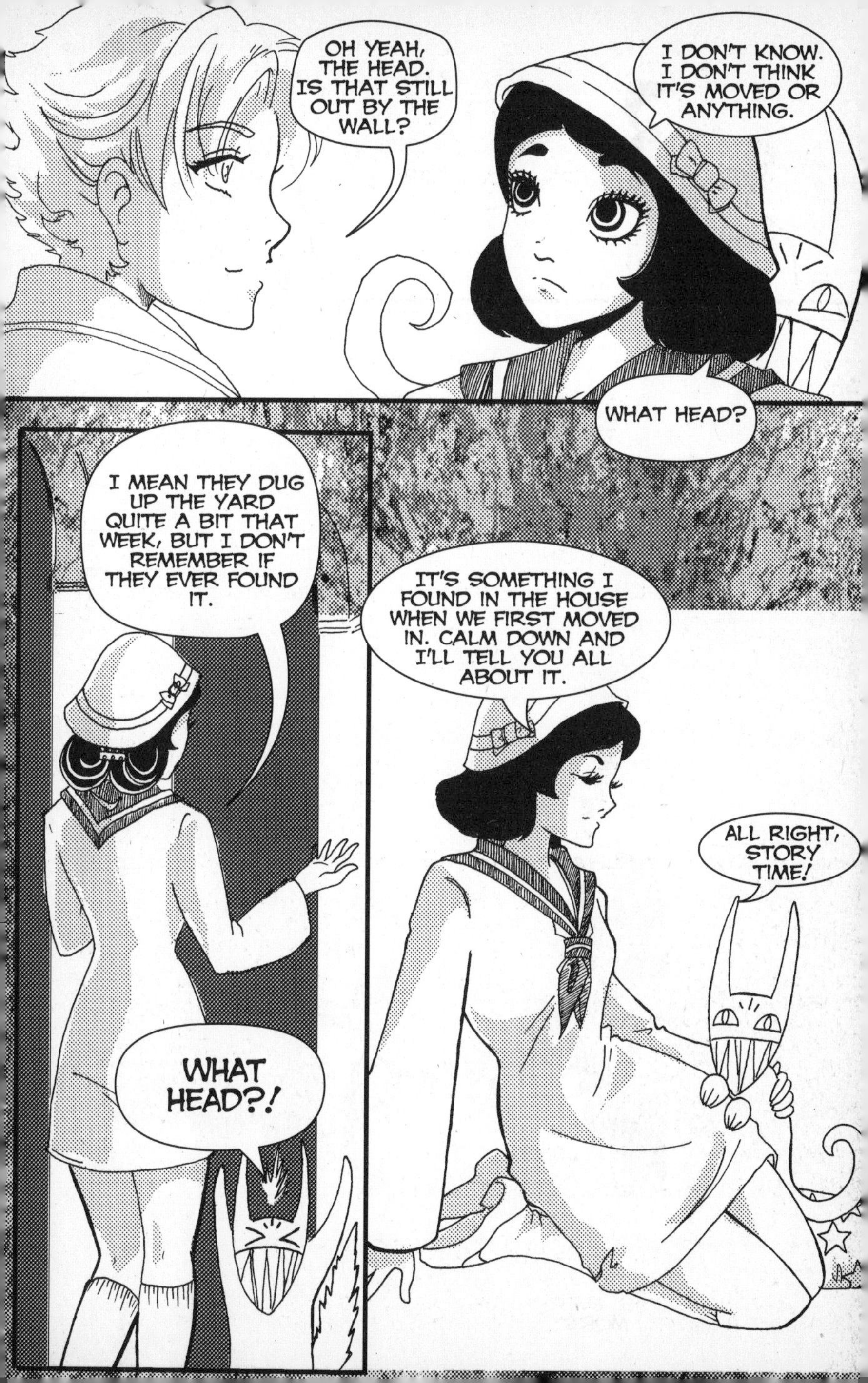
OH YEAH, THE HEAD. IS THAT STILL OUT BY THE WALL?
I DON'T KNOW. I DON'T THINK IT'S MOVED OR ANYTHING.
WHAT HEAD?
I MEAN THEY DUG UP THE YARD QUITE A BIT THAT WEEK, BUT I DON'T REMEMBER IF THEY EVER FOUND IT.
WHAT HEAD?!
IT'S SOMETHING I FOUND IN THE HOUSE WHEN WE FIRST MOVED IN. CALM DOWN AND I'LL TELL YOU ALL ABOUT IT.
ALL RIGHT, STORY TIME!

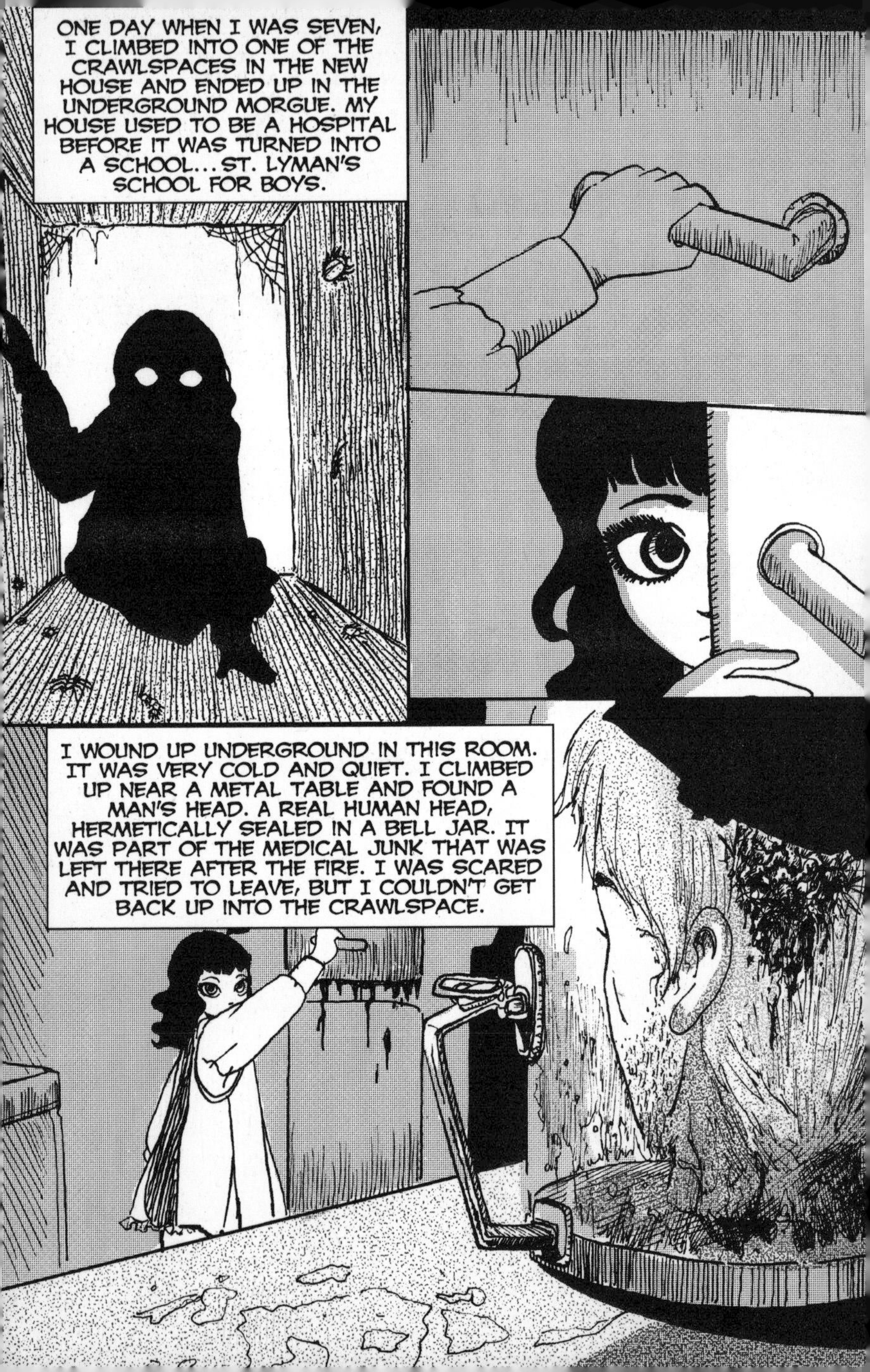
ONE DAY WHEN I WAS SEVEN, I CLIMBED INTO ONE OF THE CRAWLSPACES IN THE NEW HOUSE AND ENDED UP IN THE UNDERGROUND MORGUE. MY HOUSE USED TO BE A HOSPITAL BEFORE IT WAS TURNED INTO A SCHOOL... ST. LYMAN'S SCHOOL FOR BOYS.
I WOUND UP UNDERGROUND IN THIS ROOM. IT WAS VERY COLD AND QUIET. I CLIMBED UP NEAR A METAL TABLE AND FOUND A MAN'S HEAD. A REAL HUMAN HEAD, HERMETICALLY SEALED IN A BELL JAR. IT WAS PART OF THE MEDICAL JUNK THAT WAS LEFT THERE AFTER THE FIRE. I WAS SCARED AND TRIED TO LEAVE, BUT I COULDN'T GET BACK UP INTO THE CRAWLSPACE.

SO I JUST SAT THERE, IN THE ROOM, FOR ALMOST THREE HOURS. MY AUNT FINALLY NOTICED I WAS GONE AND WENT LOOKING FOR ME. THEY TOOK ME AWAY TO THE HOSPITAL IN WATERTOWN AND KEPT ME THERE FOR A LONG TIME. I DIDN'T SAY MUCH WHILE I WAS THERE. I JUST KEPT THINKING ABOUT THE HEAD.
WHEN I GOT HOME, I REALIZED I WANTED THE SEALED HEAD, SO I STOLE IT FROM THE MORGUE BEFORE IT WAS REMOVED FROM THE HOUSE. I DECIDED TO BURY IT AT NIGHT IN THE BACKYARD SO THEY COULDN'T TAKE IT AWAY.
WOW. THAT'S TRULY MESSED UP.

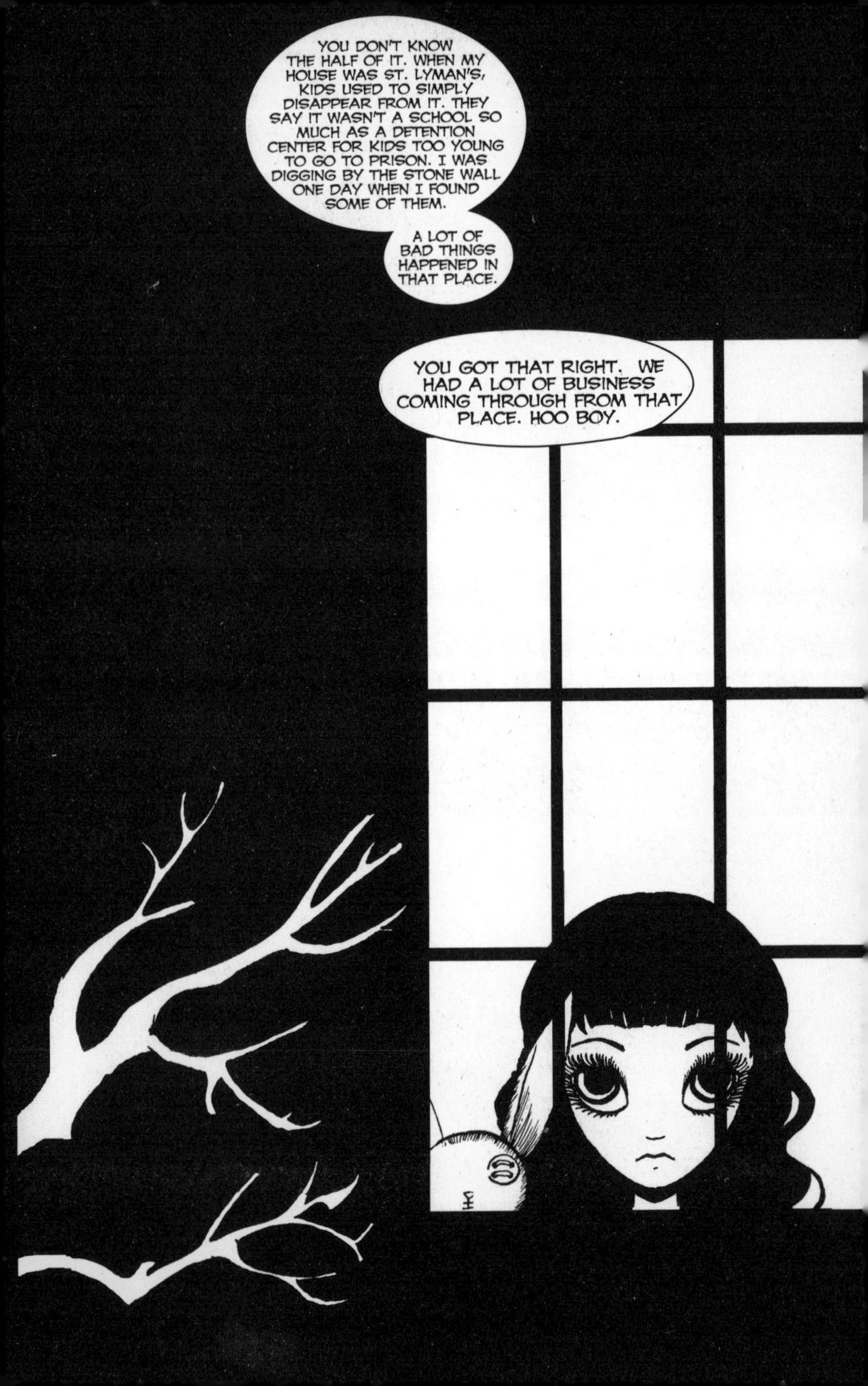
YOU DON'T KNOW THE HALF OF IT. WHEN MY HOUSE WAS ST. LYMAN'S, KIDS USED TO SIMPLY DISAPPEAR FROM IT. THEY SAY IT WASN'T A SCHOOL SO MUCH AS A DETENTION CENTER FOR KIDS TOO YOUNG TO GO TO PRISON. I WAS DIGGING BY THE STONE WALL ONE DAY WHEN I FOUND SOME OF THEM.
A LOT OF BAD THINGS HAPPENED IN THAT PLACE.
YOU GOT THAT RIGHT. WE HAD A LOT OF BUSINESS COMING THROUGH FROM THAT PLACE. HOO BOY.

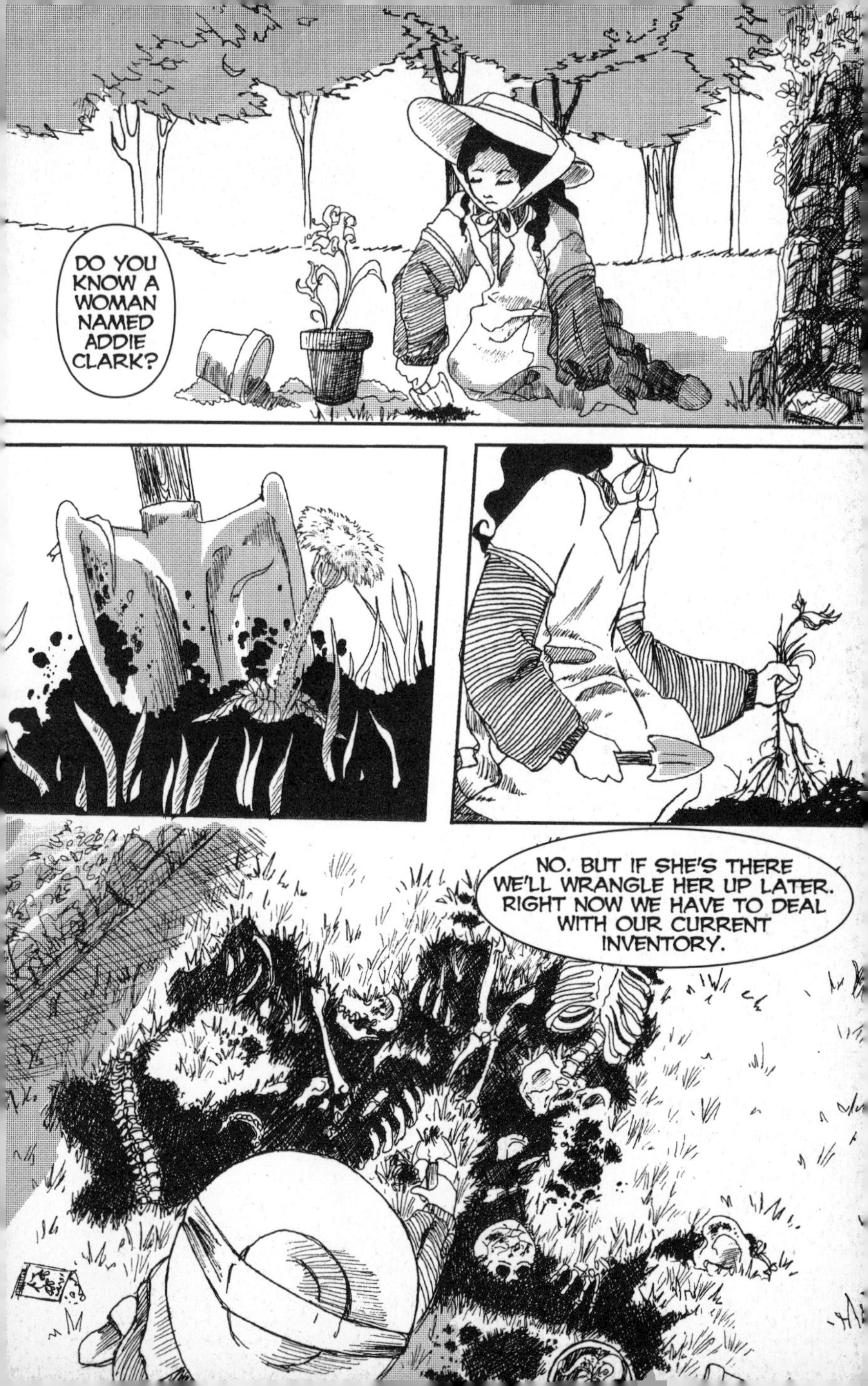
DO YOU KNOW A WOMAN NAMED ADDIE CLARK?
NO. BUT IF SHE'S THERE WE'LL WRANGLE HER UP LATER. RIGHT NOW WE HAVE TO DEAL WITH OUR CURRENT INVENTORY.

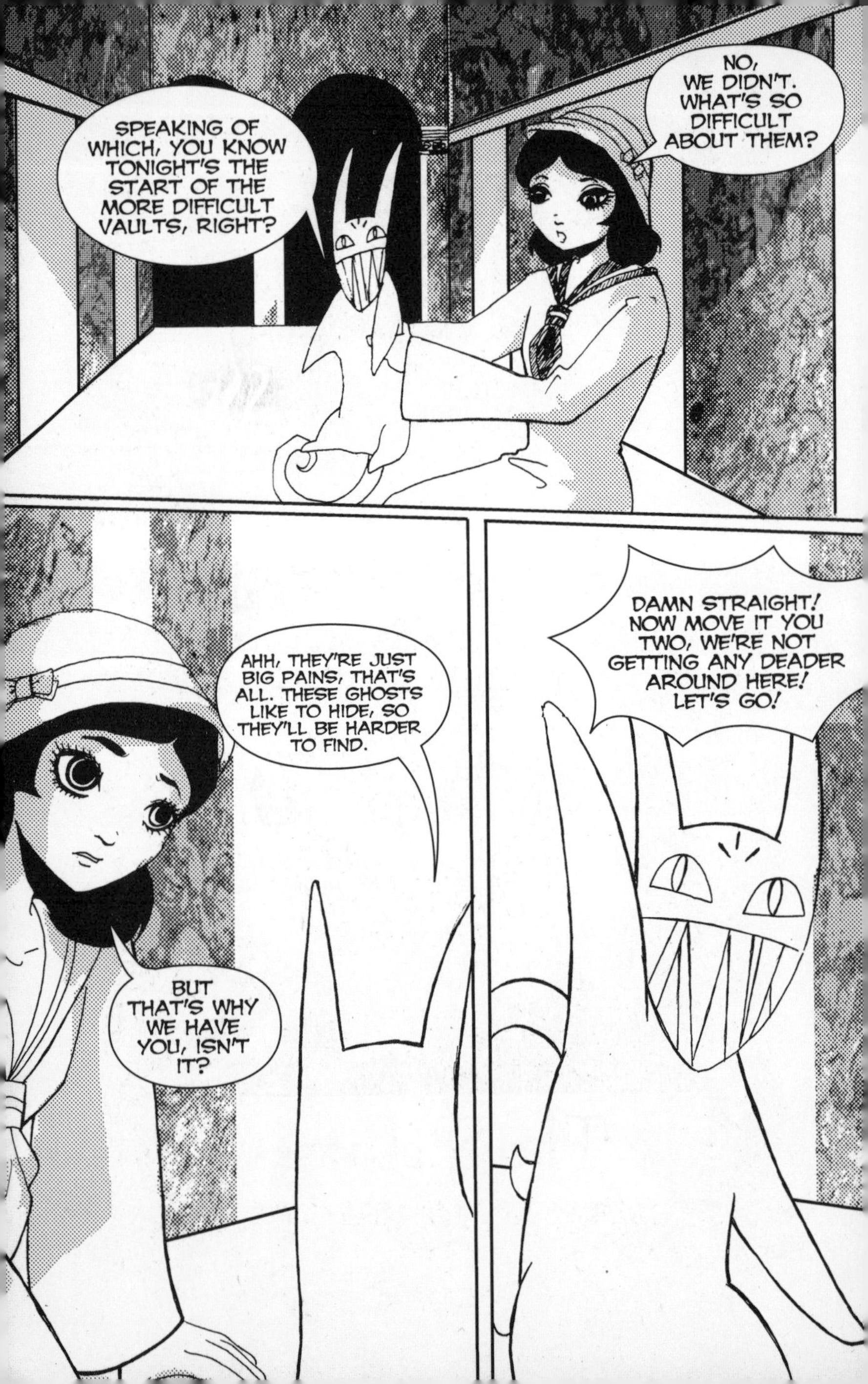
SPEAKING OF WHICH, YOU KNOW TONIGHT'S THE START OF THE MORE DIFFICULT VAULTS, RIGHT?
NO, WE DIDN'T. WHAT'S SO DIFFICULT ABOUT THEM?
AHH, THEY'RE JUST BIG PAINS, THAT'S ALL. THESE GHOSTS LIKE TO HIDE, SO THEY'LL BE HARDER TO FIND.
BUT THAT'S WHY WE HAVE YOU, ISN'T IT?
DAMN STRAIGHT! NOW MOVE IT YOU TWO, WE'RE NOT GETTING ANY DEADER AROUND HERE! LET'S GO!

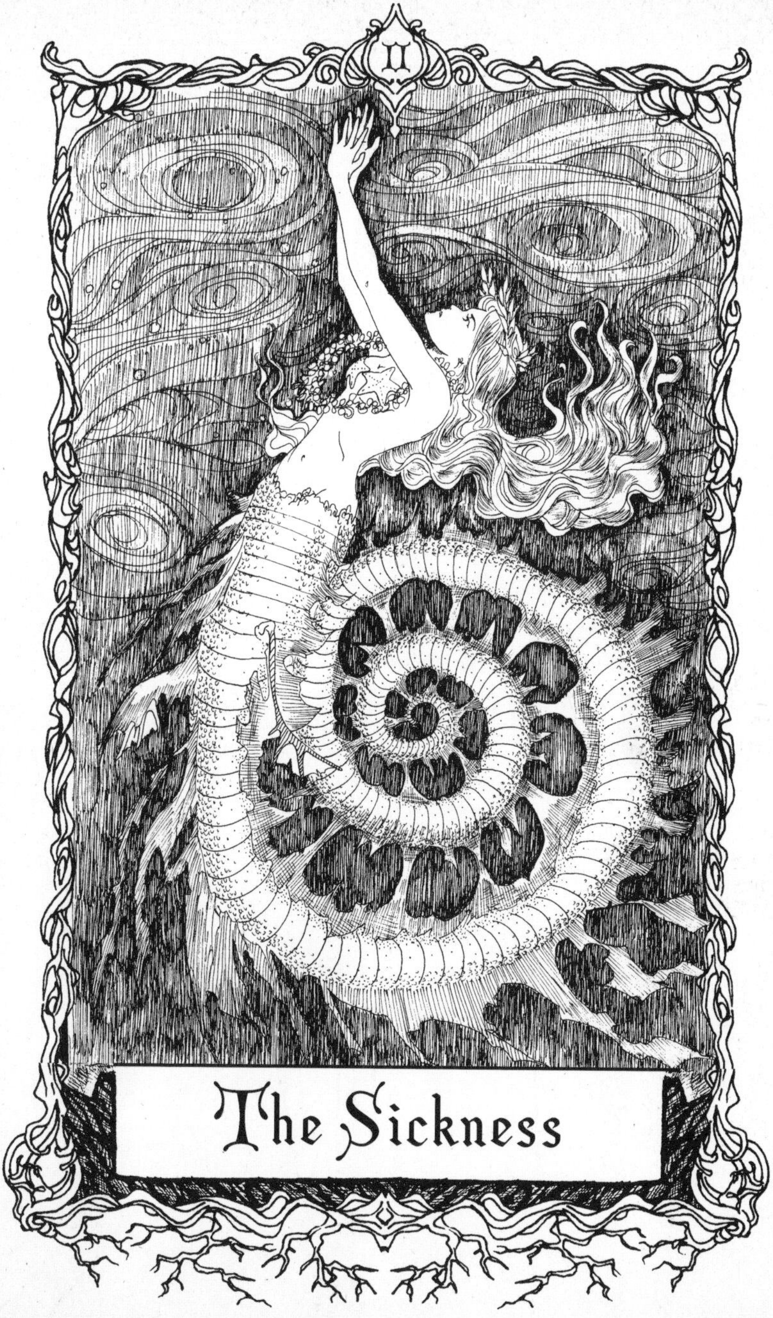
The Sickness

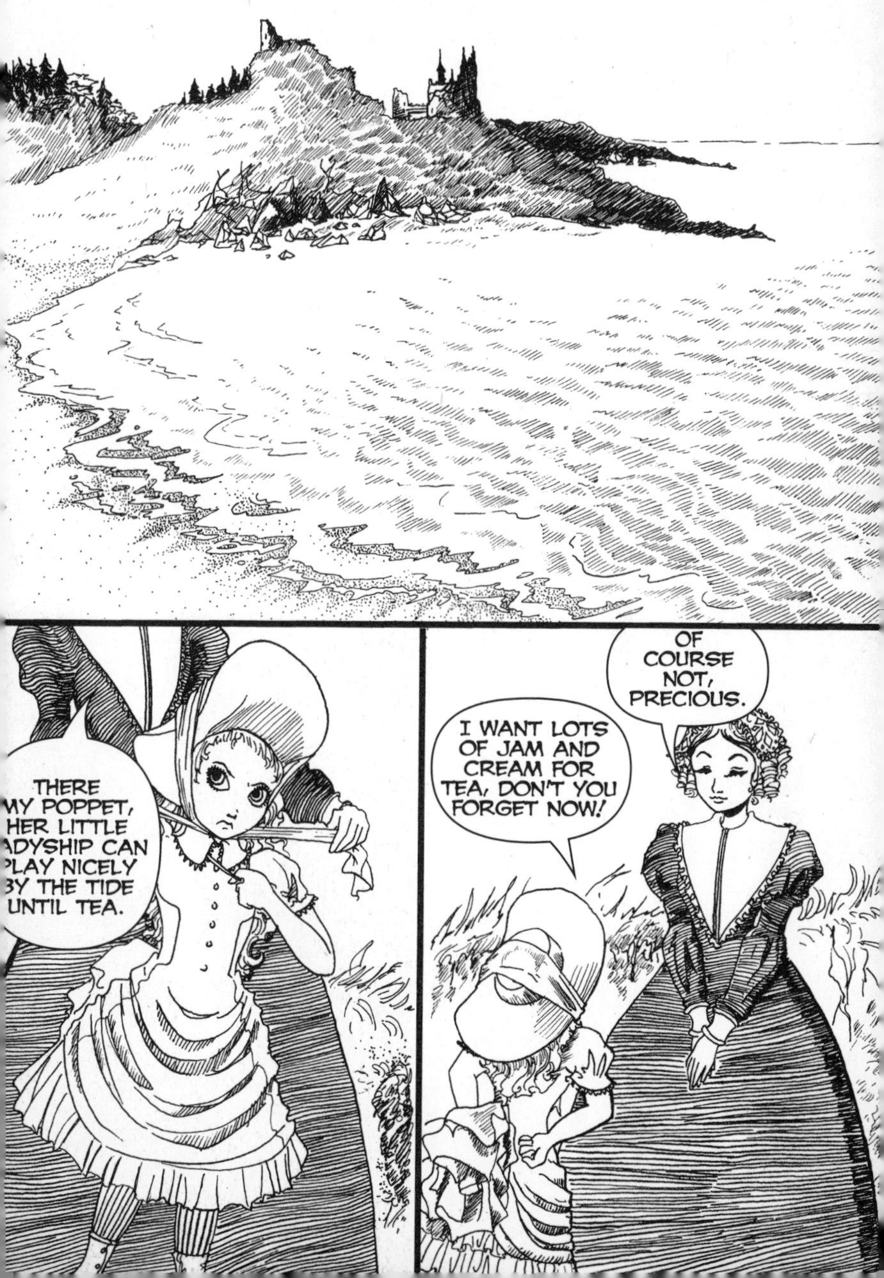
THERE MY POPPET, HER LITTLE ADYSHIP CAN PLAY NICELY BY THE TIDE UNTIL TEA.
I WANT LOTS OF JAM AND CREAM FOR TEA, DON'T YOU FORGET NOW!
OF COURSE NOT, PRECIOUS.

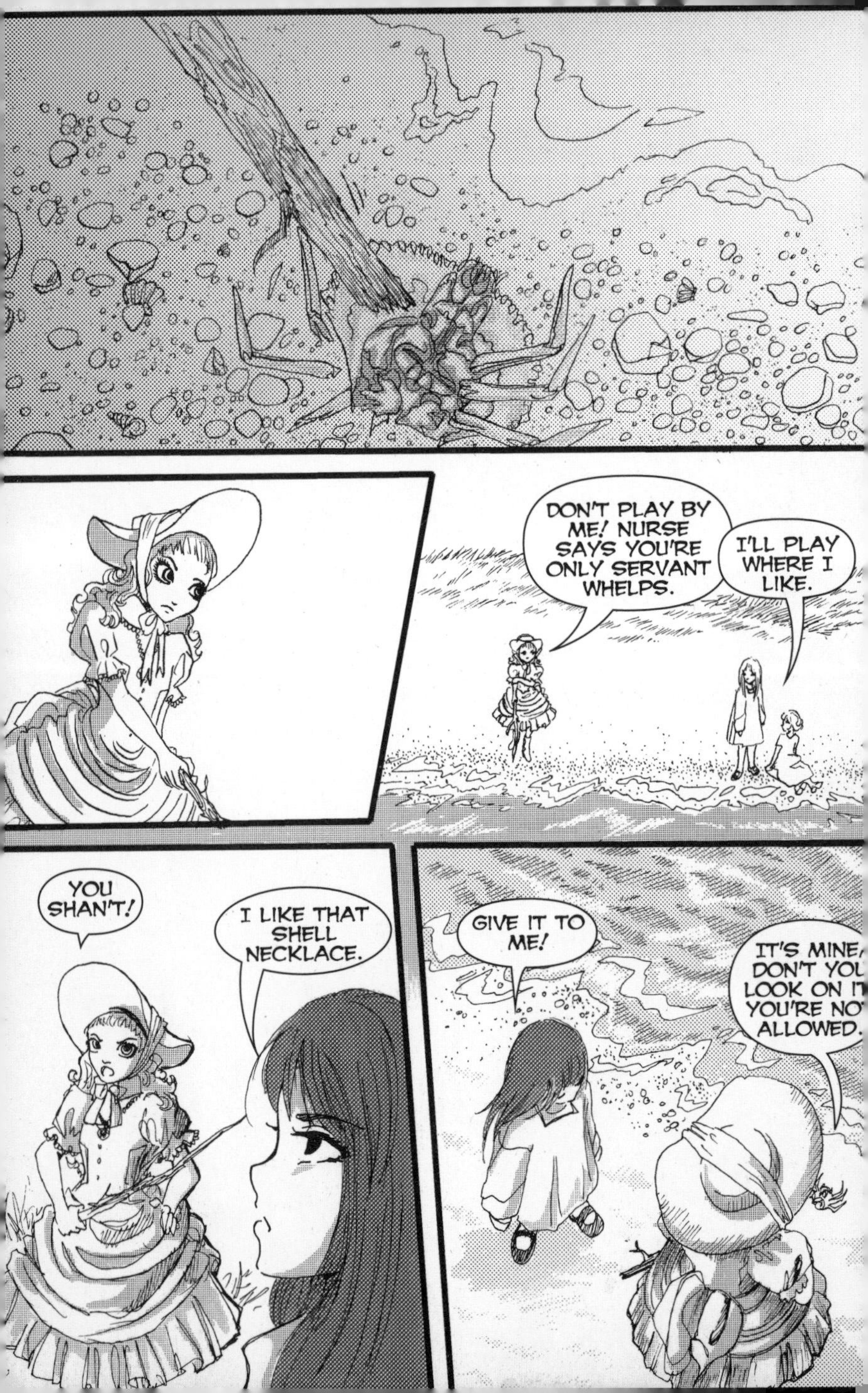
DON'T PLAY BY ME! NURSE SAYS YOU'RE ONLY SERVANT WHELPS.
I'LL PLAY WHERE I LIKE.
YOU SHAN'T!
I LIKE THAT SHELL NECKLACE.
GIVE IT TO ME!
IT'S MINE, DON'T YOU LOOK ON IT YOU'RE NOT ALLOWED.

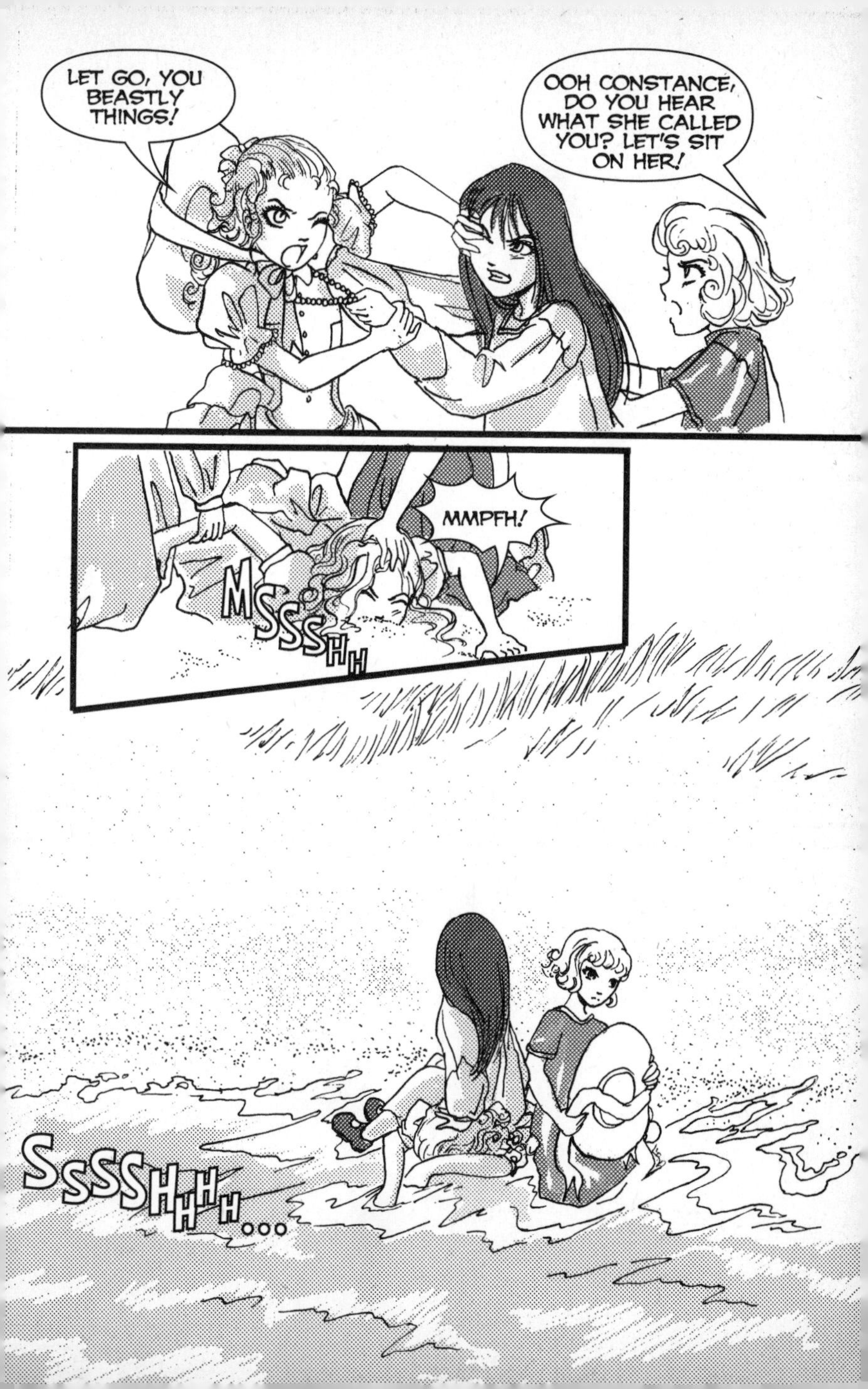
LET GO, YOU BEASTLY THINGS!
OOH CONSTANCE, DO YOU HEAR WHAT SHE CALLED YOU? LET'S SIT ON HER!
MMPFH!
MSSSHH
SSSSHHHH...

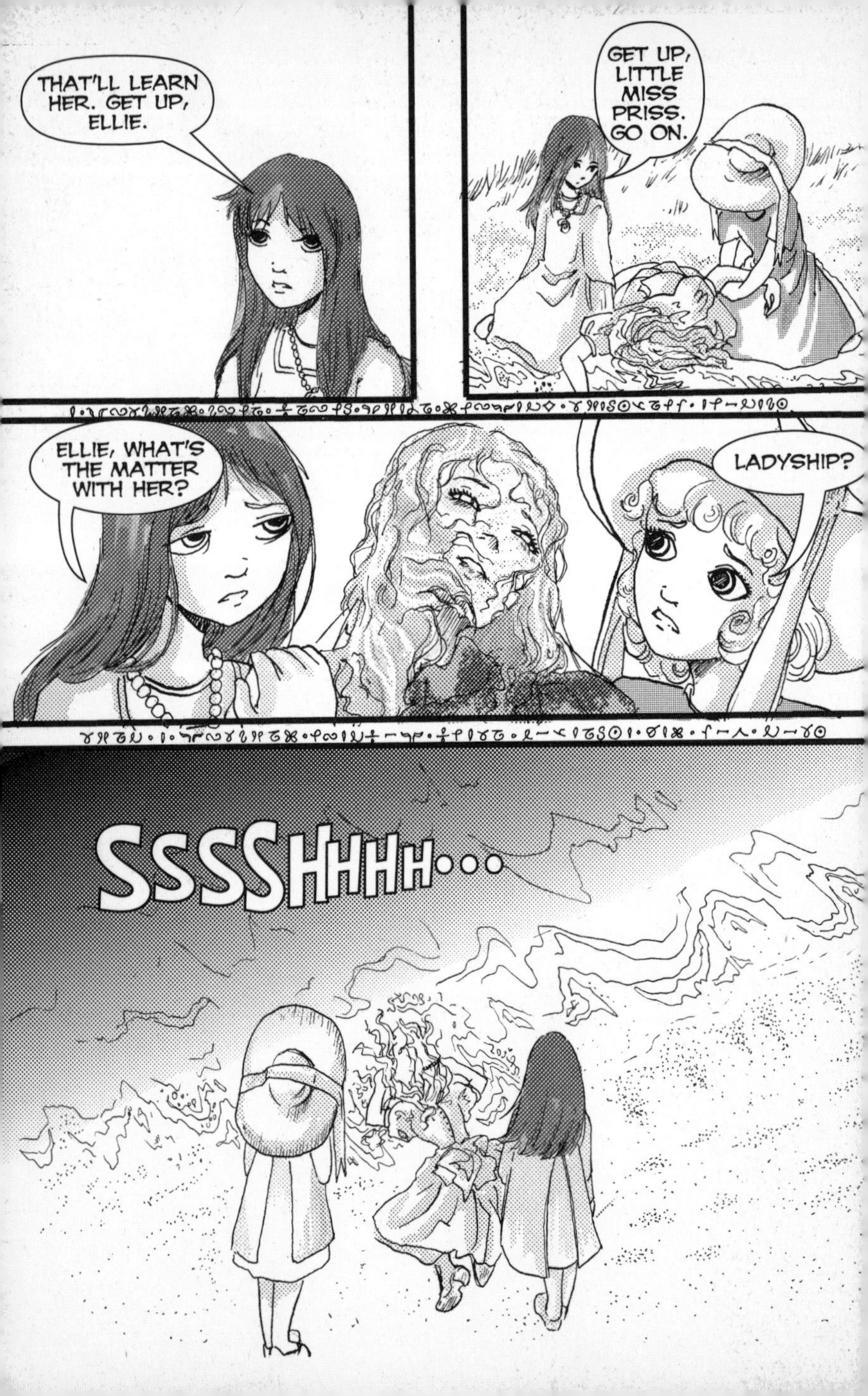
THAT'LL LEARN HER. GET UP, ELLIE.
GET UP, LITTLE MISS PRISS. GO ON.
ELLIE, WHAT'S THE MATTER WITH HER?
LADYSHIP?
SSSSHHHH...

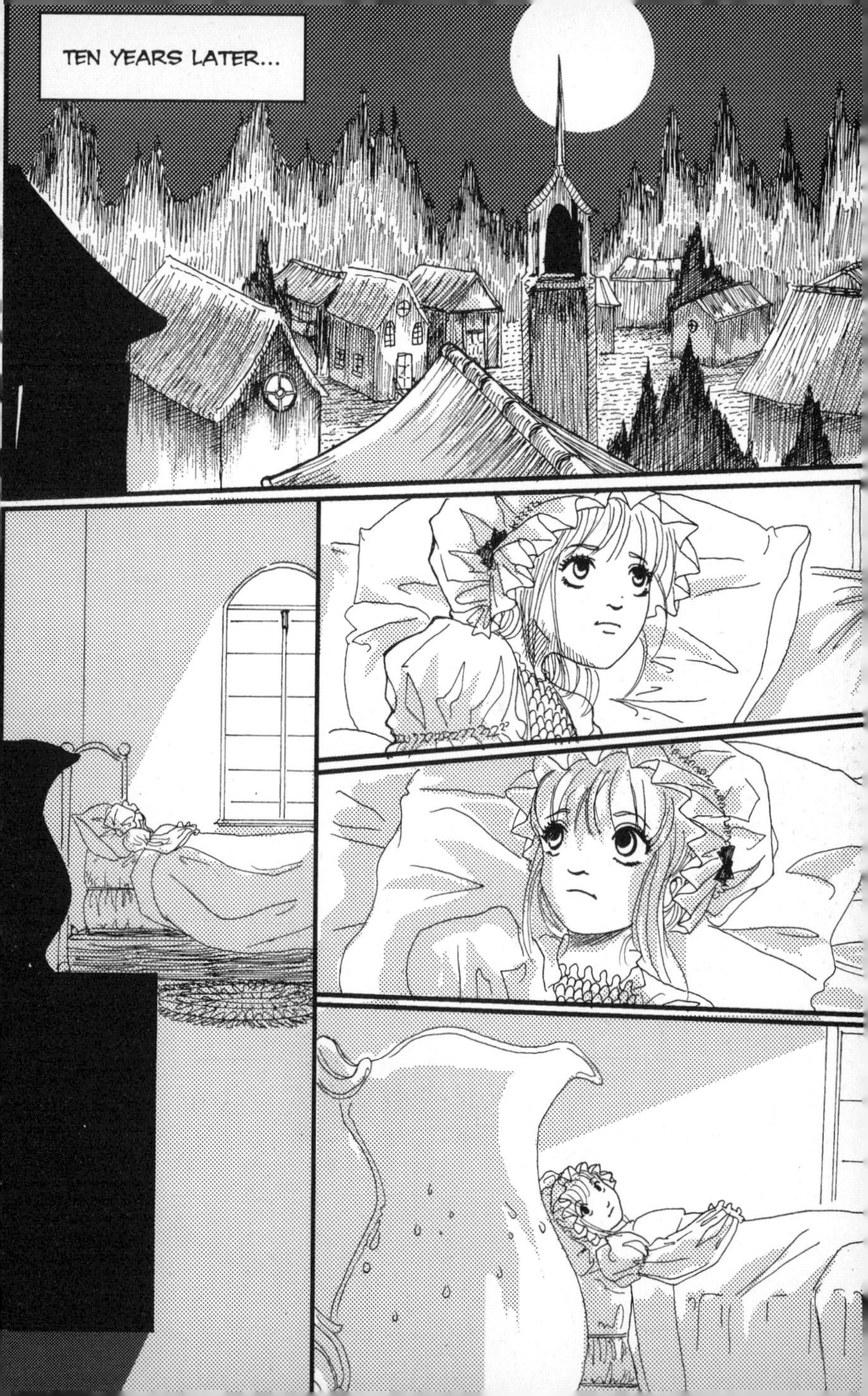
TEN YEARS LATER...

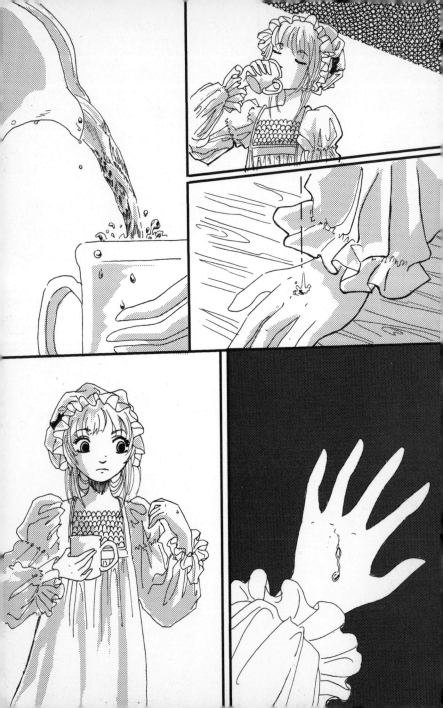

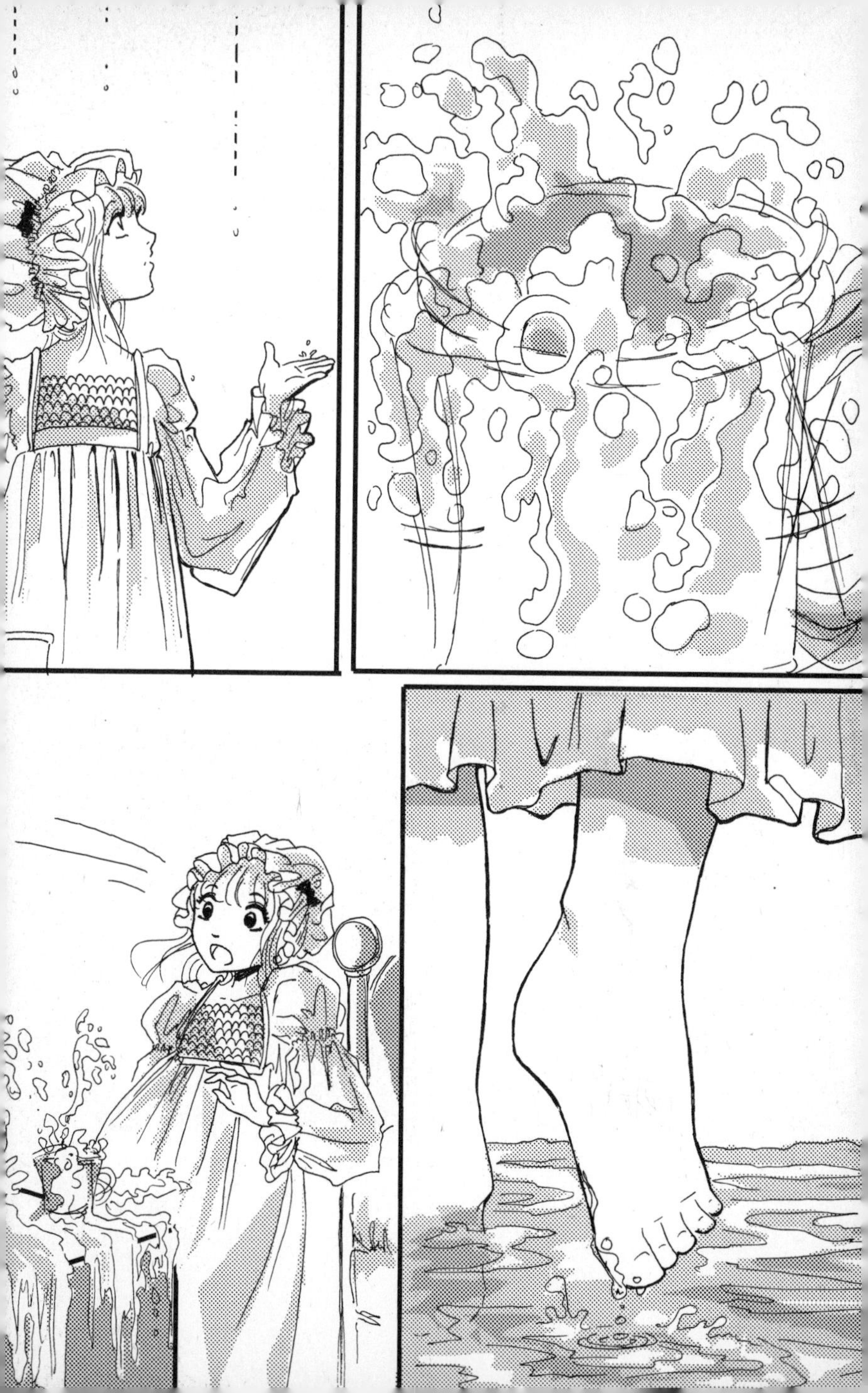

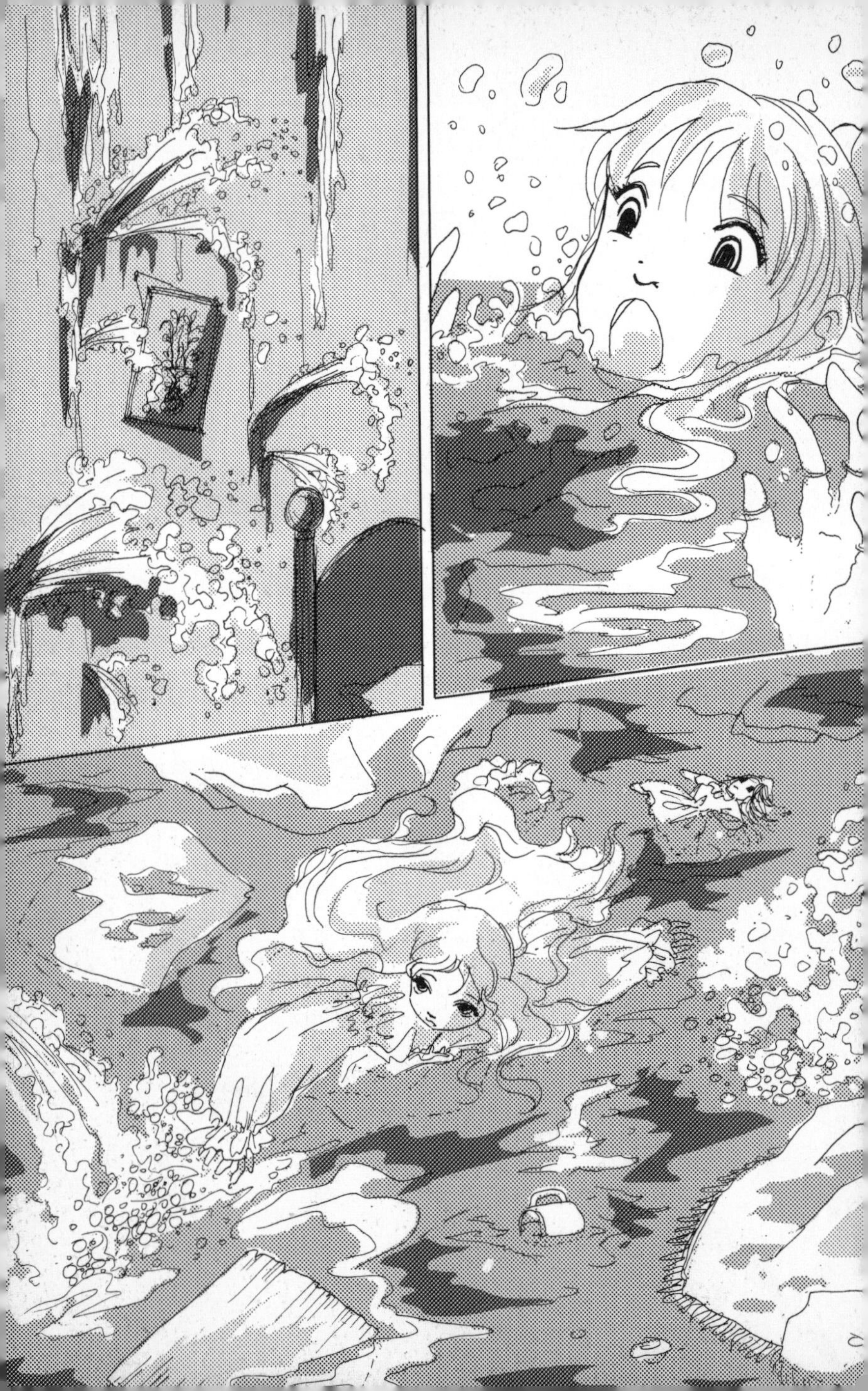

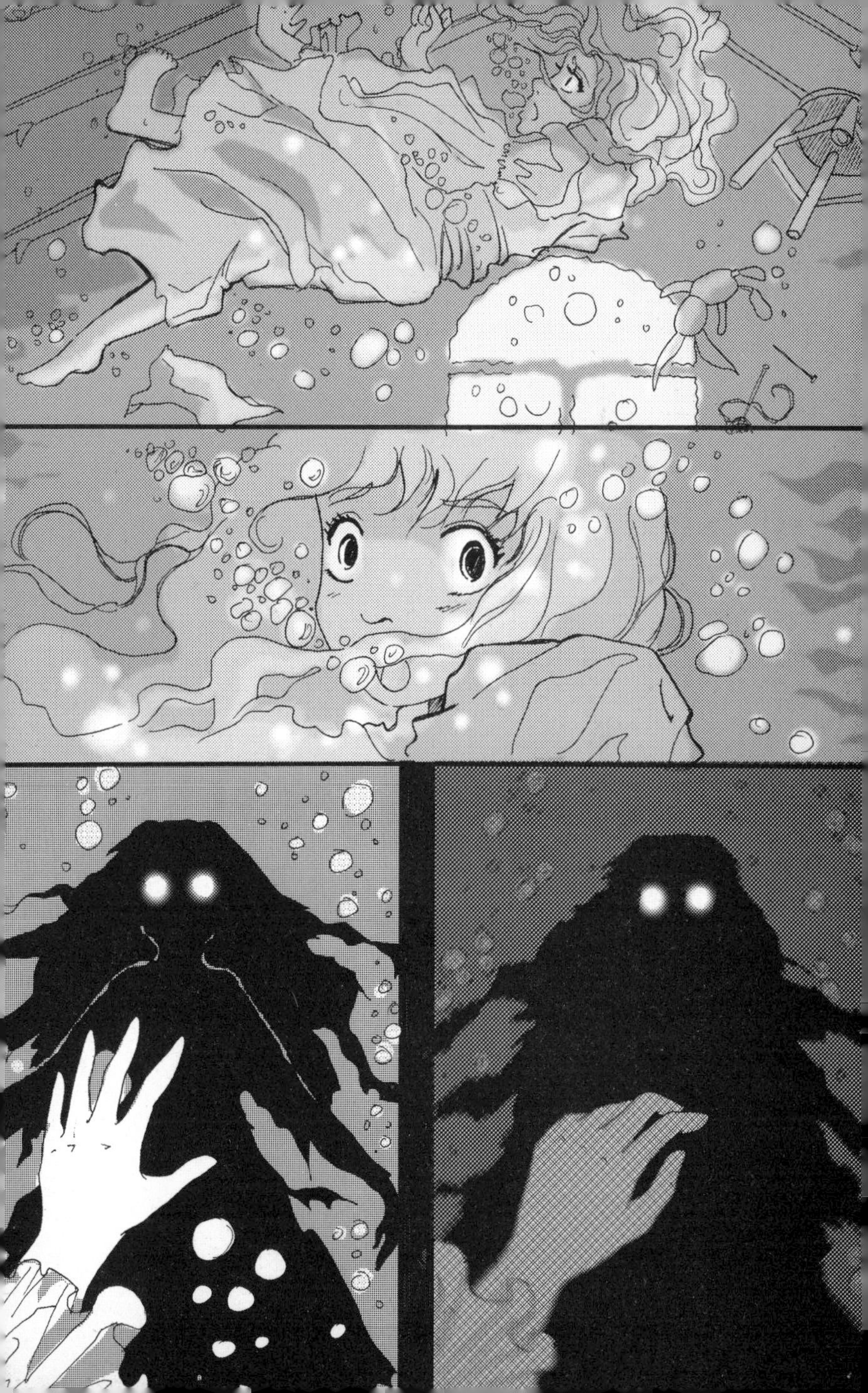

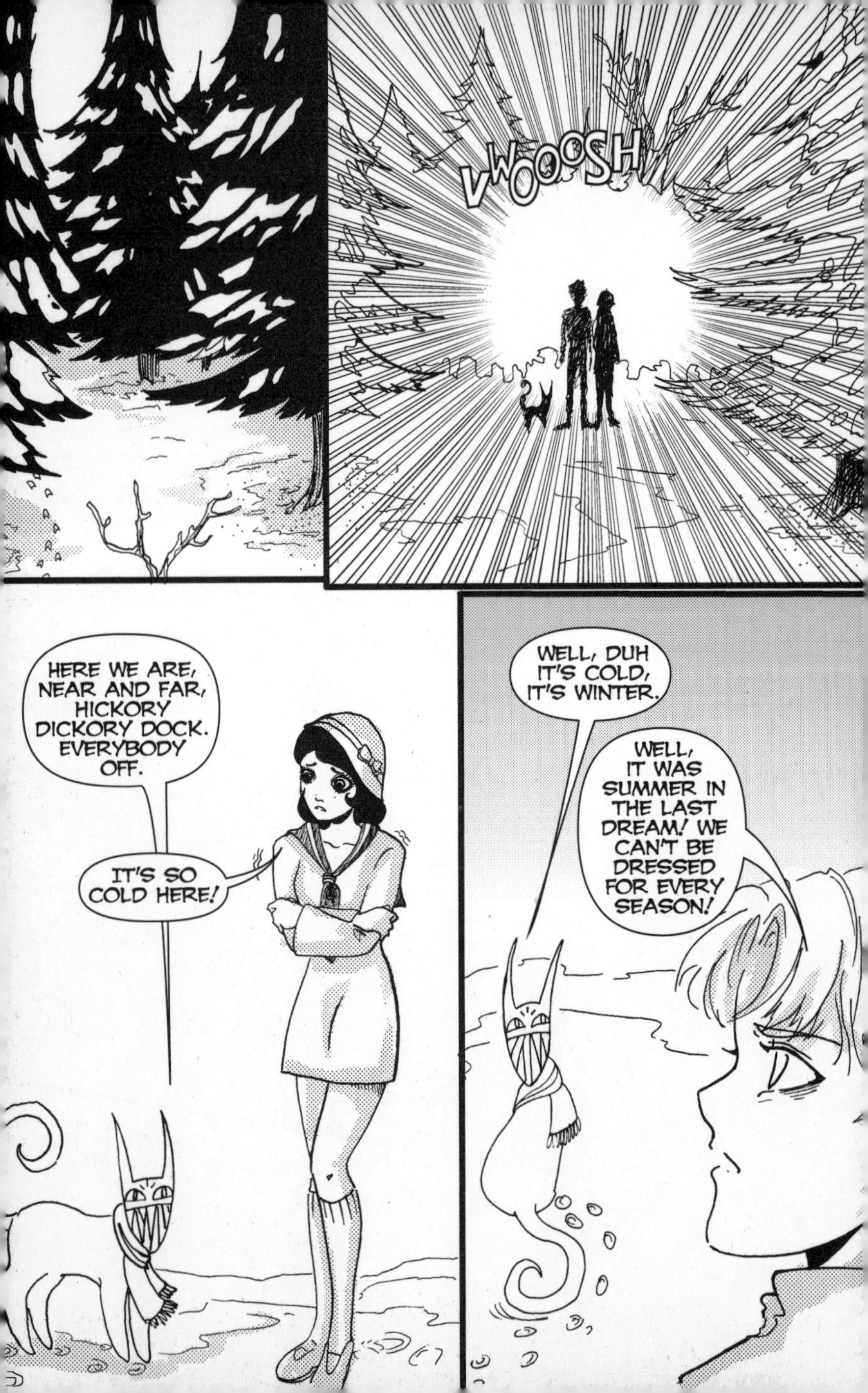
VWOOOSH
HERE WE ARE, NEAR AND FAR, HICKORY DICKORY DOCK. EVERYBODY OFF.
IT'S SO COLD HERE!
WELL, DUH IT'S COLD, IT'S WINTER.
WELL, IT WAS SUMMER IN THE LAST DREAM! WE CAN'T BE DRESSED FOR EVERY SEASON!

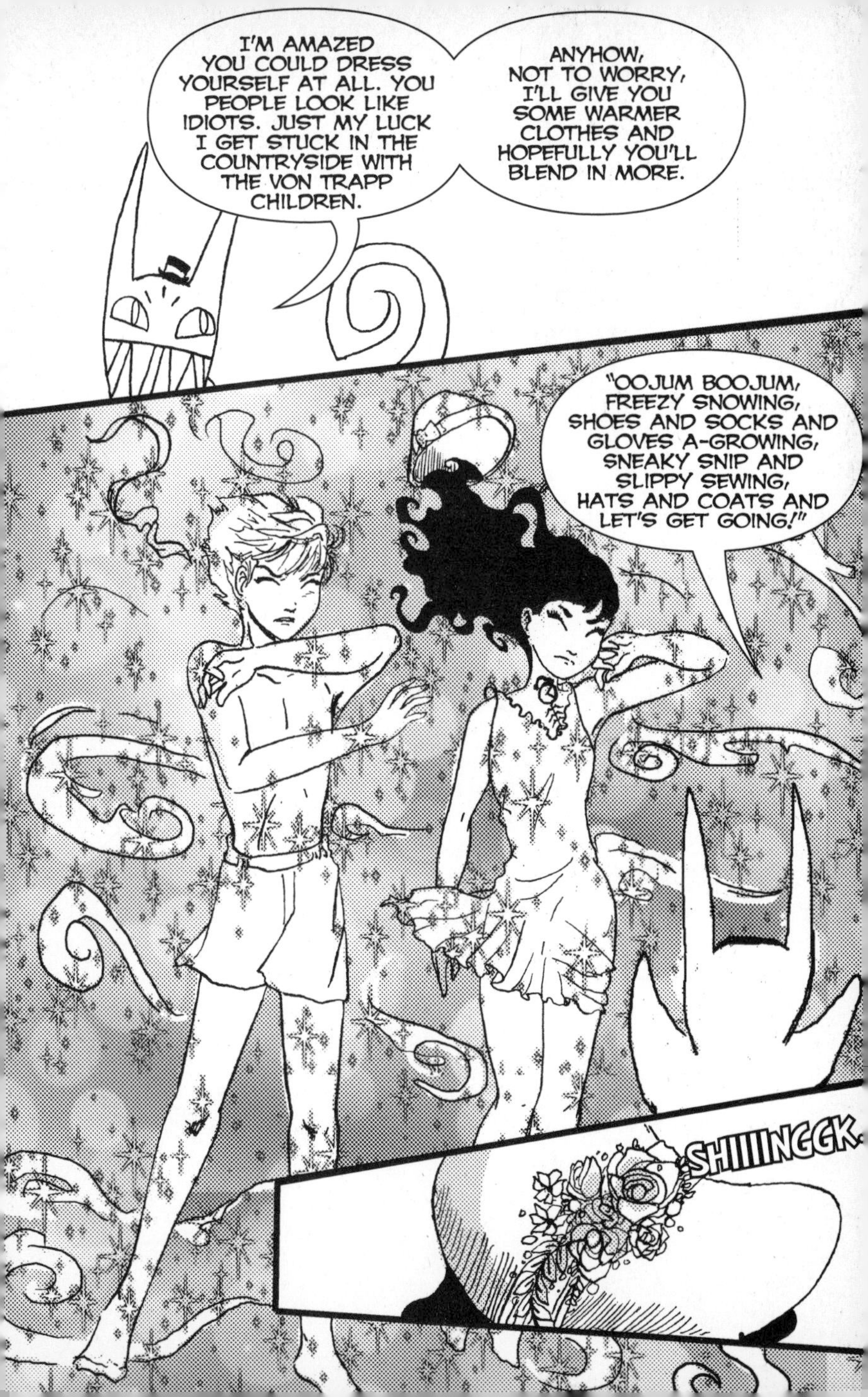
I'M AMAZED YOU COULD DRESS YOURSELF AT ALL. YOU PEOPLE LOOK LIKE IDIOTS. JUST MY LUCK I GET STUCK IN THE COUNTRYSIDE WITH THE VON TRAPP CHILDREN.
ANYHOW, NOT TO WORRY, I'LL GIVE YOU SOME WARMER CLOTHES AND HOPEFULLY YOU'LL BLEND IN MORE.
"OOJUM BOOJUM, FREEZY SNOWING, SHOES AND SOCKS AND GLOVES A-GROWING, SNEAKY SNIP AND SLIPPY SEWING, HATS AND COATS AND LET'S GET GOING!"
SHIIIINGGK.

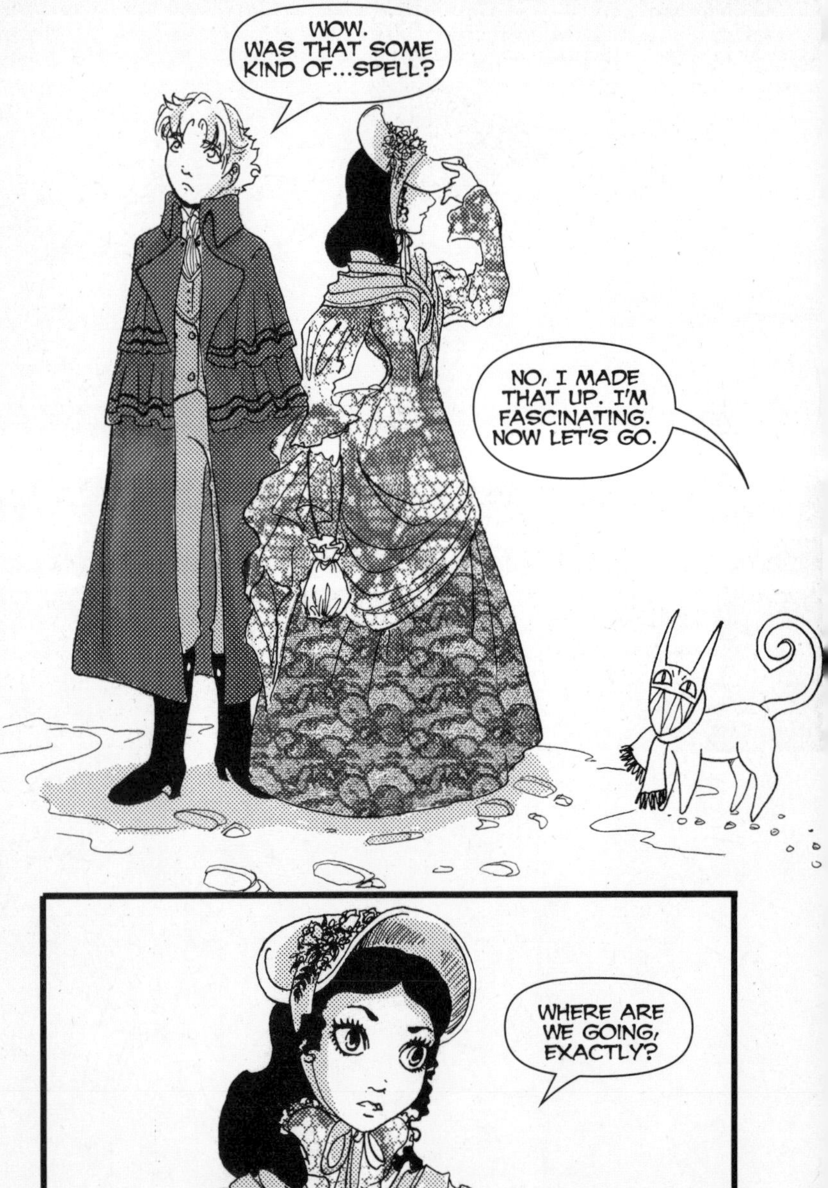
WOW. WAS THAT SOME KIND OF...SPELL?
NO, I MADE THAT UP. I'M FASCINATING. NOW LET'S GO.
WHERE ARE WE GOING, EXACTLY?

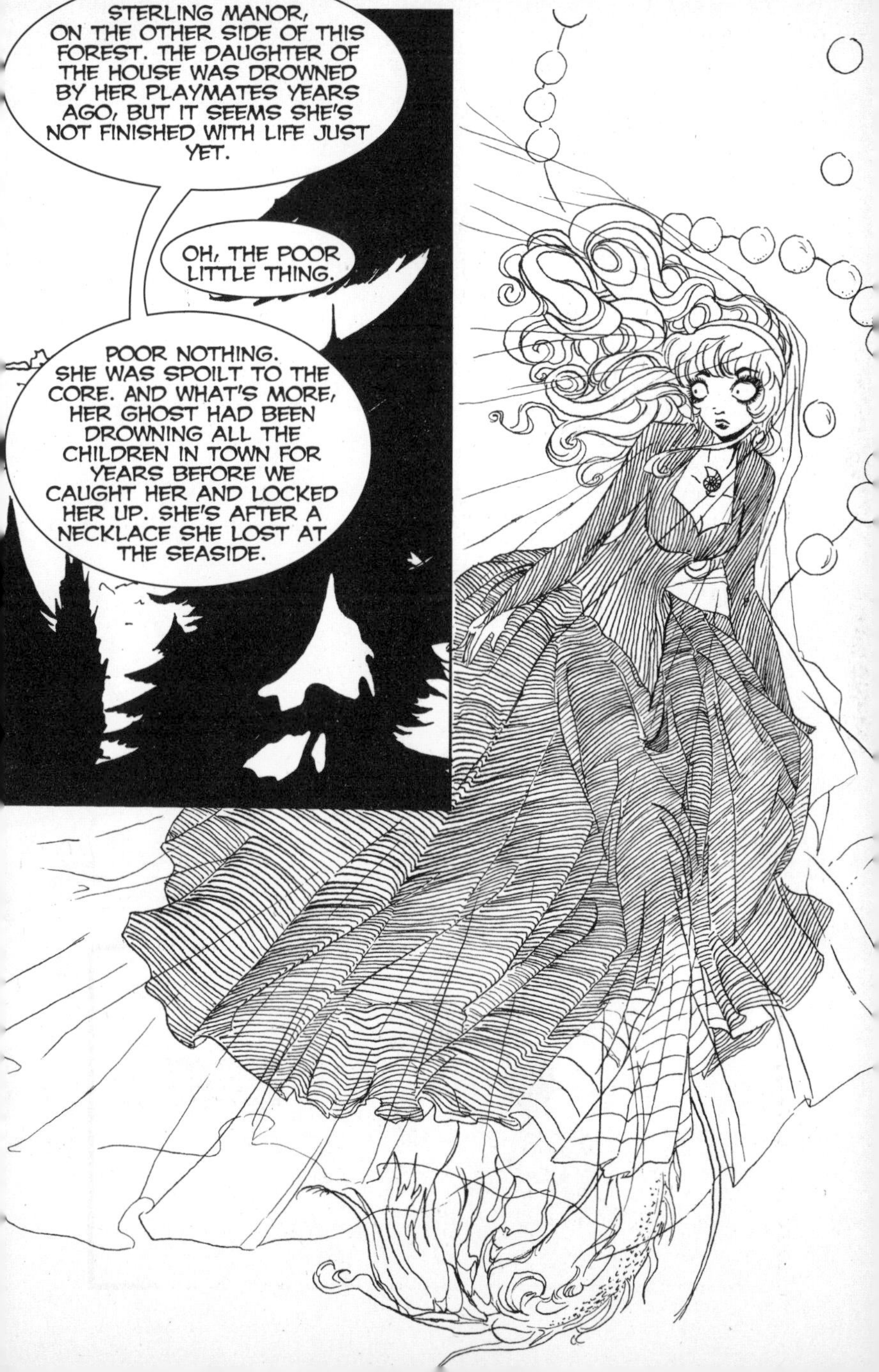
STERLING MANOR, ON THE OTHER SIDE OF THIS FOREST. THE DAUGHTER OF THE HOUSE WAS DROWNED BY HER PLAYMATES YEARS AGO, BUT IT SEEMS SHE'S NOT FINISHED WITH LIFE JUST YET.
OH, THE POOR LITTLE THING.
POOR NOTHING. SHE WAS SPOILT TO THE CORE. AND WHAT'S MORE, HER GHOST HAD BEEN DROWNING ALL THE CHILDREN IN TOWN FOR YEARS BEFORE WE CAUGHT HER AND LOCKED HER UP. SHE'S AFTER A NECKLACE SHE LOST AT THE SEASIDE.

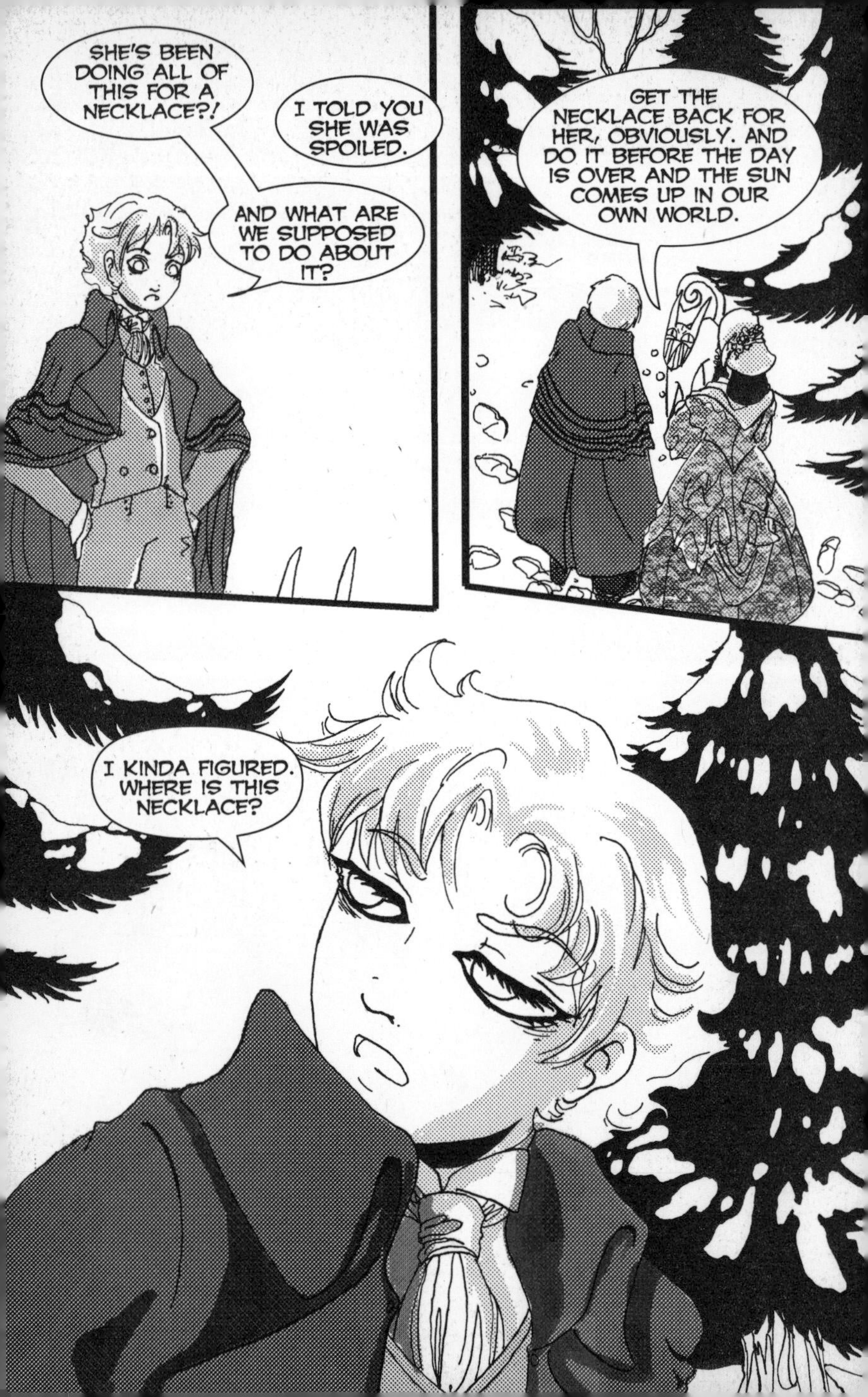
SHE'S BEEN DOING ALL OF THIS FOR A NECKLACE?!
I TOLD YOU SHE WAS SPOILED.
AND WHAT ARE WE SUPPOSED TO DO ABOUT IT?
GET THE NECKLACE BACK FOR HER, OBVIOUSLY. AND DO IT BEFORE THE DAY IS OVER AND THE SUN COMES UP IN OUR OWN WORLD.
I KINDA FIGURED. WHERE IS THIS NECKLACE?

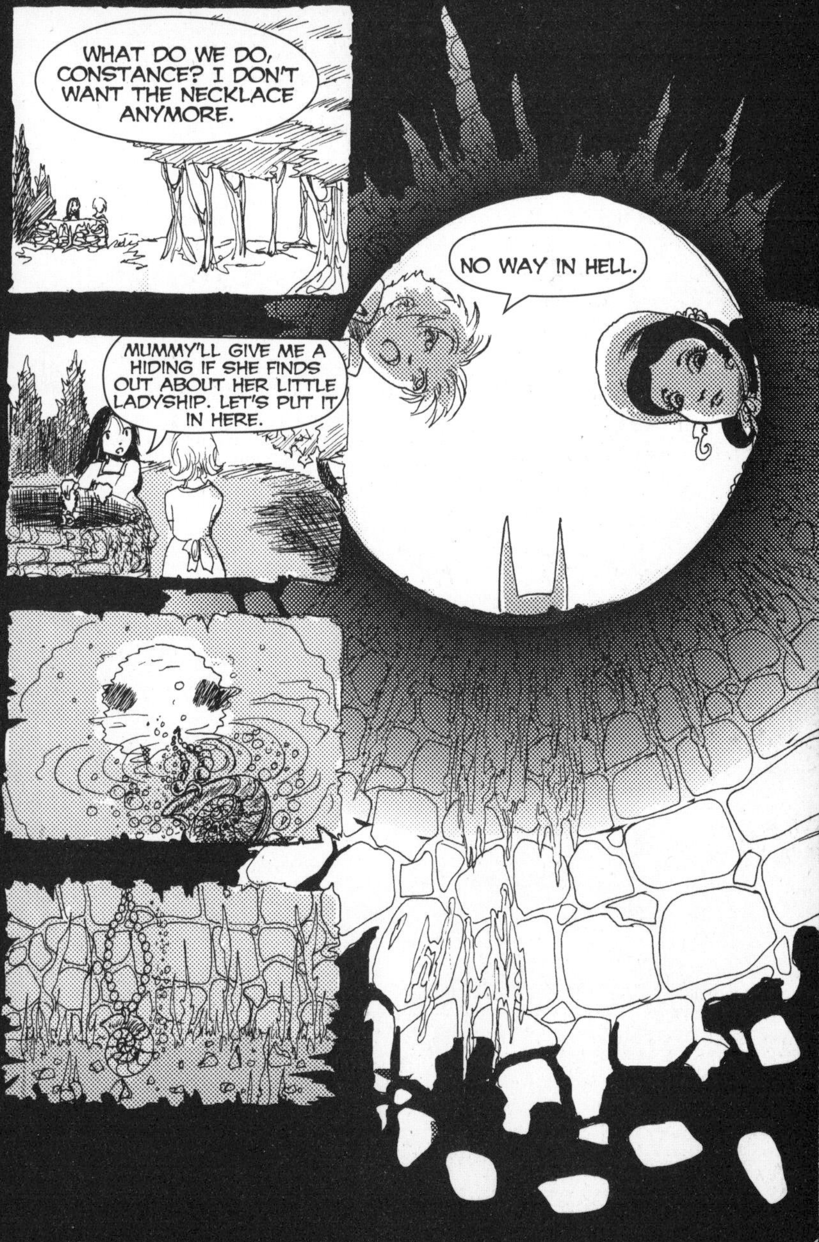
WHAT DO WE DO, CONSTANCE? I DON'T WANT THE NECKLACE ANYMORE.
NO WAY IN HELL.
MUMMY'LL GIVE ME A HIDING IF SHE FINDS OUT ABOUT HER LITTLE LADYSHIP. LET'S PUT IT IN HERE.

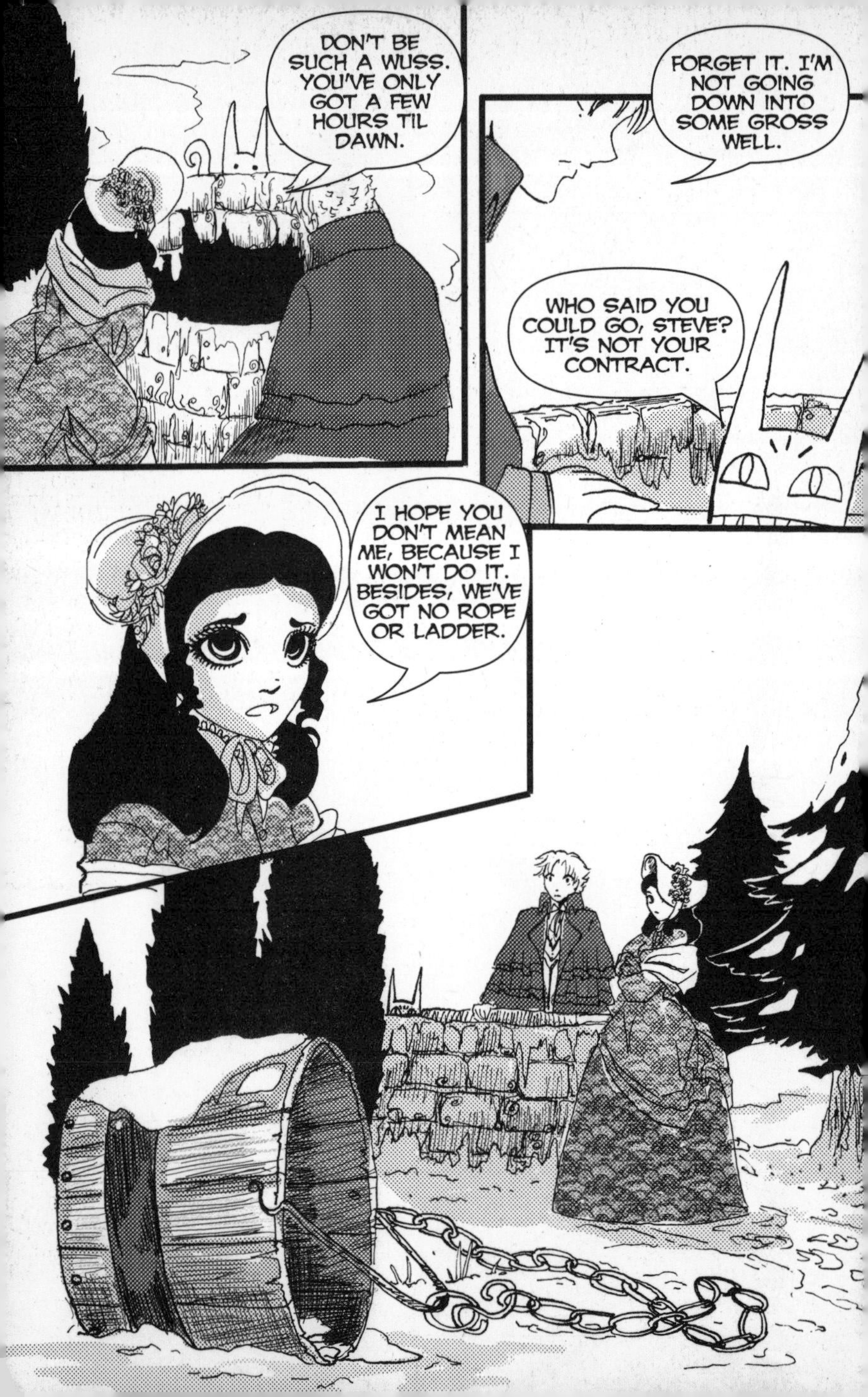
DON'T BE SUCH A WUSS. YOU'VE ONLY GOT A FEW HOURS TIL DAWN.
FORGET IT. I'M NOT GOING DOWN INTO SOME GROSS WELL.
WHO SAID YOU COULD GO, STEVE? IT'S NOT YOUR CONTRACT.
I HOPE YOU DON'T MEAN ME, BECAUSE I WON'T DO IT. BESIDES, WE'VE GOT NO ROPE OR LADDER.

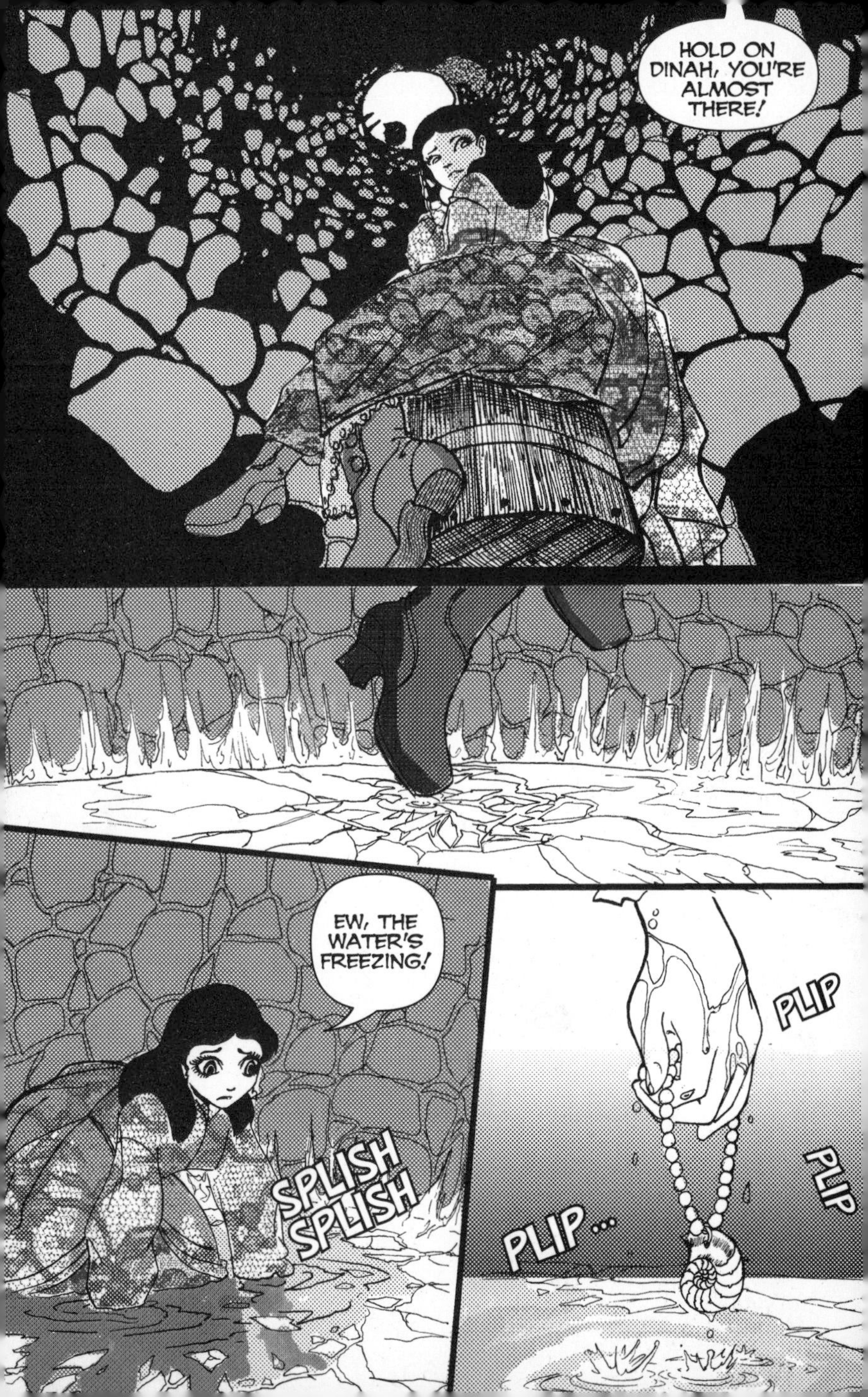
HOLD ON DINAH, YOU'RE ALMOST THERE!
EW, THE WATER'S FREEZING!
SPLISH SPLISH
PLIP
PLIP
PLIP...

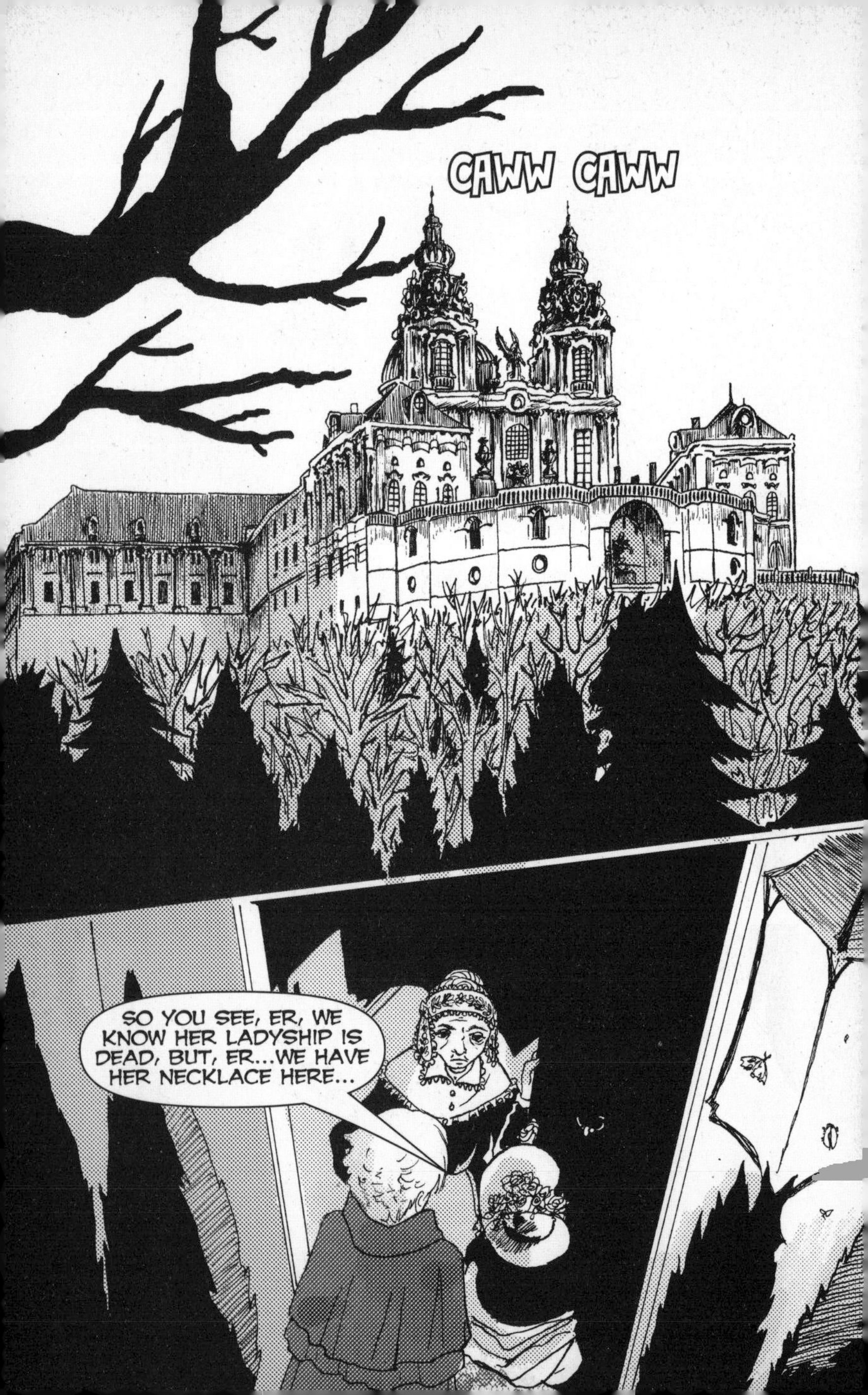
CAWW CAWW
SO YOU SEE, ER, WE KNOW HER LADYSHIP IS DEAD, BUT, ER...WE HAVE HER NECKLACE HERE...

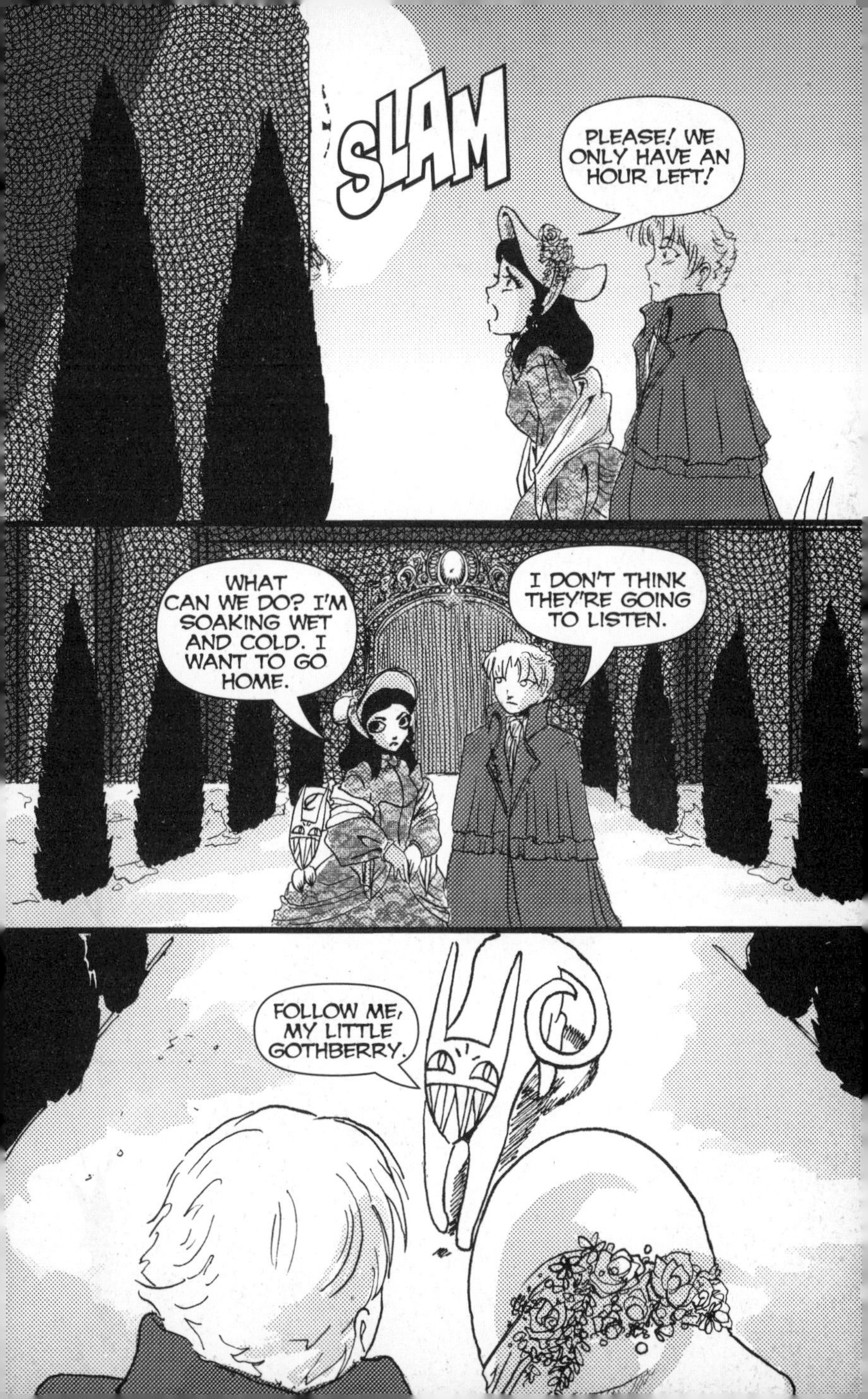
SLAM
PLEASE! WE ONLY HAVE AN HOUR LEFT!
WHAT CAN WE DO? I'M SOAKING WET AND COLD. I WANT TO GO HOME.
I DON'T THINK THEY'RE GOING TO LISTEN.
FOLLOW ME, MY LITTLE GOTHBERRY.

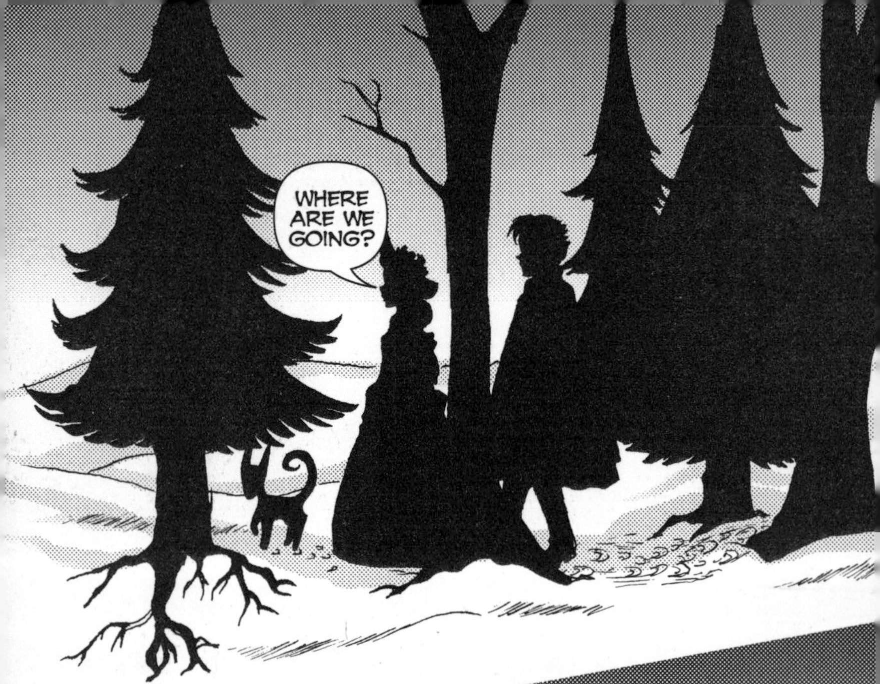
WHERE ARE WE GOING?

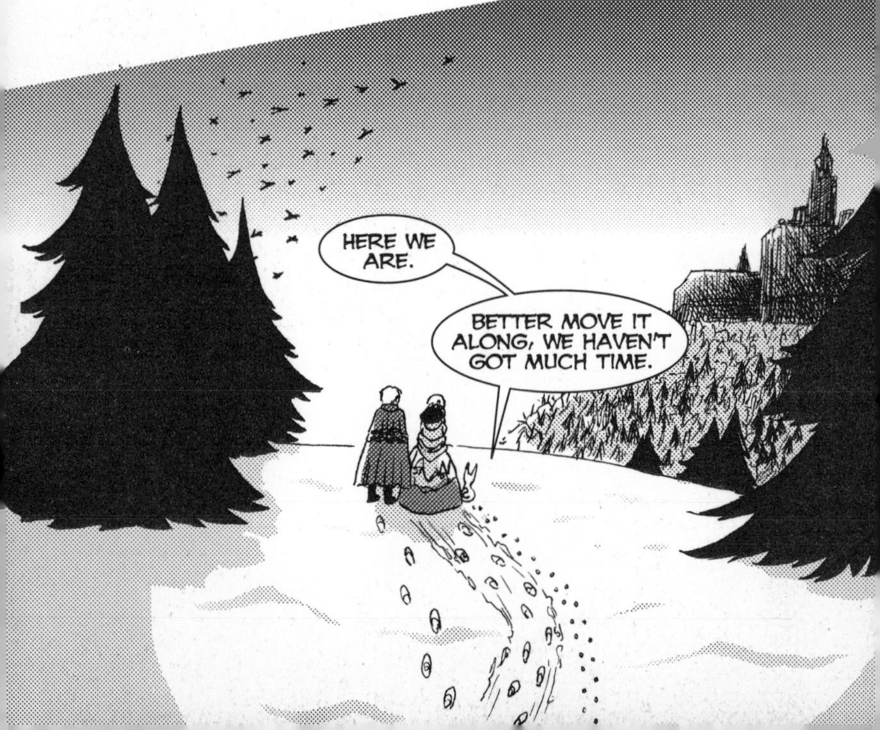
HERE WE ARE.
BETTER MOVE IT ALONG, WE HAVEN'T GOT MUCH TIME.

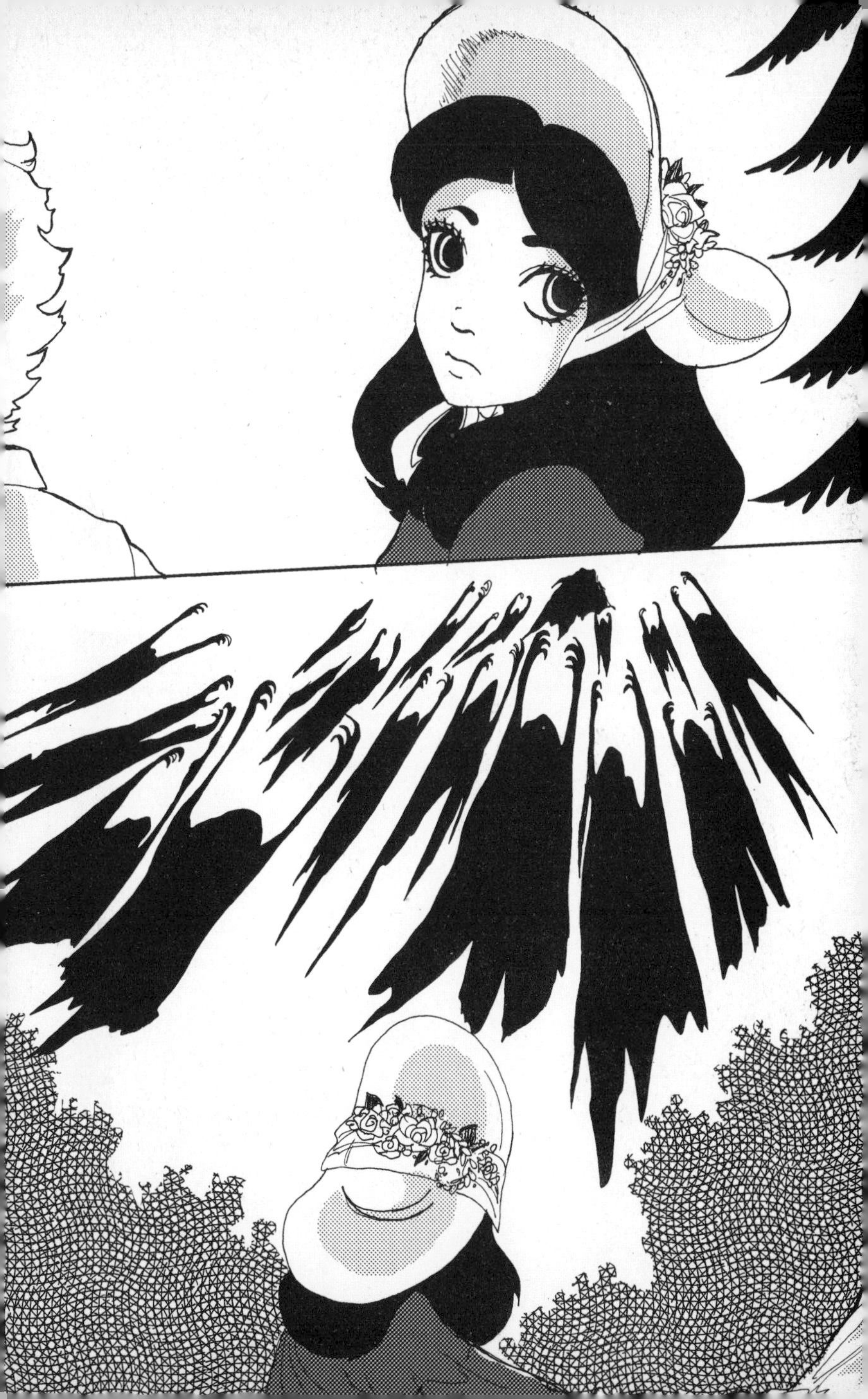

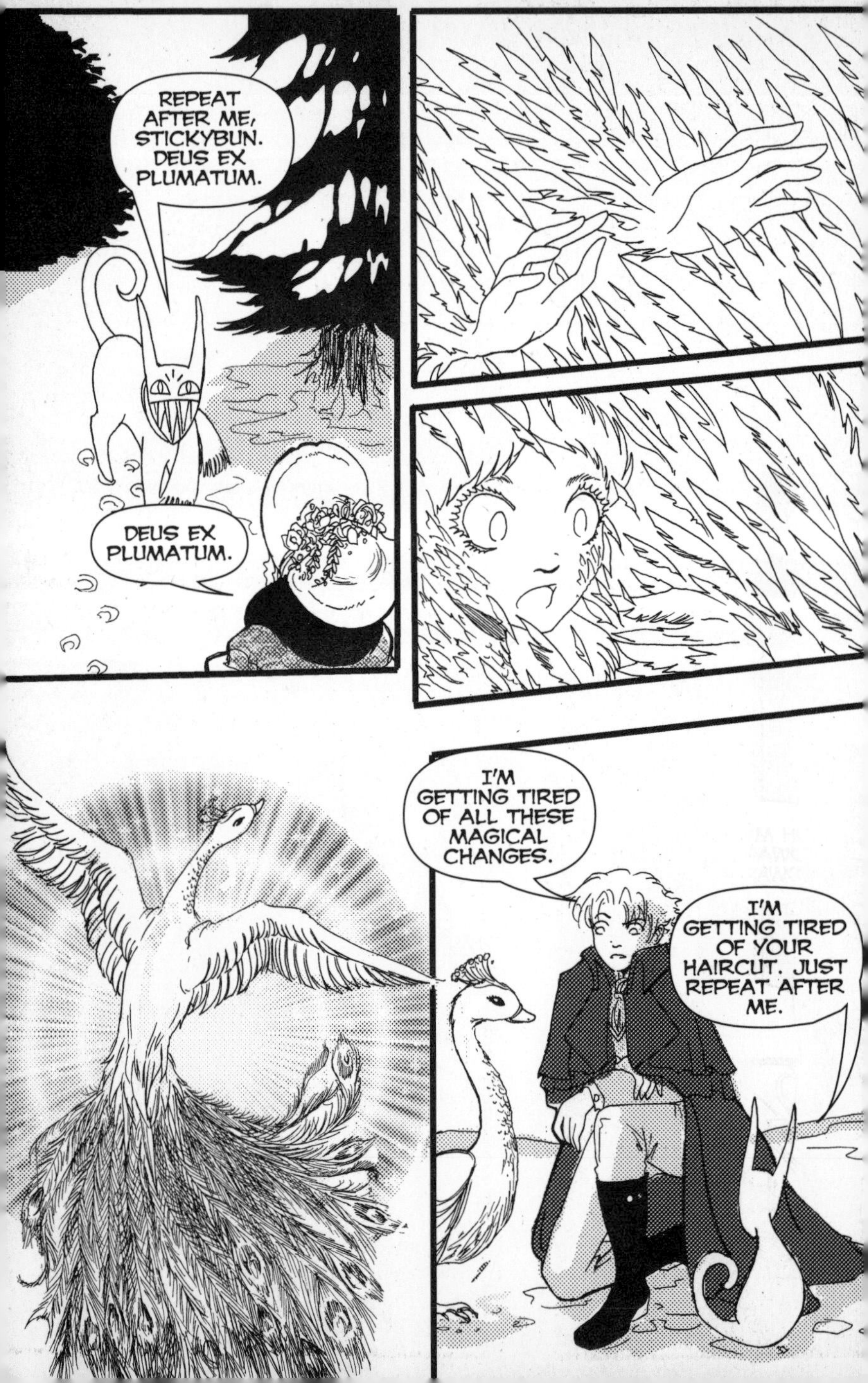

REPEAT AFTER ME, STICKYBUN. DEUS EX PLUMATUM.
DEUS EX PLUMATUM.
I'M GETTING TIRED OF ALL THESE MAGICAL CHANGES.
I'M GETTING TIRED OF YOUR HAIRCUT. JUST REPEAT AFTER ME.

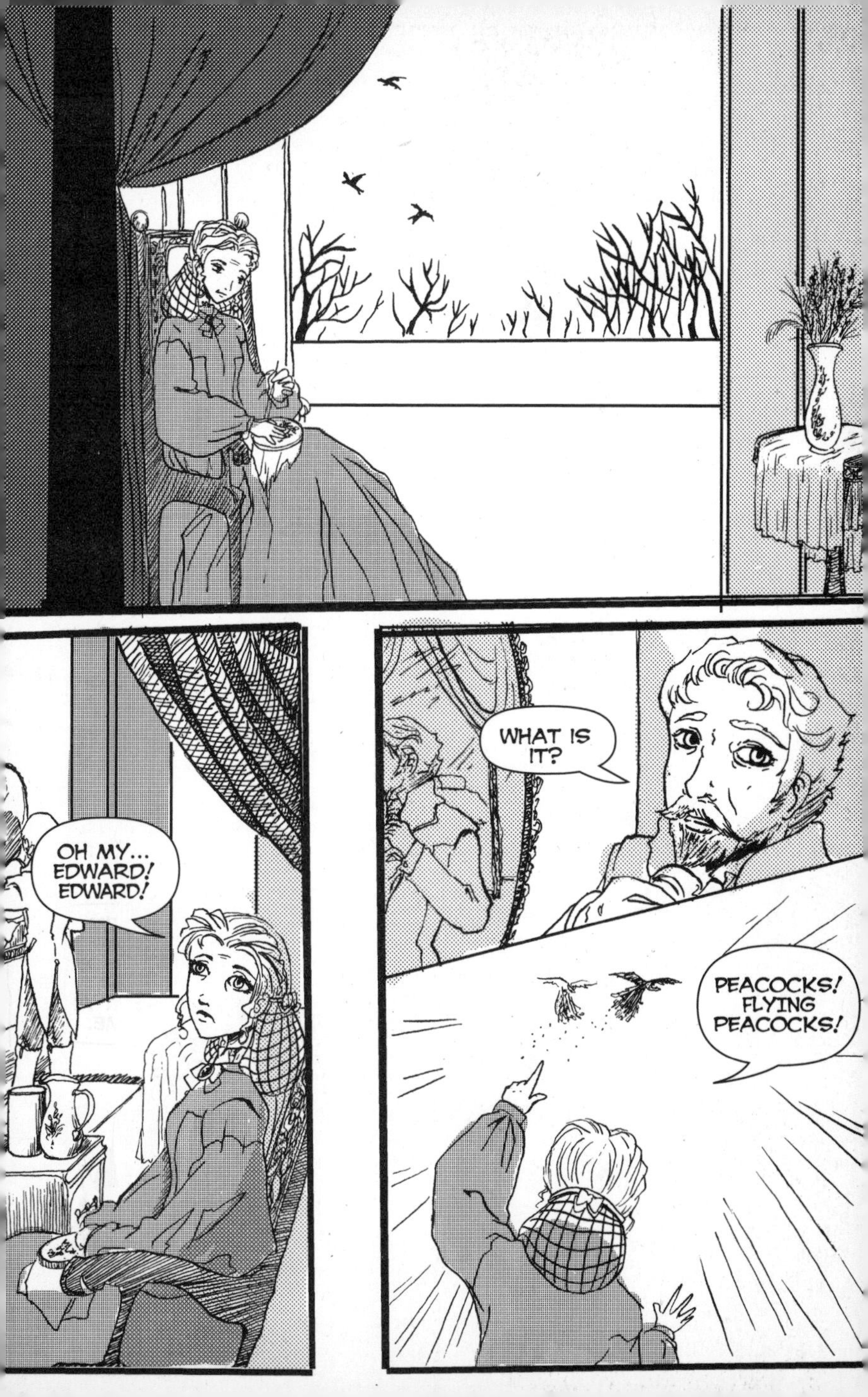
OH MY... EDWARD! EDWARD!
WHAT IS IT?
PEACOCKS! FLYING PEACOCKS!

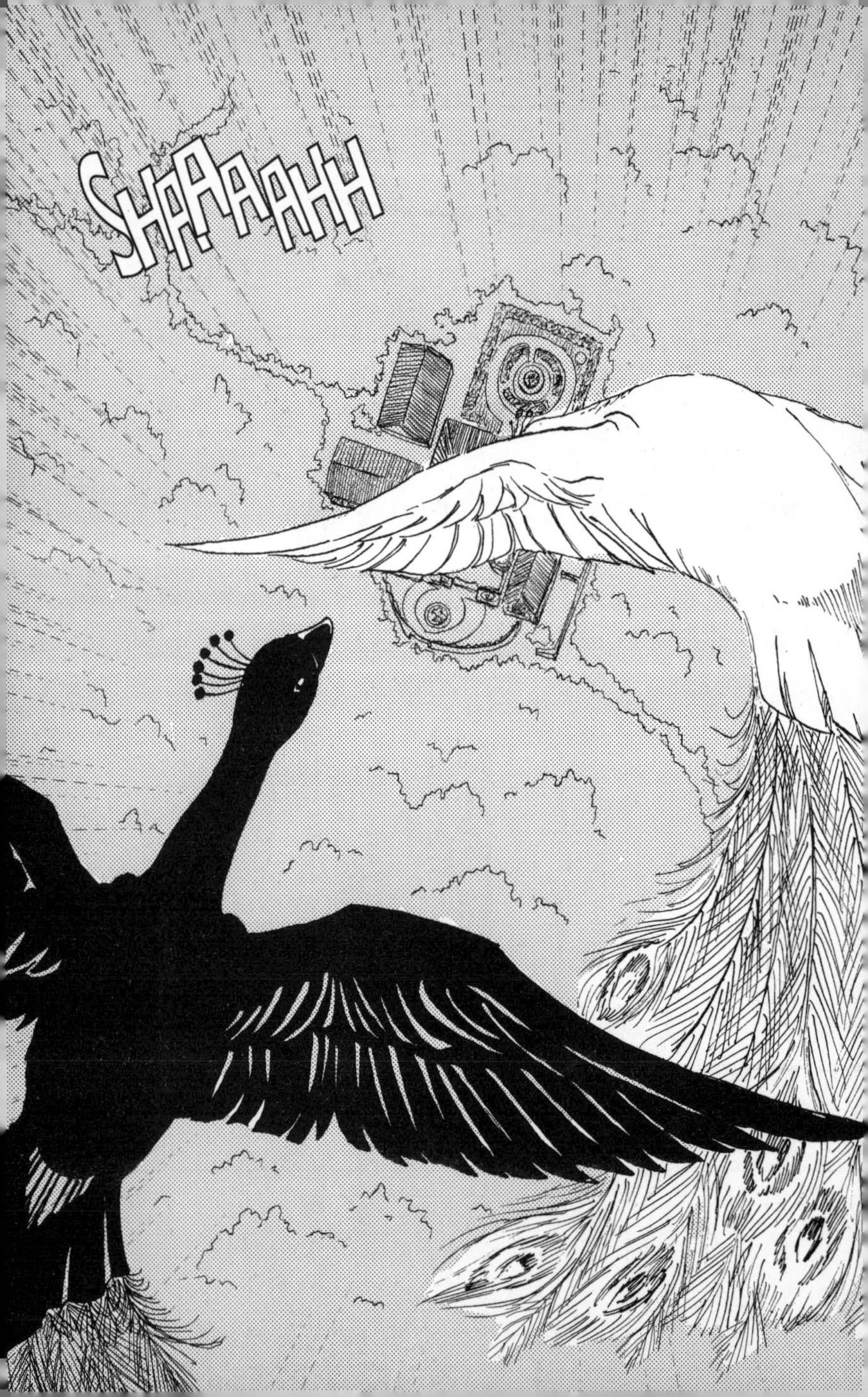
SHAAAAHH

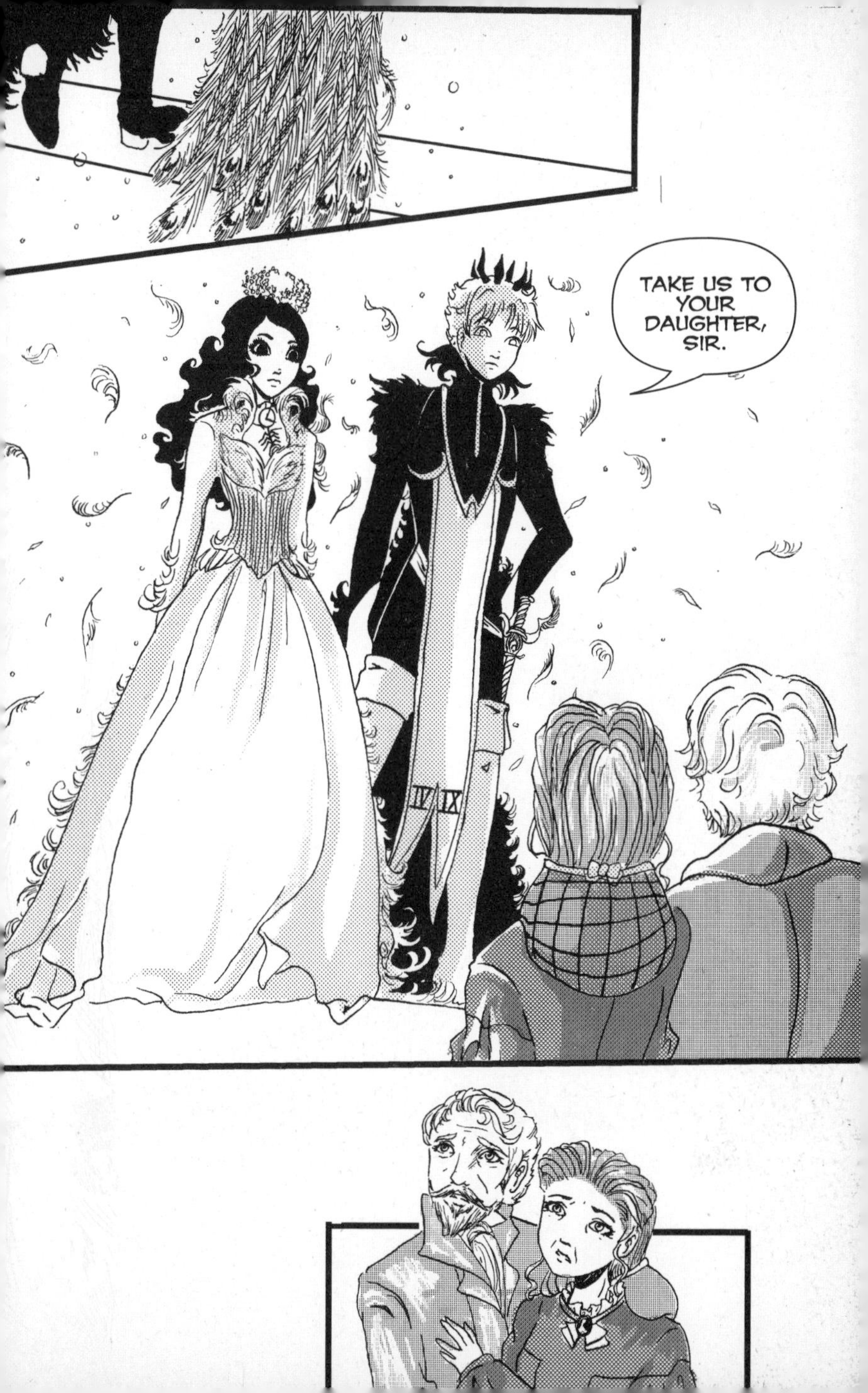
TAKE US TO YOUR DAUGHTER, SIR.

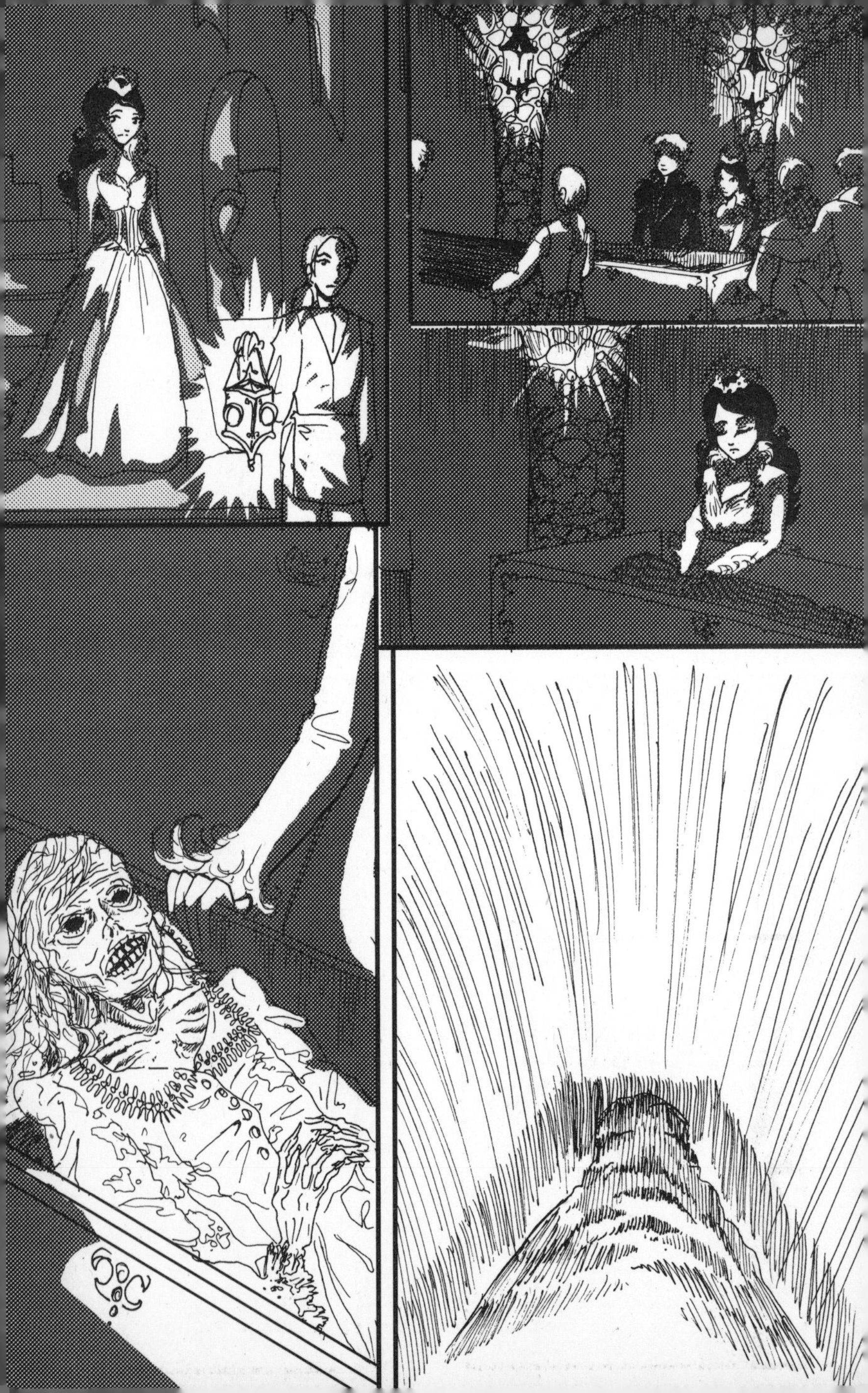

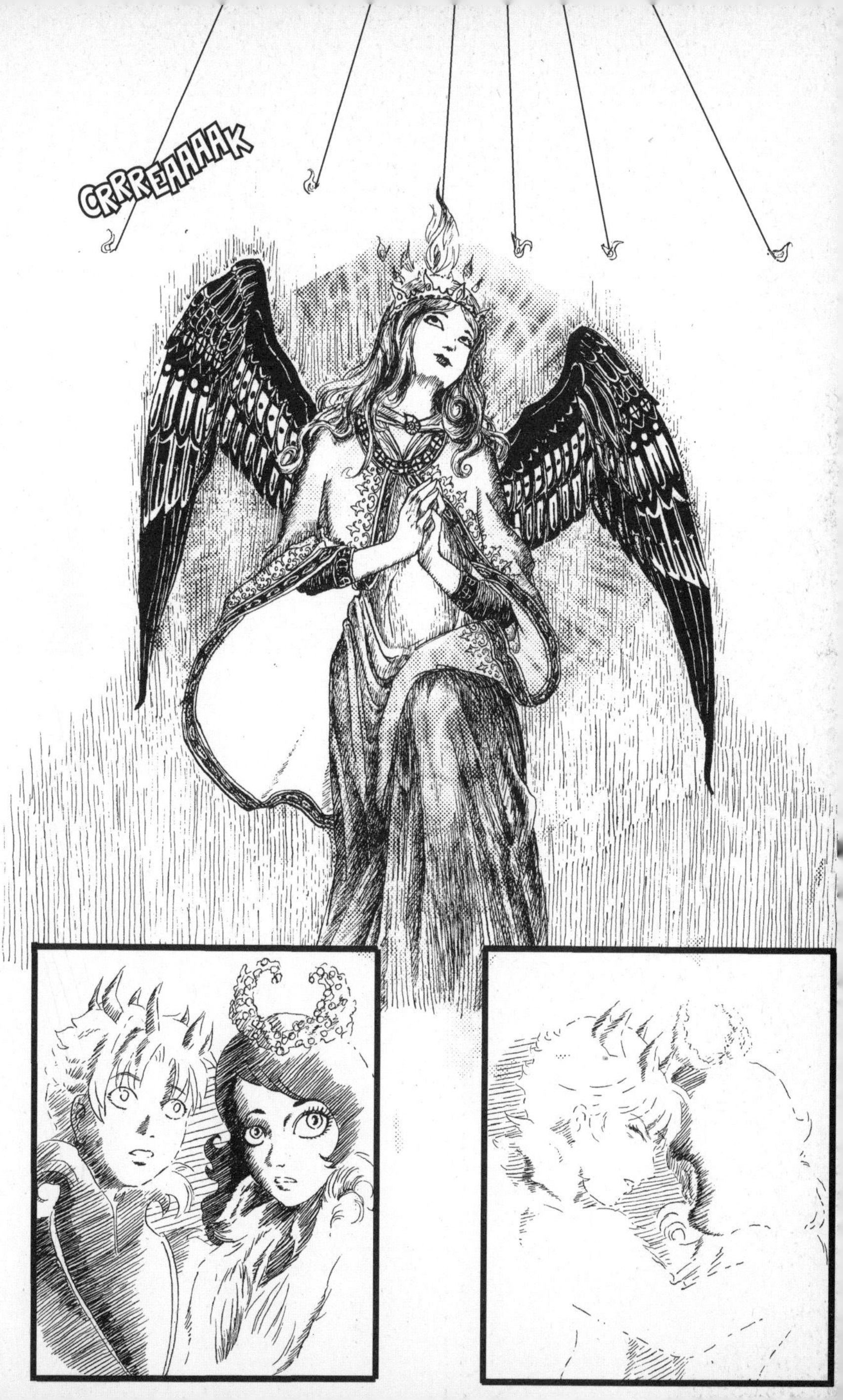
CRRREAAAAK

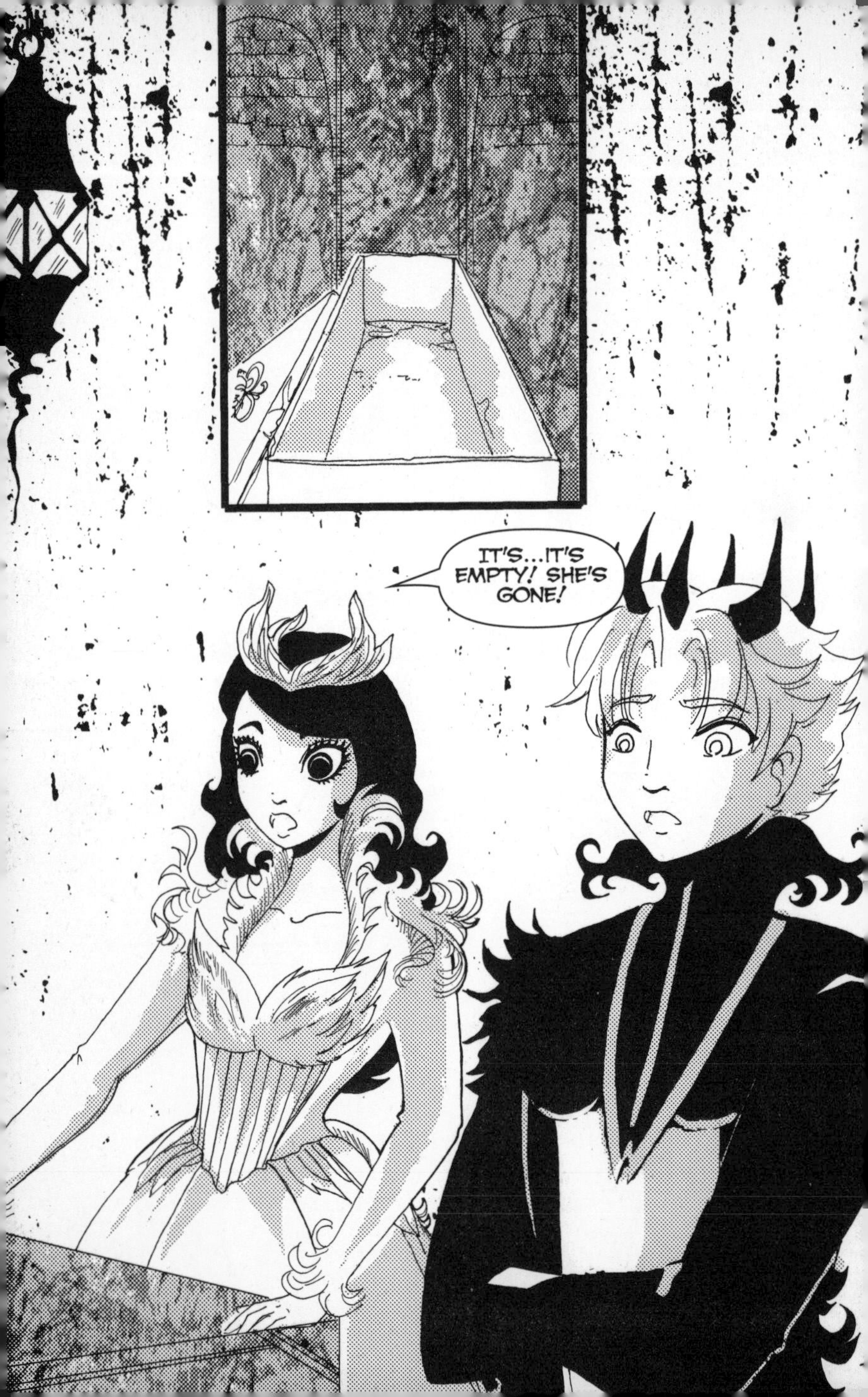
IT'S...IT'S EMPTY! SHE'S GONE!

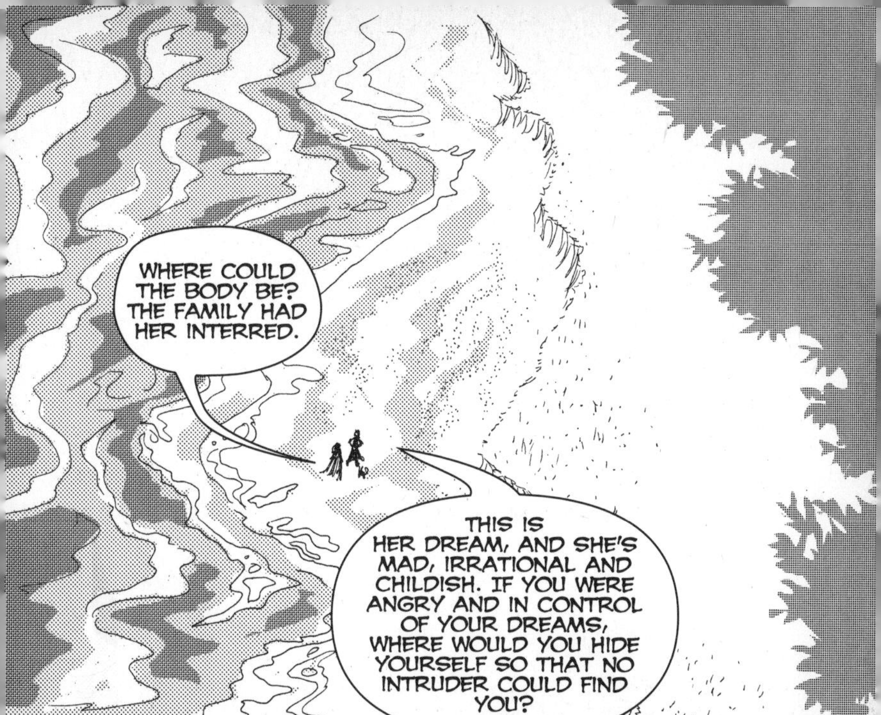
WHERE COULD THE BODY BE? THE FAMILY HAD HER INTERRED.
THIS IS HER DREAM, AND SHE'S MAD, IRRATIONAL AND CHILDISH. IF YOU WERE ANGRY AND IN CONTROL OF YOUR DREAMS, WHERE WOULD YOU HIDE YOURSELF SO THAT NO INTRUDER COULD FIND YOU?

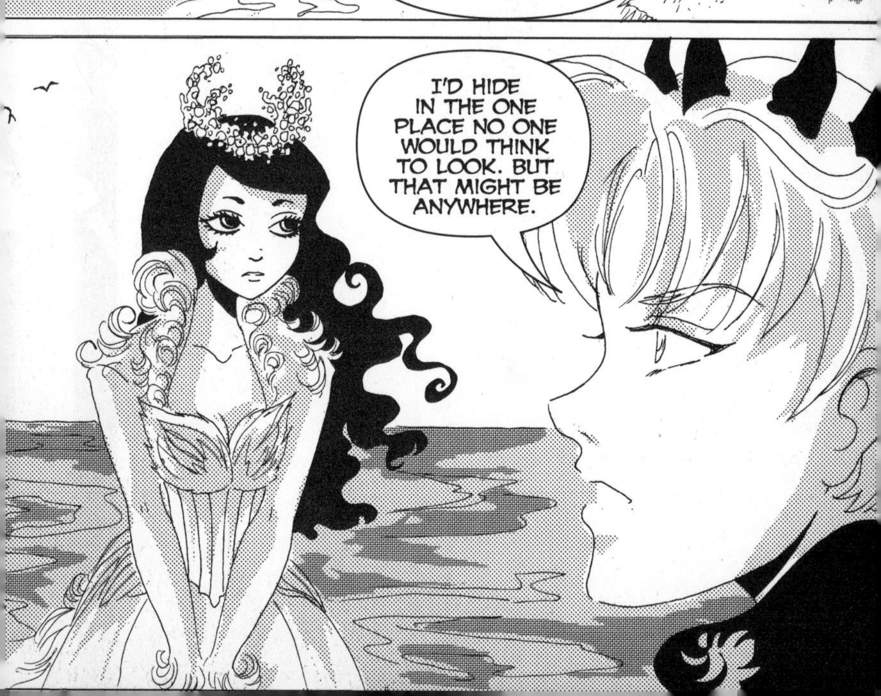
I'D HIDE IN THE ONE PLACE NO ONE WOULD THINK TO LOOK. BUT THAT MIGHT BE ANYWHERE.

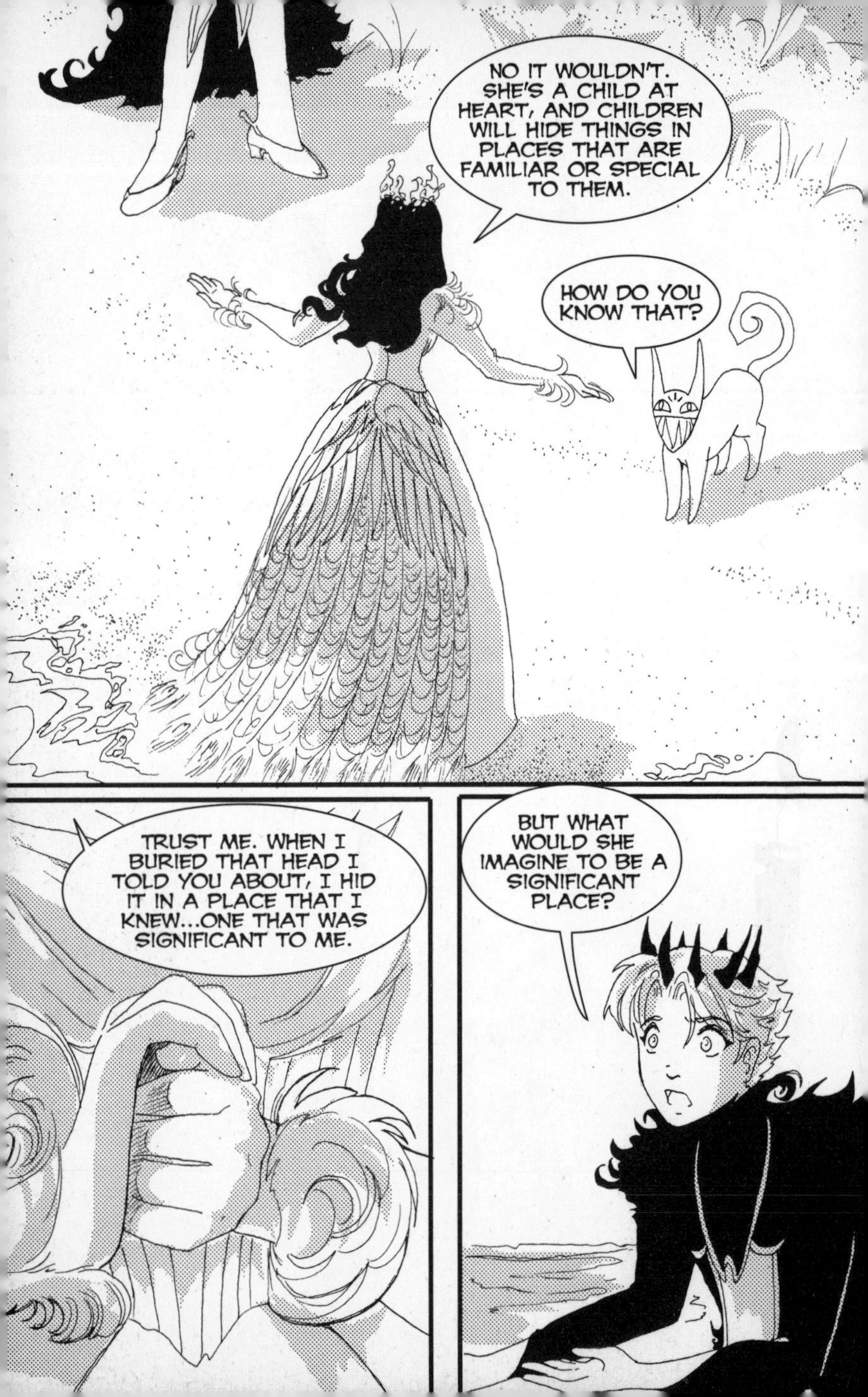
NO IT WOULDN'T. SHE'S A CHILD AT HEART, AND CHILDREN WILL HIDE THINGS IN PLACES THAT ARE FAMILIAR OR SPECIAL TO THEM.
HOW DO YOU KNOW THAT?
TRUST ME. WHEN I BURIED THAT HEAD I TOLD YOU ABOUT, I HID IT IN A PLACE THAT I KNEW...ONE THAT WAS SIGNIFICANT TO ME.
BUT WHAT WOULD SHE IMAGINE TO BE A SIGNIFICANT PLACE?

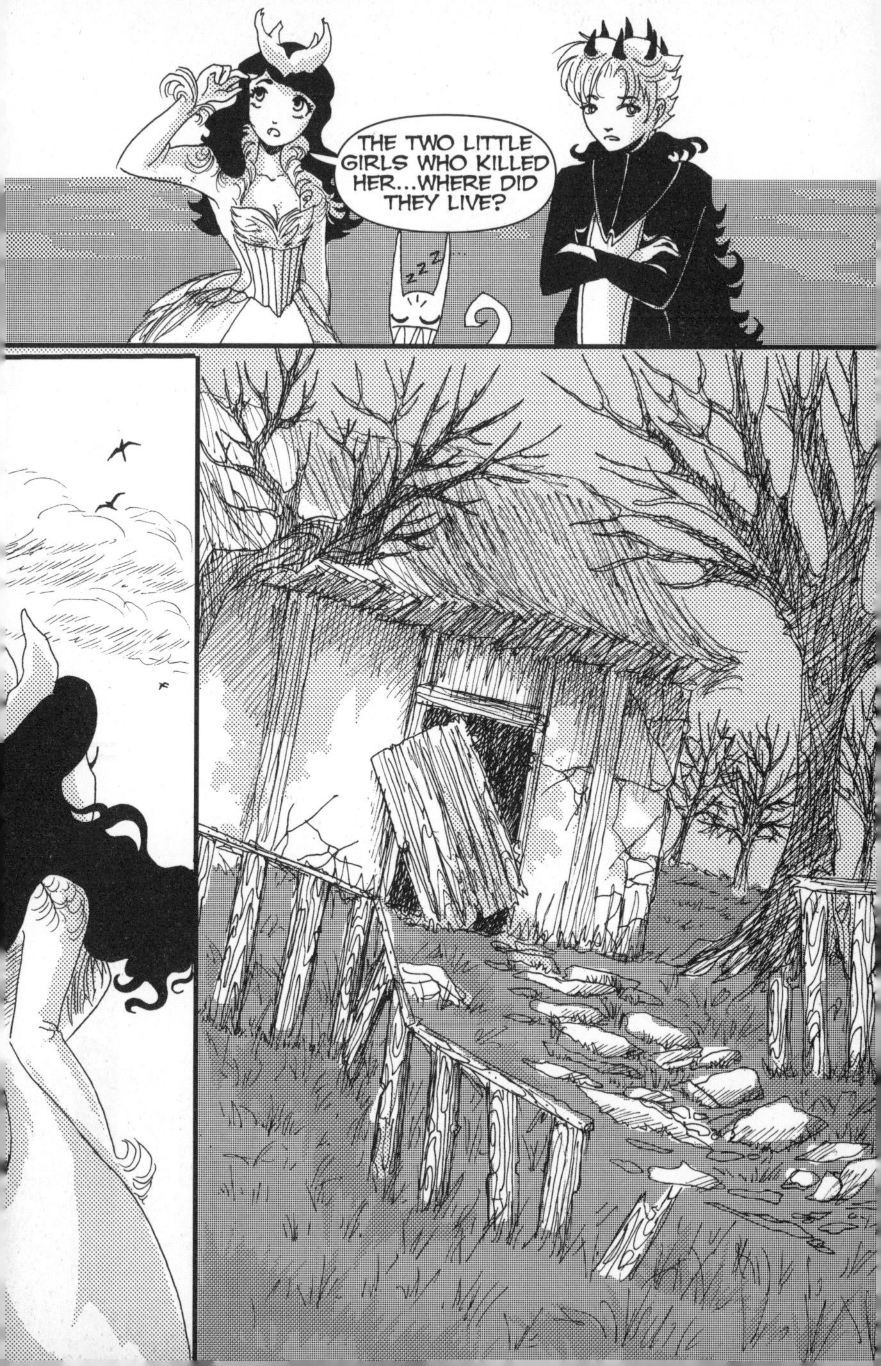
THE TWO LITTLE GIRLS WHO KILLED HER...WHERE DID THEY LIVE?
ZZZ

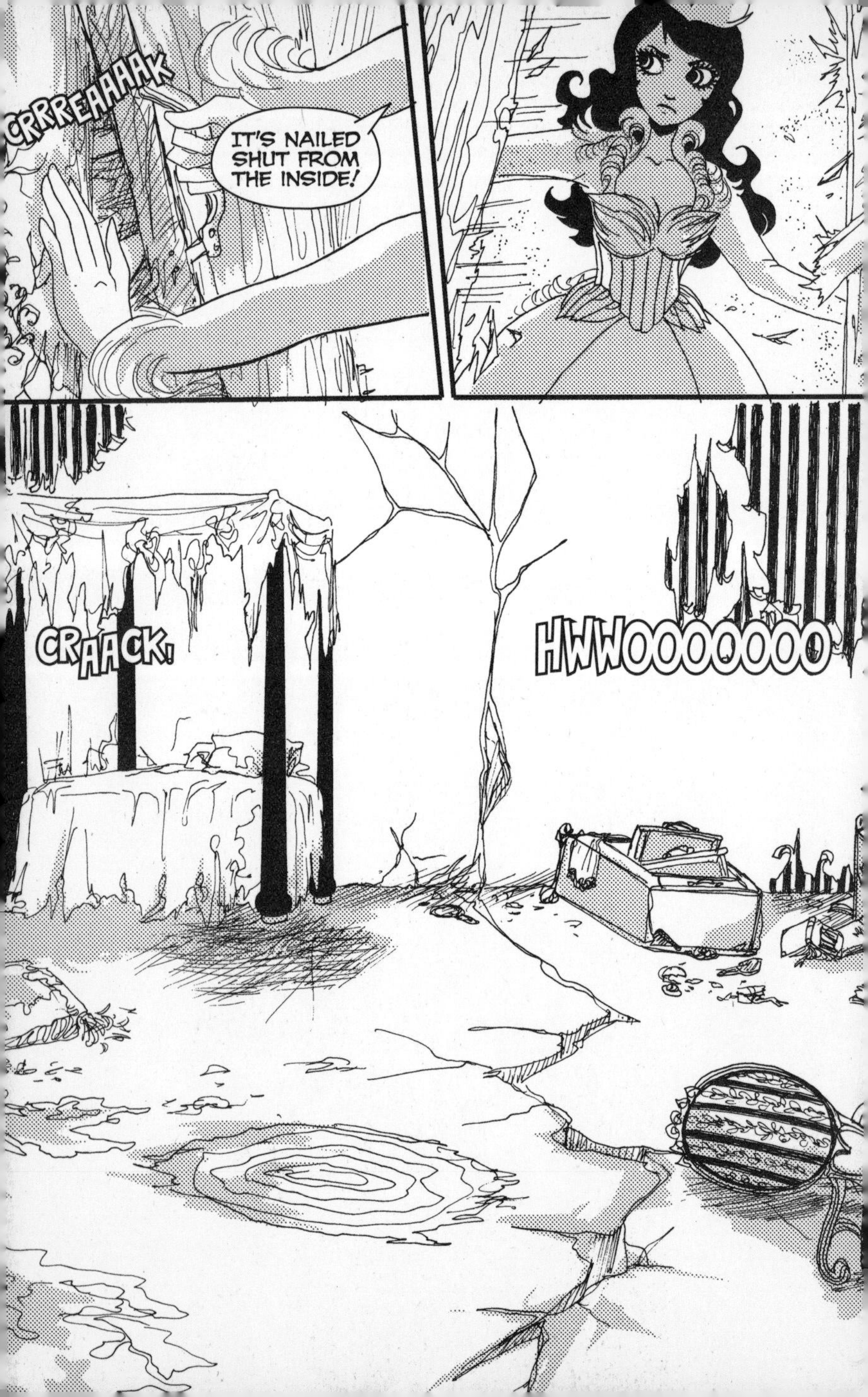
CRRREAAAAK
IT'S NAILED SHUT FROM THE INSIDE!
CRAACK!
HWWOOOOOOO

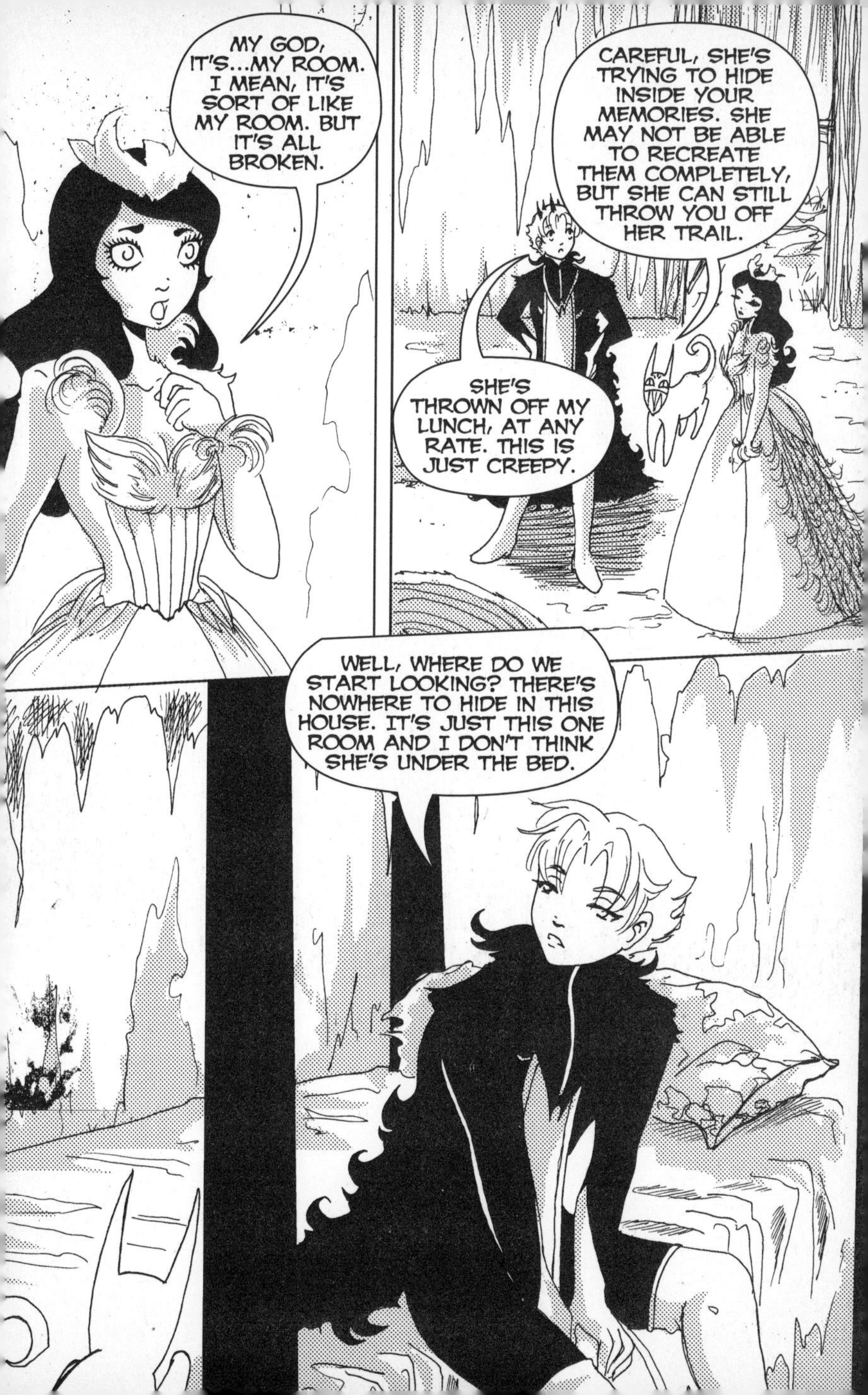
MY GOD, IT'S...MY ROOM. I MEAN, IT'S SORT OF LIKE MY ROOM. BUT IT'S ALL BROKEN.
CAREFUL, SHE'S TRYING TO HIDE INSIDE YOUR MEMORIES. SHE MAY NOT BE ABLE TO RECREATE THEM COMPLETELY, BUT SHE CAN STILL THROW YOU OFF HER TRAIL.
SHE'S THROWN OFF MY LUNCH, AT ANY RATE. THIS IS JUST CREEPY.
WELL, WHERE DO WE START LOOKING? THERE'S NOWHERE TO HIDE IN THIS HOUSE. IT'S JUST THIS ONE ROOM AND I DON'T THINK SHE'S UNDER THE BED.

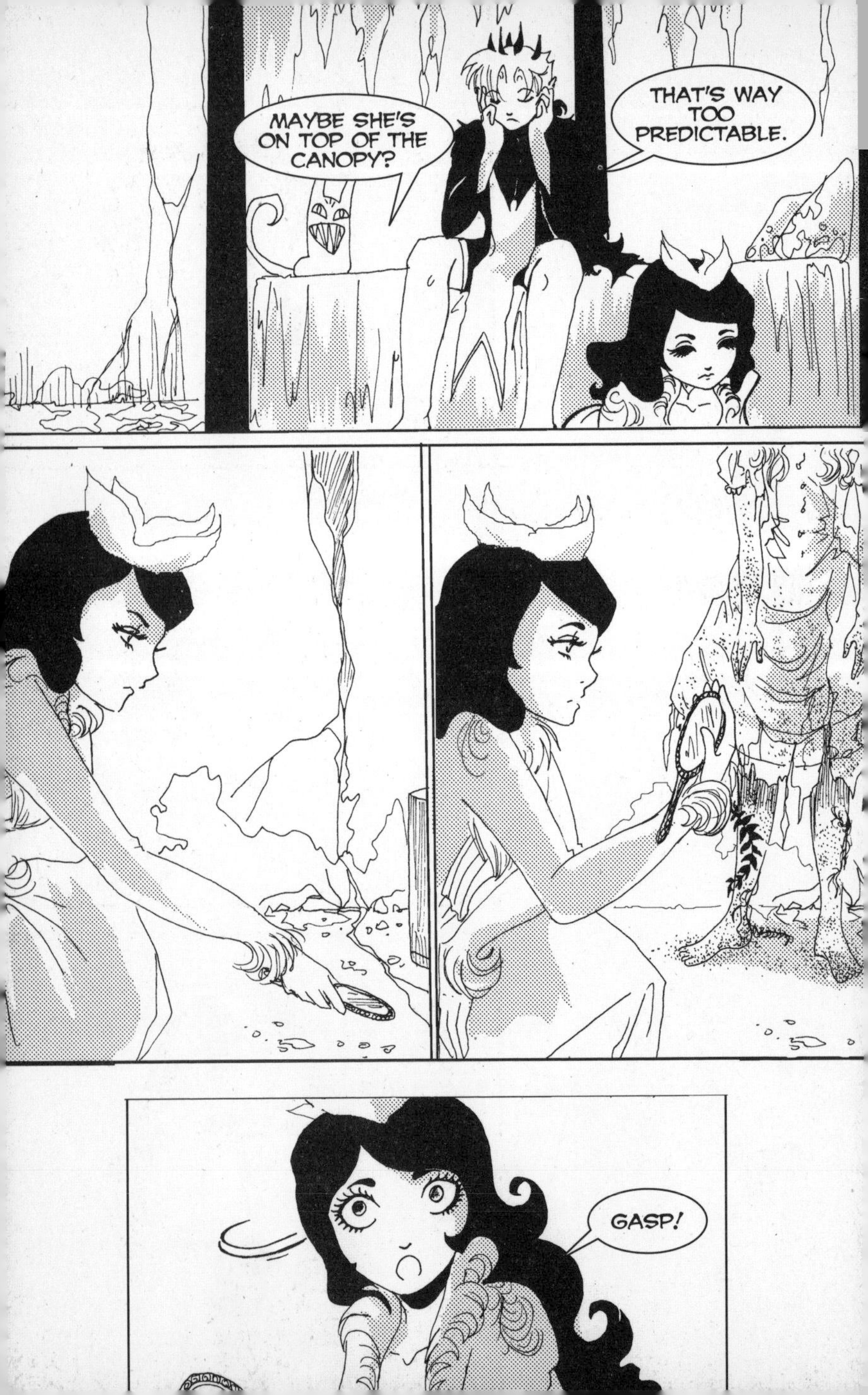
MAYBE SHE'S ON TOP OF THE CANOPY?
THAT'S WAY TOO PREDICTABLE.
GASP!

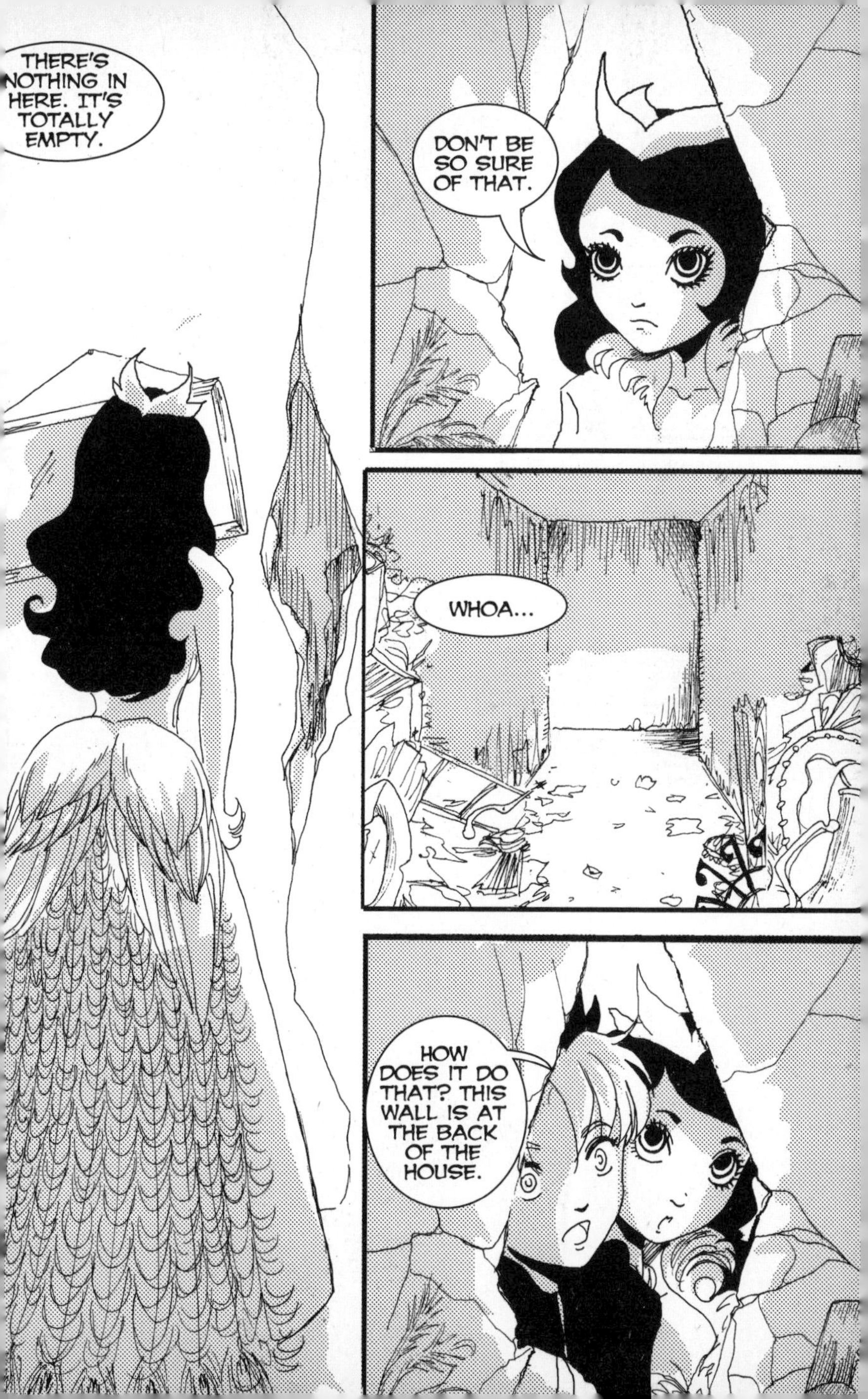
THERE'S NOTHING IN HERE. IT'S TOTALLY EMPTY.
DON'T BE SO SURE OF THAT.
WHOA...
HOW DOES IT DO THAT? THIS WALL IS AT THE BACK OF THE HOUSE.

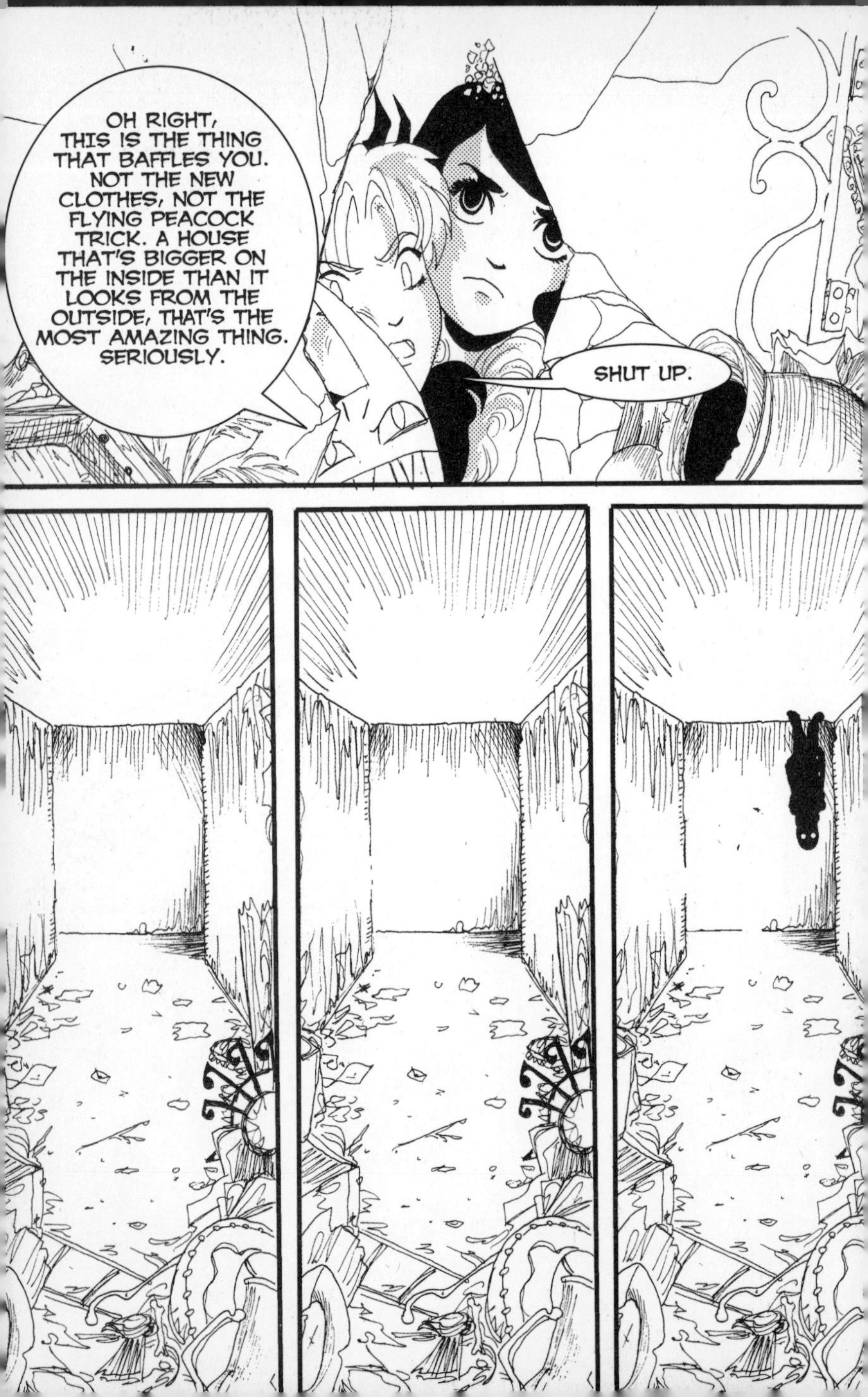
OH RIGHT, THIS IS THE THING THAT BAFFLES YOU. NOT THE NEW CLOTHES, NOT THE FLYING PEACOCK TRICK. A HOUSE THAT'S BIGGER ON THE INSIDE THAN IT LOOKS FROM THE OUTSIDE, THAT'S THE MOST AMAZING THING. SERIOUSLY.
SHUT UP.

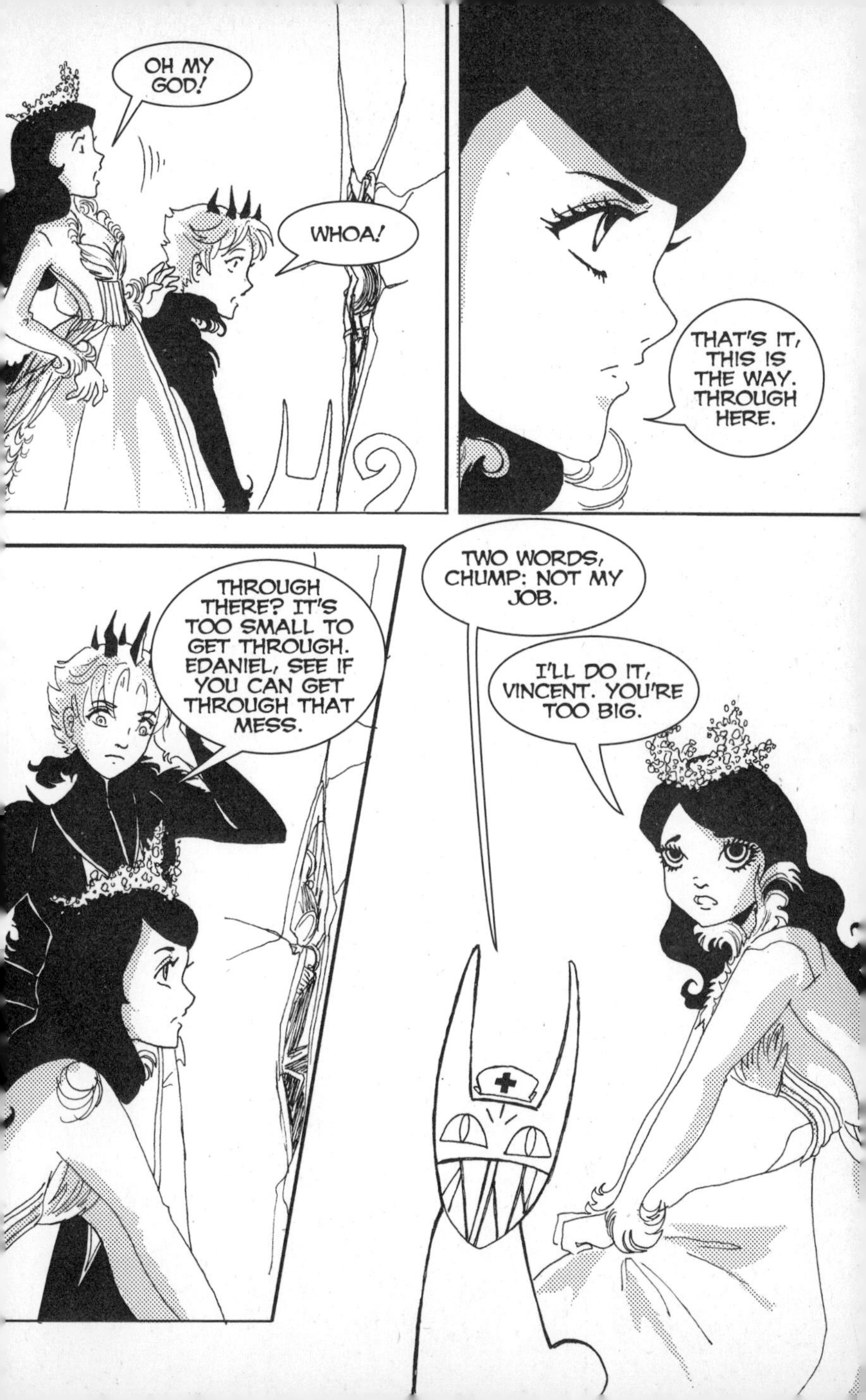
OH MY GOD!
WHOA!
THAT'S IT, THIS IS THE WAY. THROUGH HERE.
THROUGH THERE? IT'S TOO SMALL TO GET THROUGH. EDANIEL, SEE IF YOU CAN GET THROUGH THAT MESS.
TWO WORDS, CHUMP: NOT MY JOB.
I'LL DO IT, VINCENT. YOU'RE TOO BIG.

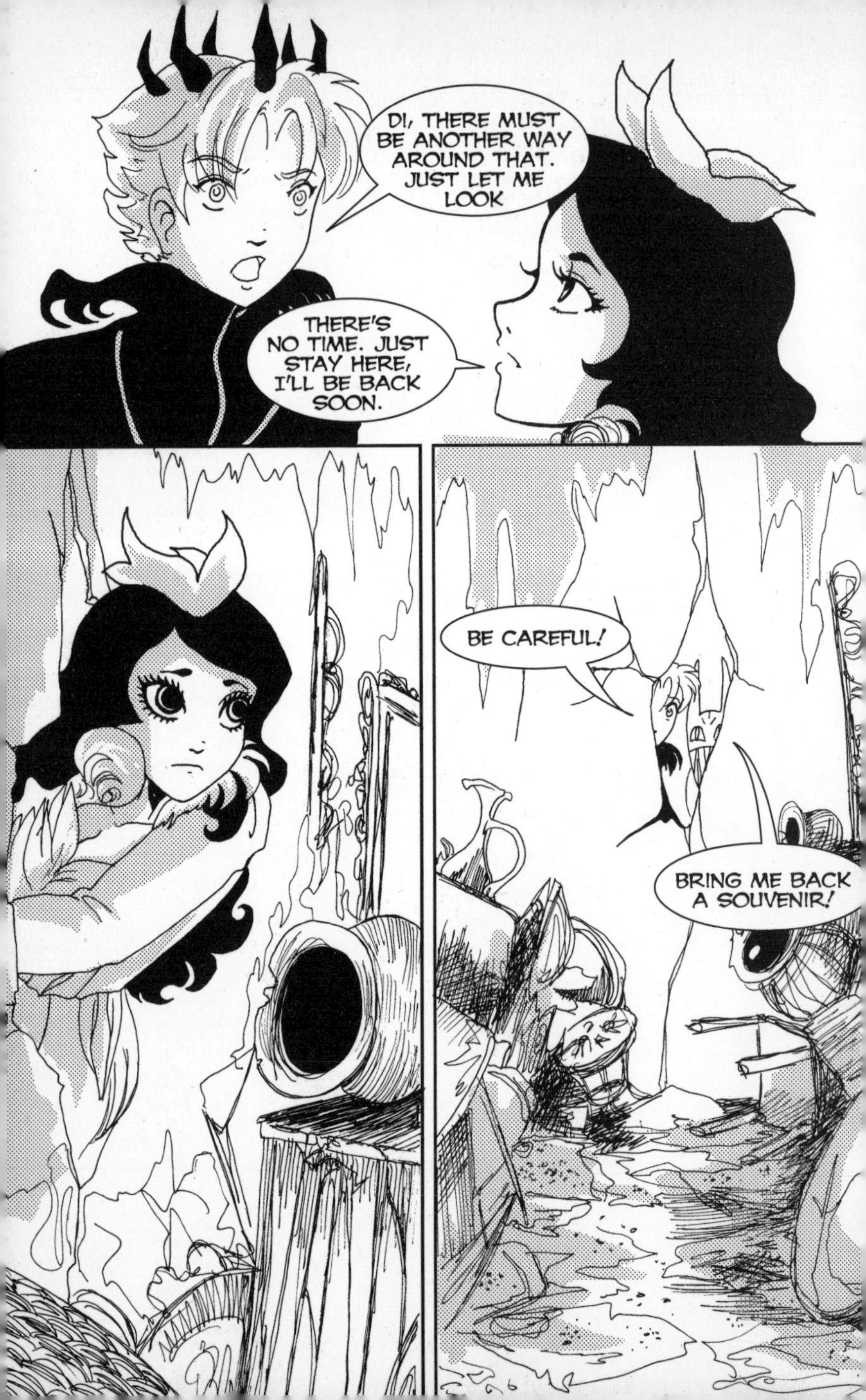
DI, THERE MUST BE ANOTHER WAY AROUND THAT. JUST LET ME LOOK
THERE'S NO TIME. JUST STAY HERE, I'LL BE BACK SOON.
BE CAREFUL!
BRING ME BACK A SOUVENIR!

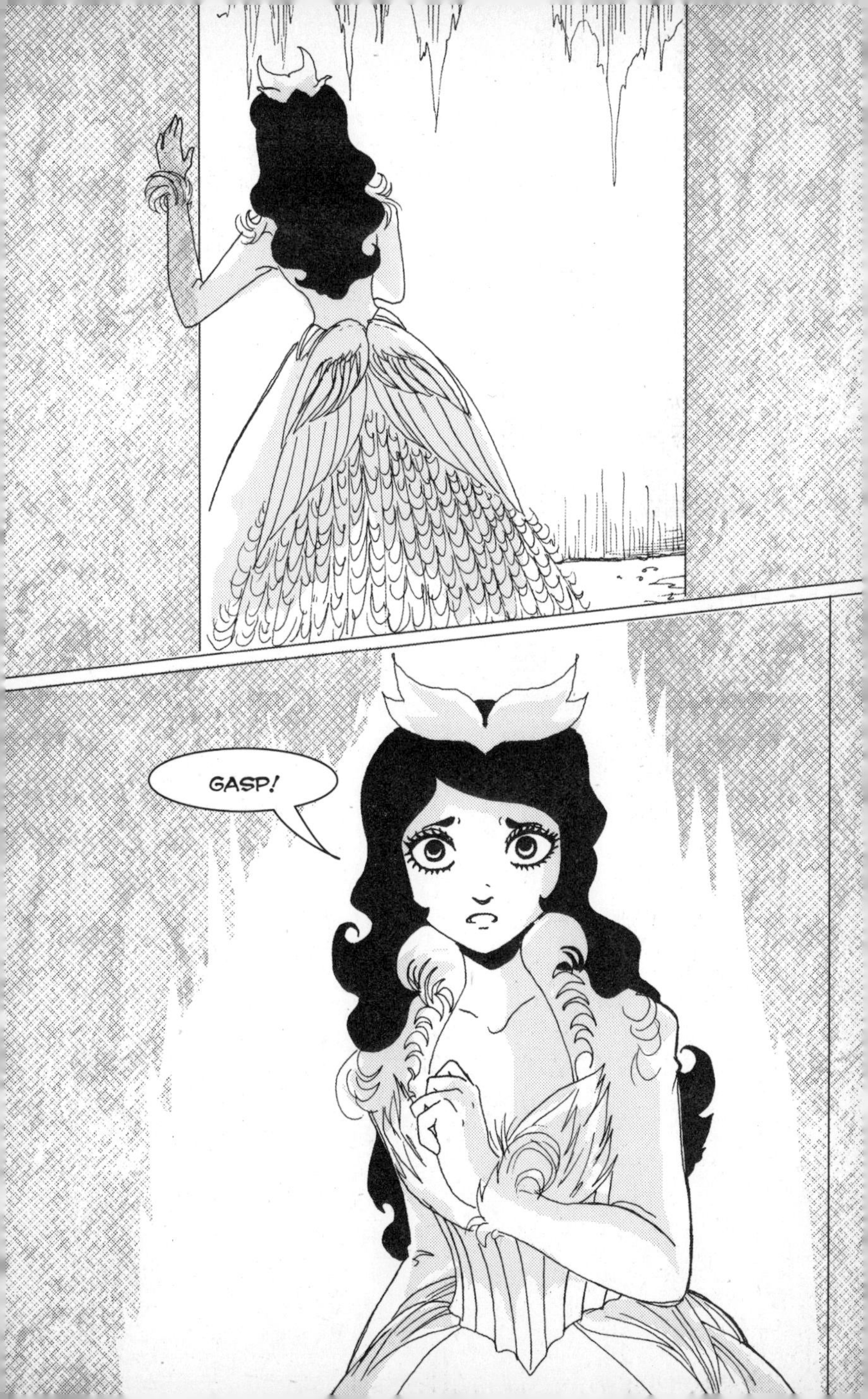
GASP!

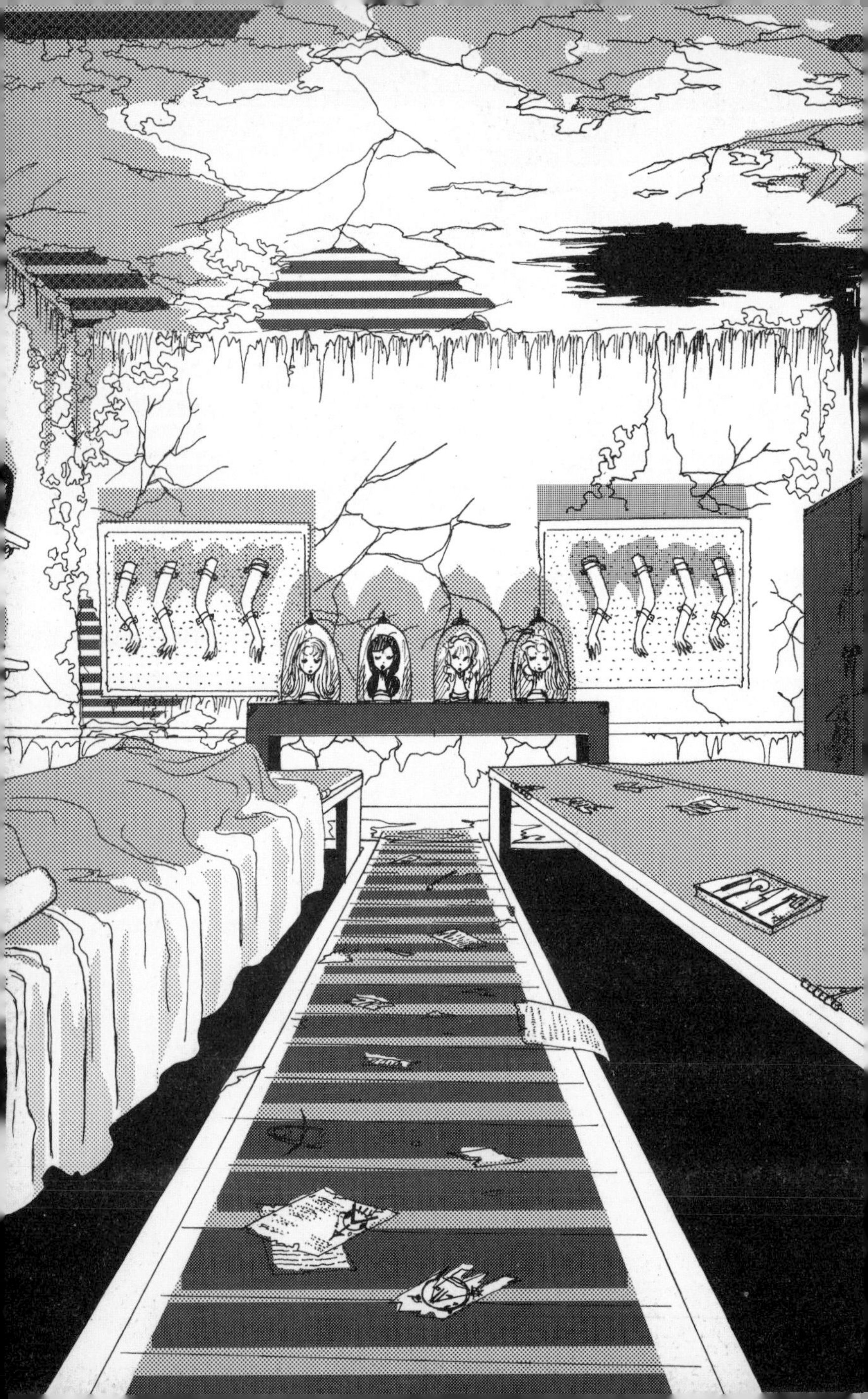

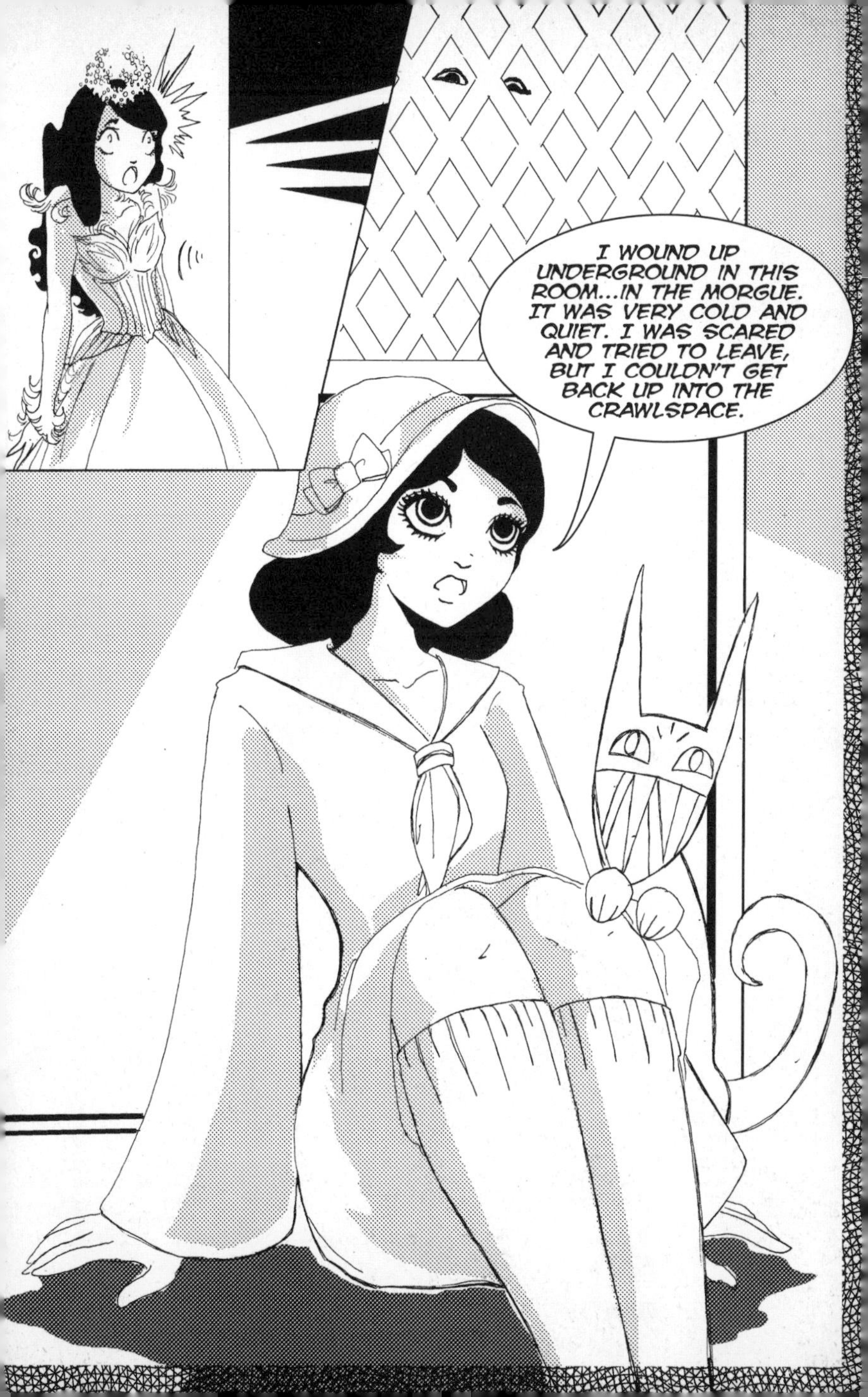
I WOUND UP UNDERGROUND IN THIS ROOM...IN THE MORGUE. IT WAS VERY COLD AND QUIET. I WAS SCARED AND TRIED TO LEAVE, BUT I COULDN'T GET BACK UP INTO THE CRAWLSPACE.

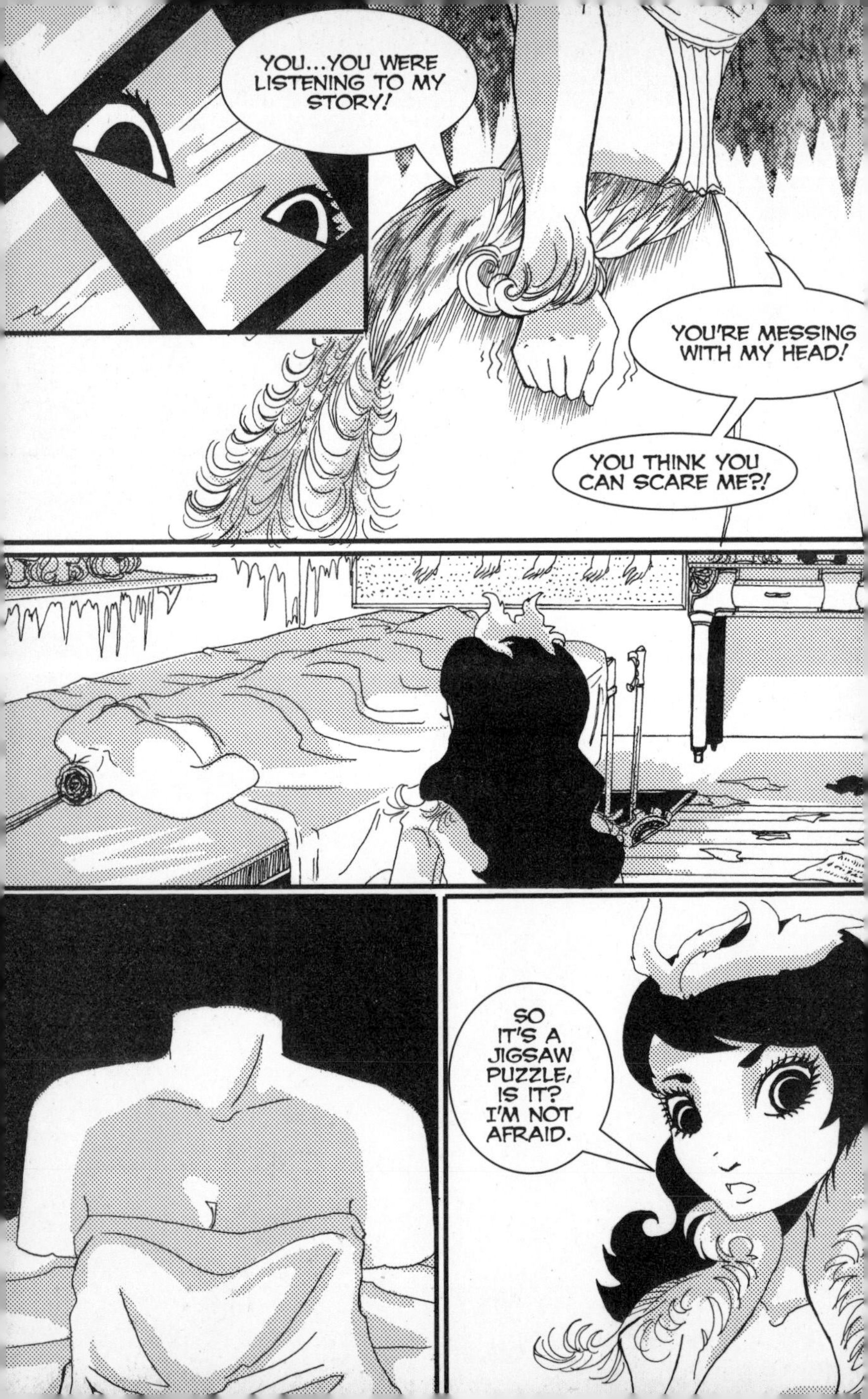
YOU...YOU WERE LISTENING TO MY STORY!
YOU'RE MESSING WITH MY HEAD!
YOU THINK YOU CAN SCARE ME?!
SO IT'S A JIGSAW PUZZLE, IS IT? I'M NOT AFRAID.

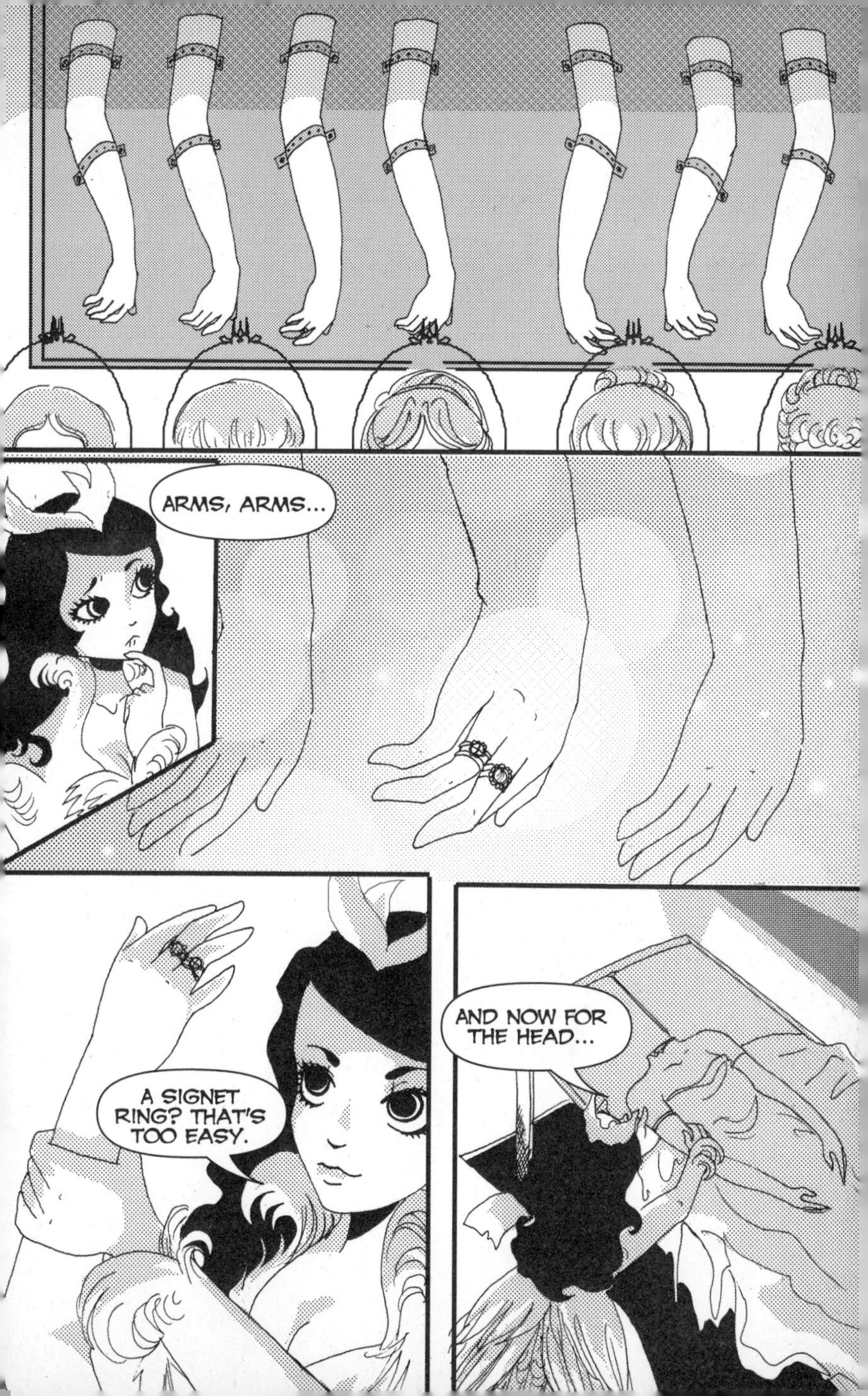
ARMS, ARMS...
A SIGNET RING? THAT'S TOO EASY.
AND NOW FOR THE HEAD...

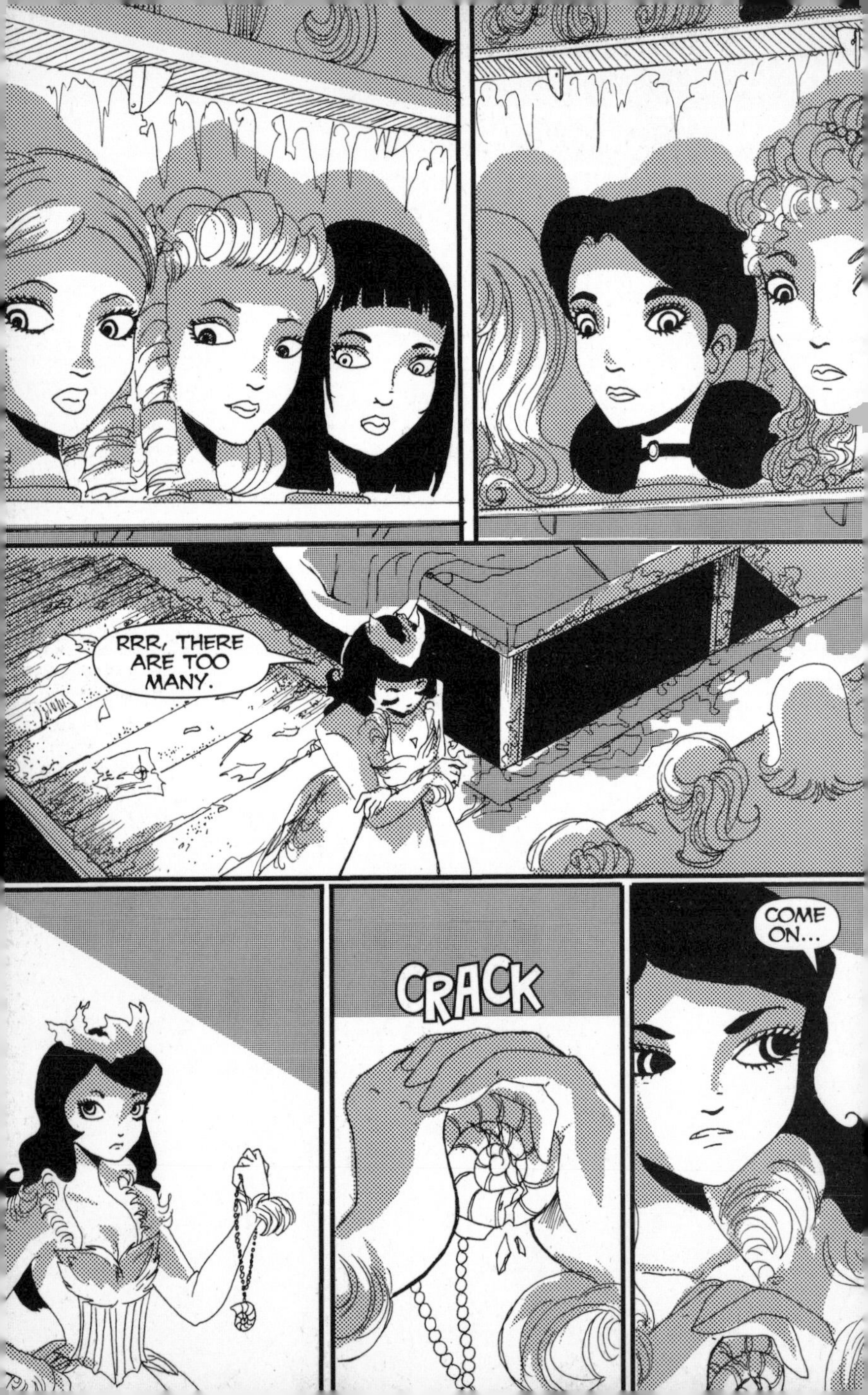
RRR, THERE ARE TOO MANY.
CRACK
COME ON...

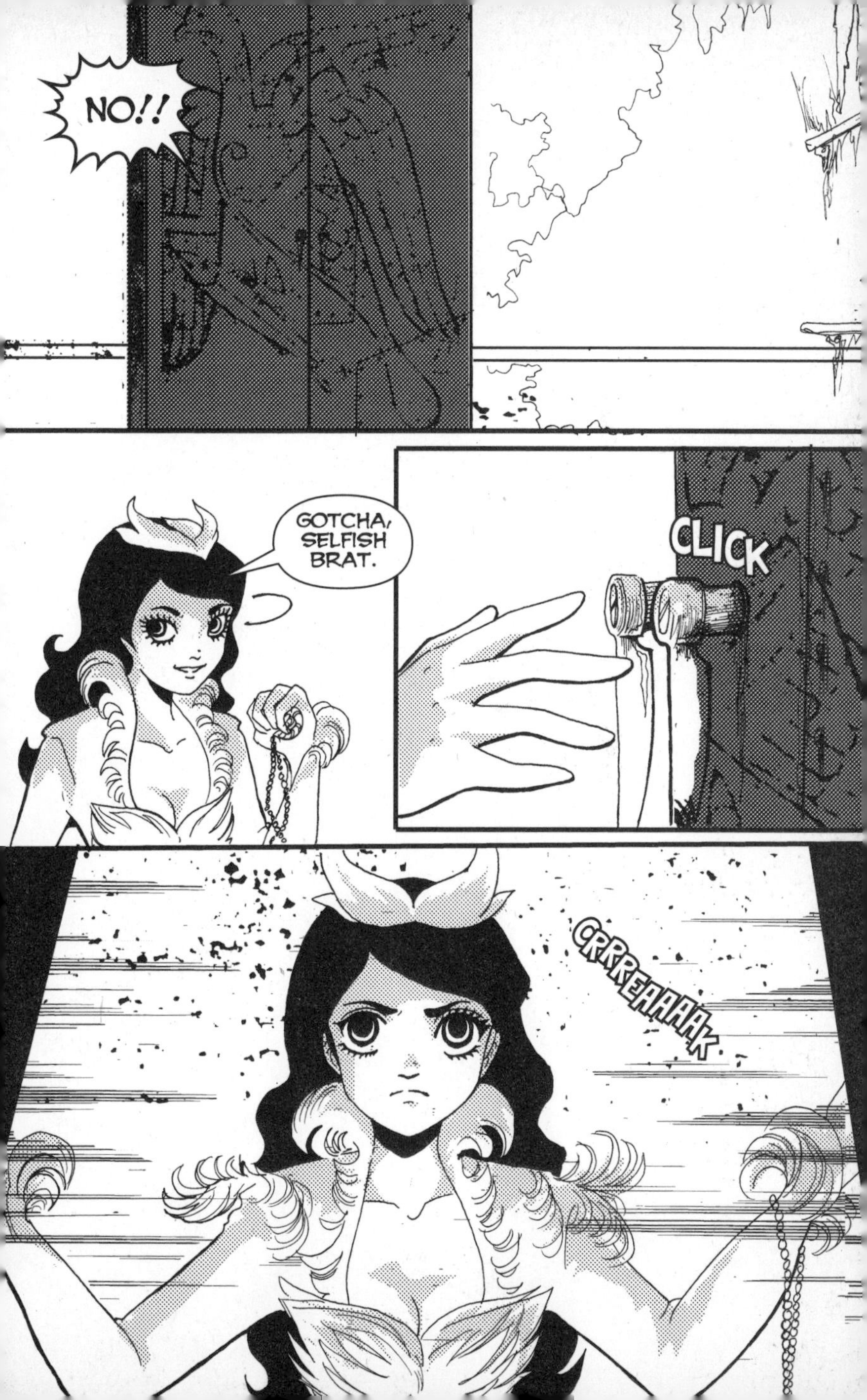
NO!!
GOTCHA, SELFISH BRAT.
CLICK
CRRREAAAAK

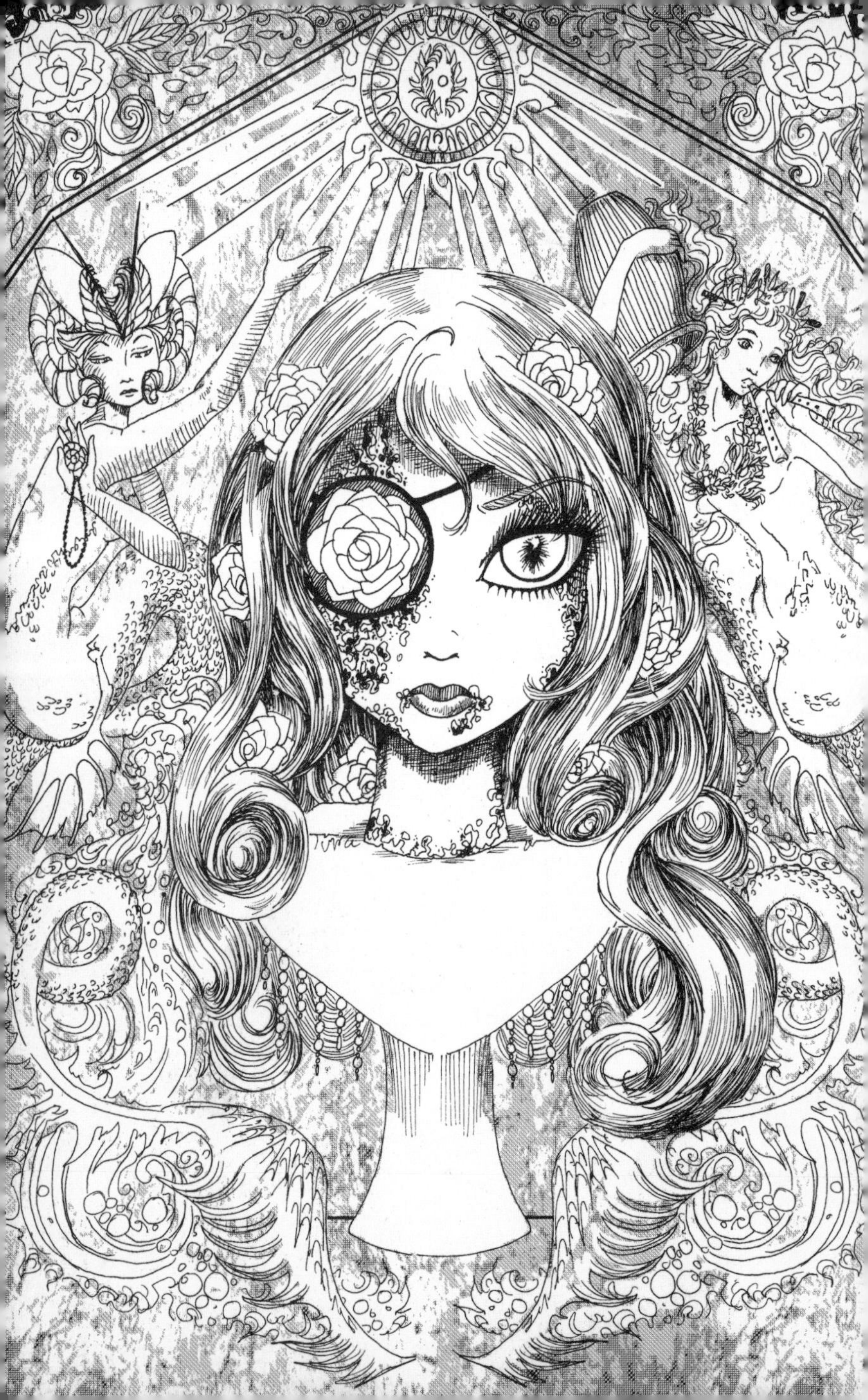

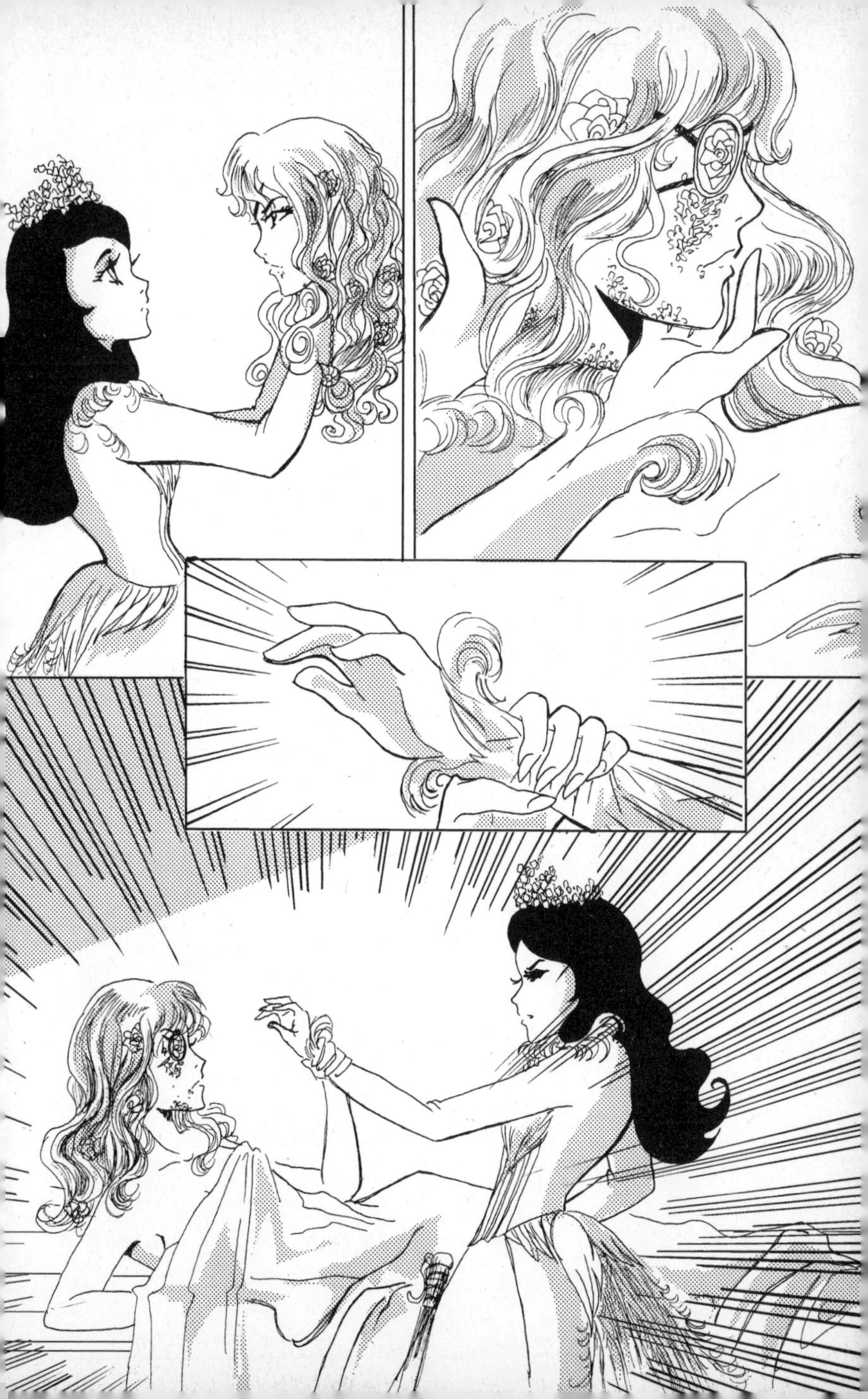

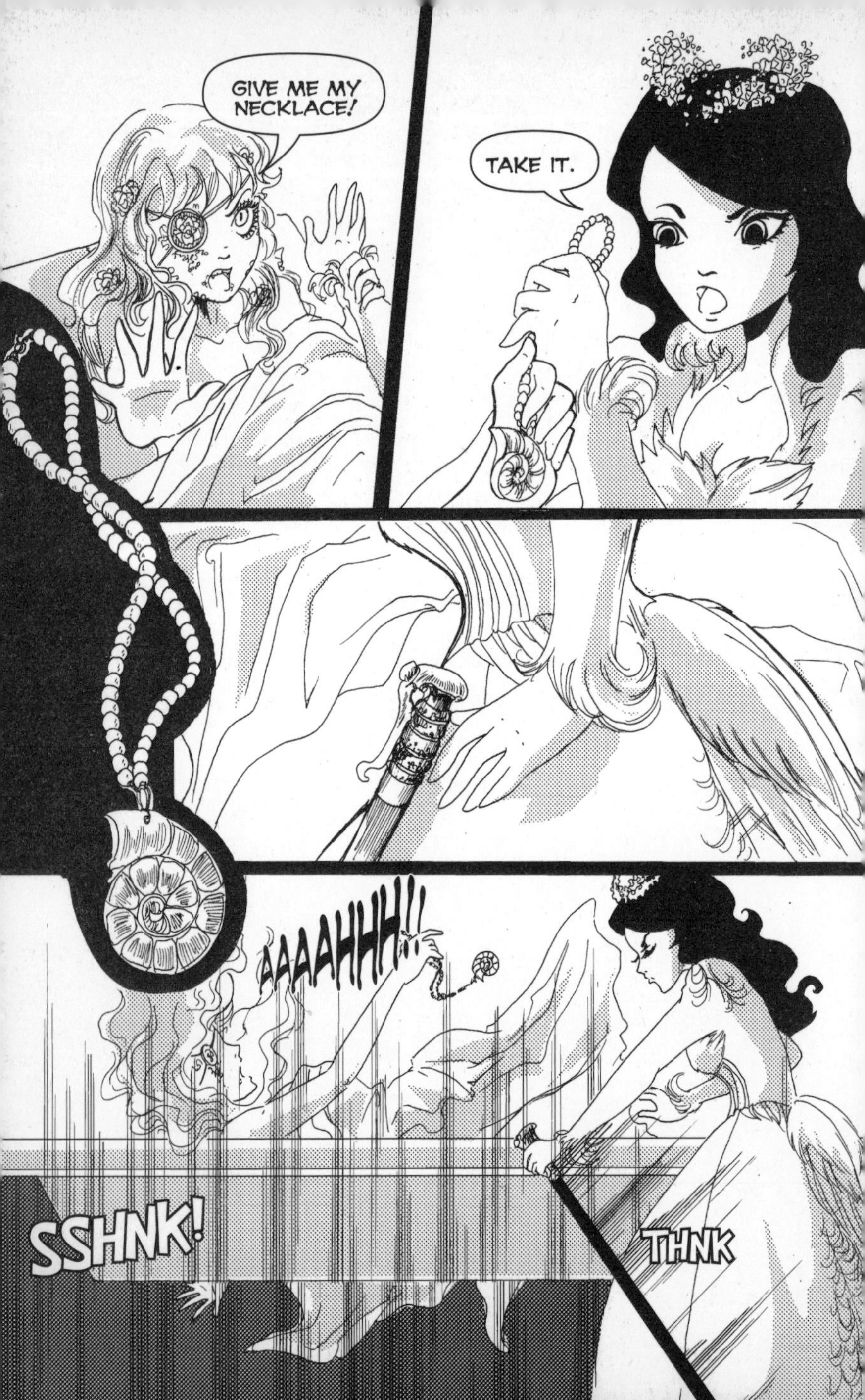
GIVE ME MY NECKLACE!
TAKE IT.
AAAAHHH!!!
SSHNK!
THNK

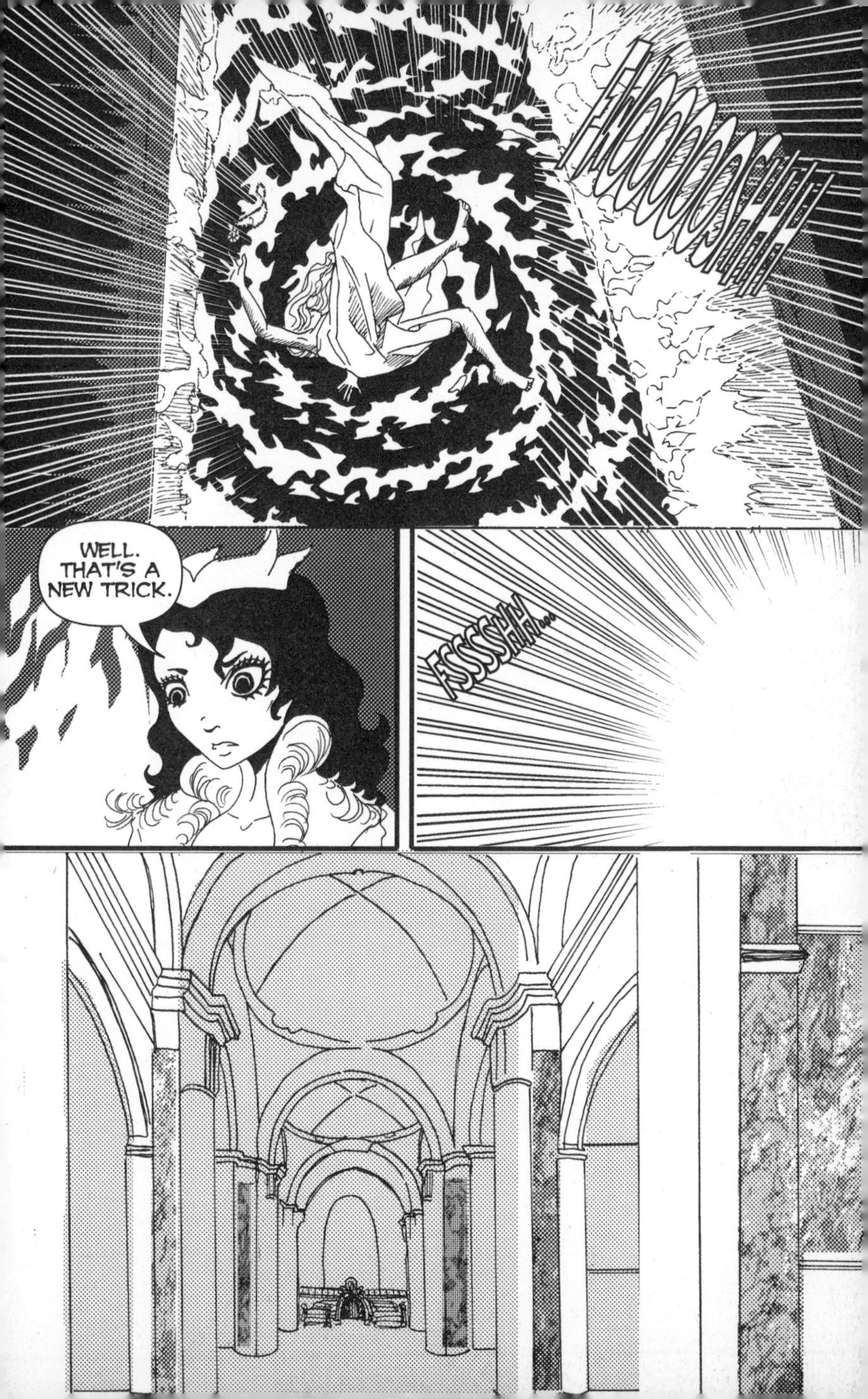

FHOOOOOSHHH
WELL. THAT'S A NEW TRICK.
FSSSSHH...

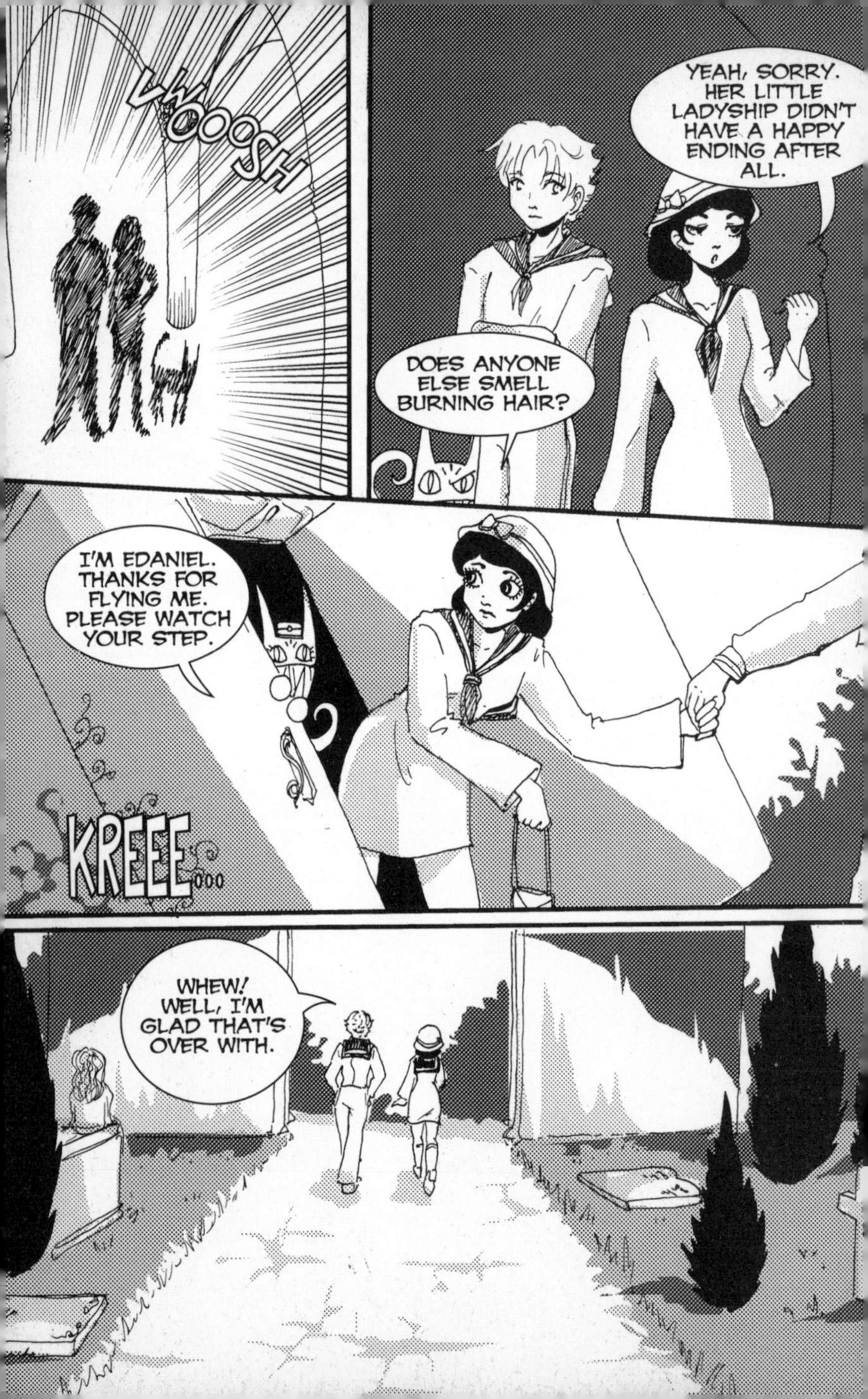

WOOOSH
YEAH, SORRY. HER LITTLE LADYSHIP DIDN'T HAVE A HAPPY ENDING AFTER ALL.
DOES ANYONE ELSE SMELL BURNING HAIR?
I'M EDANIEL. THANKS FOR FLYING ME. PLEASE WATCH YOUR STEP.
KREEE...
WHEW! WELL, I'M GLAD THAT'S OVER WITH.

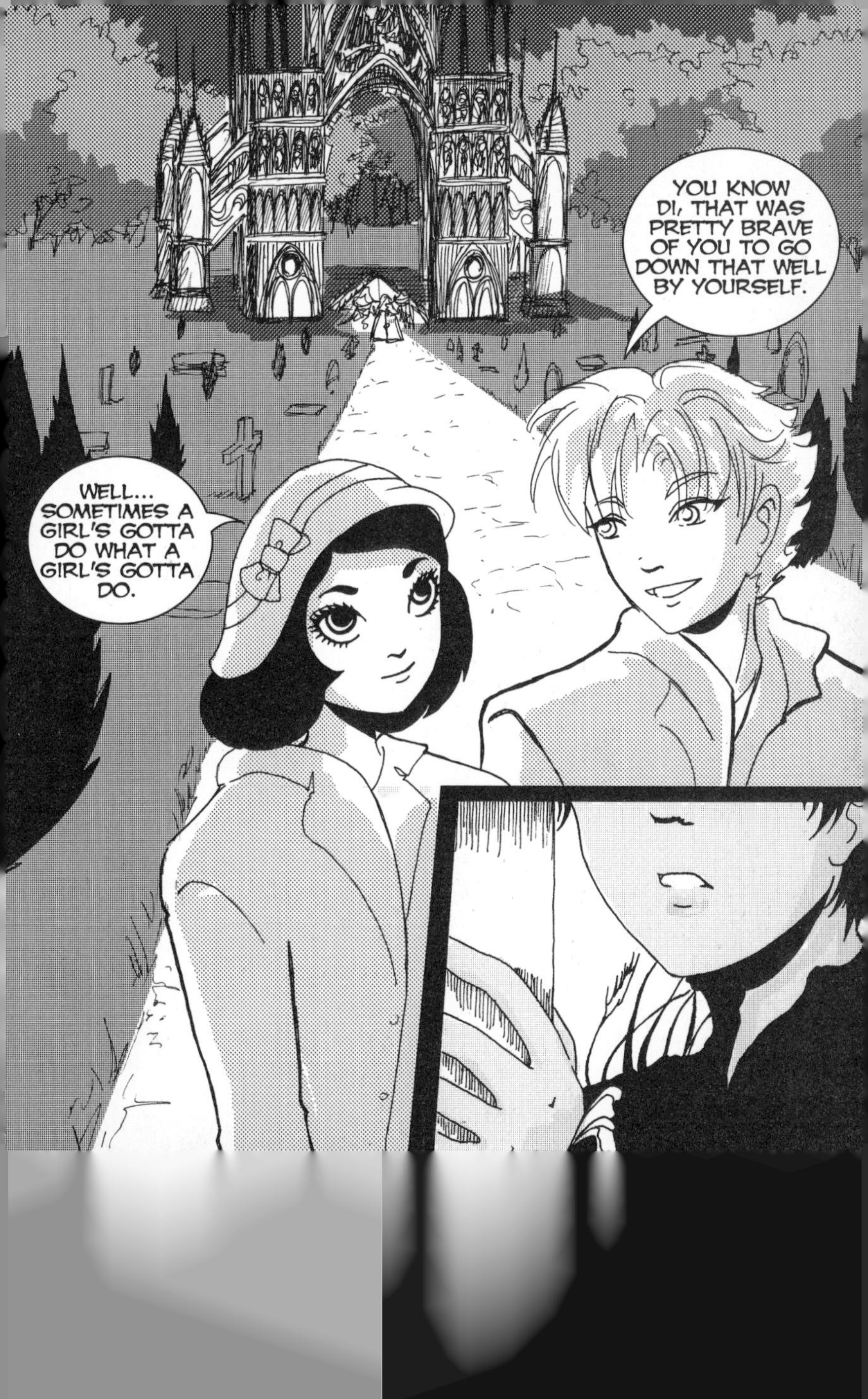
YOU KNOW DI, THAT WAS PRETTY BRAVE OF YOU TO GO DOWN THAT WELL BY YOURSELF.
WELL... SOMETIMES A GIRL'S GOTTA DO WHAT A GIRL'S GOTTA DO.

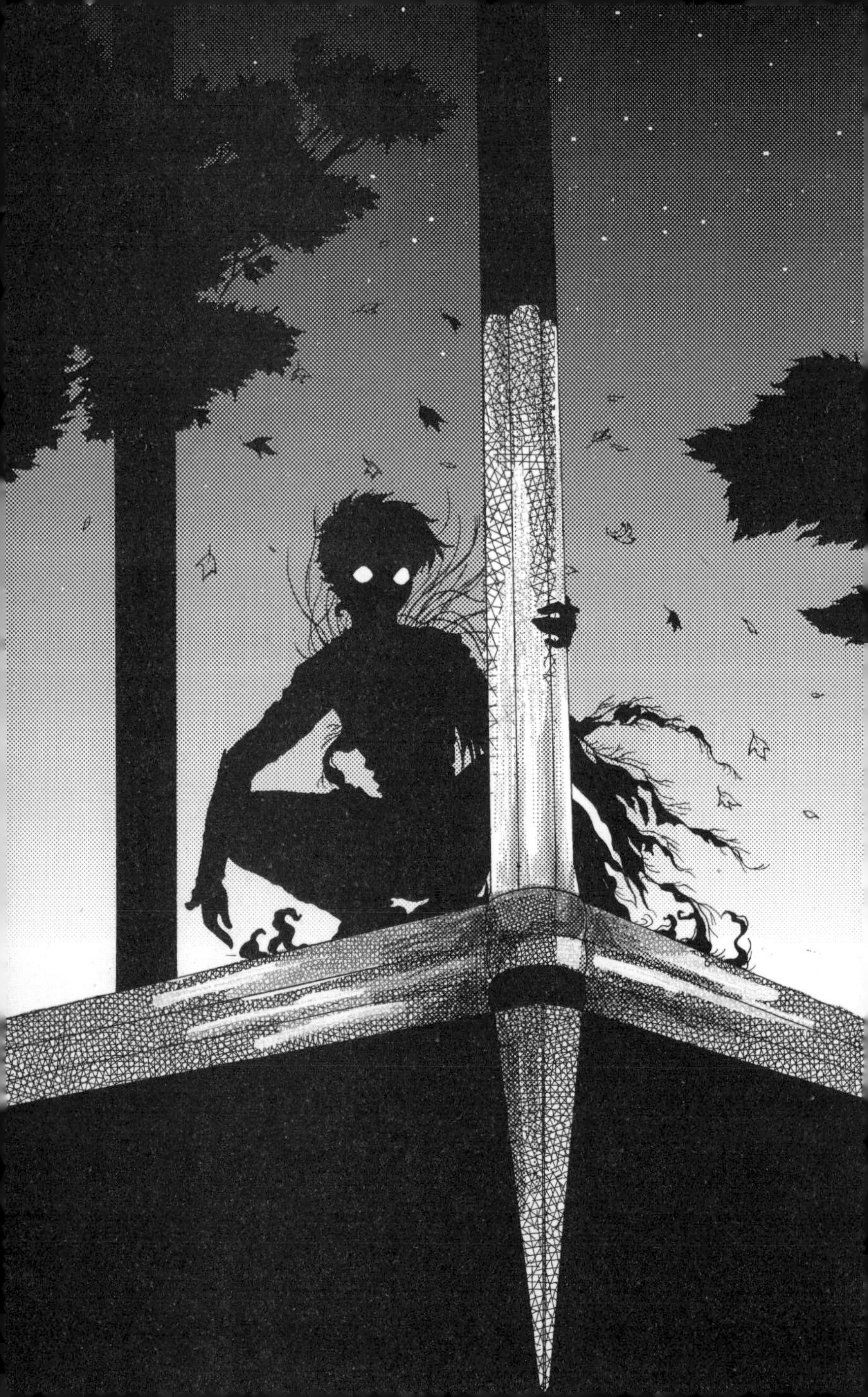

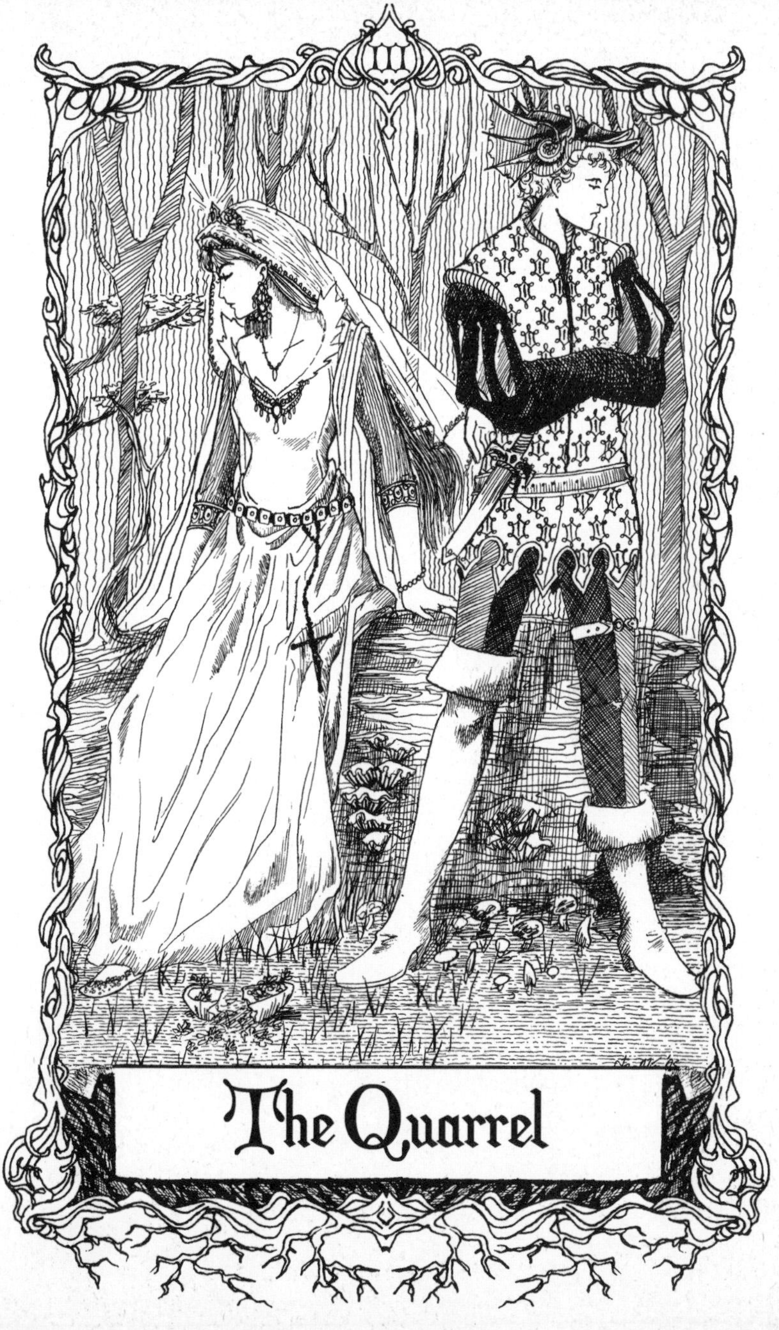
III
The Quarrel

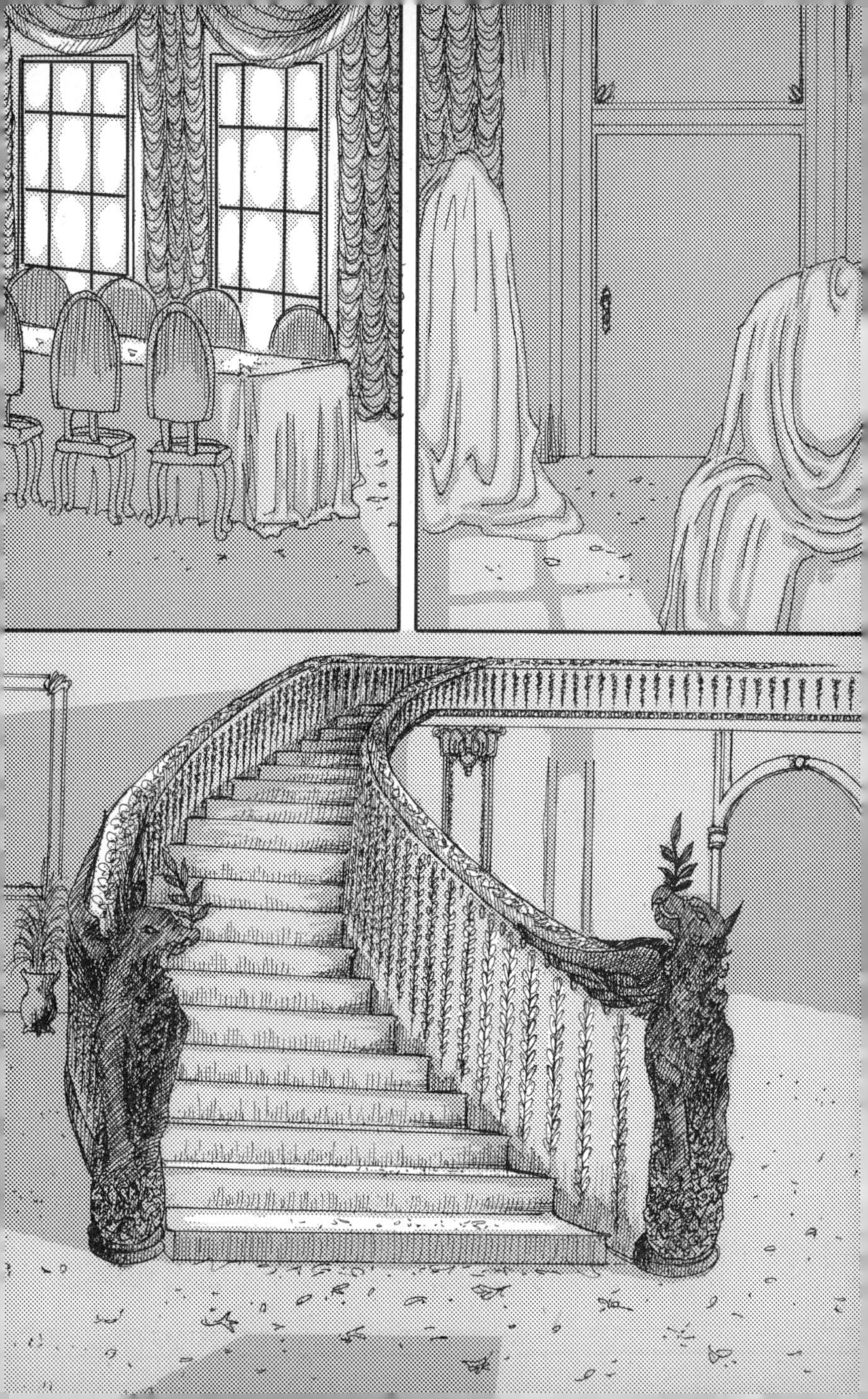

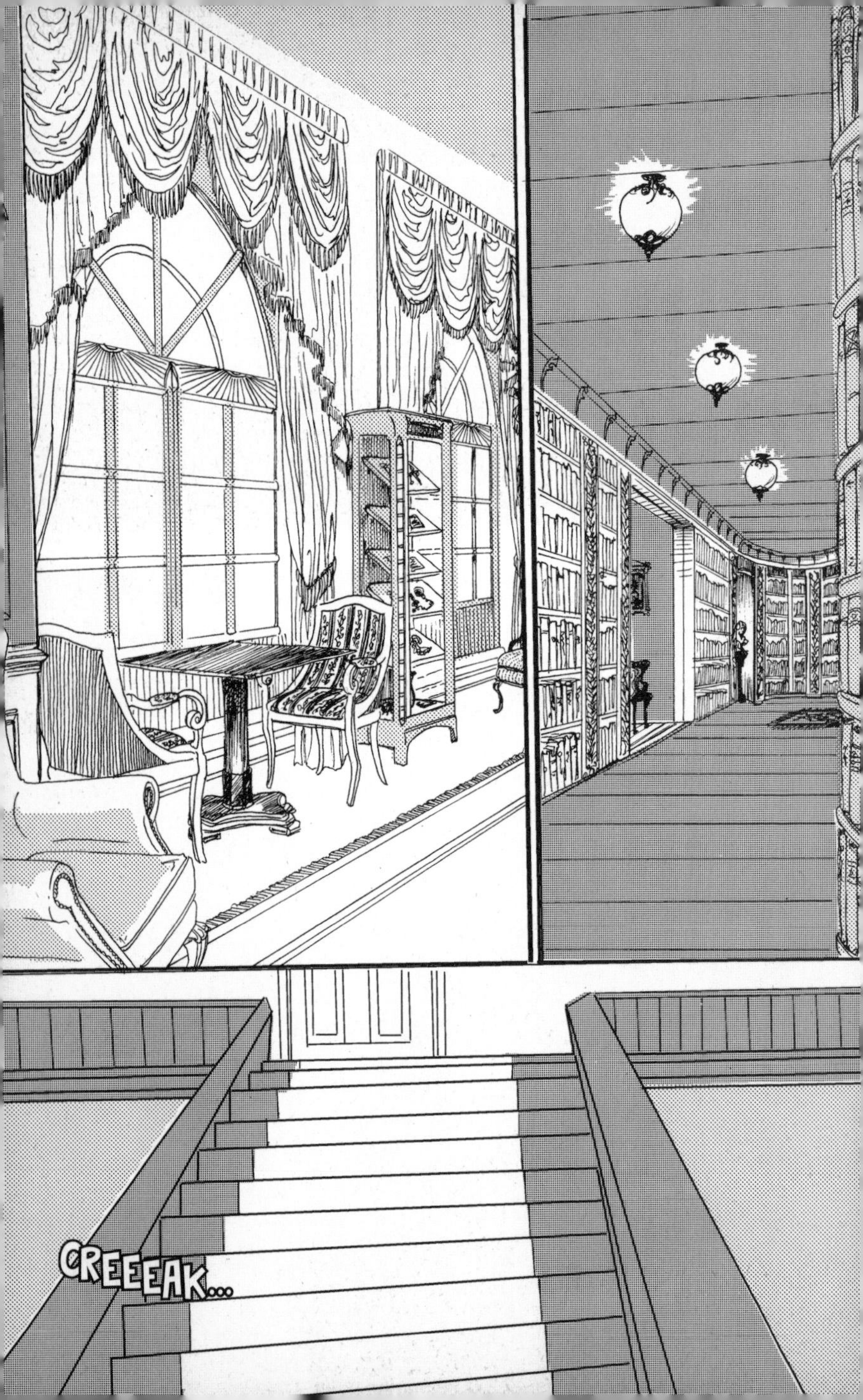
CREEEAK...

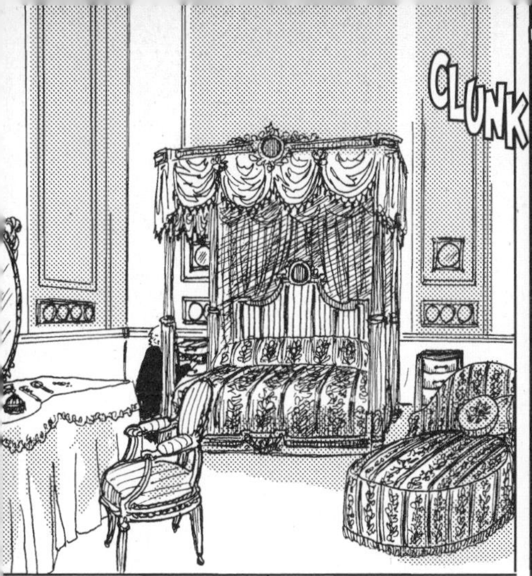
CLUNK

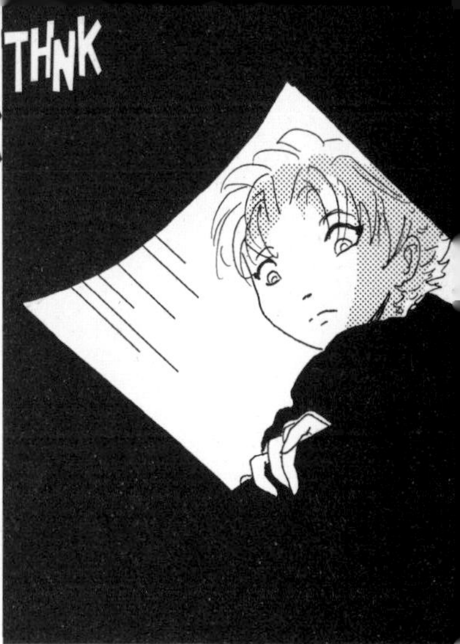
THNK

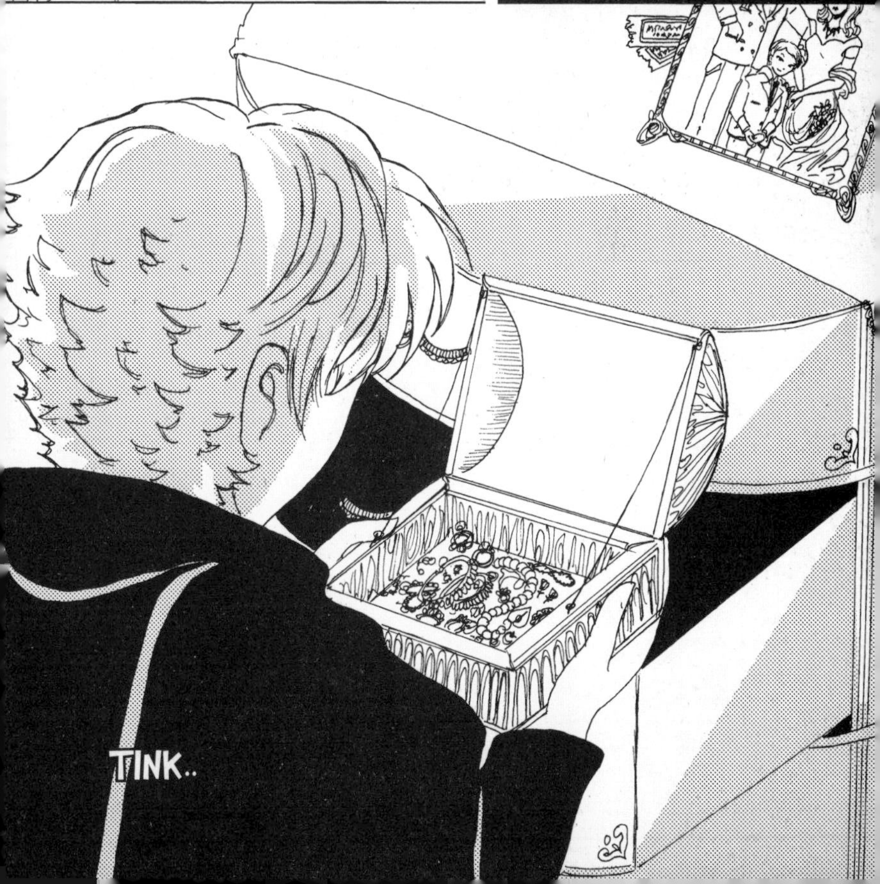
TINK..

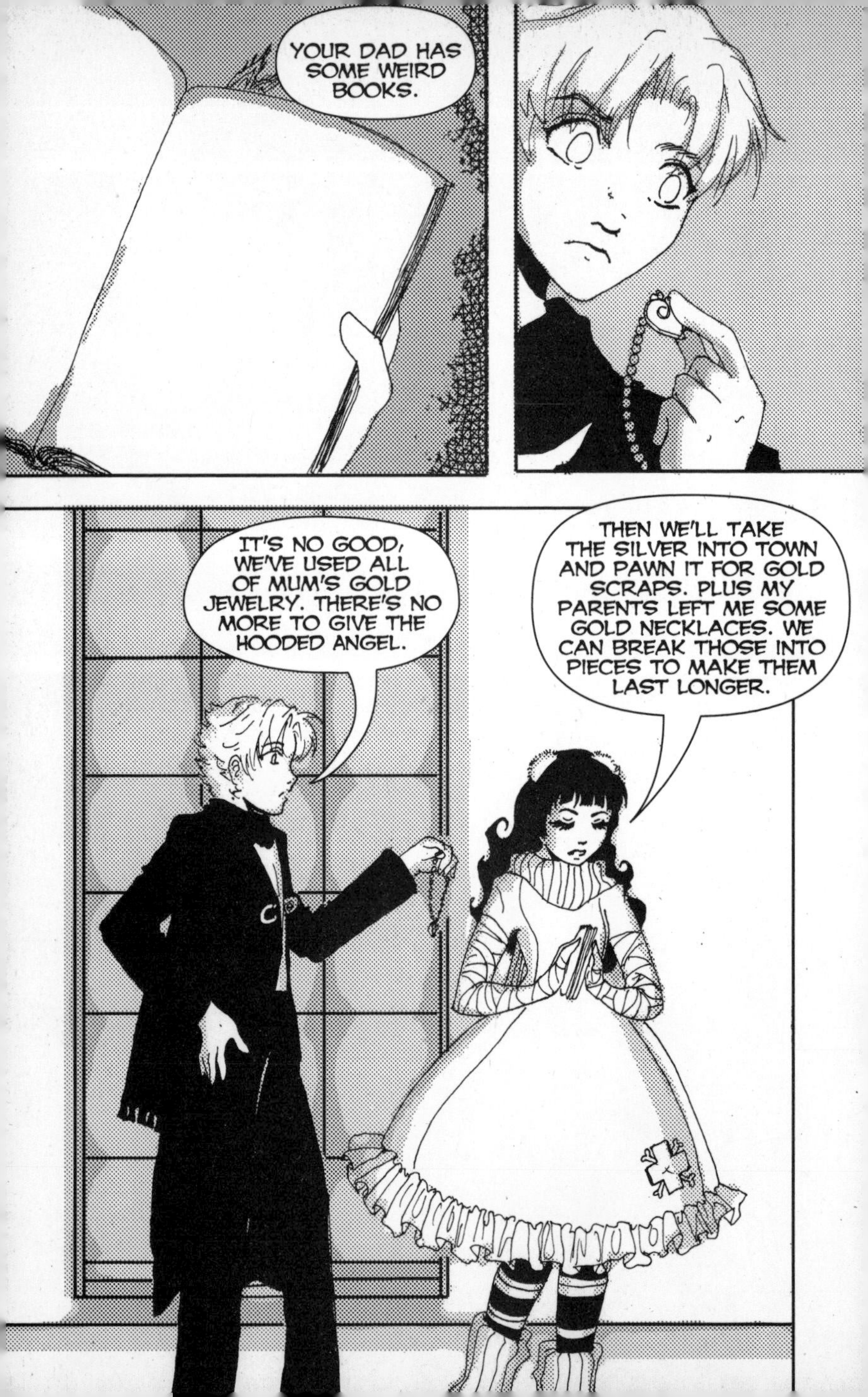
YOUR DAD HAS SOME WEIRD BOOKS.
IT'S NO GOOD, WE'VE USED ALL OF MUM'S GOLD JEWELRY. THERE'S NO MORE TO GIVE THE HOODED ANGEL.
THEN WE'LL TAKE THE SILVER INTO TOWN AND PAWN IT FOR GOLD SCRAPS. PLUS MY PARENTS LEFT ME SOME GOLD NECKLACES. WE CAN BREAK THOSE INTO PIECES TO MAKE THEM LAST LONGER.

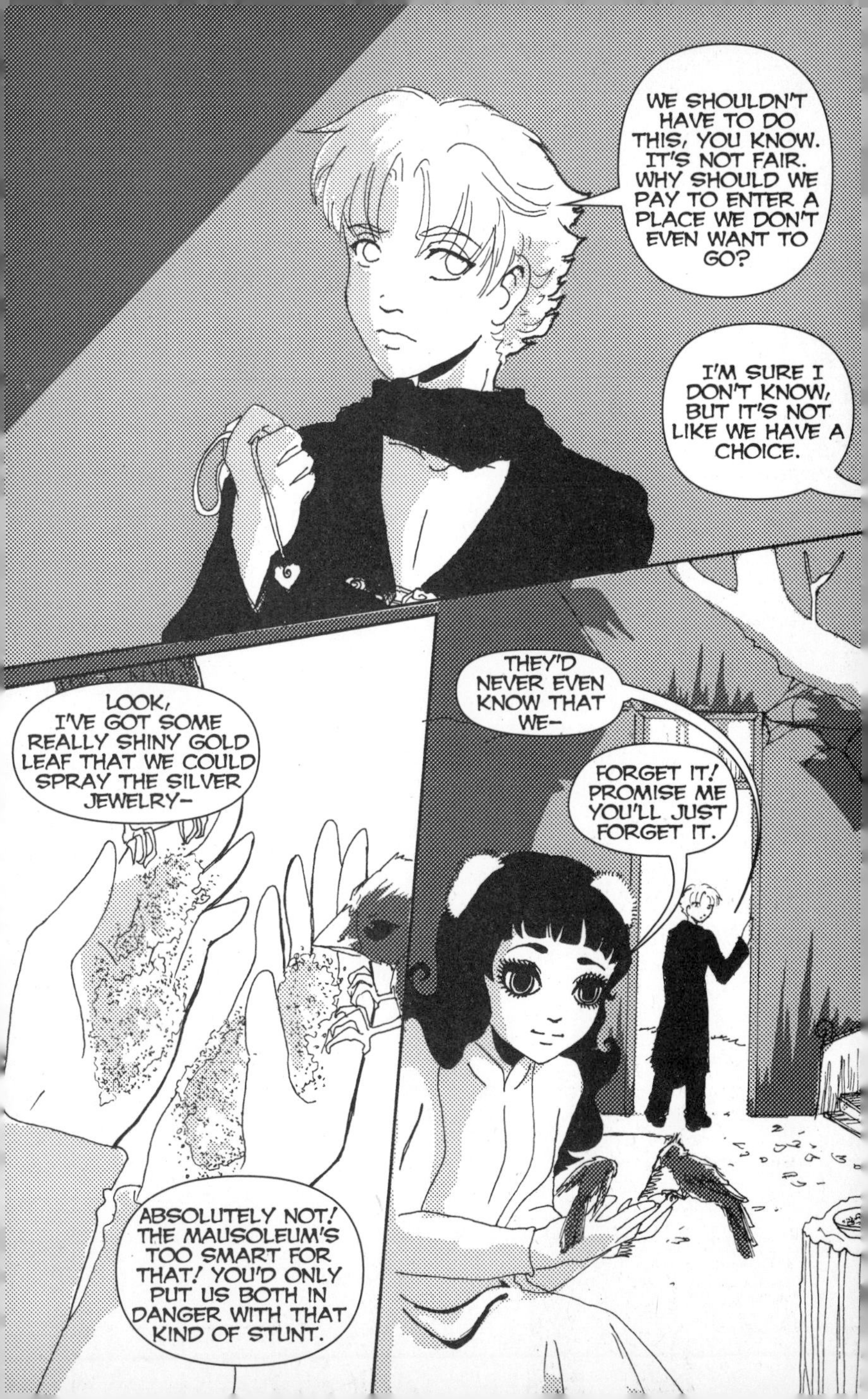
WE SHOULDN'T HAVE TO DO THIS, YOU KNOW. IT'S NOT FAIR. WHY SHOULD WE PAY TO ENTER A PLACE WE DON'T EVEN WANT TO GO?
I'M SURE I DON'T KNOW, BUT IT'S NOT LIKE WE HAVE A CHOICE.
LOOK, I'VE GOT SOME REALLY SHINY GOLD LEAF THAT WE COULD SPRAY THE SILVER JEWELRY-
ABSOLUTELY NOT! THE MAUSOLEUM'S TOO SMART FOR THAT! YOU'D ONLY PUT US BOTH IN DANGER WITH THAT KIND OF STUNT.
THEY'D NEVER EVEN KNOW THAT WE-
FORGET IT! PROMISE ME YOU'LL JUST FORGET IT.

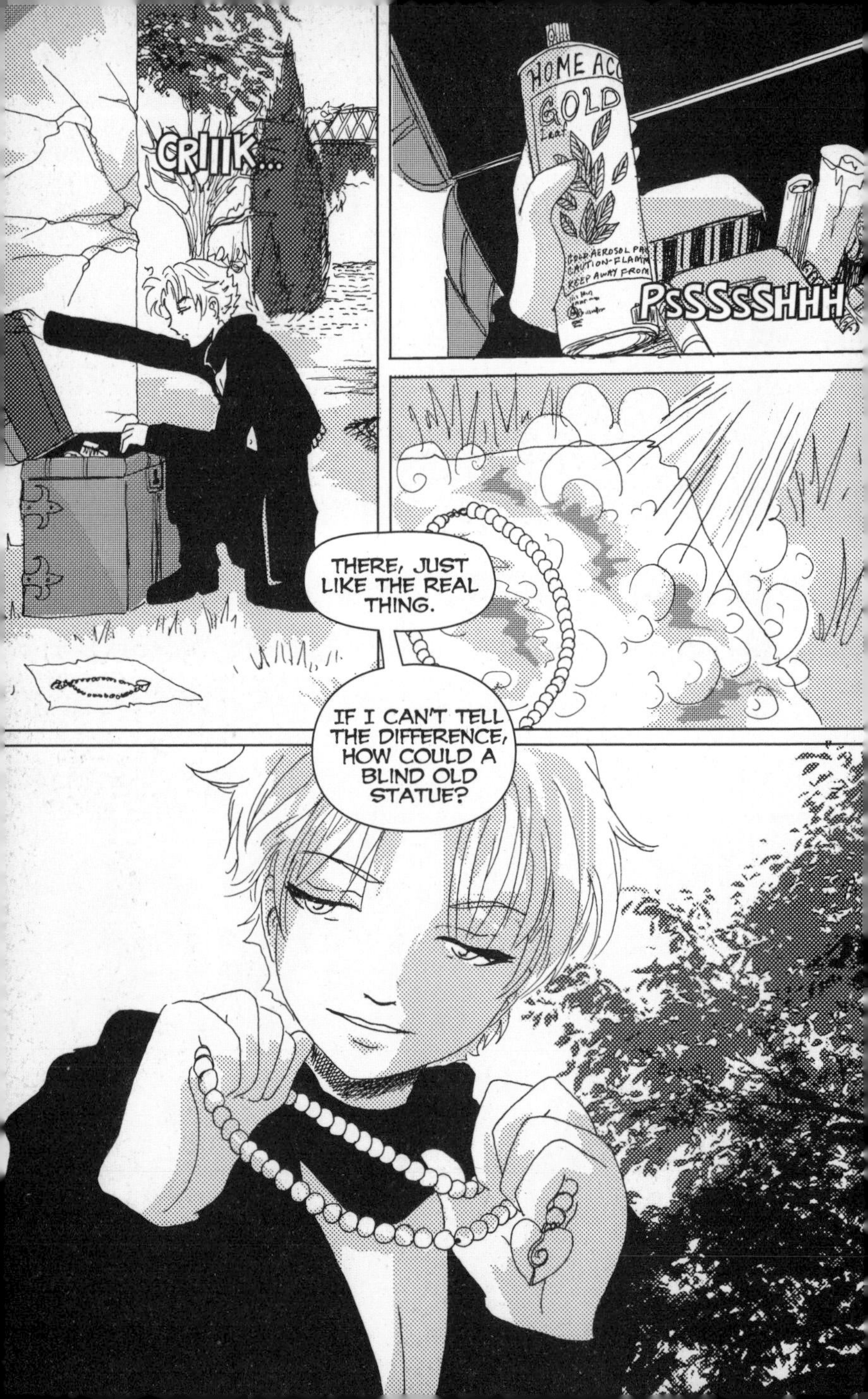
CRIIIK...
HOME ACC
GOLD
Leaf
PSSSSSHHH
THERE, JUST LIKE THE REAL THING.
IF I CAN'T TELL THE DIFFERENCE, HOW COULD A BLIND OLD STATUE?

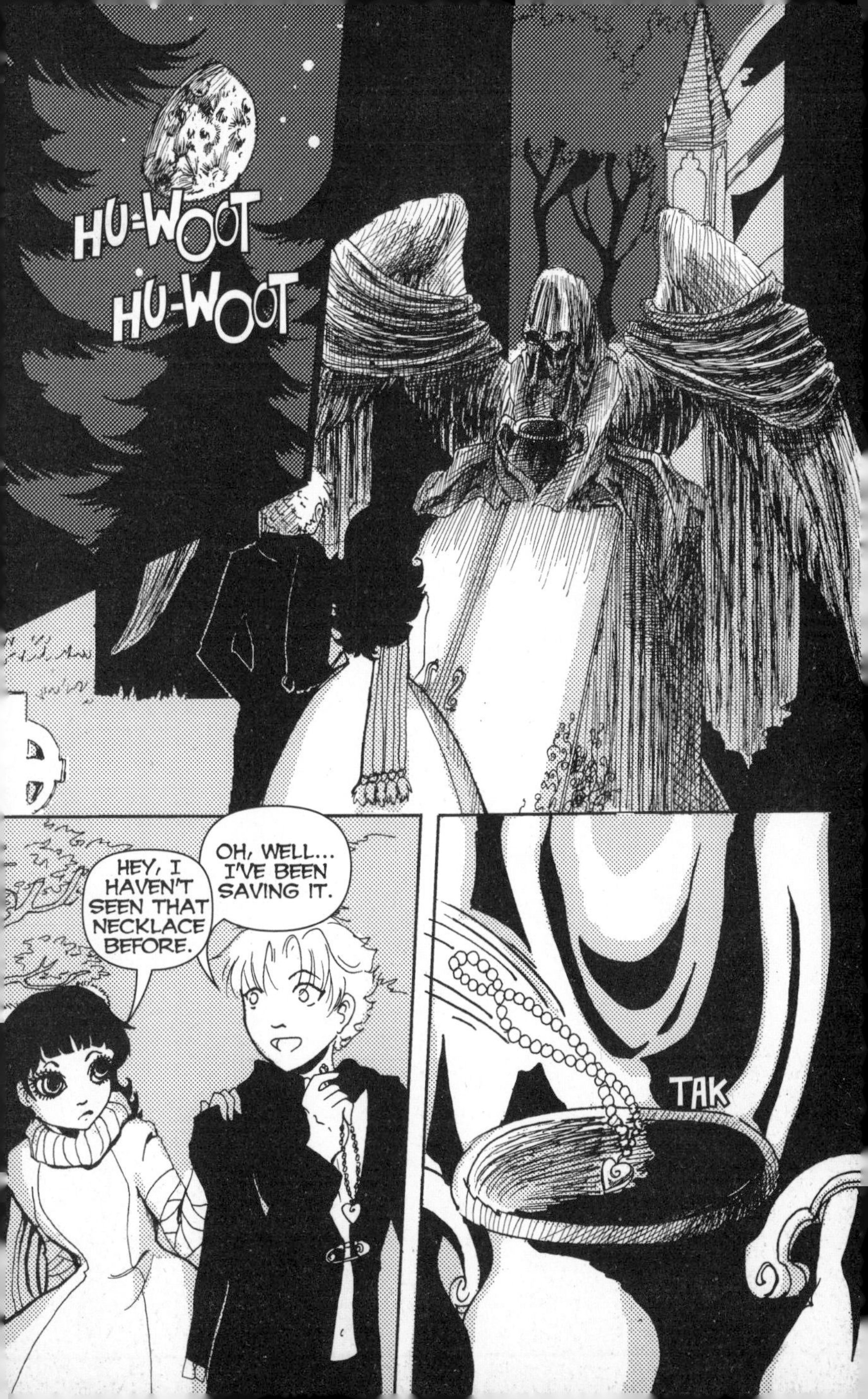
HU-WOOT
HU-WOOT
HEY, I HAVEN'T SEEN THAT NECKLACE BEFORE.
OH, WELL... I'VE BEEN SAVING IT.
TAK

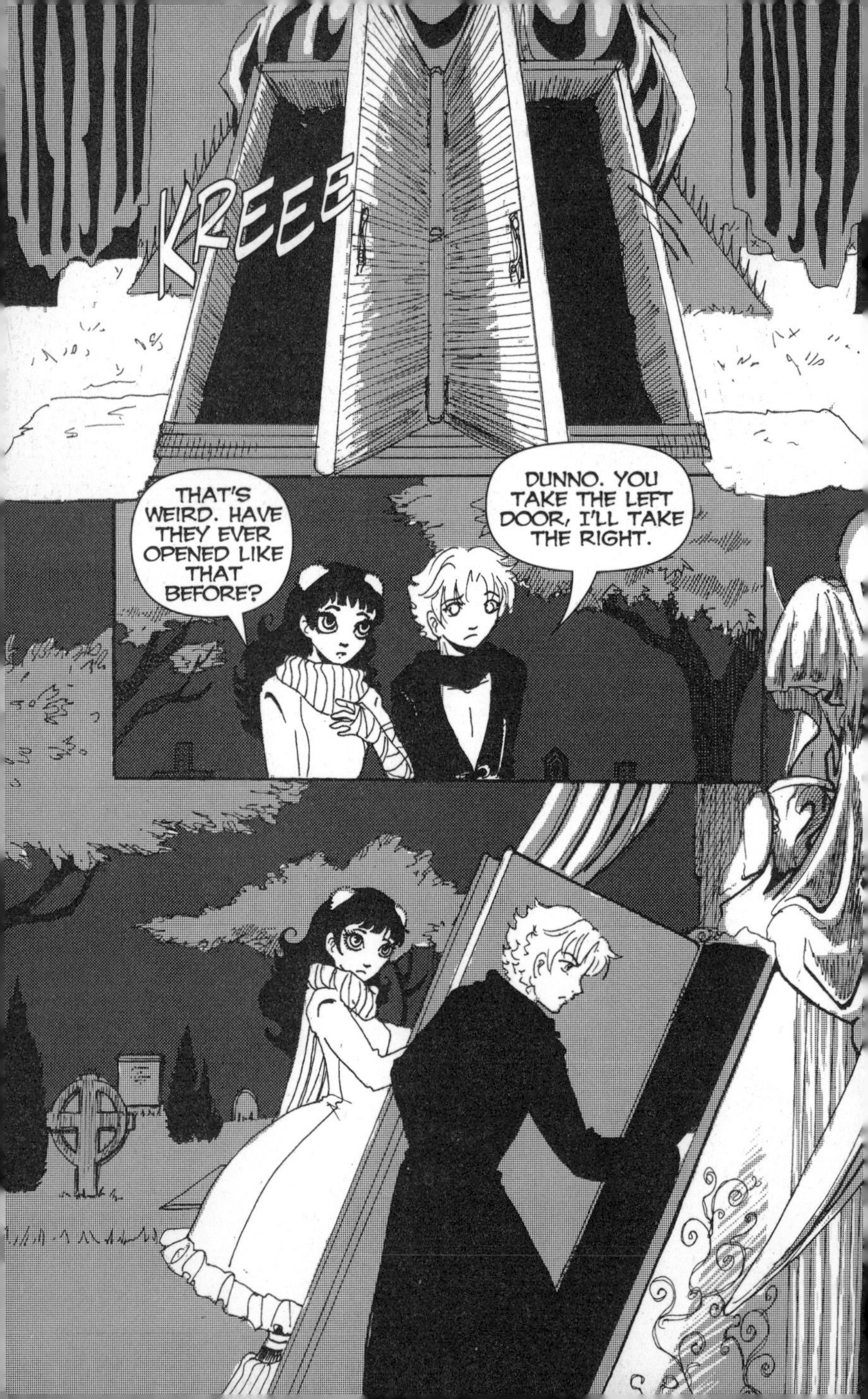
KREEE
THAT'S WEIRD. HAVE THEY EVER OPENED LIKE THAT BEFORE?
DUNNO. YOU TAKE THE LEFT DOOR, I'LL TAKE THE RIGHT.

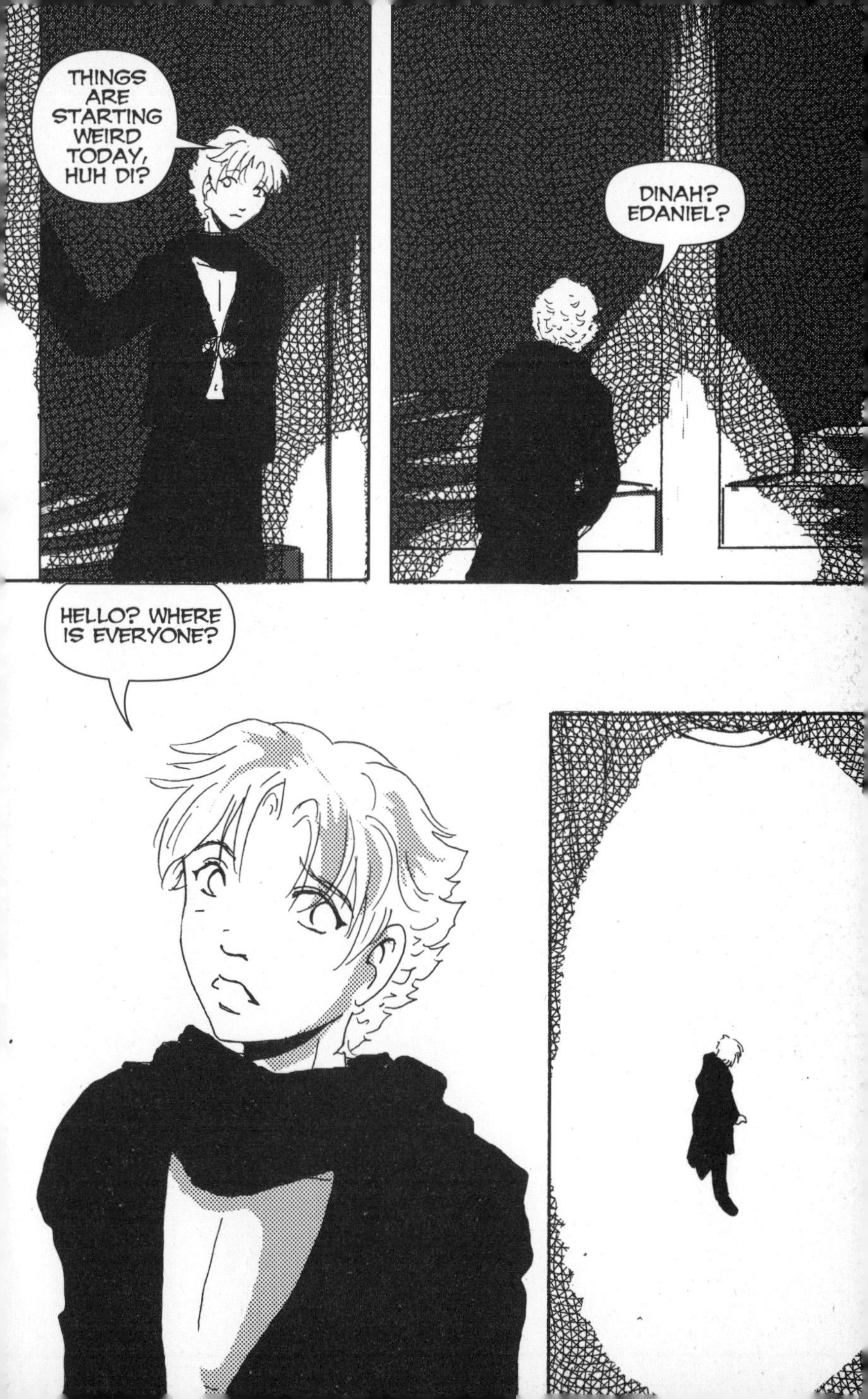
THINGS ARE STARTING WEIRD TODAY, HUH DI?
DINAH? EDANIEL?
HELLO? WHERE IS EVERYONE?

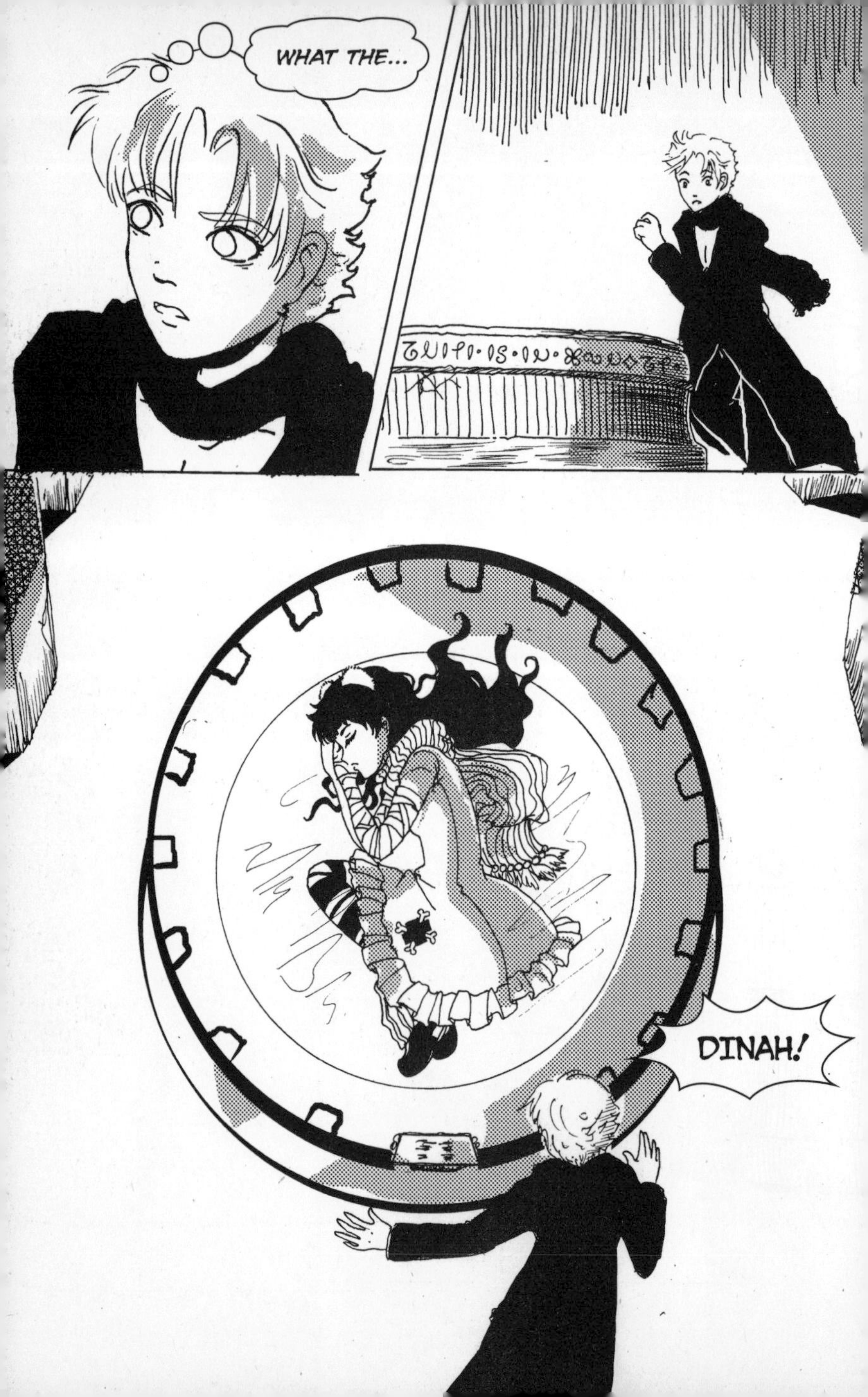
WHAT THE...
DINAH!

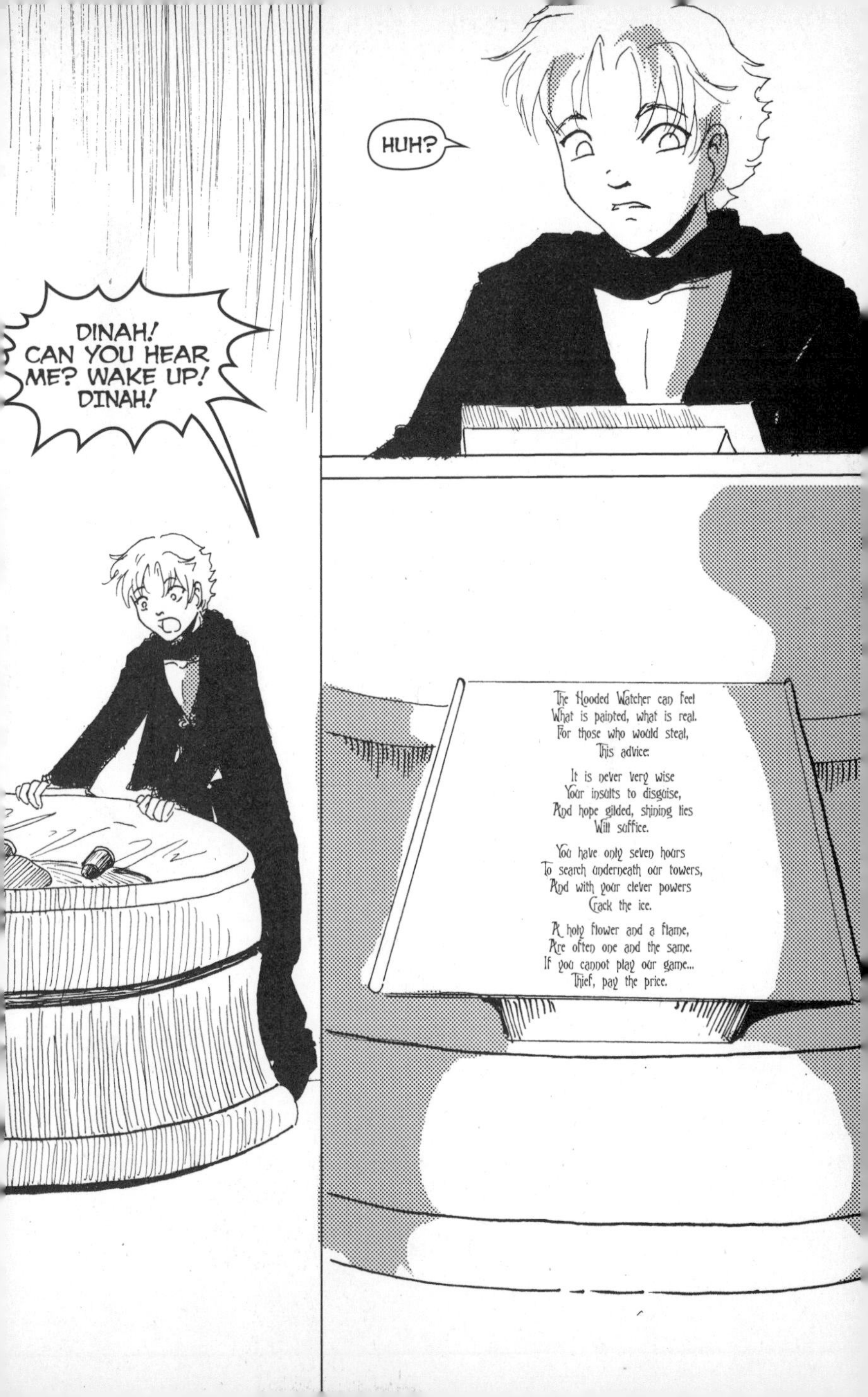
DINAH! CAN YOU HEAR ME? WAKE UP! DINAH!
HUH?
The Hooded Watcher can feel
What is painted, what is real.
For those who would steal,
This advice:
It is never very wise
Your insults to disguise,
And hope gilded, shining lies
Will suffice.
You have only seven hours
To search underneath our towers,
And with your clever powers
Crack the ice.
A holy flower and a flame,
Are often one and the same.
If you cannot play our game...
Thief, pay the price.

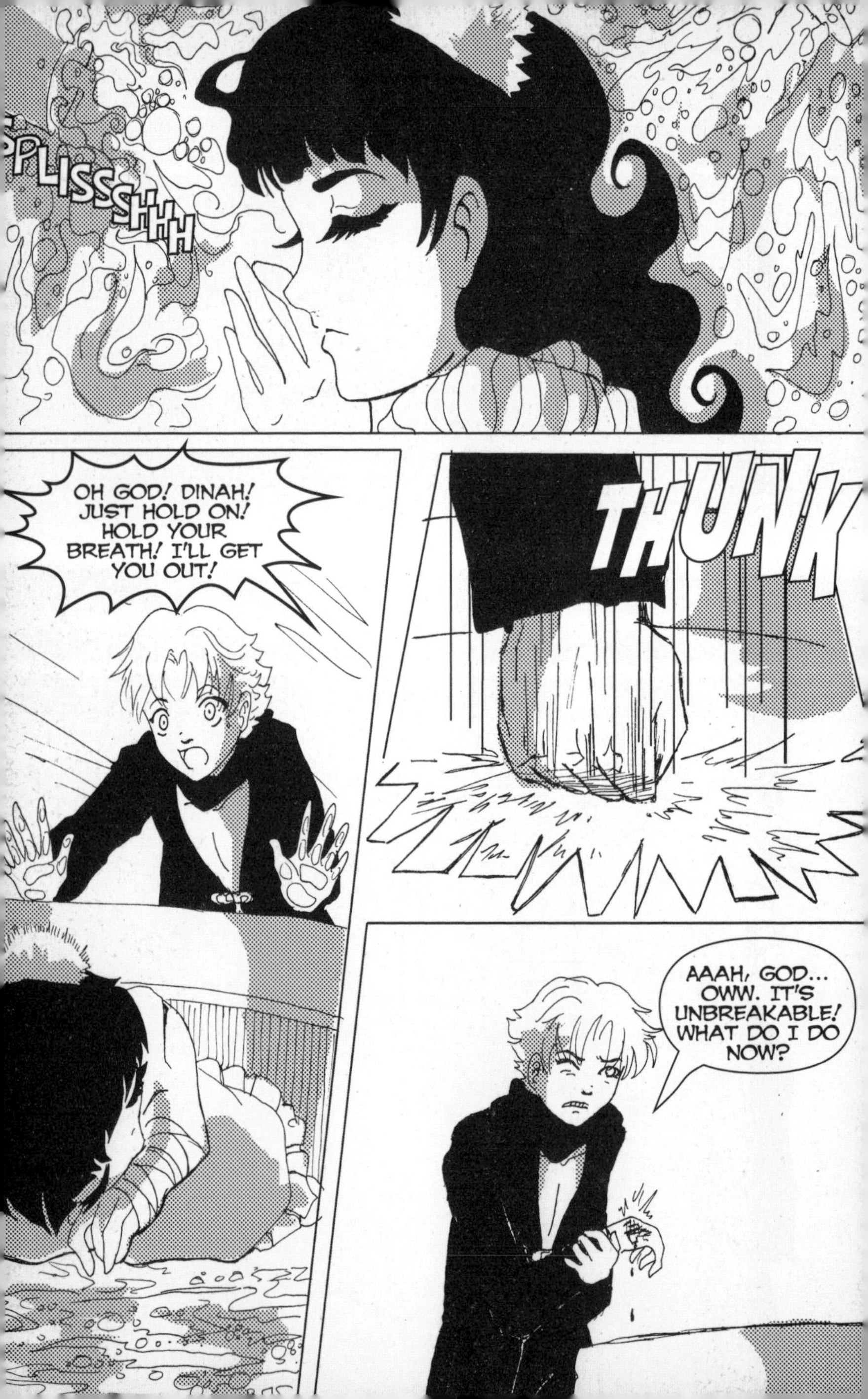
SPLISSSHHH
OH GOD! DINAH! JUST HOLD ON! HOLD YOUR BREATH! I'LL GET YOU OUT!
THUNK
AAAH, GOD... OWW. IT'S UNBREAKABLE! WHAT DO I DO NOW?

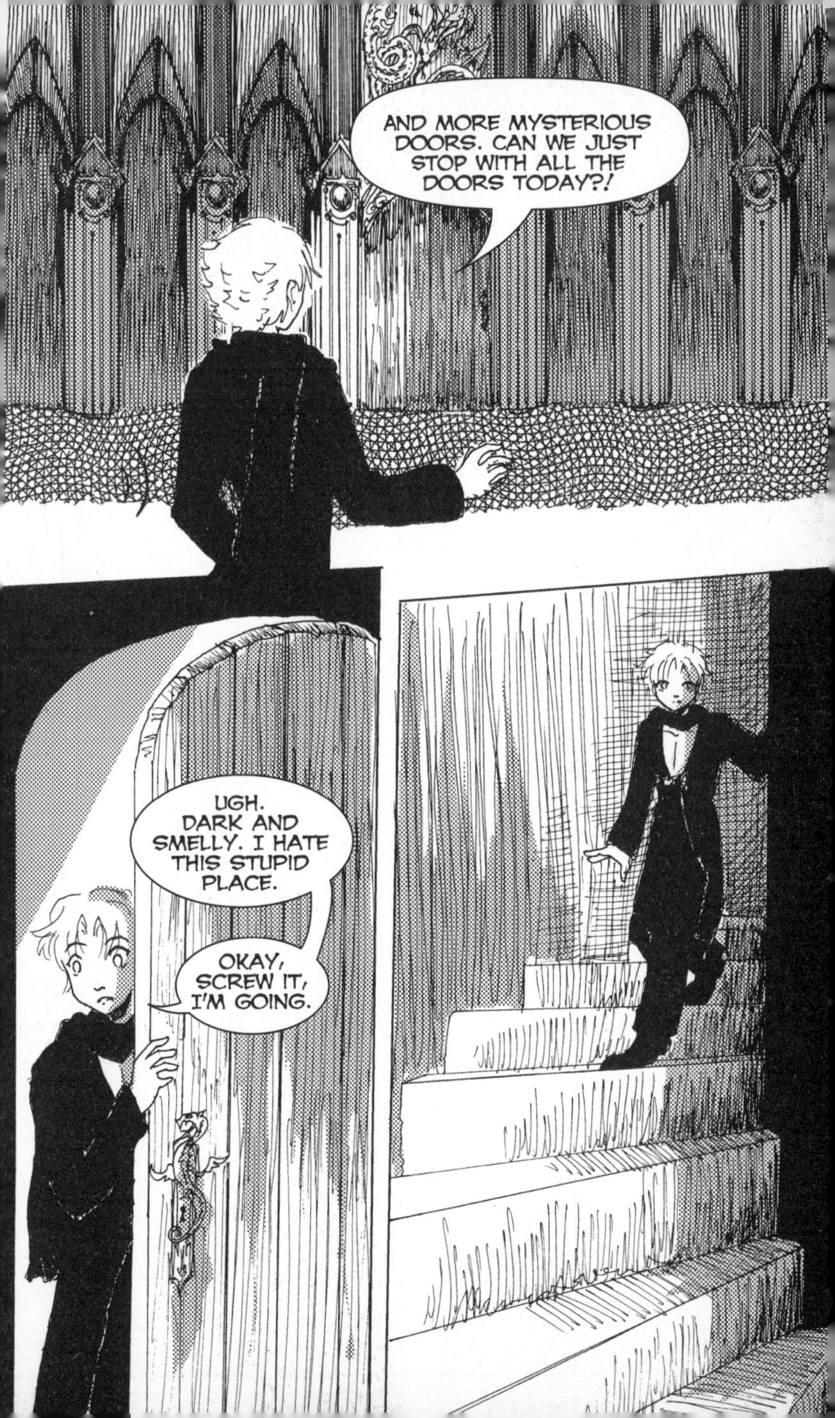
AND MORE MYSTERIOUS DOORS. CAN WE JUST STOP WITH ALL THE DOORS TODAY?!
UGH. DARK AND SMELLY. I HATE THIS STUPID PLACE.
OKAY, SCREW IT, I'M GOING.

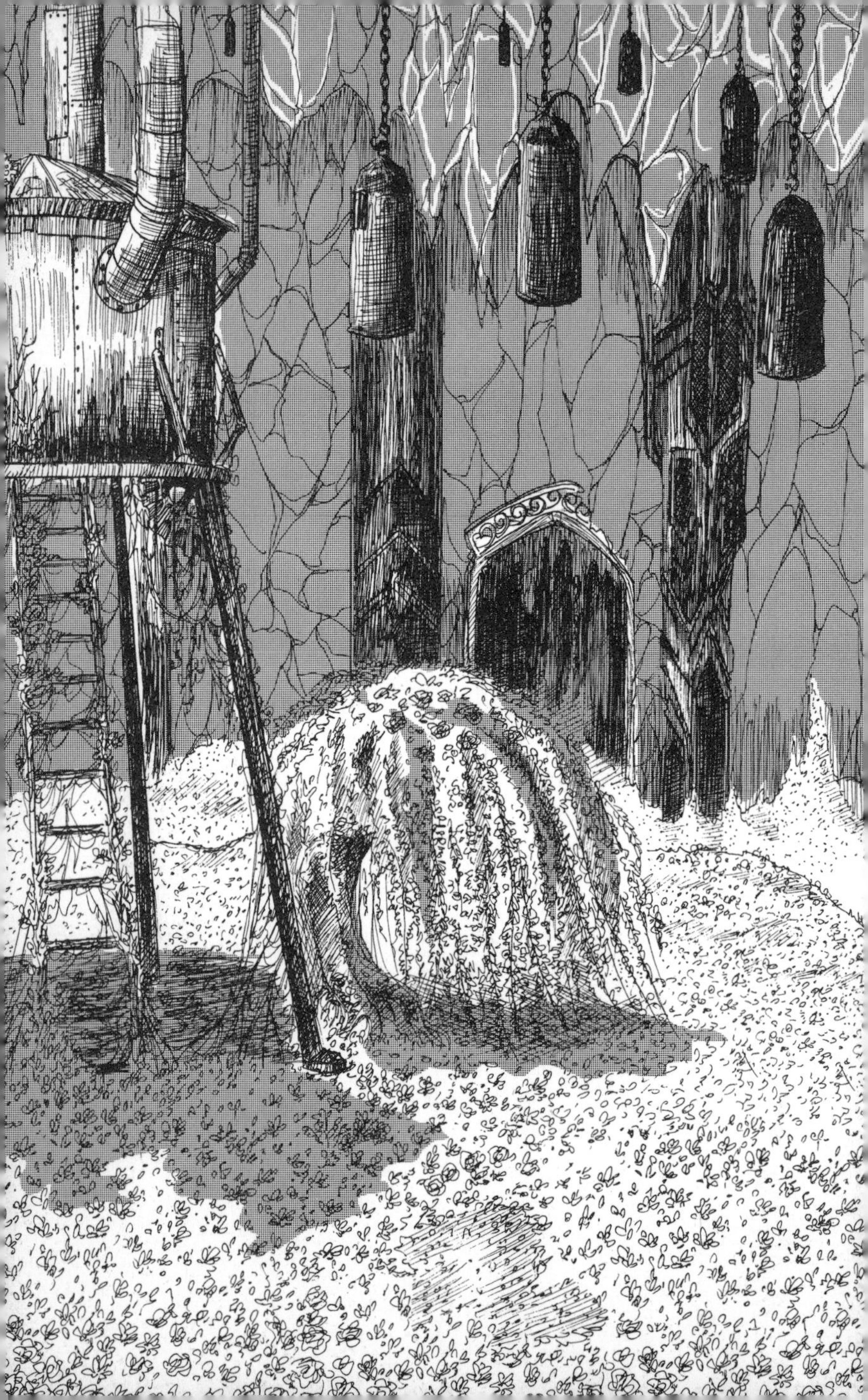

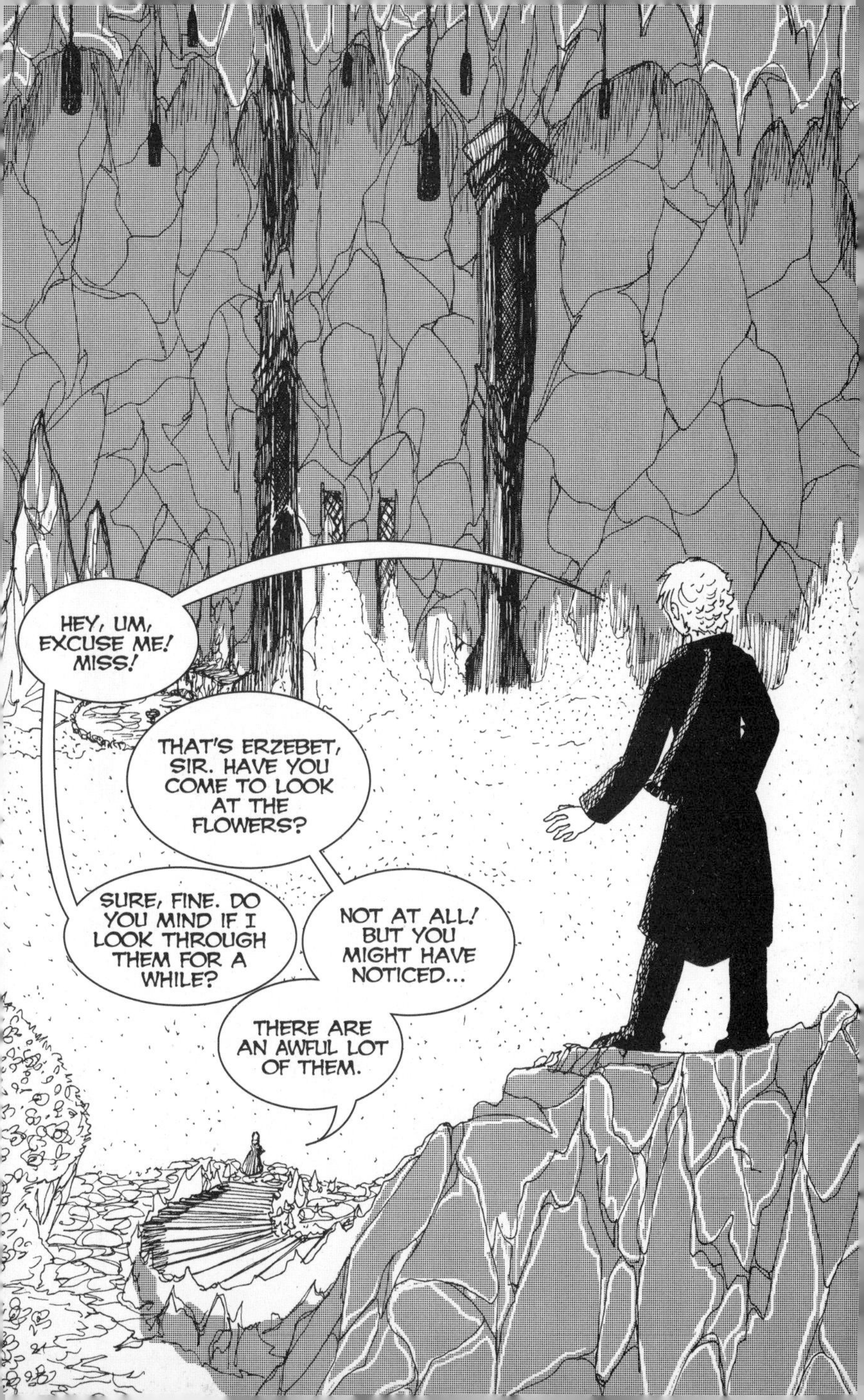
HEY, UM, EXCUSE ME! MISS!
THAT'S ERZEBET, SIR. HAVE YOU COME TO LOOK AT THE FLOWERS?
SURE, FINE. DO YOU MIND IF I LOOK THROUGH THEM FOR A WHILE?
NOT AT ALL! BUT YOU MIGHT HAVE NOTICED...
THERE ARE AN AWFUL LOT OF THEM.

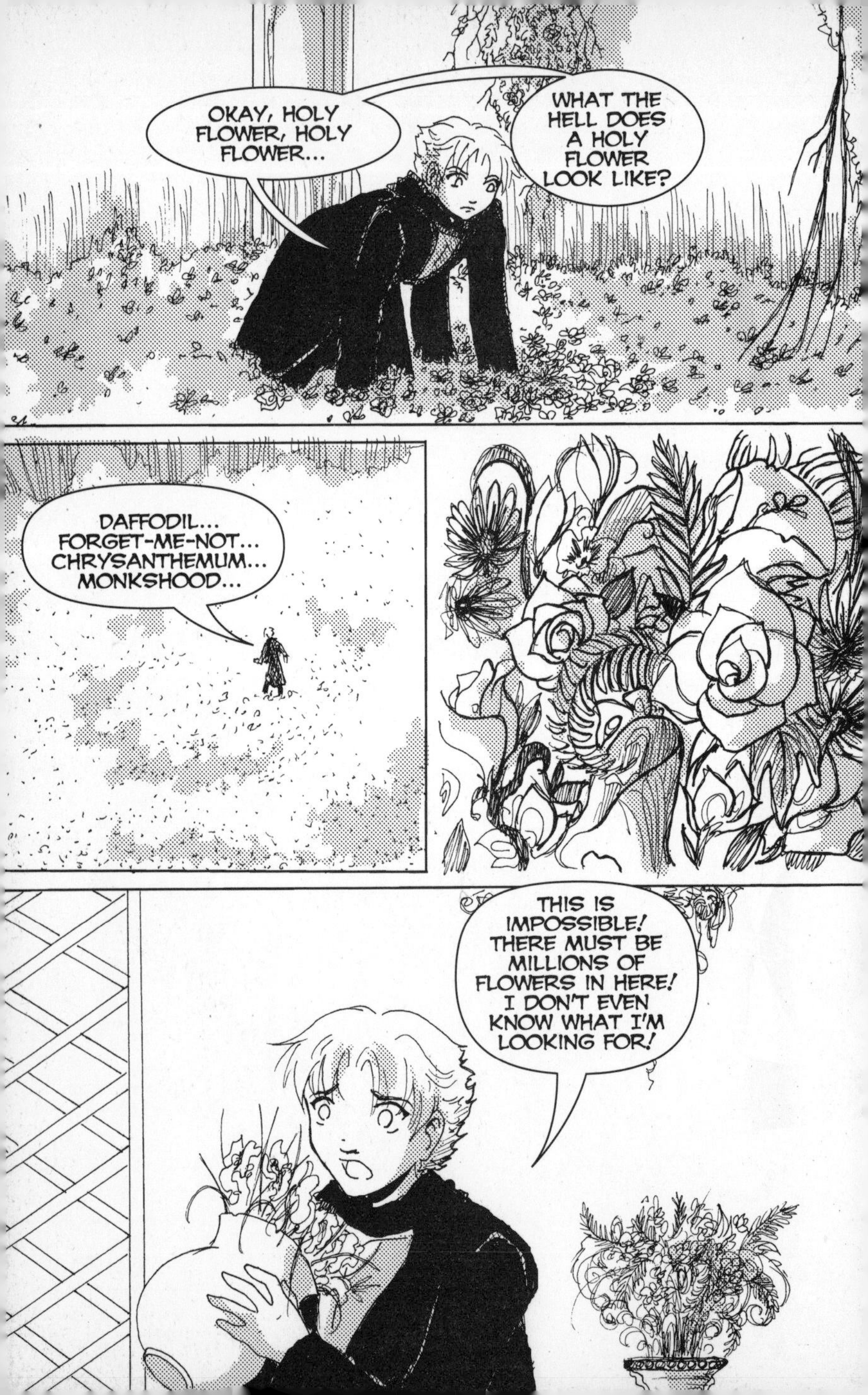
OKAY, HOLY FLOWER, HOLY FLOWER...
WHAT THE HELL DOES A HOLY FLOWER LOOK LIKE?
DAFFODIL... FORGET-ME-NOT... CHRYSANTHEMUM... MONKSHOOD...
THIS IS IMPOSSIBLE! THERE MUST BE MILLIONS OF FLOWERS IN HERE! I DON'T EVEN KNOW WHAT I'M LOOKING FOR!

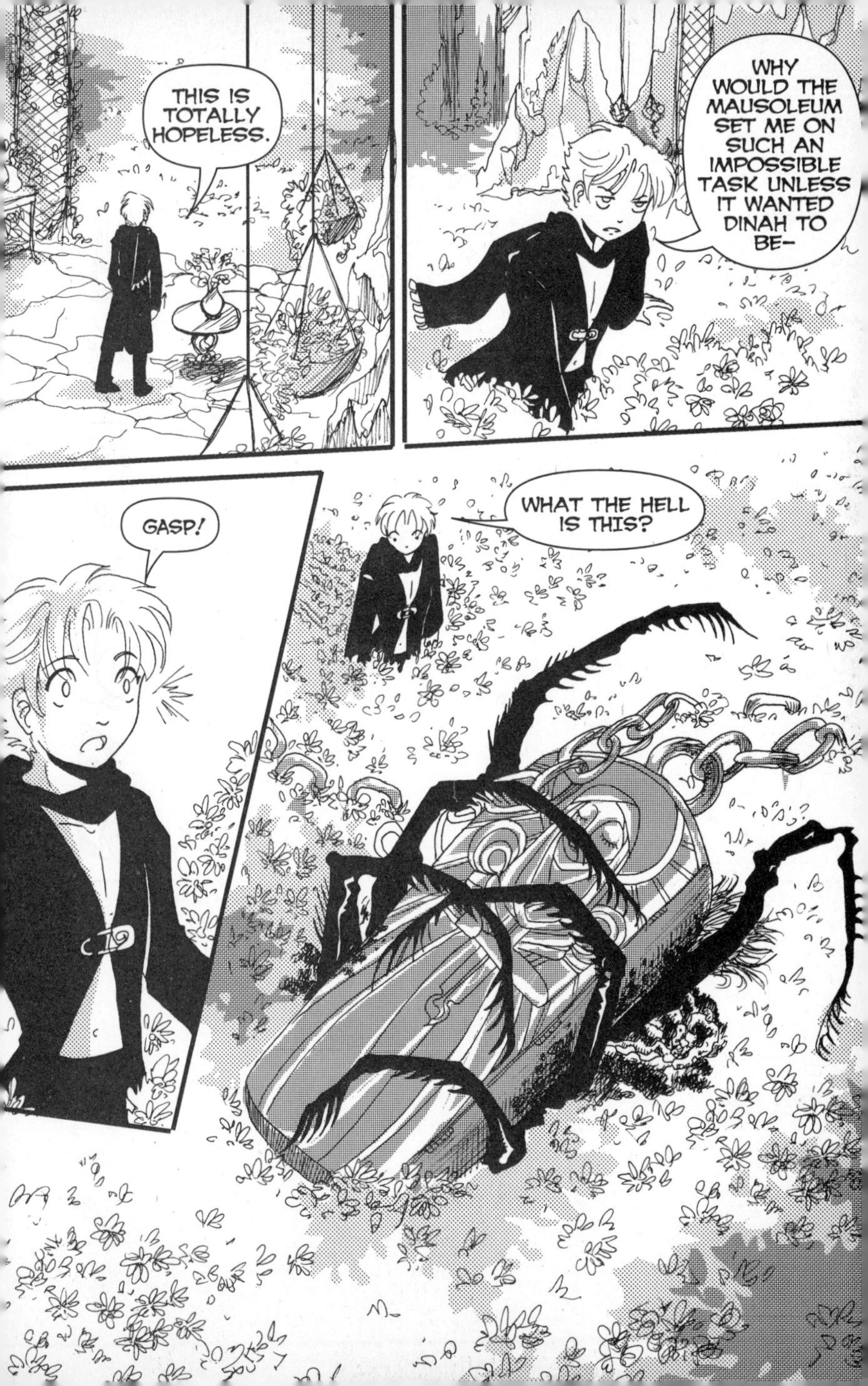
THIS IS TOTALLY HOPELESS.
WHY WOULD THE MAUSOLEUM SET ME ON SUCH AN IMPOSSIBLE TASK UNLESS IT WANTED DINAH TO BE-
GASP!
WHAT THE HELL IS THIS?

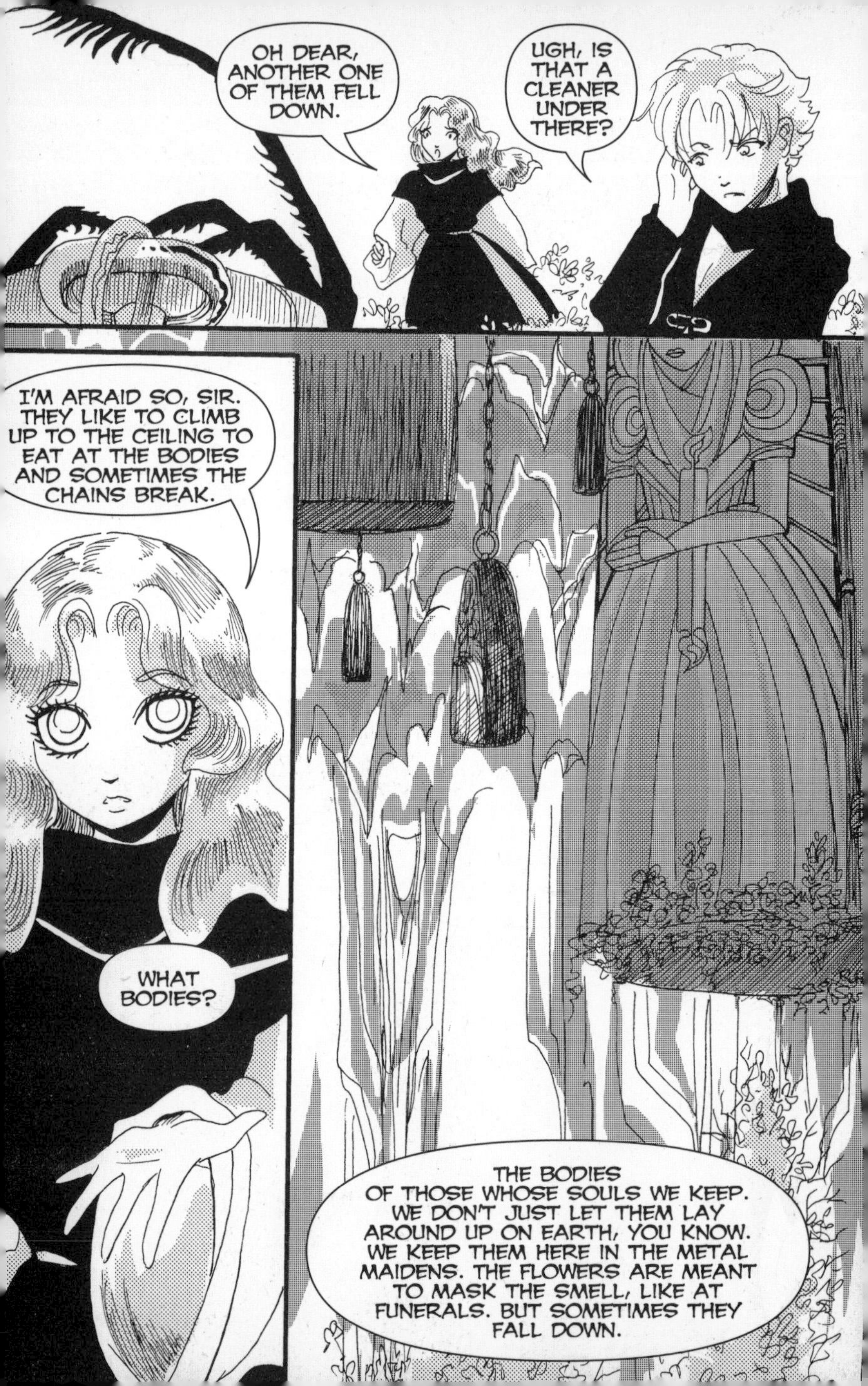
OH DEAR, ANOTHER ONE OF THEM FELL DOWN.
UGH, IS THAT A CLEANER UNDER THERE?
I'M AFRAID SO, SIR. THEY LIKE TO CLIMB UP TO THE CEILING TO EAT AT THE BODIES AND SOMETIMES THE CHAINS BREAK.
WHAT BODIES?
THE BODIES OF THOSE WHOSE SOULS WE KEEP. WE DON'T JUST LET THEM LAY AROUND UP ON EARTH, YOU KNOW. WE KEEP THEM HERE IN THE METAL MAIDENS. THE FLOWERS ARE MEANT TO MASK THE SMELL, LIKE AT FUNERALS. BUT SOMETIMES THEY FALL DOWN.

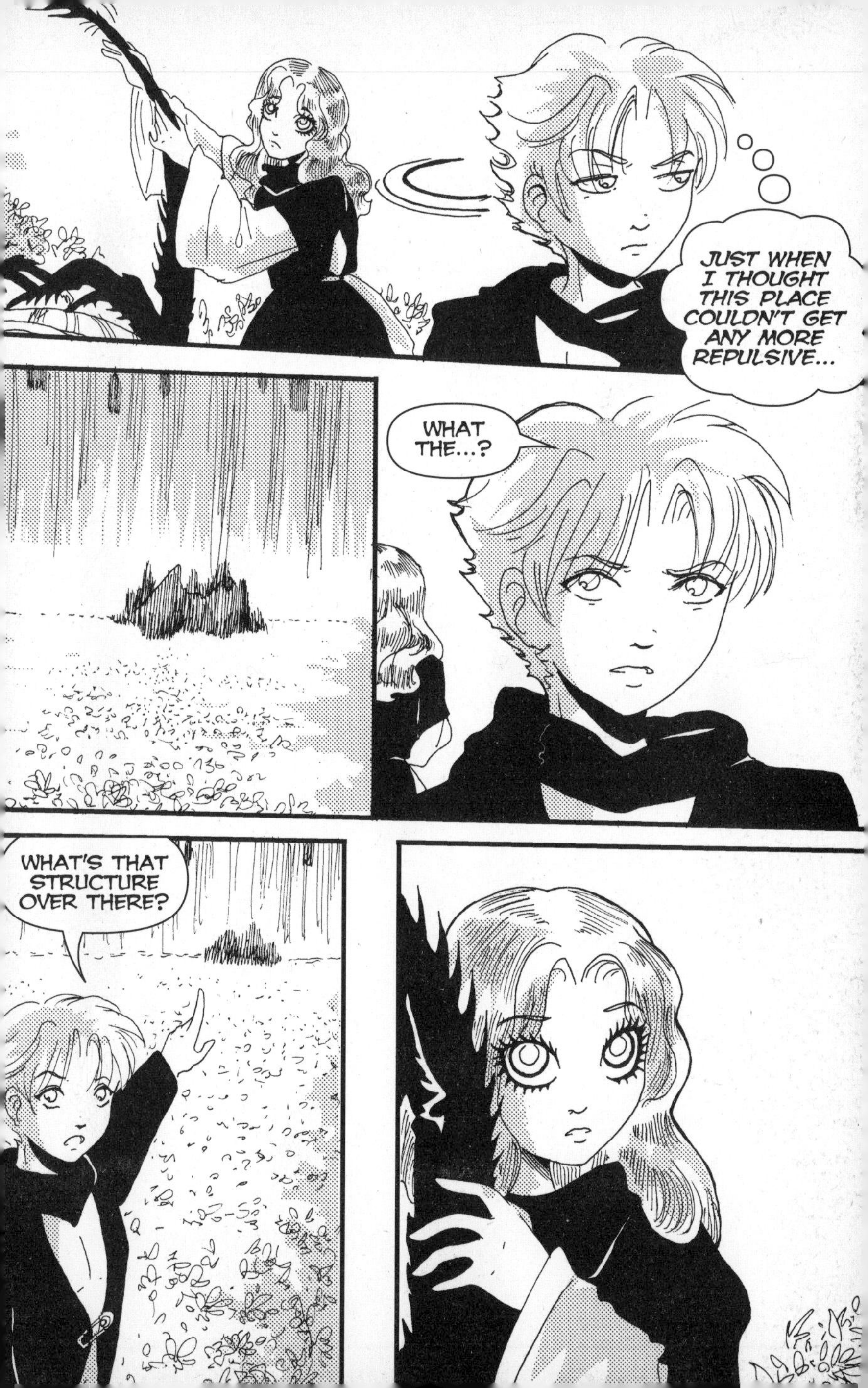
JUST WHEN I THOUGHT THIS PLACE COULDN'T GET ANY MORE REPULSIVE...
WHAT THE...?
WHAT'S THAT STRUCTURE OVER THERE?

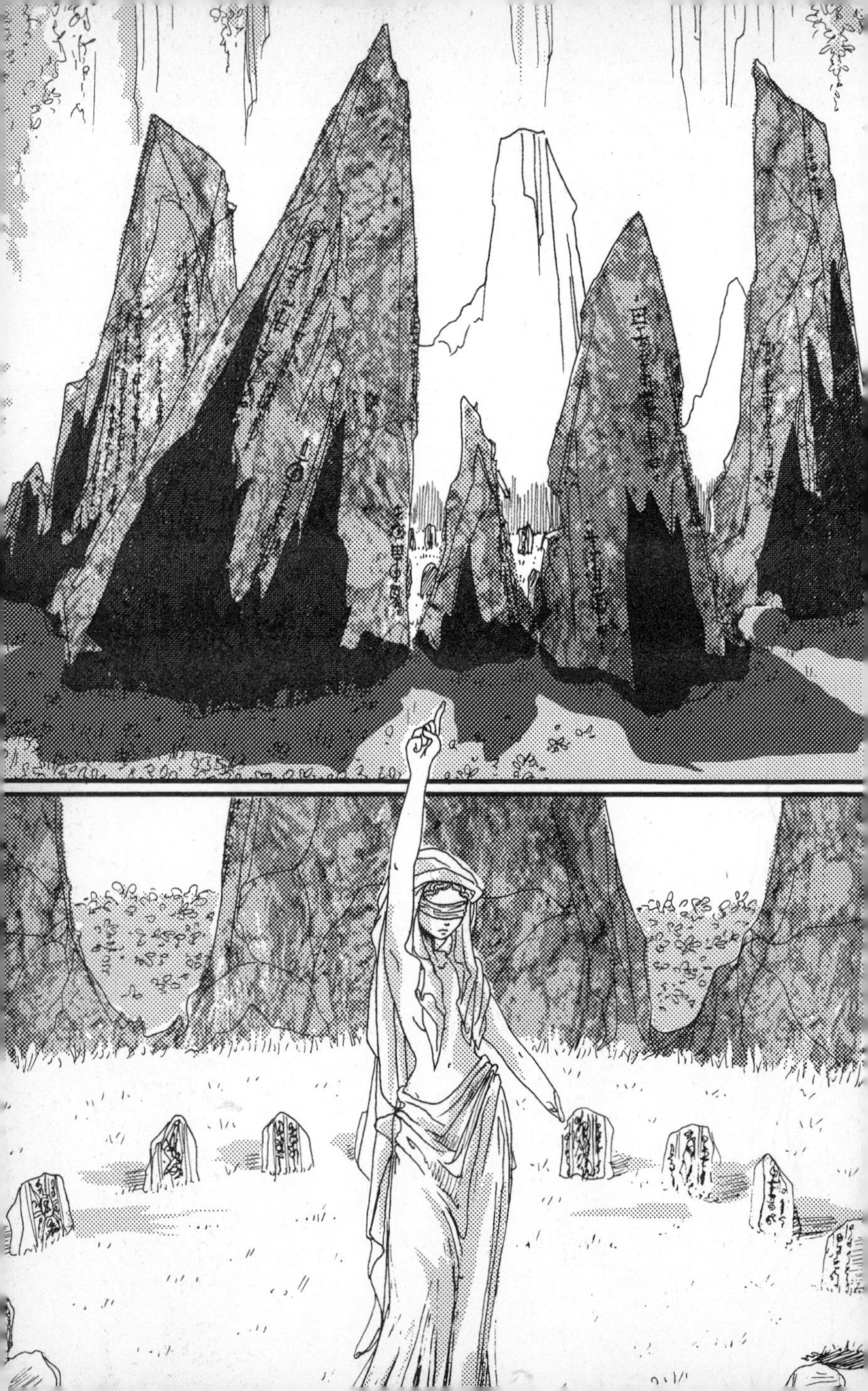

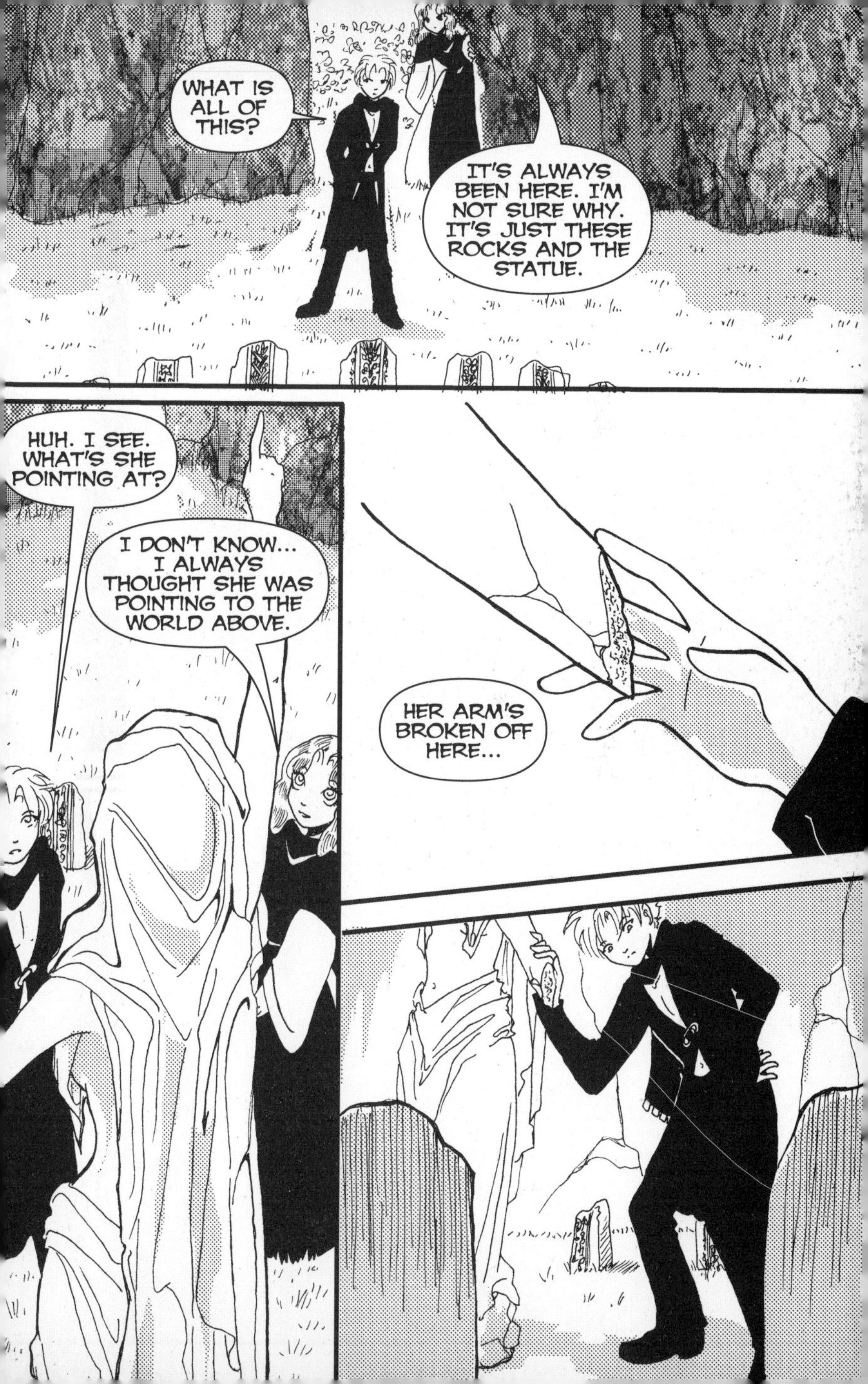
WHAT IS ALL OF THIS?
IT'S ALWAYS BEEN HERE. I'M NOT SURE WHY. IT'S JUST THESE ROCKS AND THE STATUE.
HUH. I SEE. WHAT'S SHE POINTING AT?
I DON'T KNOW... I ALWAYS THOUGHT SHE WAS POINTING TO THE WORLD ABOVE.
HER ARM'S BROKEN OFF HERE...

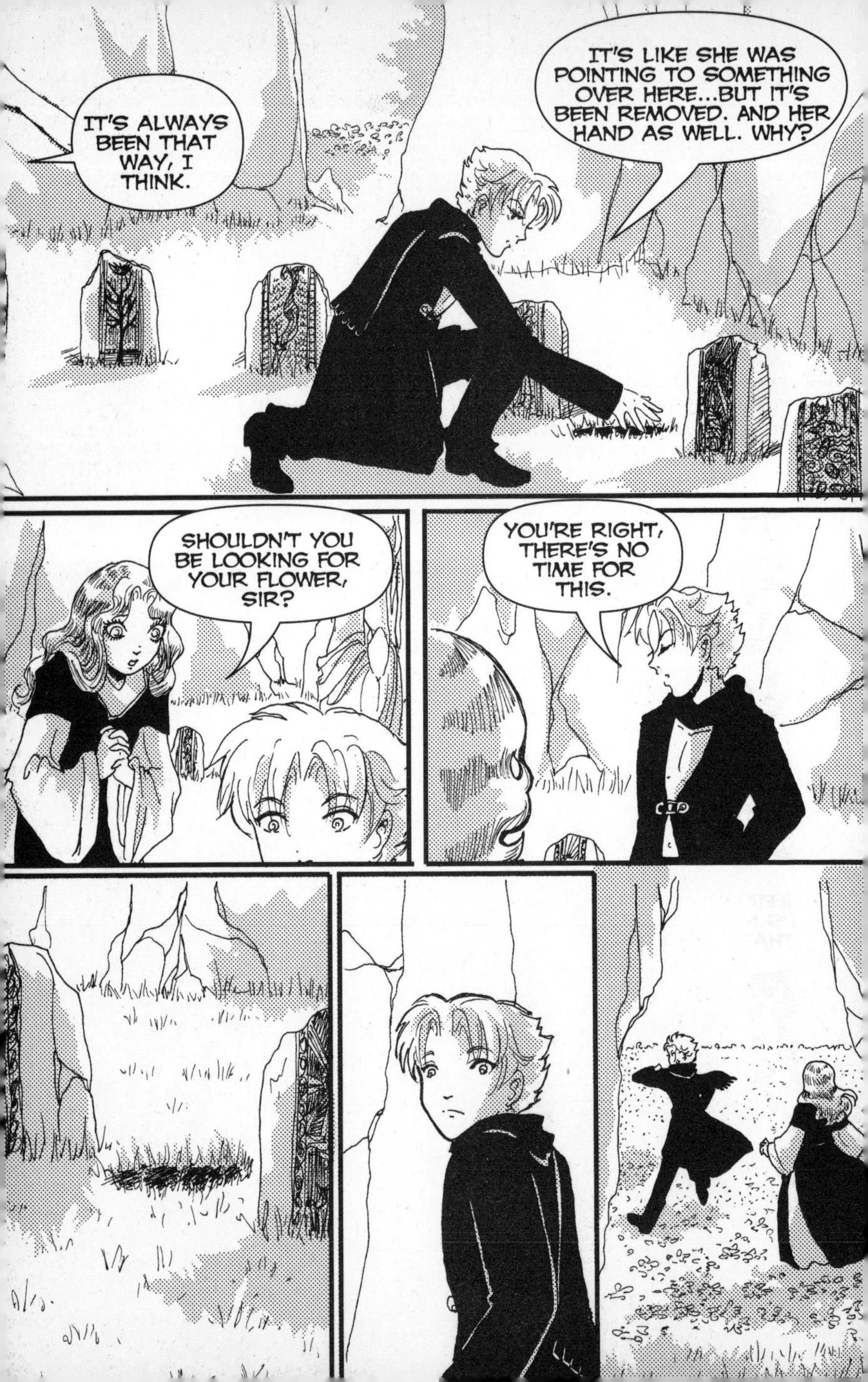
IT'S LIKE SHE WAS POINTING TO SOMETHING OVER HERE...BUT IT'S BEEN REMOVED. AND HER HAND AS WELL. WHY?
IT'S ALWAYS BEEN THAT WAY, I THINK.
SHOULDN'T YOU BE LOOKING FOR YOUR FLOWER, SIR?
YOU'RE RIGHT, THERE'S NO TIME FOR THIS.

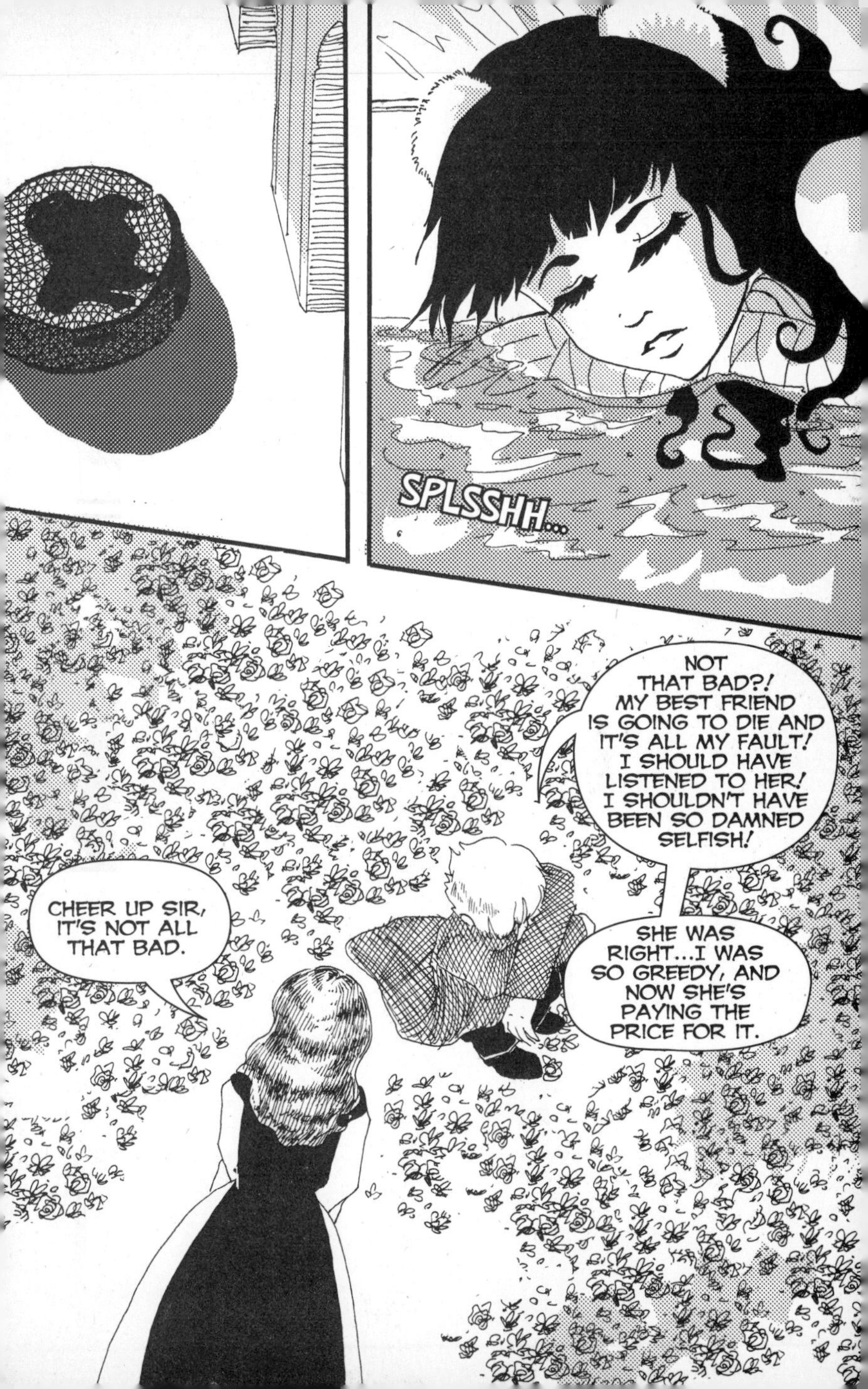
SPLSSHH...
CHEER UP SIR, IT'S NOT ALL THAT BAD.
NOT THAT BAD?! MY BEST FRIEND IS GOING TO DIE AND IT'S ALL MY FAULT! I SHOULD HAVE LISTENED TO HER! I SHOULDN'T HAVE BEEN SO DAMNED SELFISH!
SHE WAS RIGHT...I WAS SO GREEDY, AND NOW SHE'S PAYING THE PRICE FOR IT.

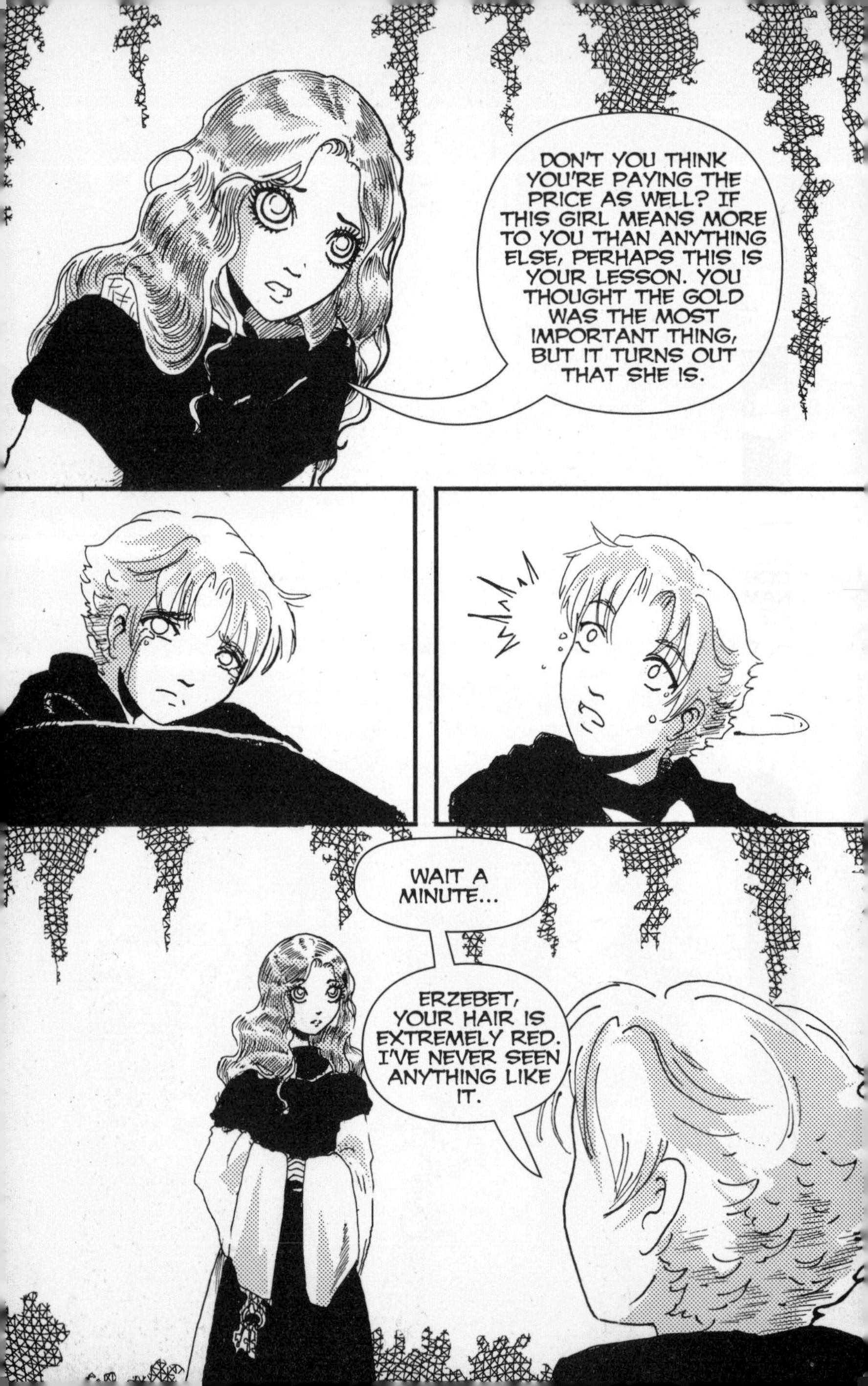
DON'T YOU THINK YOU'RE PAYING THE PRICE AS WELL? IF THIS GIRL MEANS MORE TO YOU THAN ANYTHING ELSE, PERHAPS THIS IS YOUR LESSON. YOU THOUGHT THE GOLD WAS THE MOST IMPORTANT THING, BUT IT TURNS OUT THAT SHE IS.
WAIT A MINUTE...
ERZEBET, YOUR HAIR IS EXTREMELY RED. I'VE NEVER SEEN ANYTHING LIKE IT.

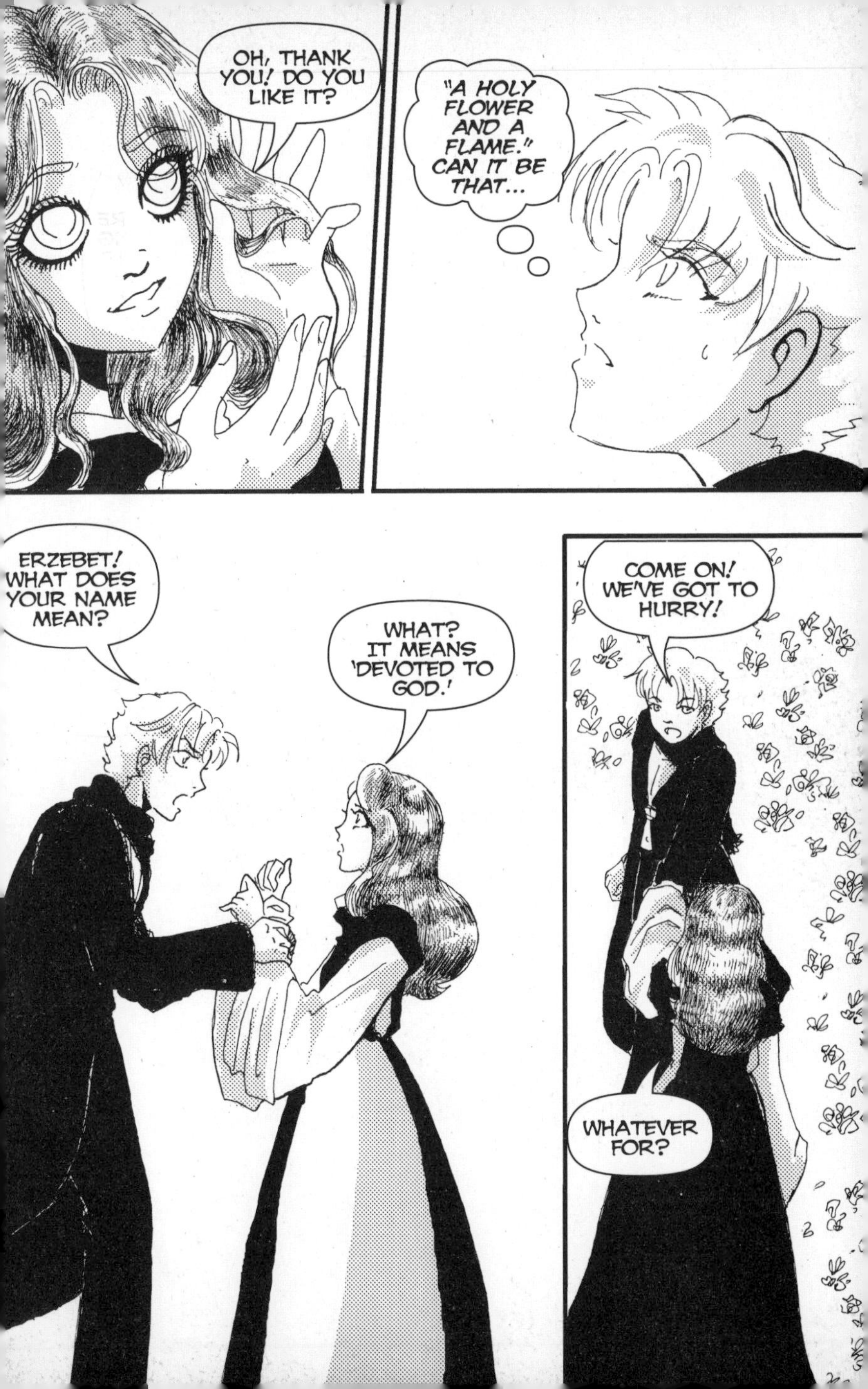

OH, THANK YOU! DO YOU LIKE IT?
"A HOLY FLOWER AND A FLAME." CAN IT BE THAT...
ERZEBET! WHAT DOES YOUR NAME MEAN?
WHAT? IT MEANS 'DEVOTED TO GOD.'
COME ON! WE'VE GOT TO HURRY!
WHATEVER FOR?

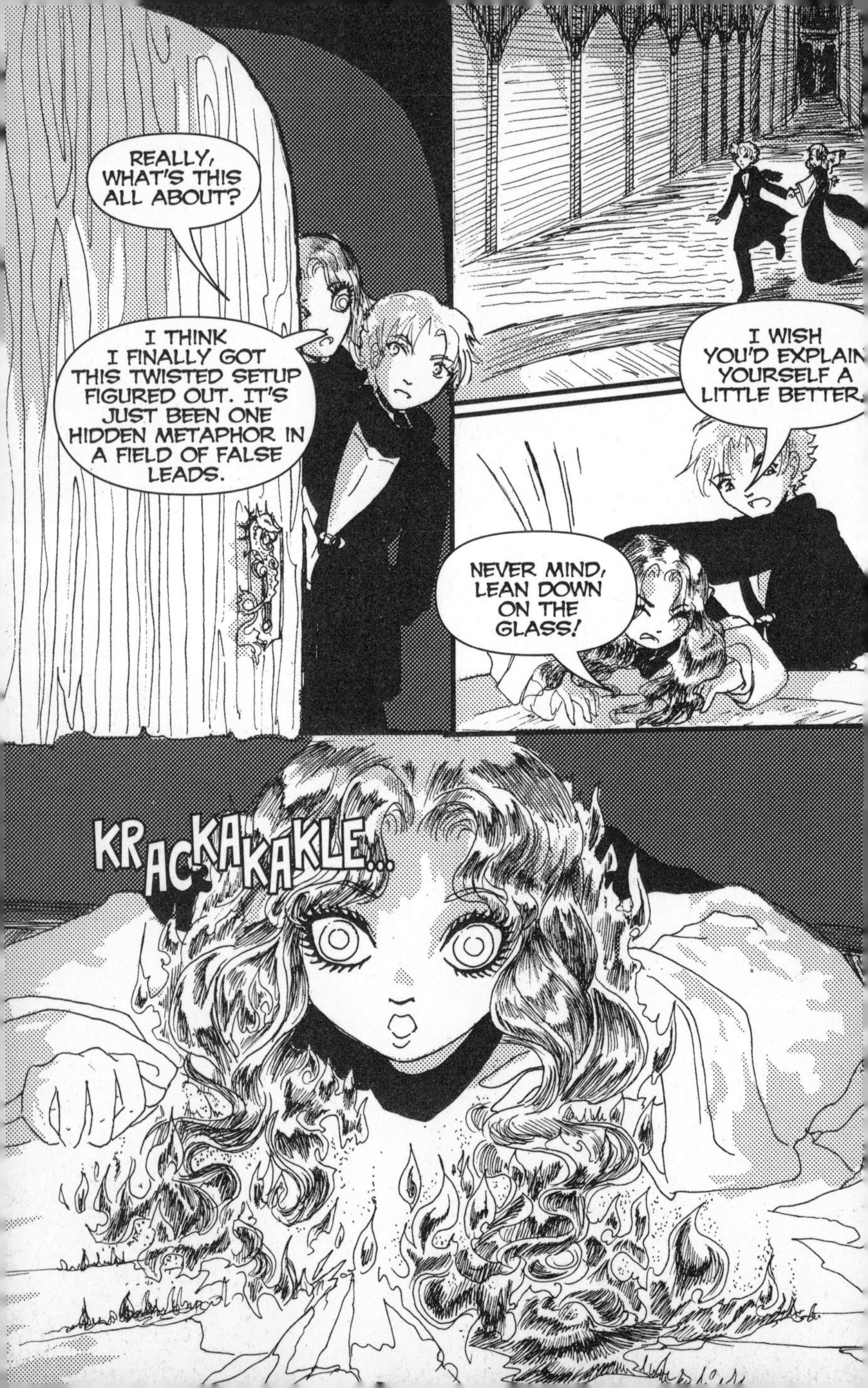
REALLY, WHAT'S THIS ALL ABOUT?
I THINK I FINALLY GOT THIS TWISTED SETUP FIGURED OUT. IT'S JUST BEEN ONE HIDDEN METAPHOR IN A FIELD OF FALSE LEADS.
I WISH YOU'D EXPLAIN YOURSELF A LITTLE BETTER.
NEVER MIND, LEAN DOWN ON THE GLASS!
KRACKAKAKLE...

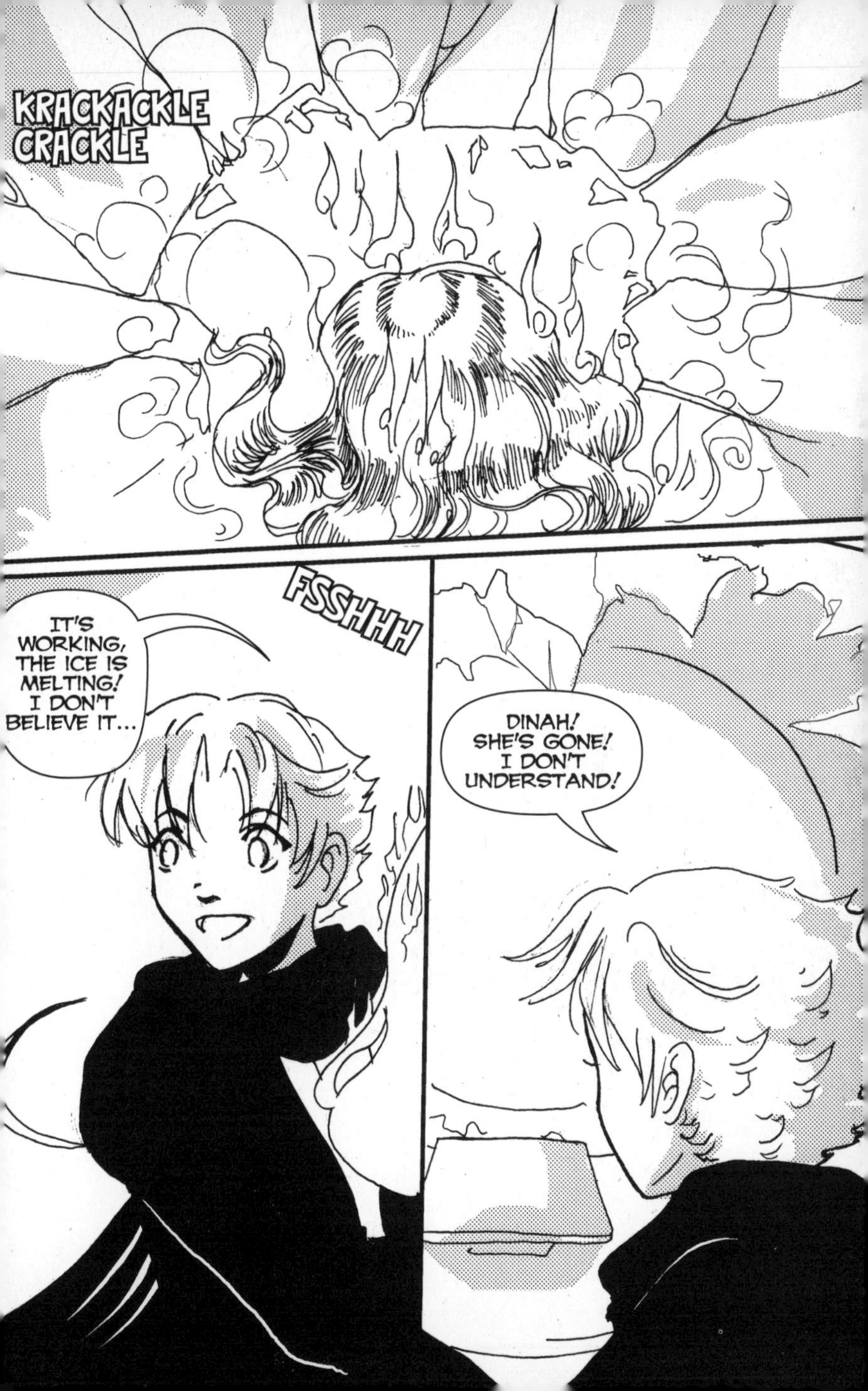
KRACKACKLE CRACKLE
FSSHHH
IT'S WORKING, THE ICE IS MELTING! I DON'T BELIEVE IT...
DINAH! SHE'S GONE! I DON'T UNDERSTAND!

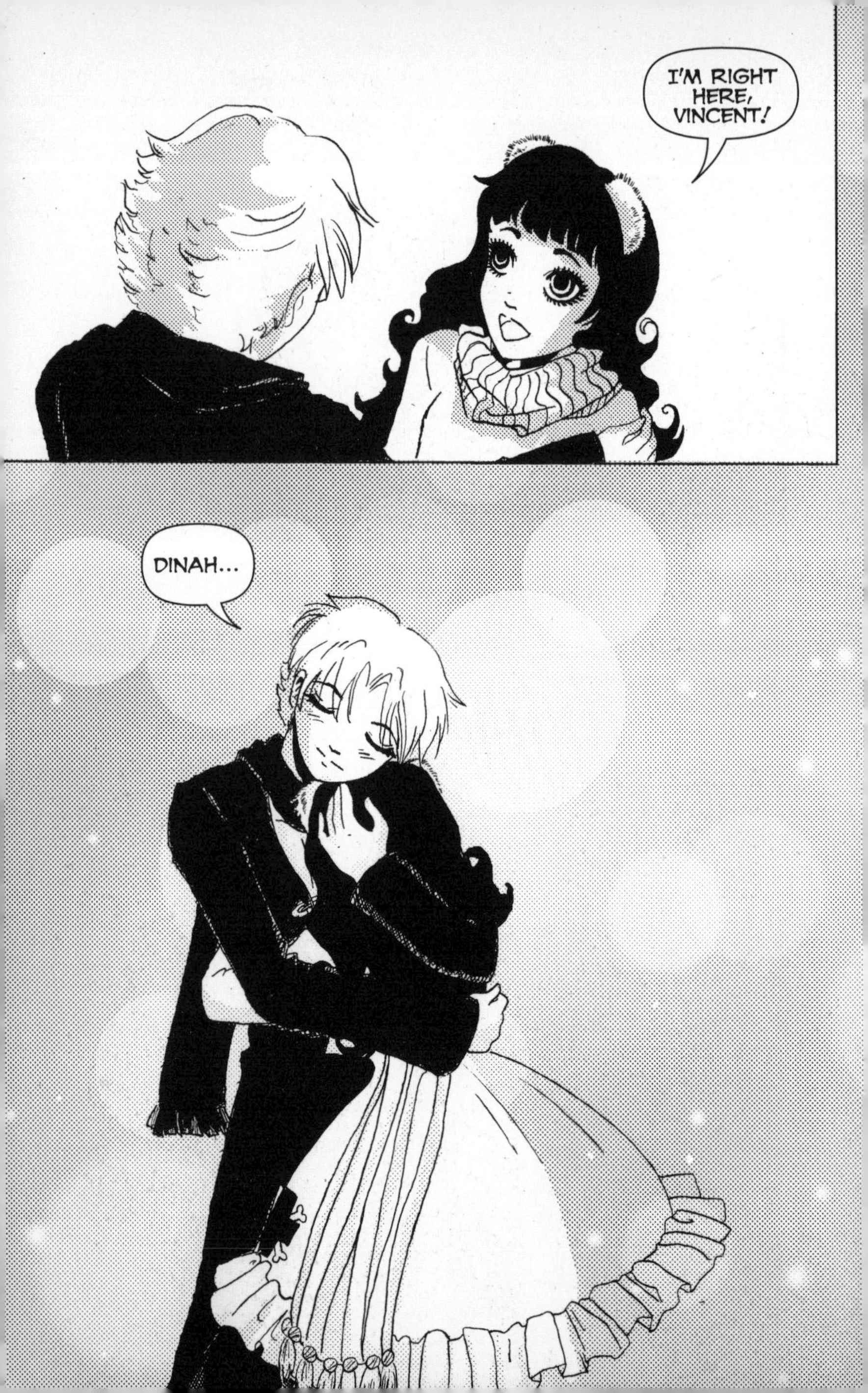
I'M RIGHT HERE, VINCENT!
DINAH...

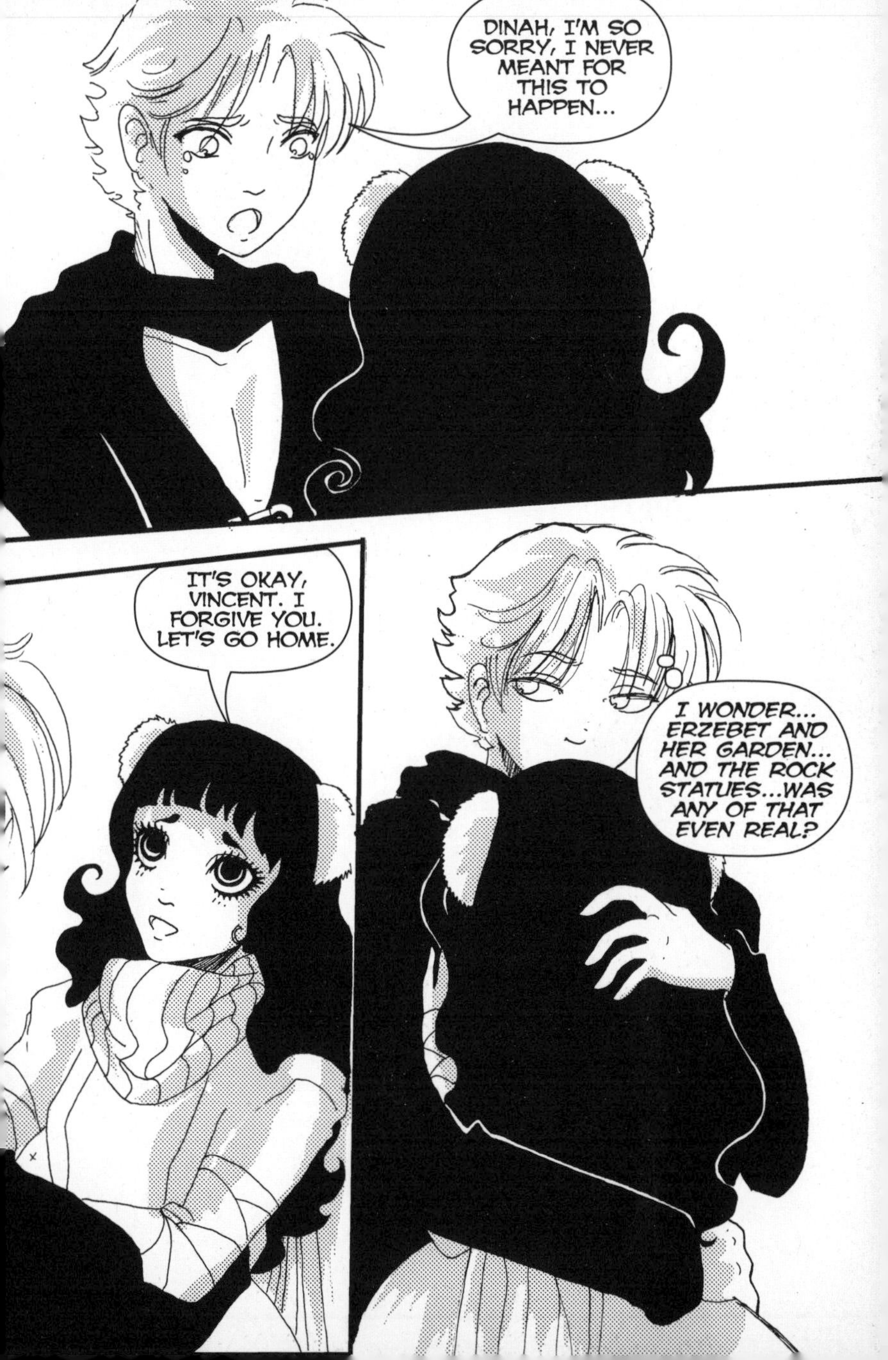
DINAH, I'M SO SORRY, I NEVER MEANT FOR THIS TO HAPPEN...
IT'S OKAY, VINCENT. I FORGIVE YOU. LET'S GO HOME.
I WONDER... ERZEBET AND HER GARDEN... AND THE ROCK STATUES...WAS ANY OF THAT EVEN REAL?

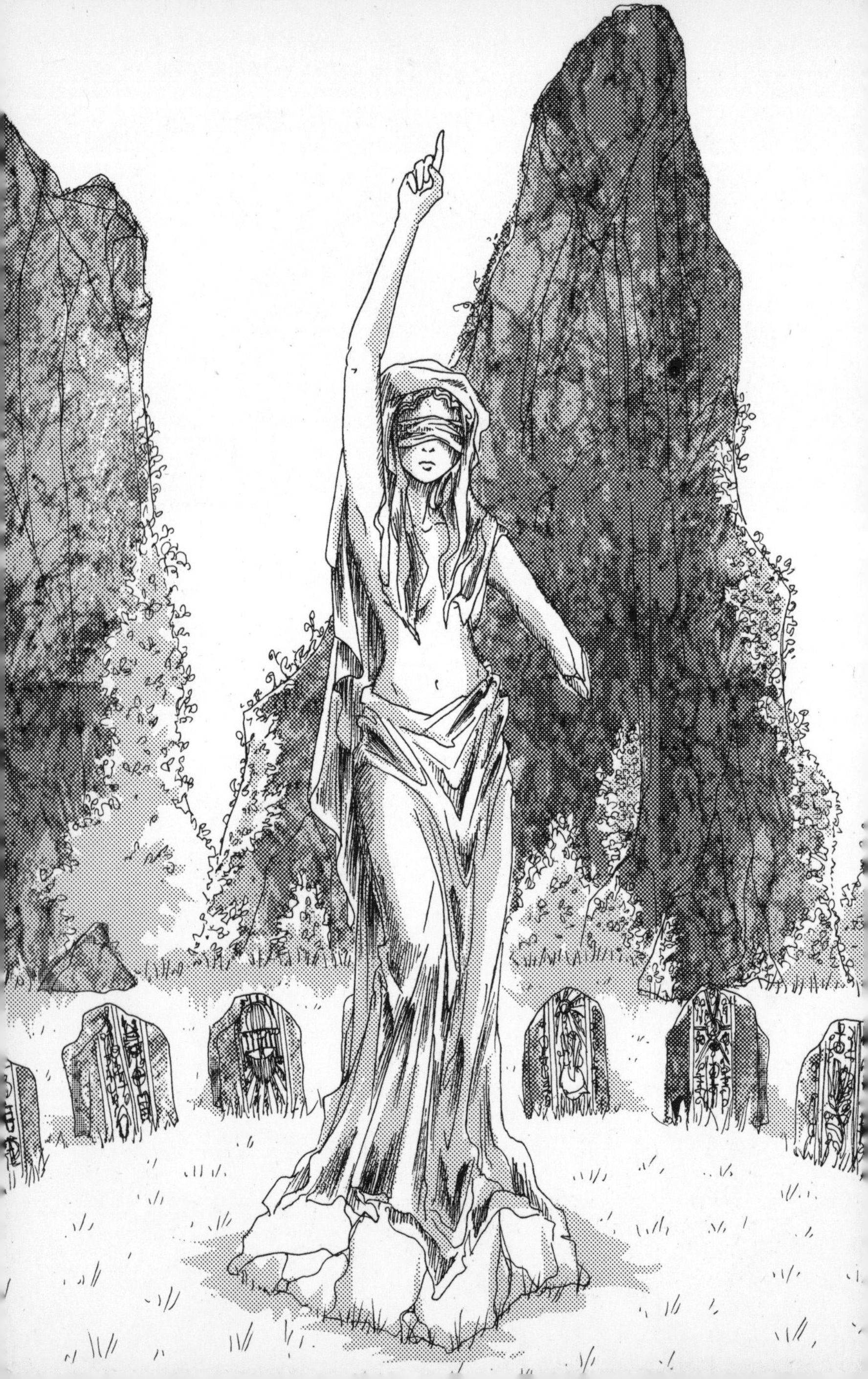

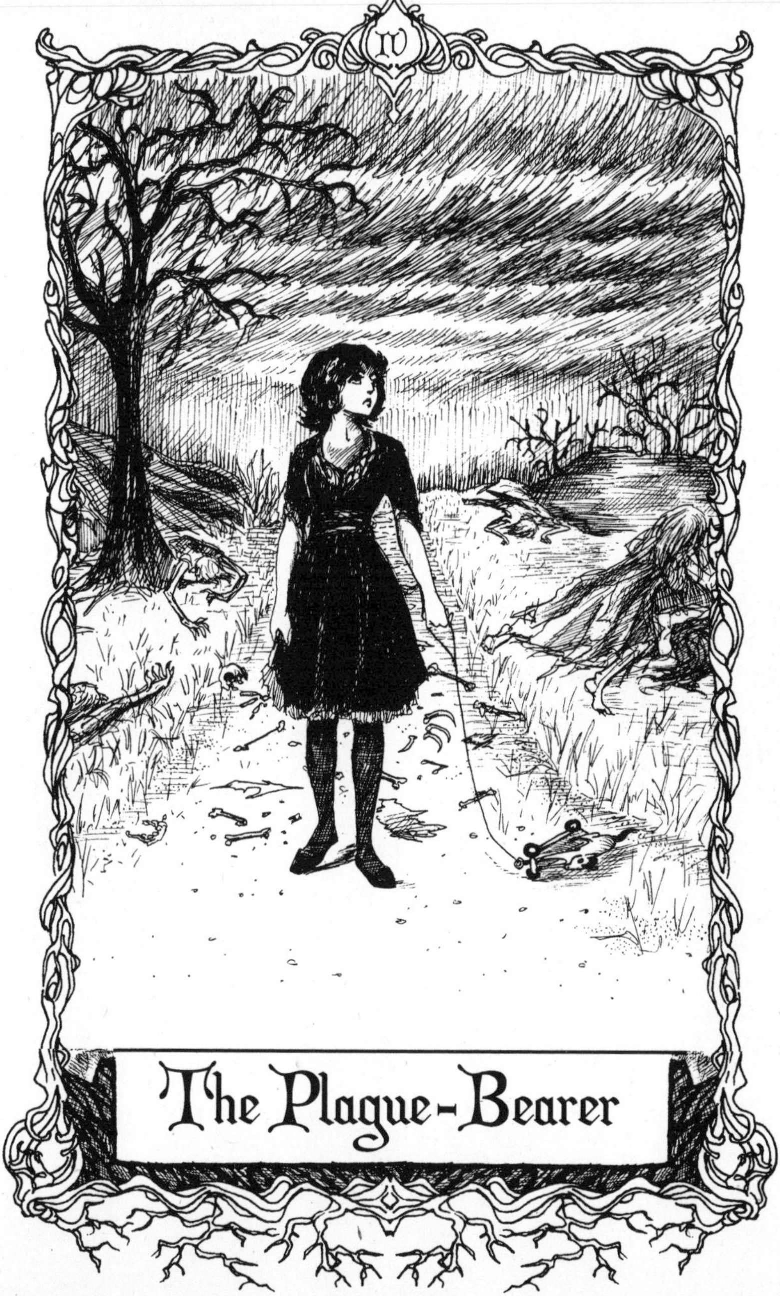
IV
The Plague-Bearer

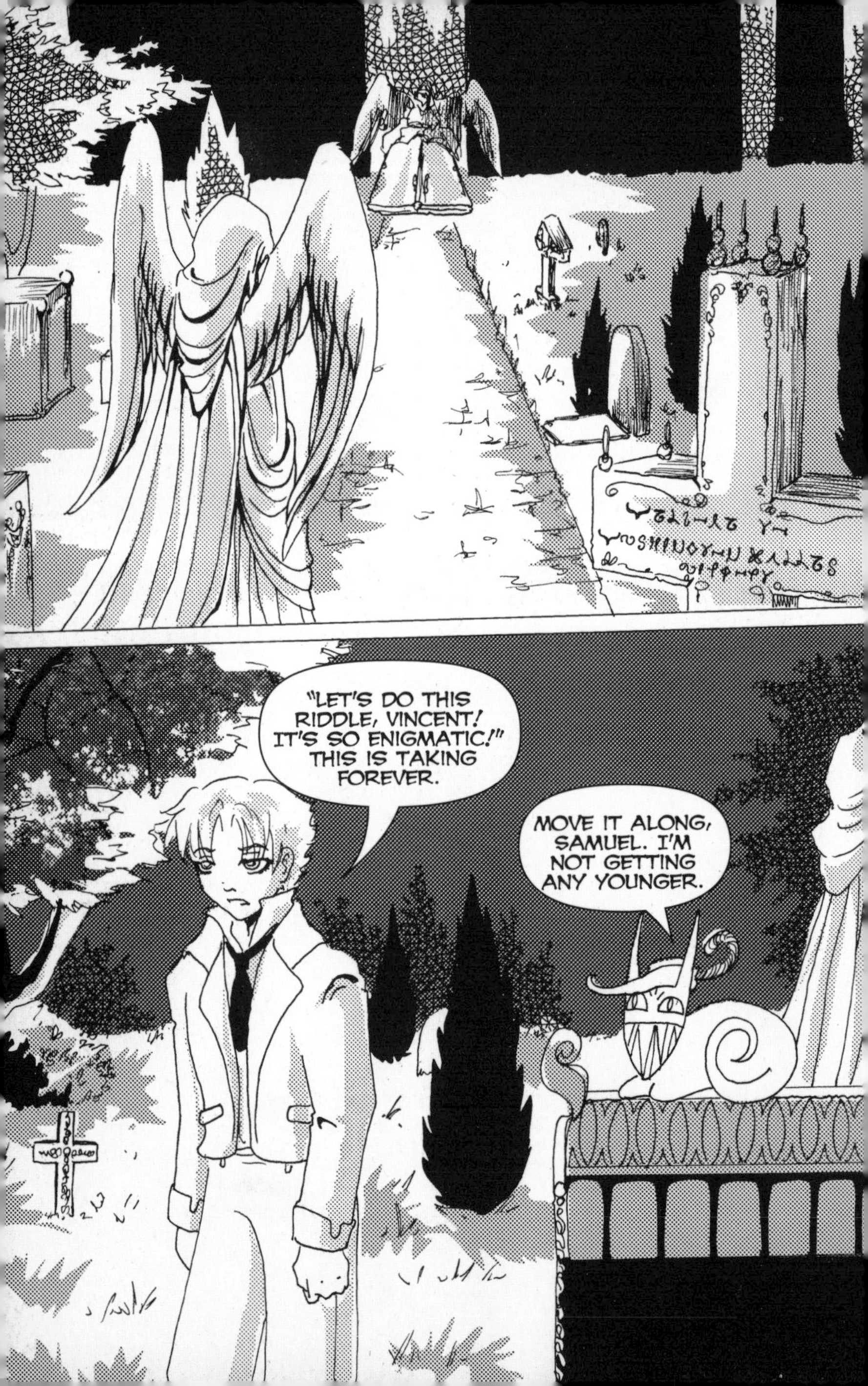
"LET'S DO THIS RIDDLE, VINCENT! IT'S SO ENIGMATIC!" THIS IS TAKING FOREVER.
MOVE IT ALONG, SAMUEL. I'M NOT GETTING ANY YOUNGER.

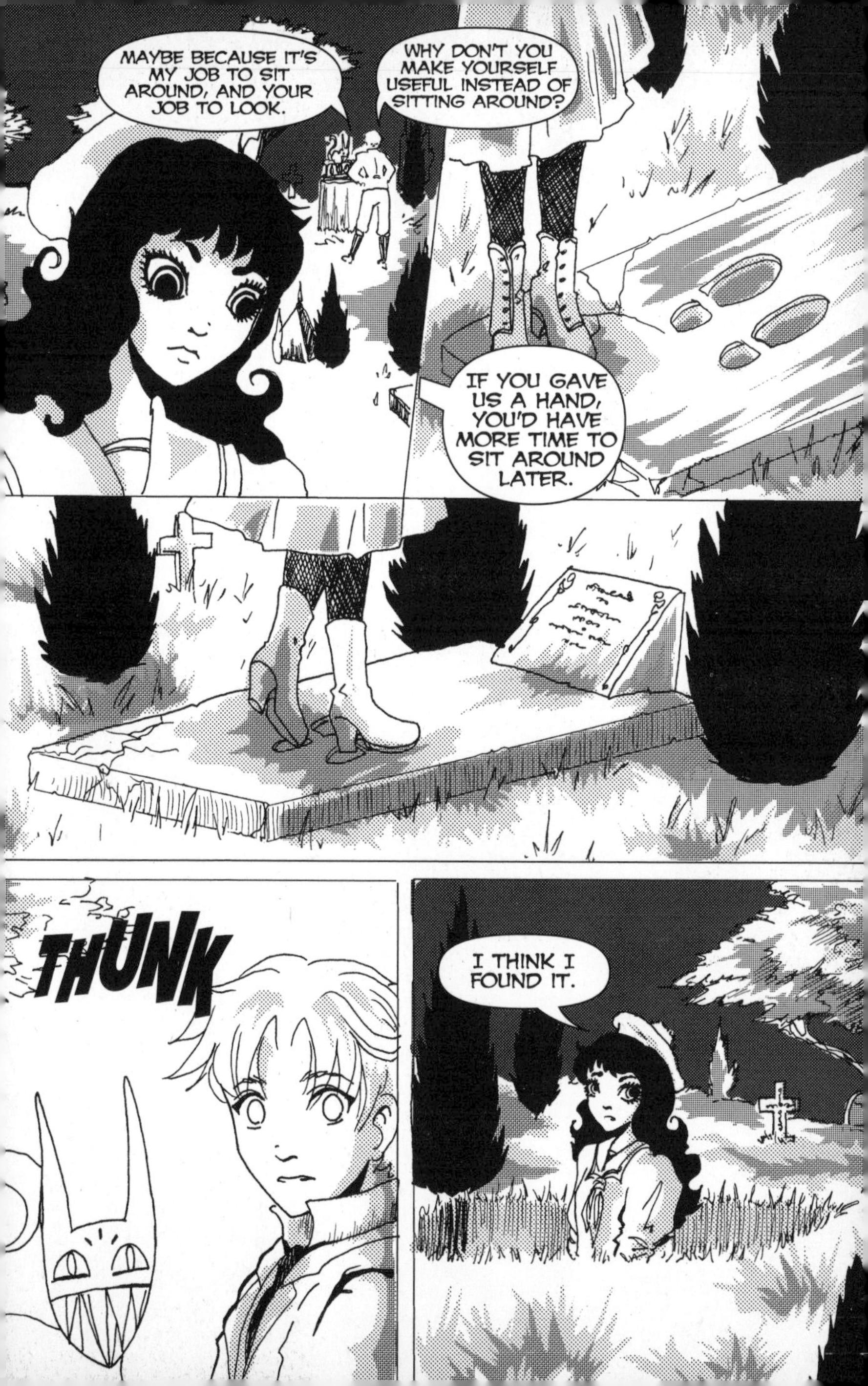
MAYBE BECAUSE IT'S MY JOB TO SIT AROUND, AND YOUR JOB TO LOOK.
WHY DON'T YOU MAKE YOURSELF USEFUL INSTEAD OF SITTING AROUND?
IF YOU GAVE US A HAND, YOU'D HAVE MORE TIME TO SIT AROUND LATER.
THUNK
I THINK I FOUND IT.

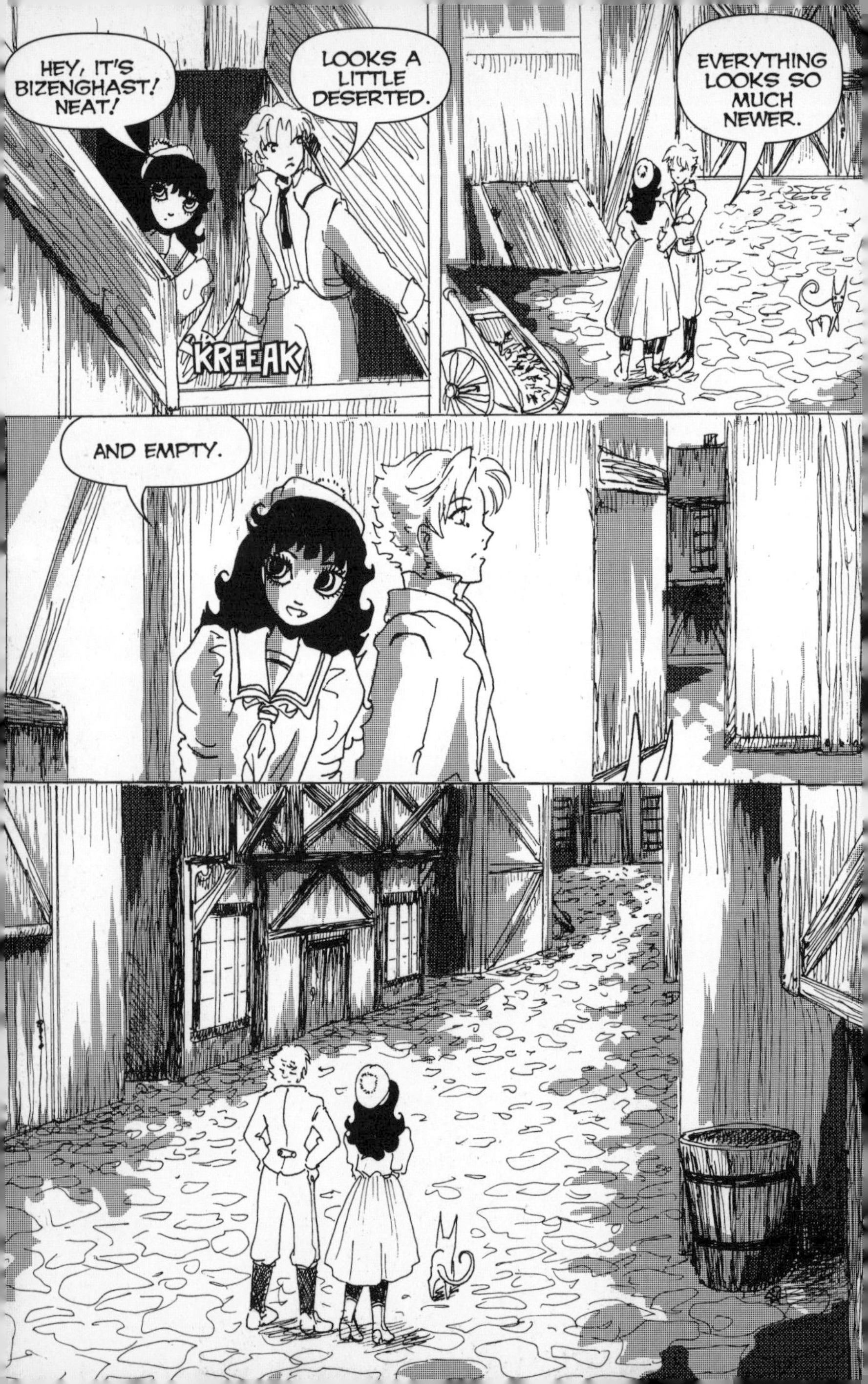
HEY, IT'S BIZENGHAST! NEAT!
KREEAK
LOOKS A LITTLE DESERTED.
EVERYTHING LOOKS SO MUCH NEWER.
AND EMPTY.

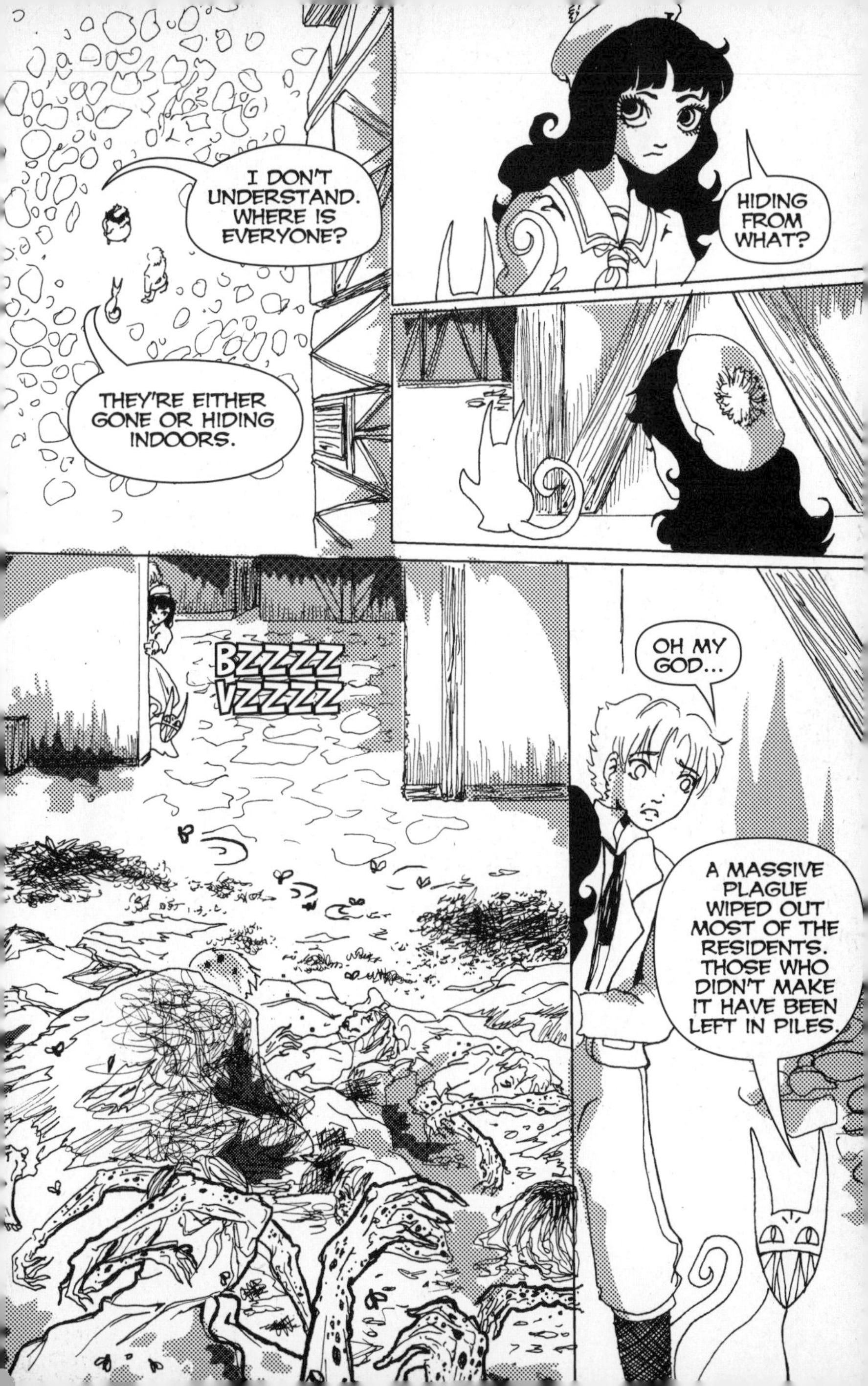
I DON'T UNDERSTAND. WHERE IS EVERYONE?
THEY'RE EITHER GONE OR HIDING INDOORS.
HIDING FROM WHAT?
BZZZZZ VZZZZZ
OH MY GOD...
A MASSIVE PLAGUE WIPED OUT MOST OF THE RESIDENTS. THOSE WHO DIDN'T MAKE IT HAVE BEEN LEFT IN PILES.

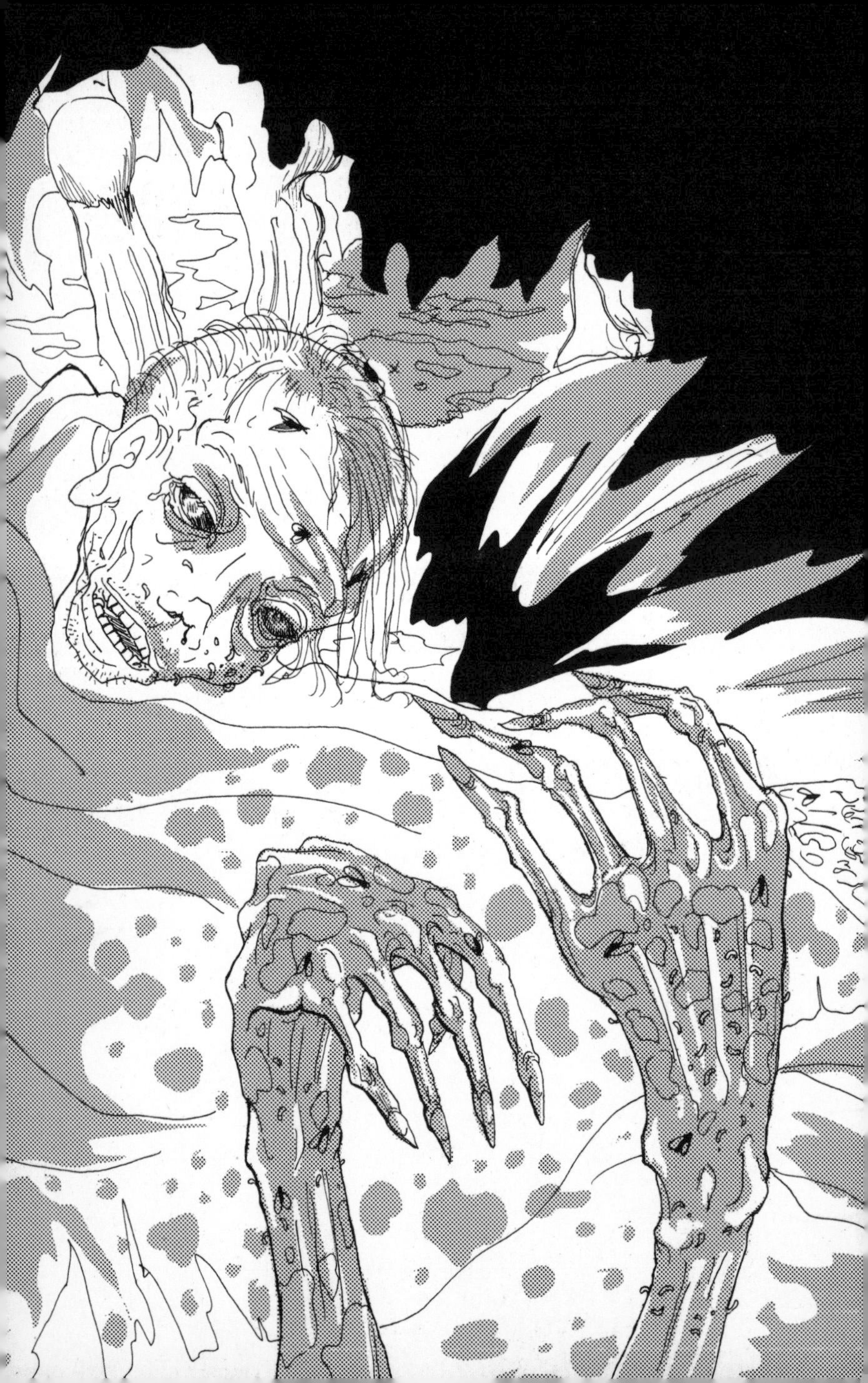

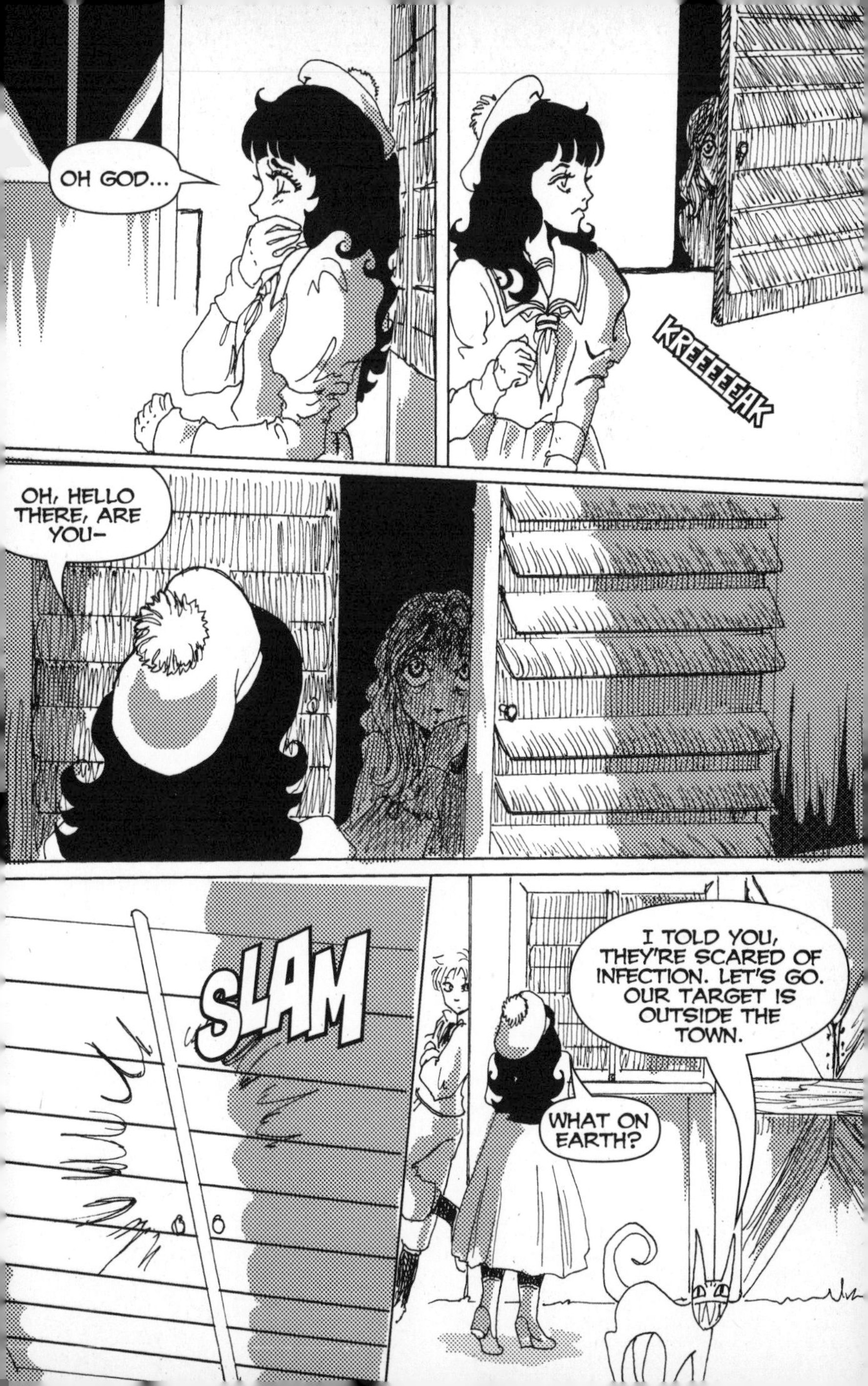
OH GOD...
KREEEEEAK
OH, HELLO THERE, ARE YOU-
SLAM
WHAT ON EARTH?
I TOLD YOU, THEY'RE SCARED OF INFECTION. LET'S GO. OUR TARGET IS OUTSIDE THE TOWN.

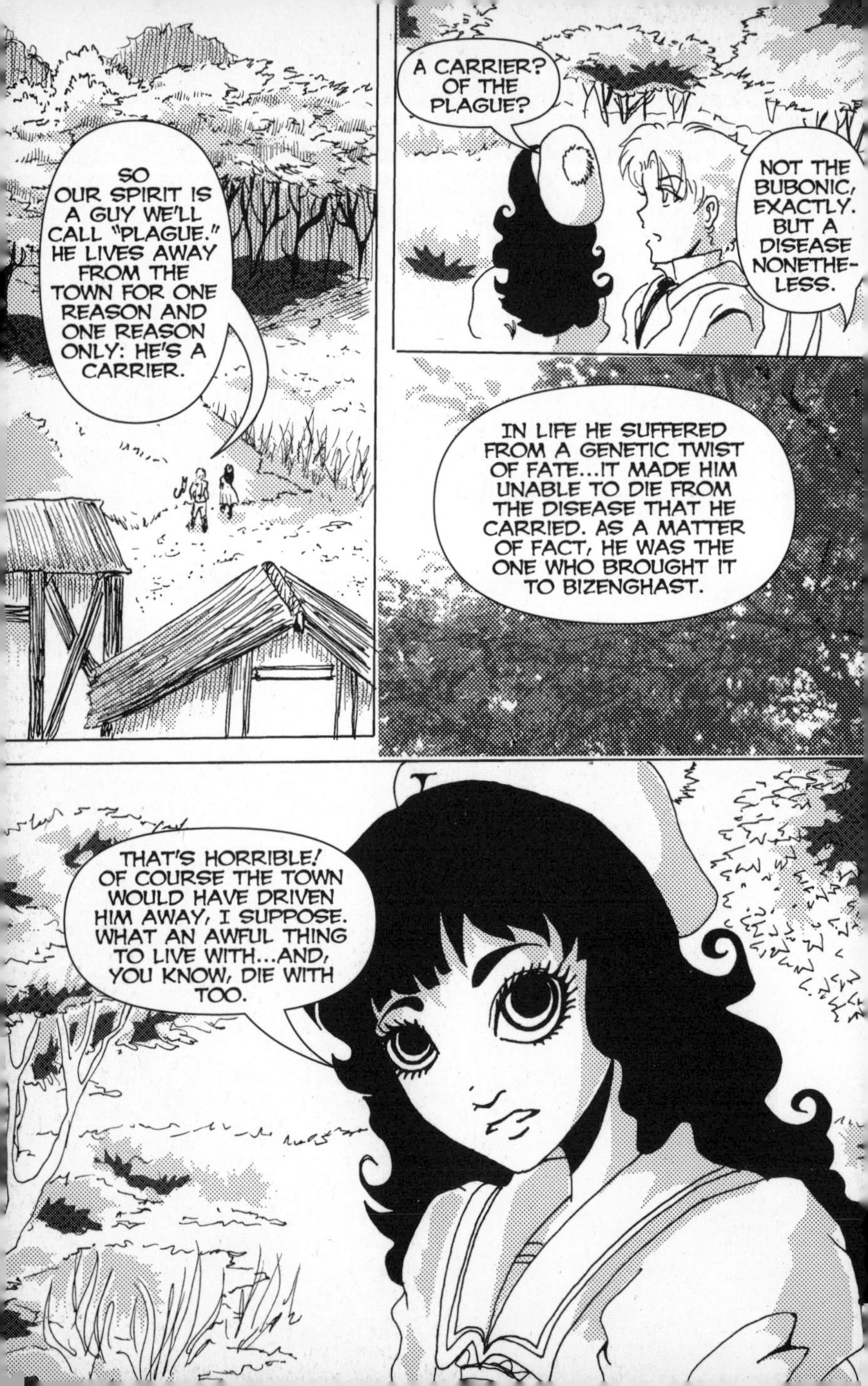
SO OUR SPIRIT IS A GUY WE'LL CALL "PLAGUE." HE LIVES AWAY FROM THE TOWN FOR ONE REASON AND ONE REASON ONLY: HE'S A CARRIER.
A CARRIER? OF THE PLAGUE?
NOT THE BUBONIC, EXACTLY. BUT A DISEASE NONETHELESS.
IN LIFE HE SUFFERED FROM A GENETIC TWIST OF FATE...IT MADE HIM UNABLE TO DIE FROM THE DISEASE THAT HE CARRIED. AS A MATTER OF FACT, HE WAS THE ONE WHO BROUGHT IT TO BIZENGHAST.
THAT'S HORRIBLE! OF COURSE THE TOWN WOULD HAVE DRIVEN HIM AWAY, I SUPPOSE. WHAT AN AWFUL THING TO LIVE WITH...AND, YOU KNOW, DIE WITH TOO.

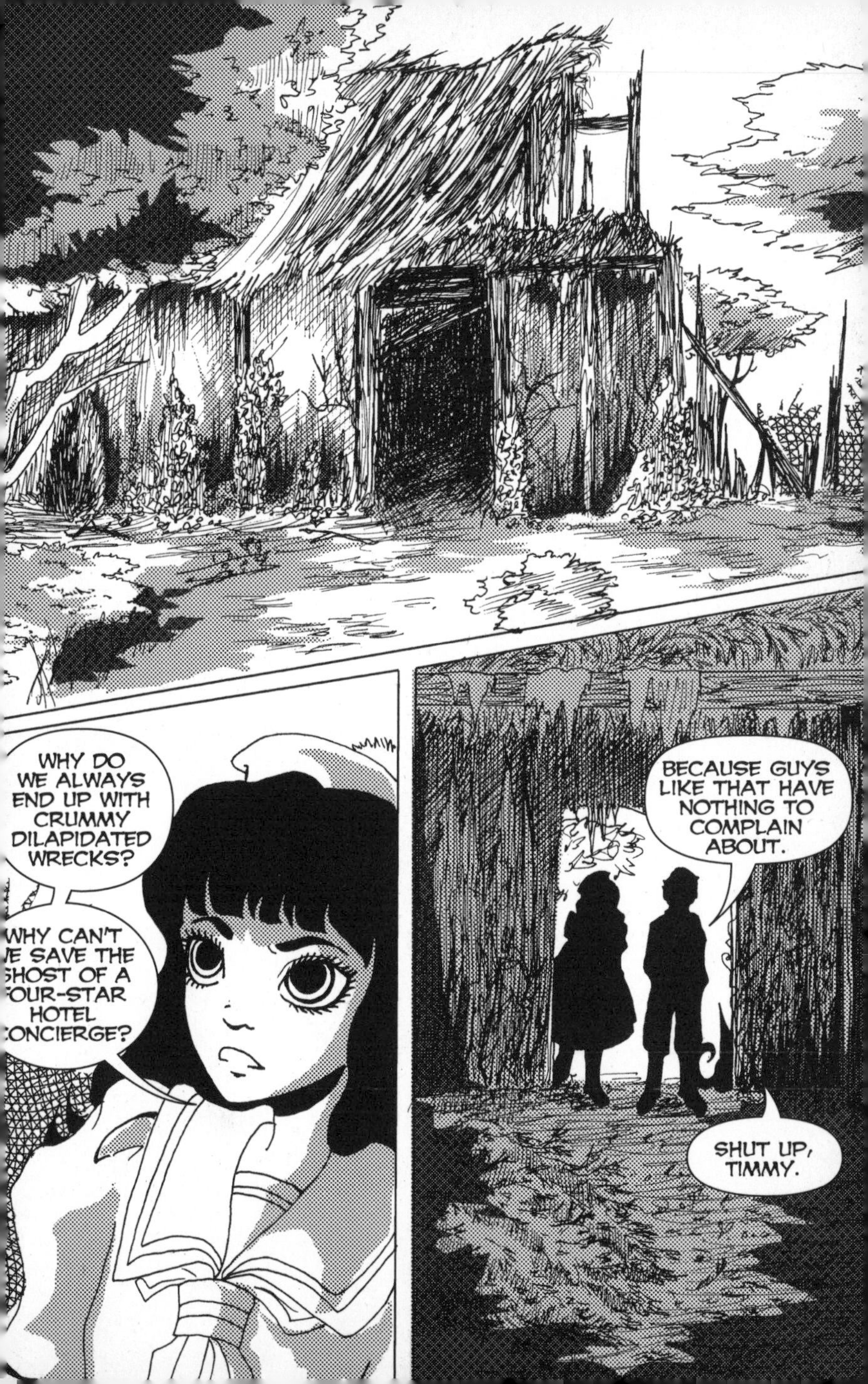
WHY DO WE ALWAYS END UP WITH CRUMMY DILAPIDATED WRECKS?
WHY CAN'T WE SAVE THE GHOST OF A FOUR-STAR HOTEL CONCIERGE?
BECAUSE GUYS LIKE THAT HAVE NOTHING TO COMPLAIN ABOUT.
SHUT UP, TIMMY.

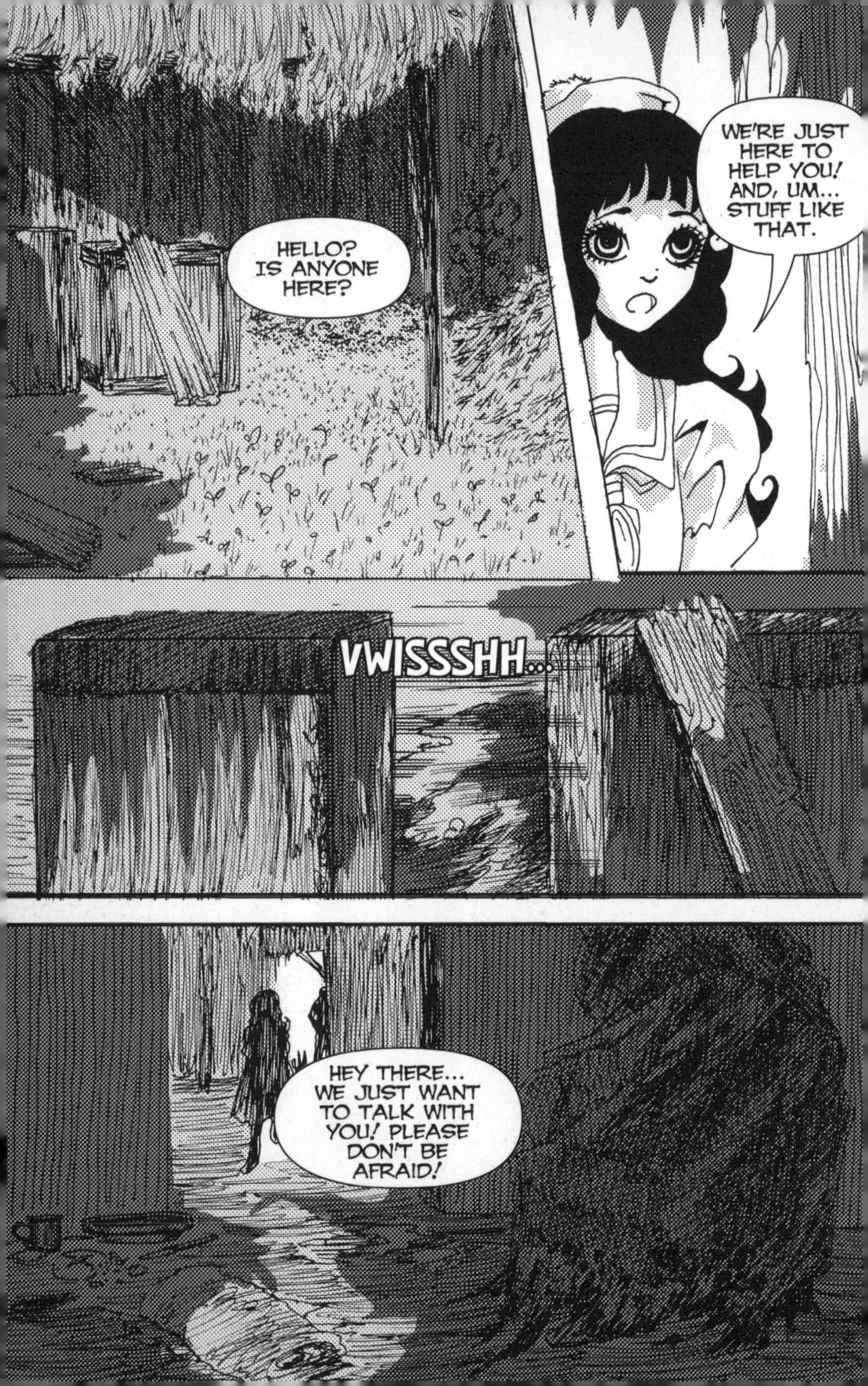
HELLO? IS ANYONE HERE?
WE'RE JUST HERE TO HELP YOU! AND, UM... STUFF LIKE THAT.
VWISSSHH...
HEY THERE... WE JUST WANT TO TALK WITH YOU! PLEASE DON'T BE AFRAID!

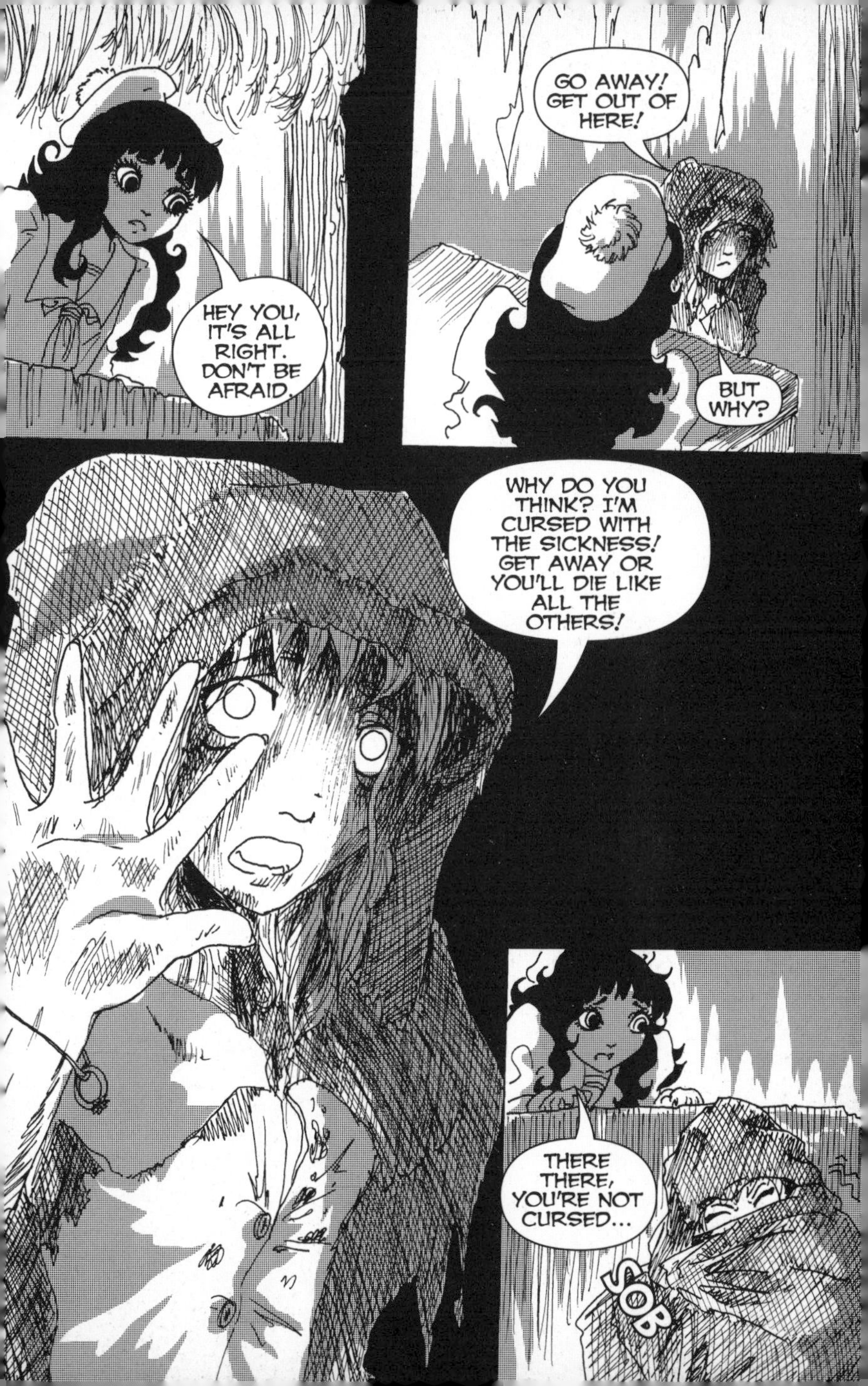
HEY YOU, IT'S ALL RIGHT. DON'T BE AFRAID.
GO AWAY! GET OUT OF HERE!
BUT WHY?
WHY DO YOU THINK? I'M CURSED WITH THE SICKNESS! GET AWAY OR YOU'LL DIE LIKE ALL THE OTHERS!
THERE THERE, YOU'RE NOT CURSED...
SOB

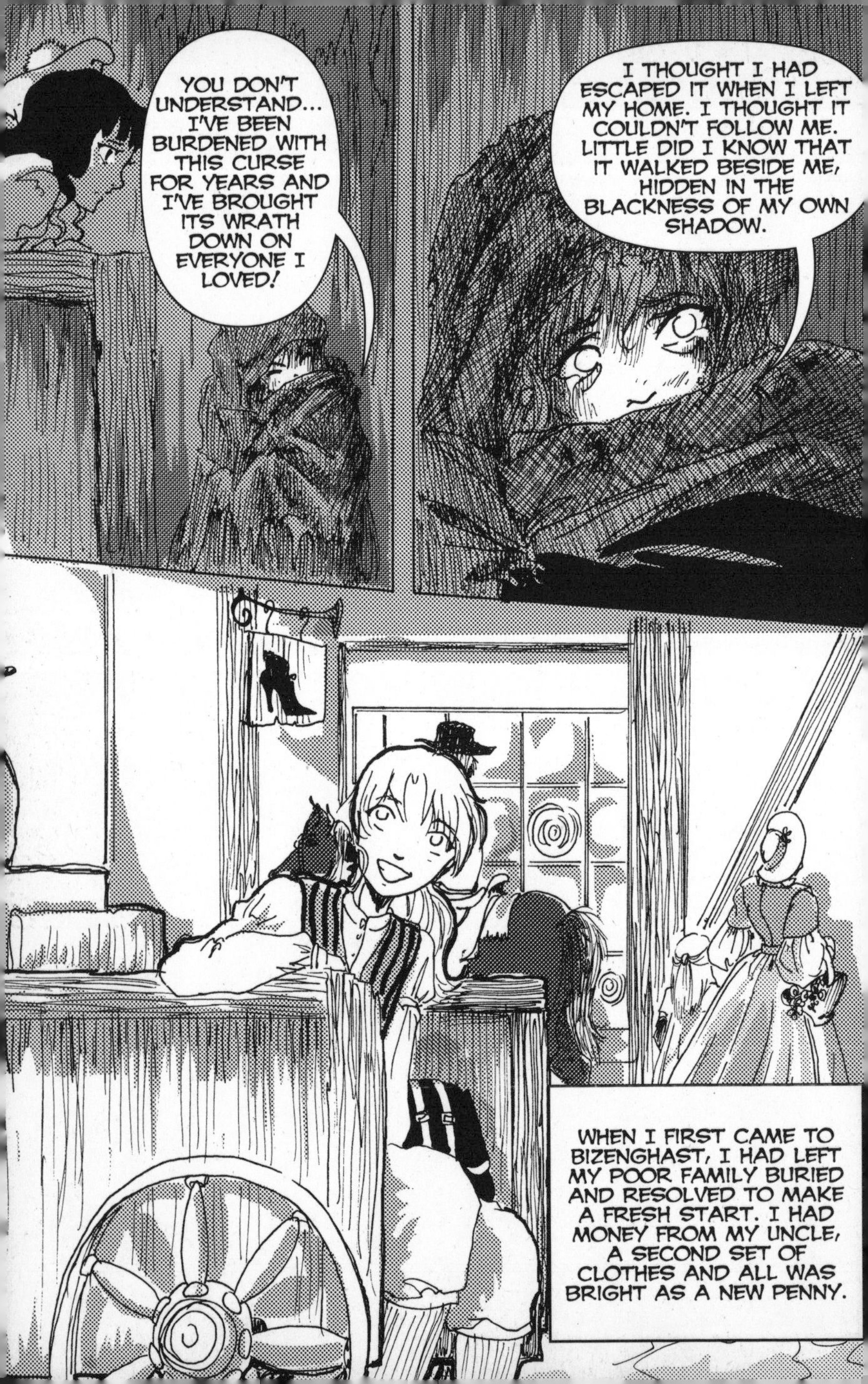
YOU DON'T UNDERSTAND... I'VE BEEN BURDENED WITH THIS CURSE FOR YEARS AND I'VE BROUGHT ITS WRATH DOWN ON EVERYONE I LOVED!
I THOUGHT I HAD ESCAPED IT WHEN I LEFT MY HOME. I THOUGHT IT COULDN'T FOLLOW ME. LITTLE DID I KNOW THAT IT WALKED BESIDE ME, HIDDEN IN THE BLACKNESS OF MY OWN SHADOW.
WHEN I FIRST CAME TO BIZENGHAST, I HAD LEFT MY POOR FAMILY BURIED AND RESOLVED TO MAKE A FRESH START. I HAD MONEY FROM MY UNCLE, A SECOND SET OF CLOTHES AND ALL WAS BRIGHT AS A NEW PENNY.

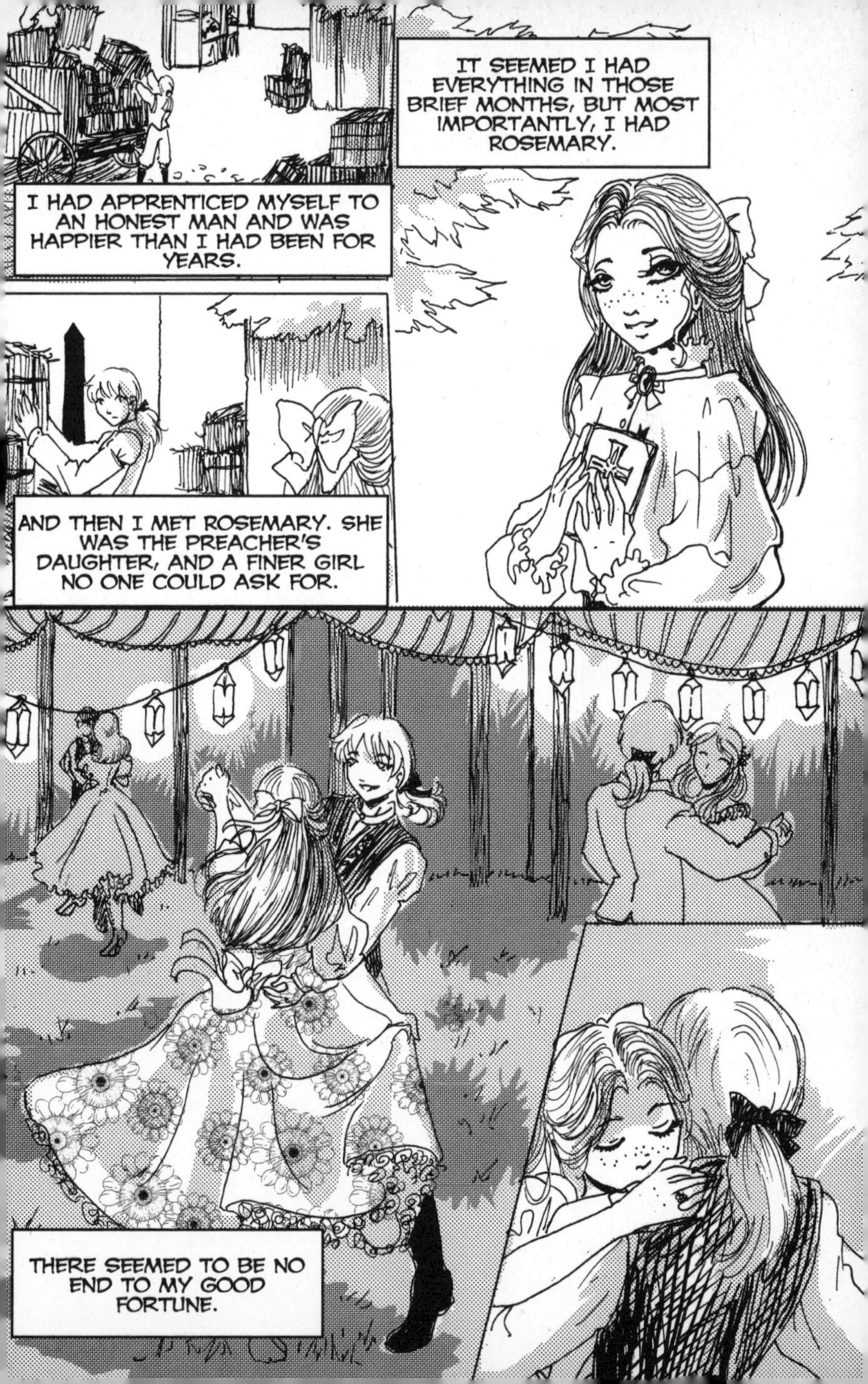
I HAD APPRENTICED MYSELF TO AN HONEST MAN AND WAS HAPPIER THAN I HAD BEEN FOR YEARS.
AND THEN I MET ROSEMARY. SHE WAS THE PREACHER'S DAUGHTER, AND A FINER GIRL NO ONE COULD ASK FOR.
IT SEEMED I HAD EVERYTHING IN THOSE BRIEF MONTHS, BUT MOST IMPORTANTLY, I HAD ROSEMARY.
THERE SEEMED TO BE NO END TO MY GOOD FORTUNE.

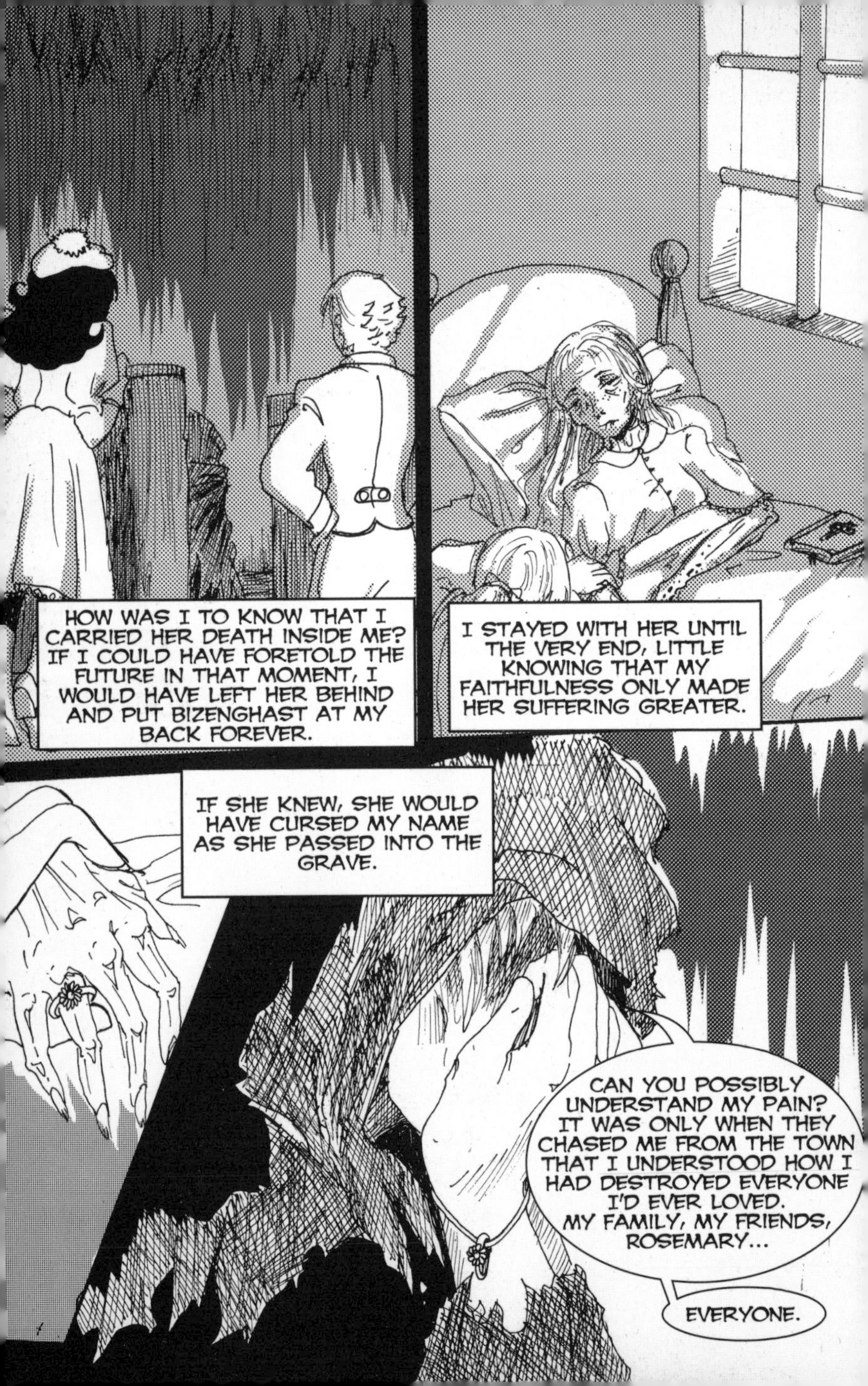
HOW WAS I TO KNOW THAT I CARRIED HER DEATH INSIDE ME? IF I COULD HAVE FORETOLD THE FUTURE IN THAT MOMENT, I WOULD HAVE LEFT HER BEHIND AND PUT BIZENGHAST AT MY BACK FOREVER.
I STAYED WITH HER UNTIL THE VERY END, LITTLE KNOWING THAT MY FAITHFULNESS ONLY MADE HER SUFFERING GREATER.
IF SHE KNEW, SHE WOULD HAVE CURSED MY NAME AS SHE PASSED INTO THE GRAVE.
CAN YOU POSSIBLY UNDERSTAND MY PAIN? IT WAS ONLY WHEN THEY CHASED ME FROM THE TOWN THAT I UNDERSTOOD HOW I HAD DESTROYED EVERYONE I'D EVER LOVED. MY FAMILY, MY FRIENDS, ROSEMARY...
EVERYONE.

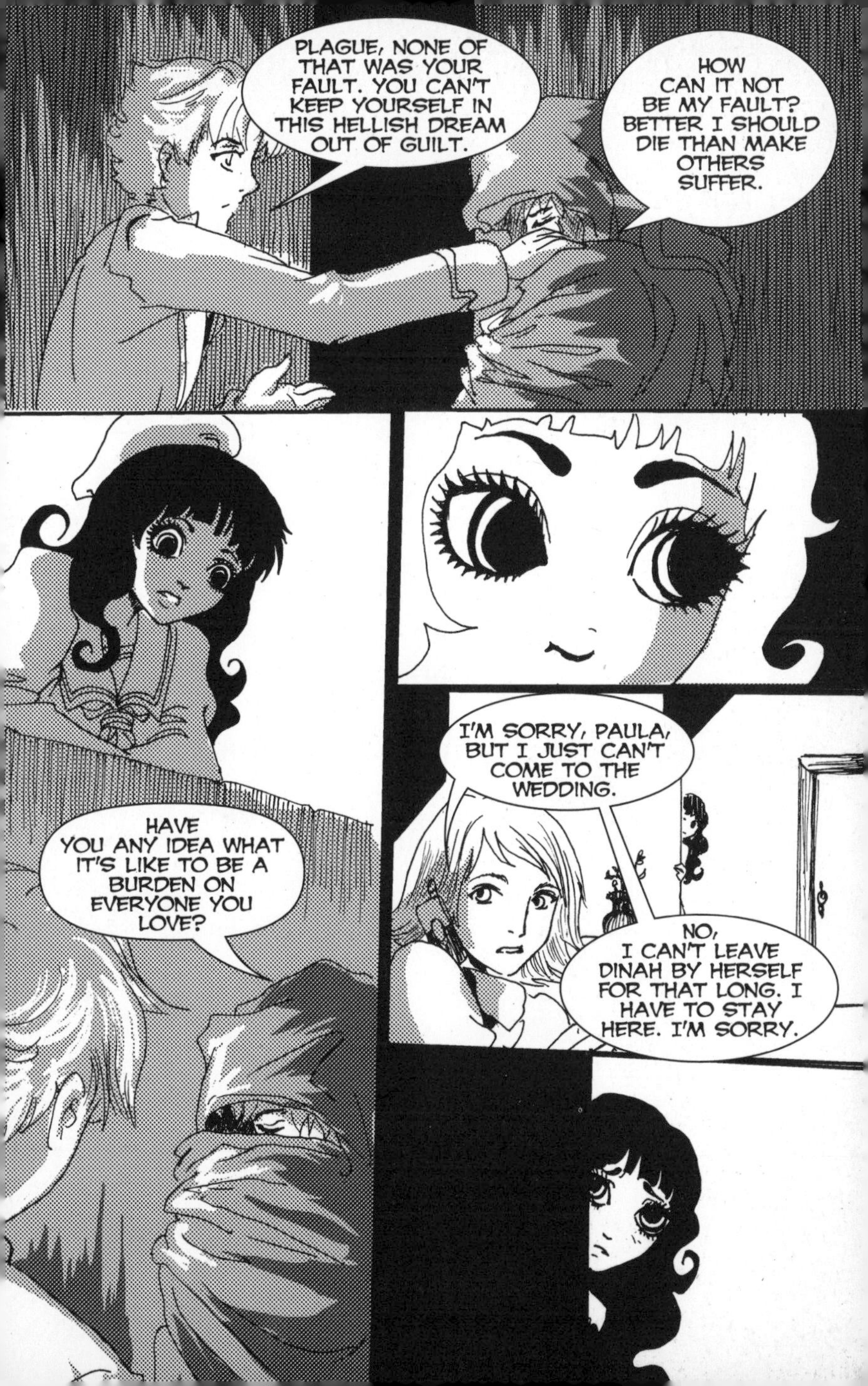
PLAGUE, NONE OF THAT WAS YOUR FAULT. YOU CAN'T KEEP YOURSELF IN THIS HELLISH DREAM OUT OF GUILT.
HOW CAN IT NOT BE MY FAULT? BETTER I SHOULD DIE THAN MAKE OTHERS SUFFER.
HAVE YOU ANY IDEA WHAT IT'S LIKE TO BE A BURDEN ON EVERYONE YOU LOVE?
I'M SORRY, PAULA, BUT I JUST CAN'T COME TO THE WEDDING.
NO, I CAN'T LEAVE DINAH BY HERSELF FOR THAT LONG. I HAVE TO STAY HERE. I'M SORRY.

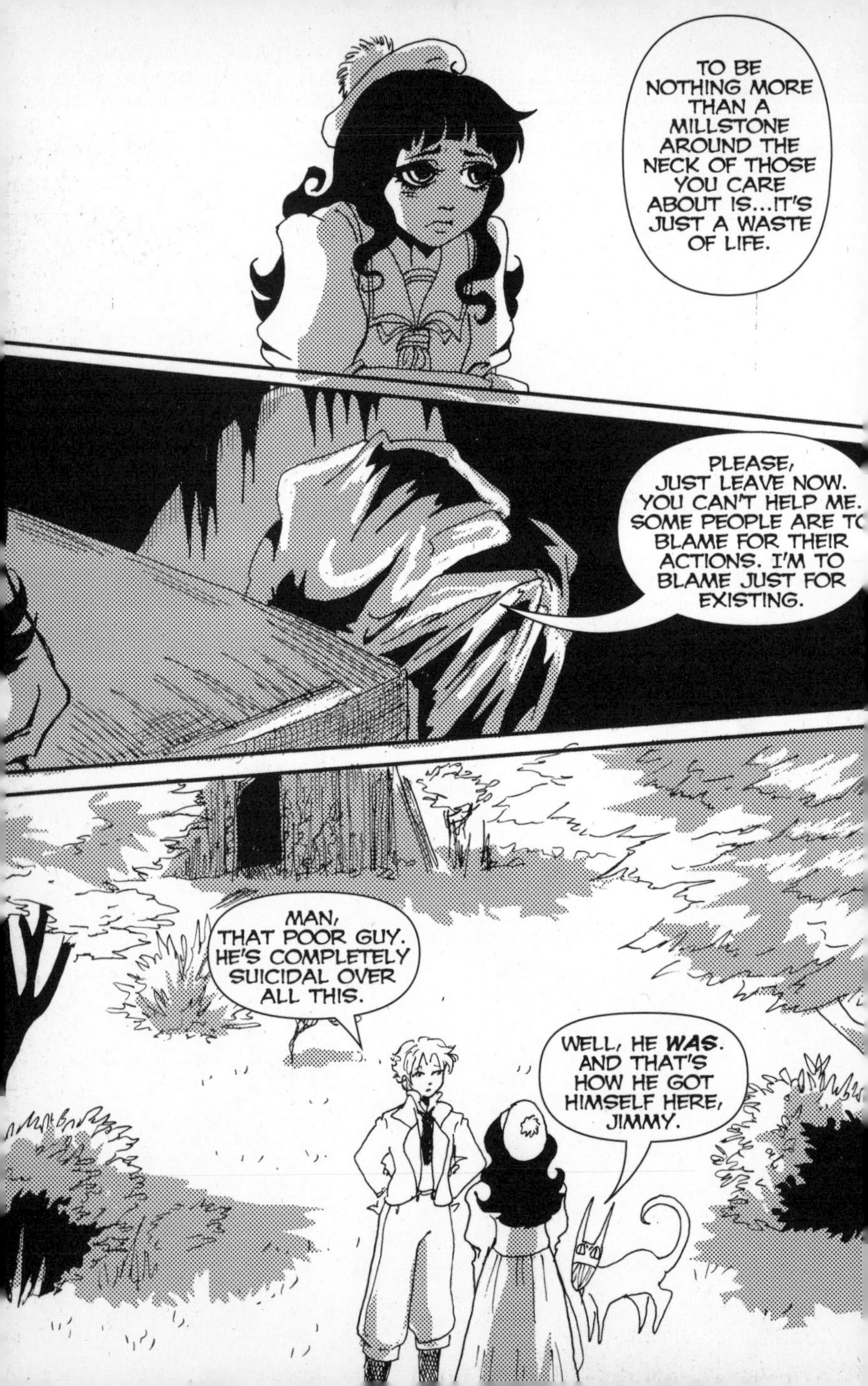
TO BE NOTHING MORE THAN A MILLSTONE AROUND THE NECK OF THOSE YOU CARE ABOUT IS...IT'S JUST A WASTE OF LIFE.
PLEASE, JUST LEAVE NOW. YOU CAN'T HELP ME. SOME PEOPLE ARE TO BLAME FOR THEIR ACTIONS. I'M TO BLAME JUST FOR EXISTING.
MAN, THAT POOR GUY. HE'S COMPLETELY SUICIDAL OVER ALL THIS.
WELL, HE *WAS*. AND THAT'S HOW HE GOT HIMSELF HERE, JIMMY.

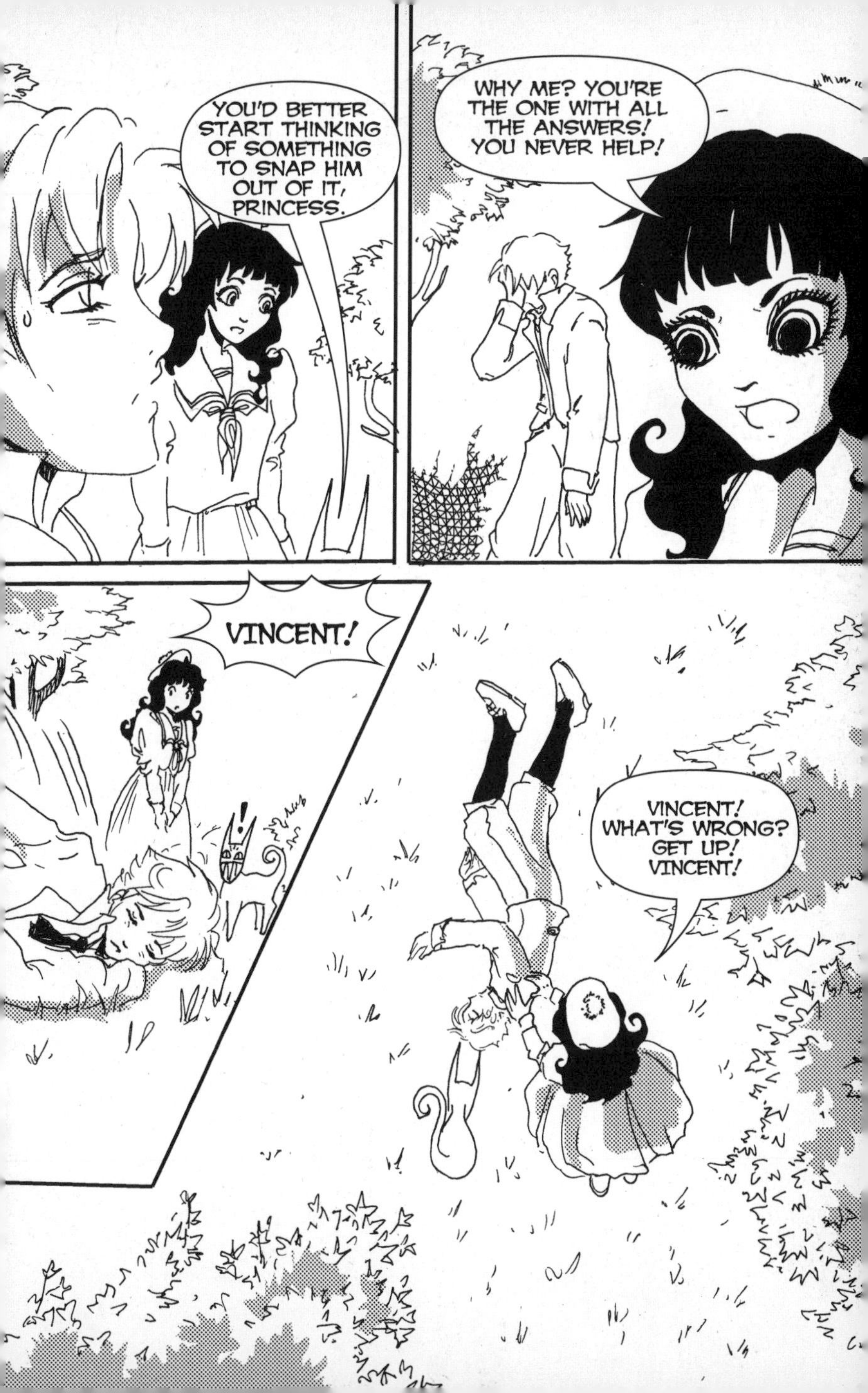
YOU'D BETTER START THINKING OF SOMETHING TO SNAP HIM OUT OF IT, PRINCESS.
WHY ME? YOU'RE THE ONE WITH ALL THE ANSWERS! YOU NEVER HELP!
VINCENT!
VINCENT! WHAT'S WRONG? GET UP! VINCENT!

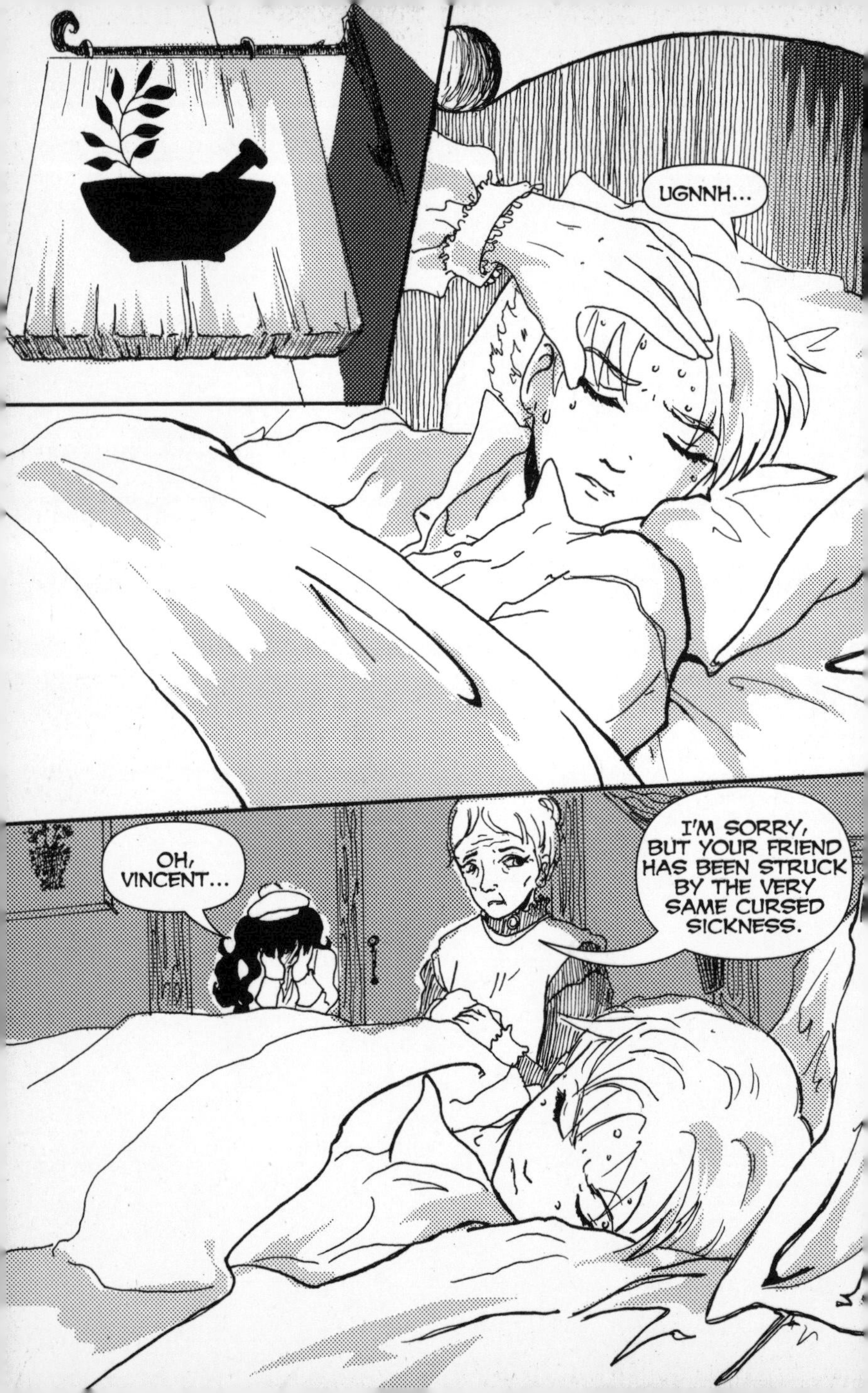
UGNNH...
OH, VINCENT...
I'M SORRY, BUT YOUR FRIEND HAS BEEN STRUCK BY THE VERY SAME CURSED SICKNESS.

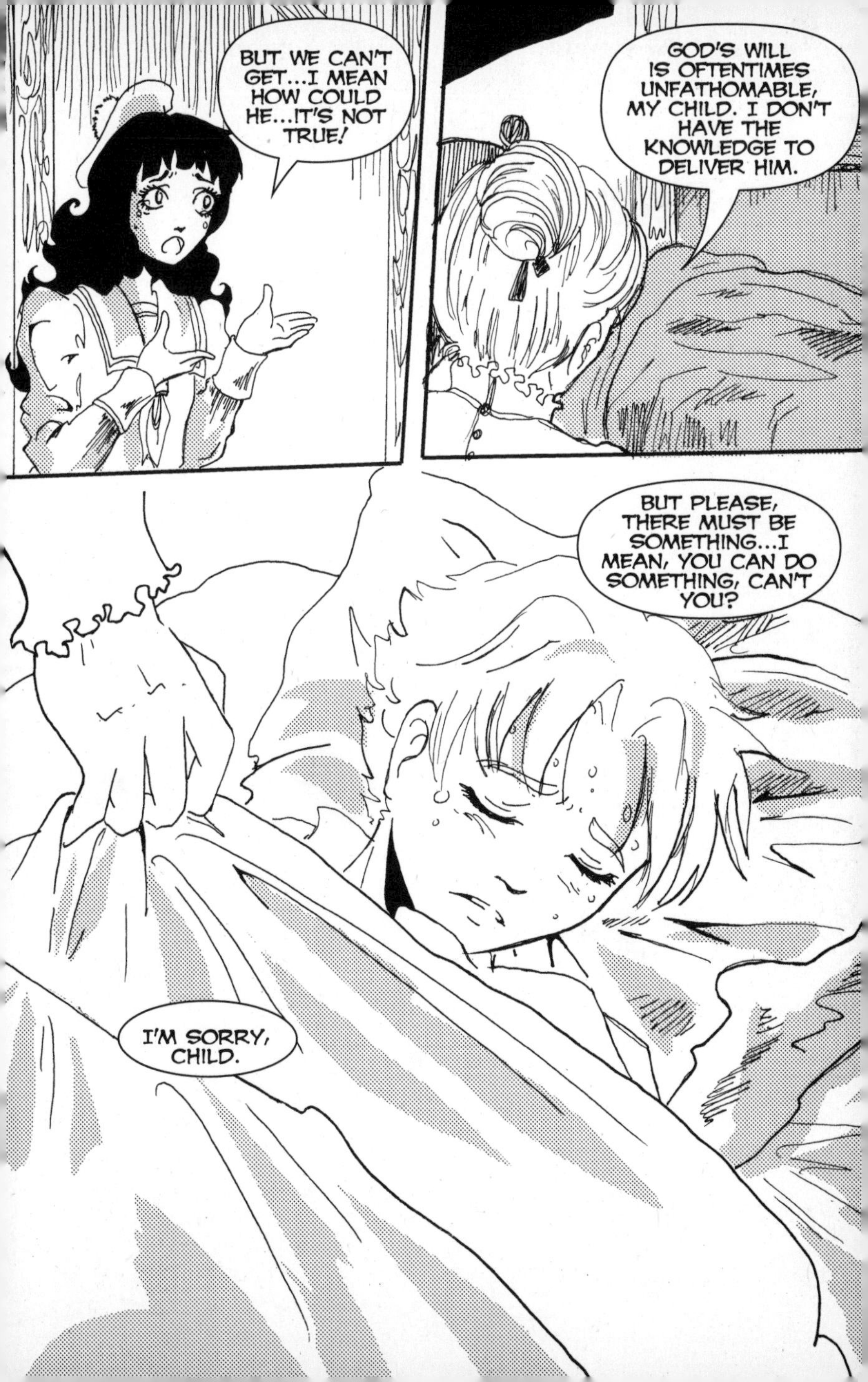
BUT WE CAN'T GET...I MEAN HOW COULD HE...IT'S NOT TRUE!
GOD'S WILL IS OFTENTIMES UNFATHOMABLE, MY CHILD. I DON'T HAVE THE KNOWLEDGE TO DELIVER HIM.
BUT PLEASE, THERE MUST BE SOMETHING...I MEAN, YOU CAN DO SOMETHING, CAN'T YOU?
I'M SORRY, CHILD.

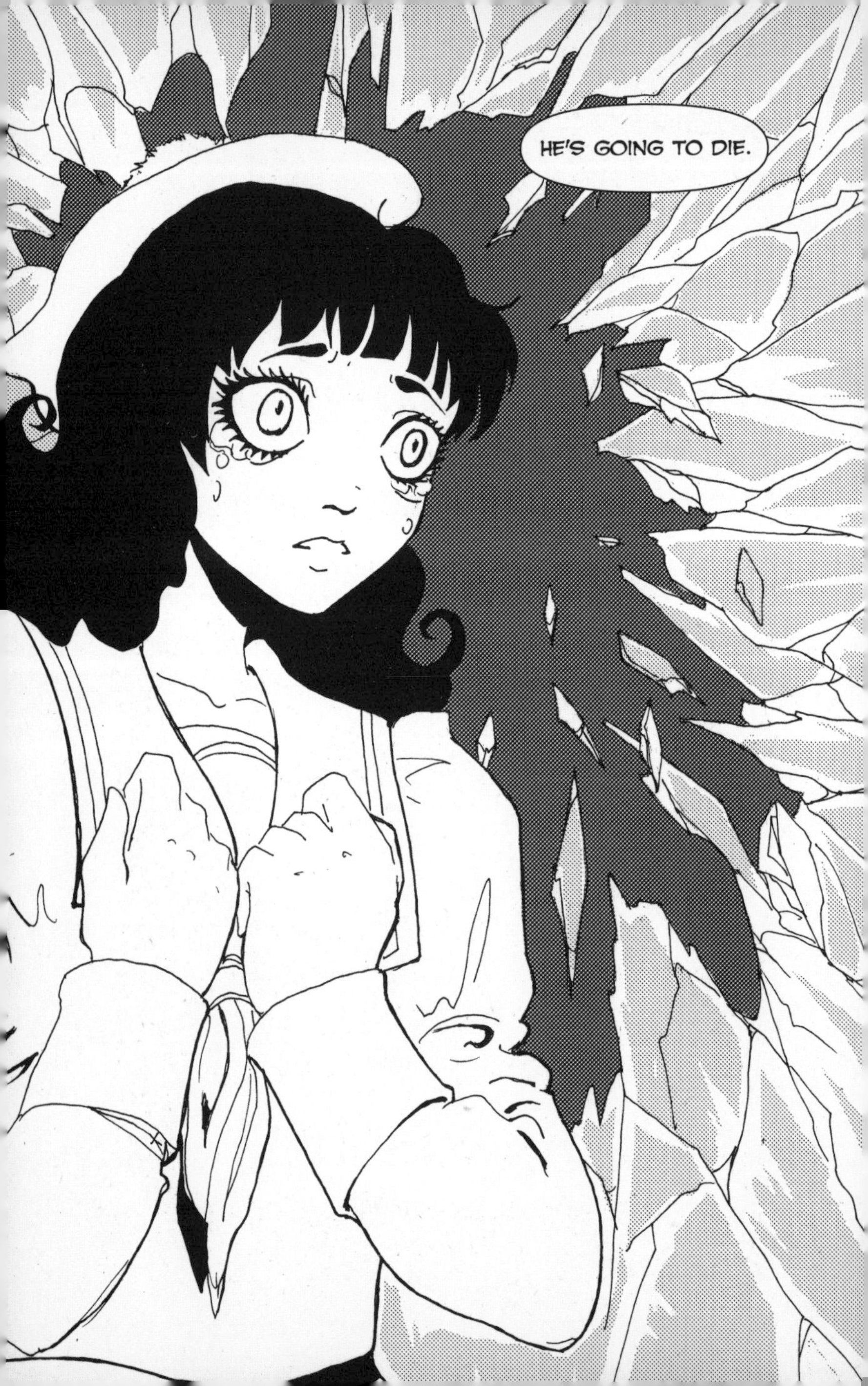
HE'S GOING TO DIE.

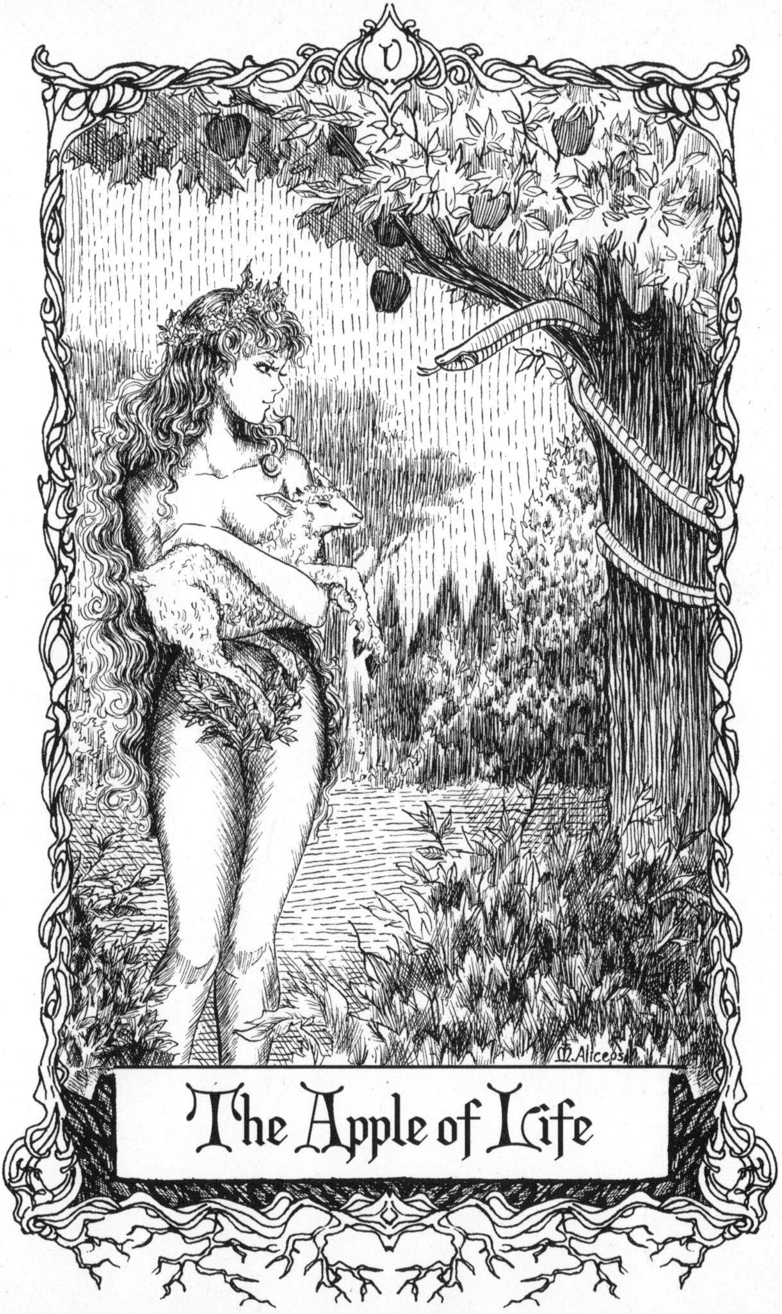
V
The Apple of Life

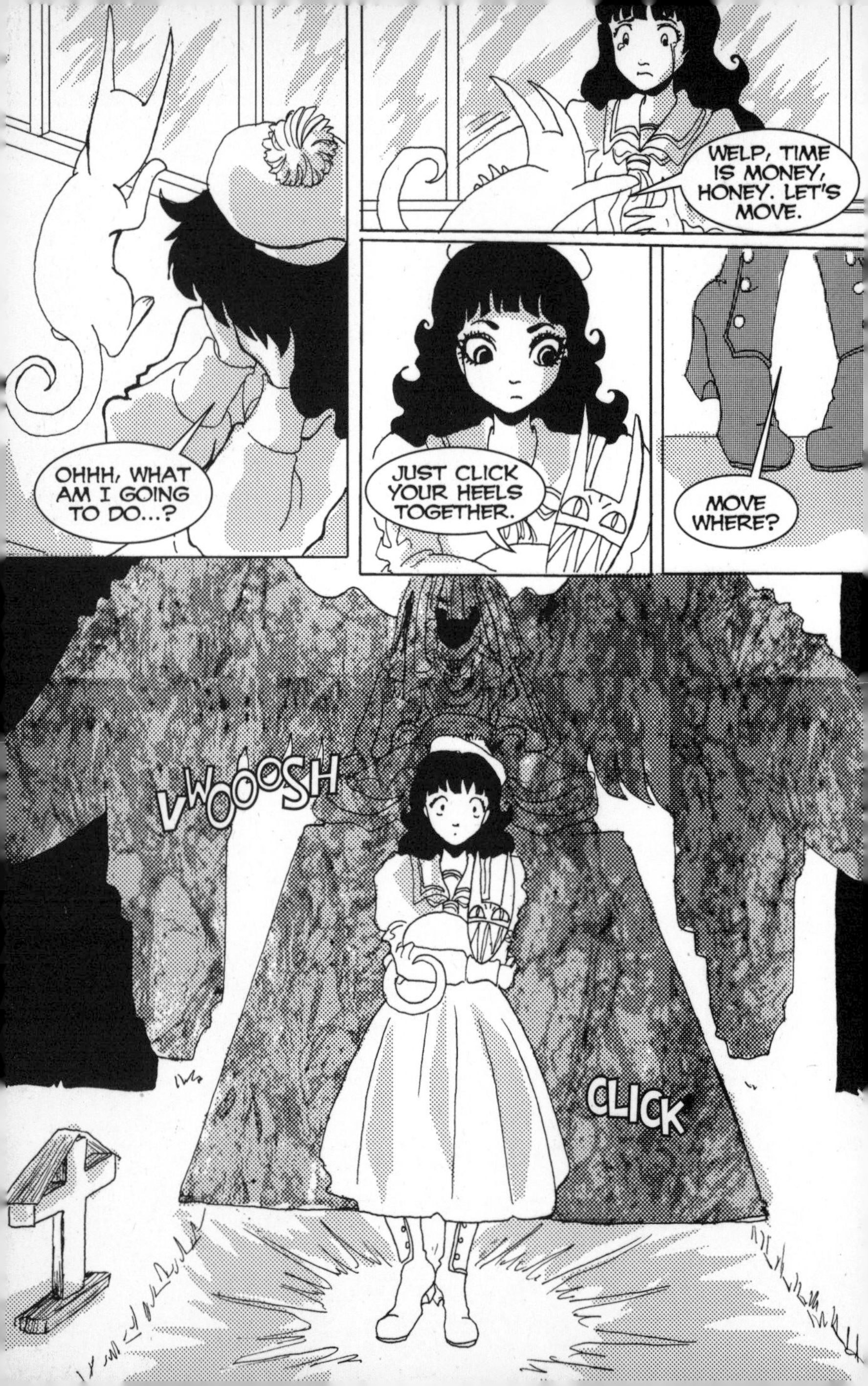
OHHH, WHAT AM I GOING TO DO...?
WELP, TIME IS MONEY, HONEY. LET'S MOVE.
JUST CLICK YOUR HEELS TOGETHER.
MOVE WHERE?
VWOOOSH
CLICK

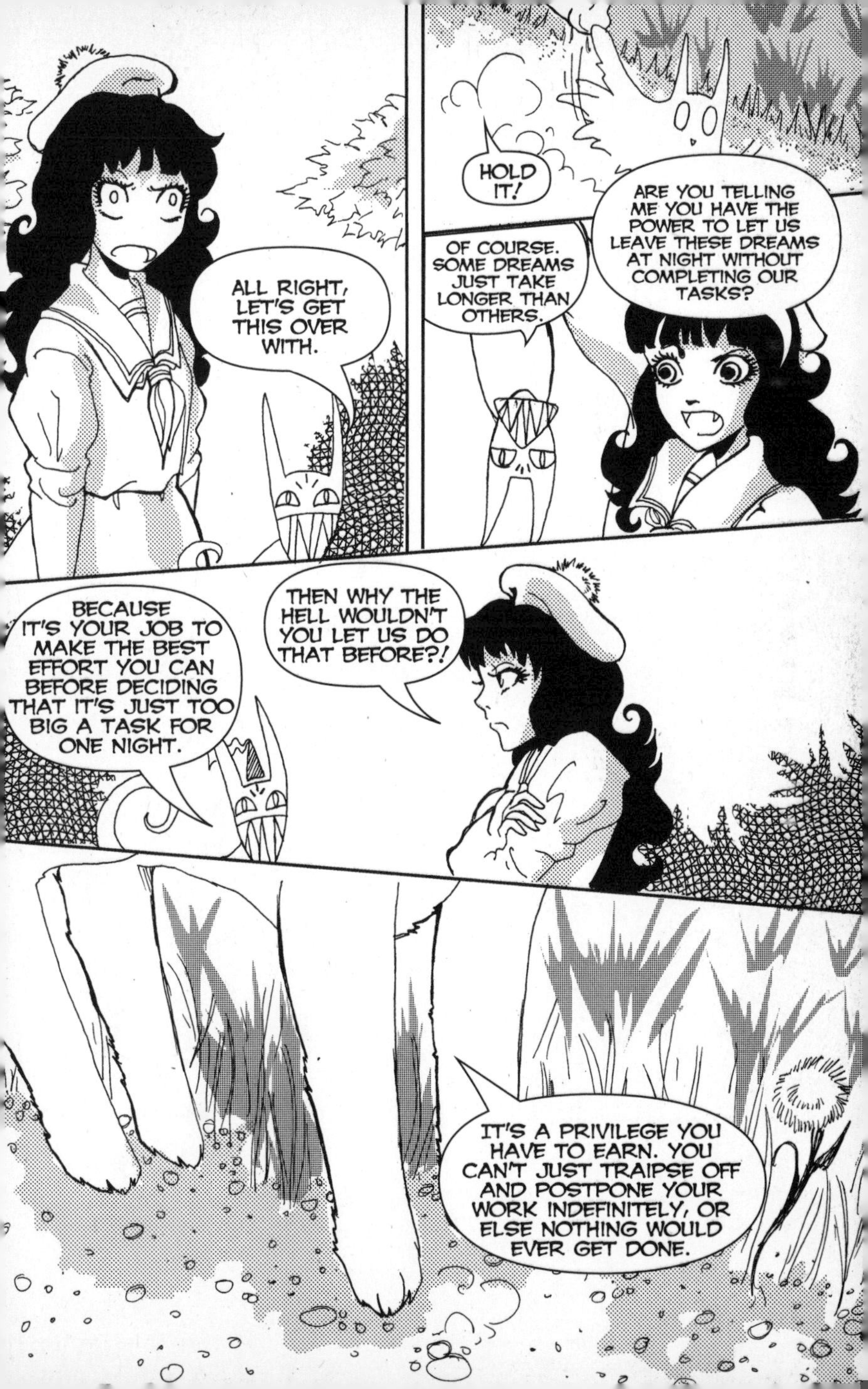
ALL RIGHT, LET'S GET THIS OVER WITH.
HOLD IT!
ARE YOU TELLING ME YOU HAVE THE POWER TO LET US LEAVE THESE DREAMS AT NIGHT WITHOUT COMPLETING OUR TASKS?
OF COURSE. SOME DREAMS JUST TAKE LONGER THAN OTHERS.
THEN WHY THE HELL WOULDN'T YOU LET US DO THAT BEFORE?!
BECAUSE IT'S YOUR JOB TO MAKE THE BEST EFFORT YOU CAN BEFORE DECIDING THAT IT'S JUST TOO BIG A TASK FOR ONE NIGHT.
IT'S A PRIVILEGE YOU HAVE TO EARN. YOU CAN'T JUST TRAIPSE OFF AND POSTPONE YOUR WORK INDEFINITELY, OR ELSE NOTHING WOULD EVER GET DONE.

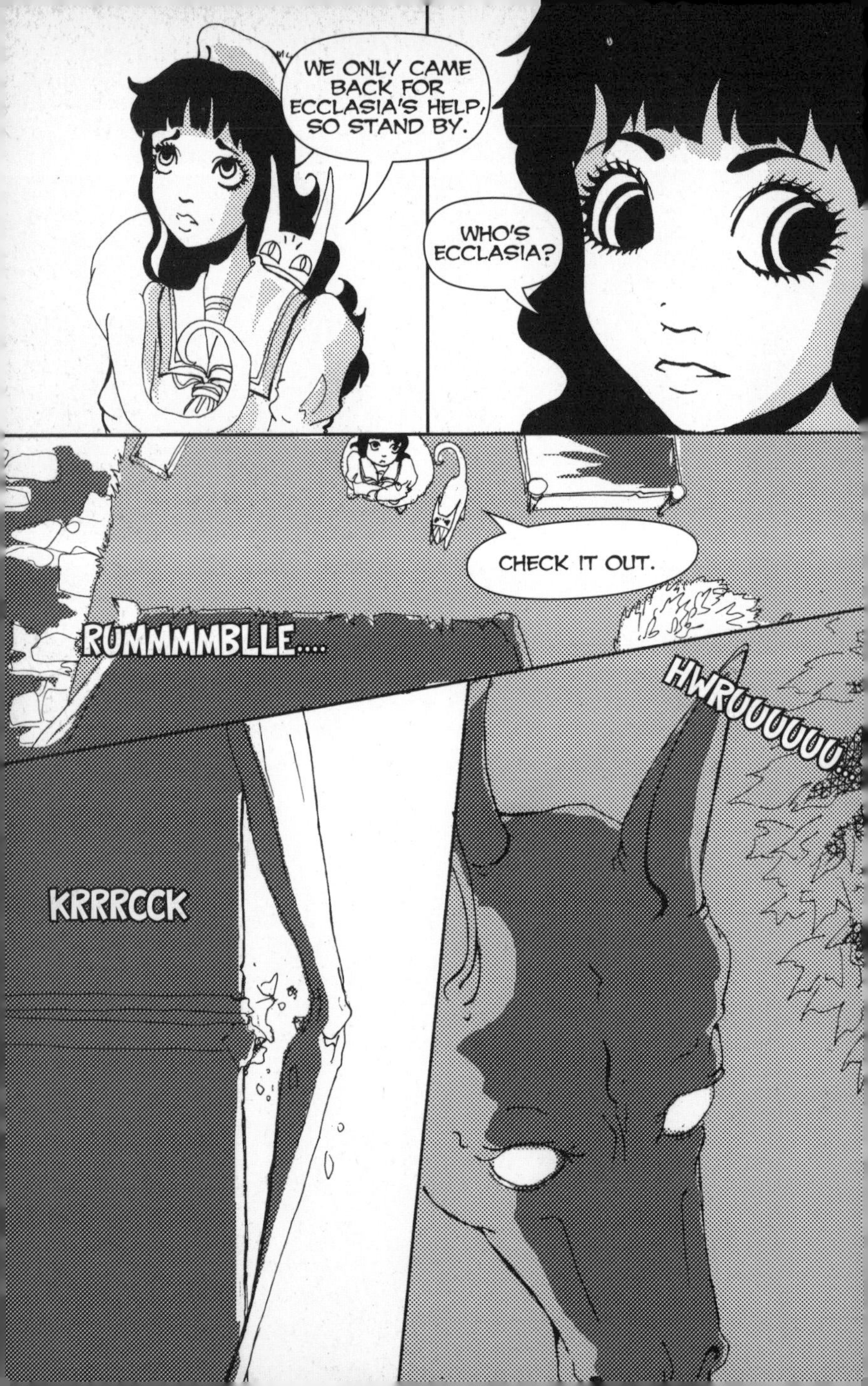
WE ONLY CAME BACK FOR ECCLASIA'S HELP, SO STAND BY.
WHO'S ECCLASIA?
CHECK IT OUT.
RUMMMMBLLE....
HWRUUUUUU...
KRRRCCK

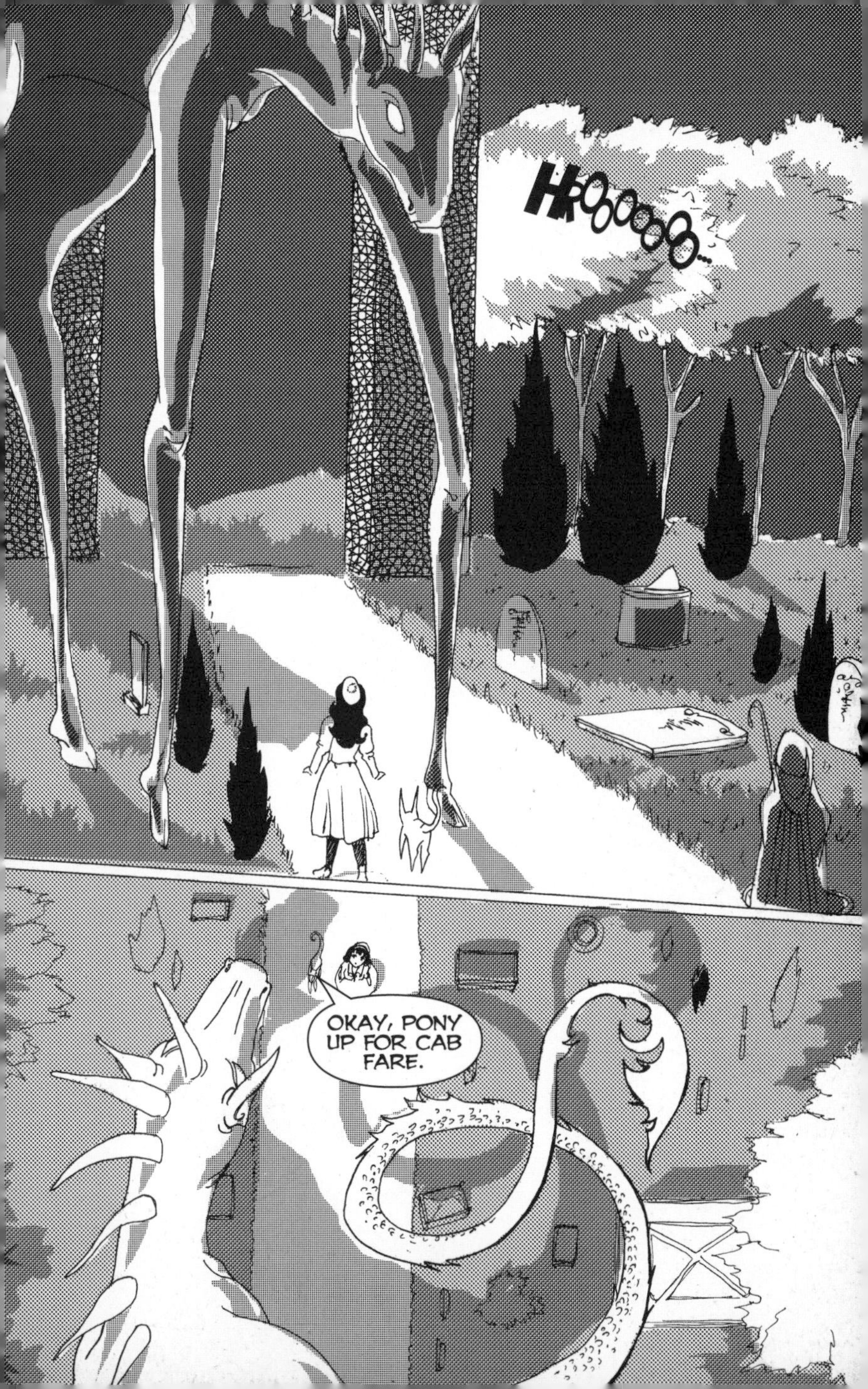
HROOOOOO...
OKAY, PONY UP FOR CAB FARE.

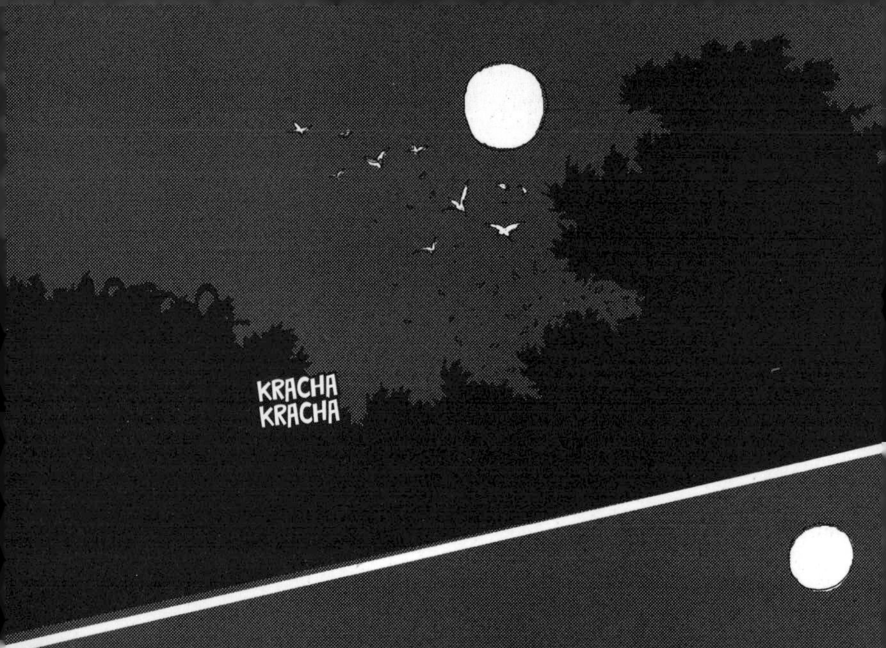
KRACHA
KRACHA
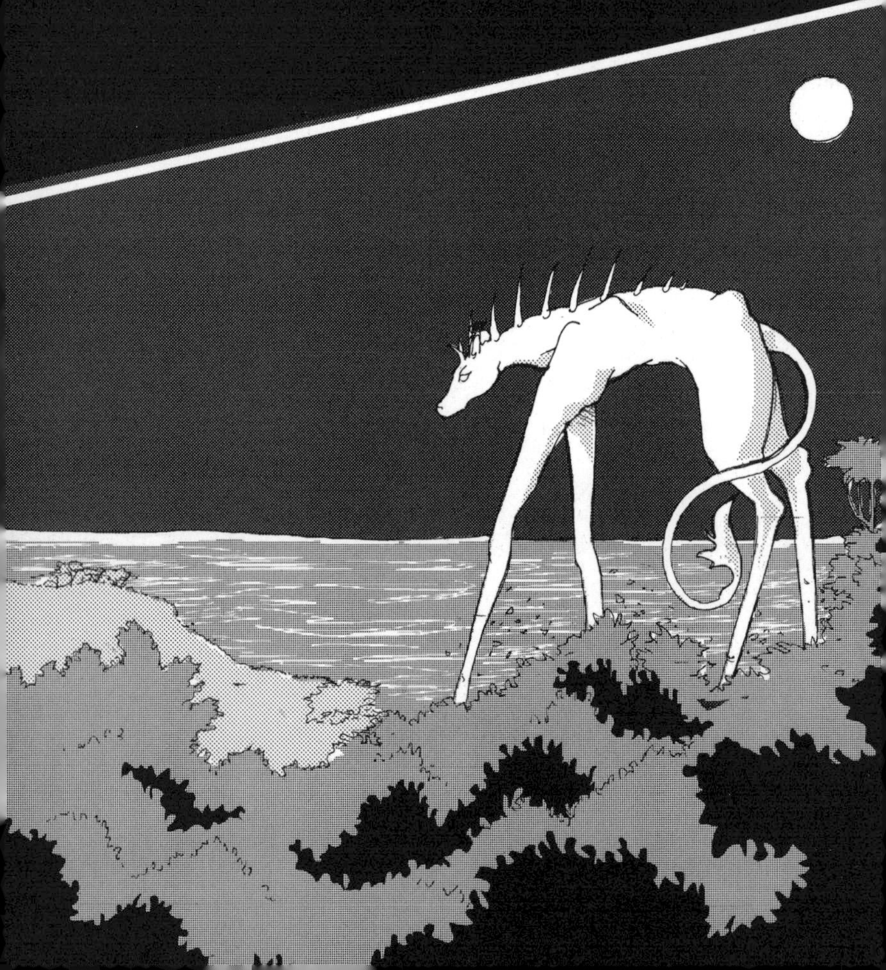

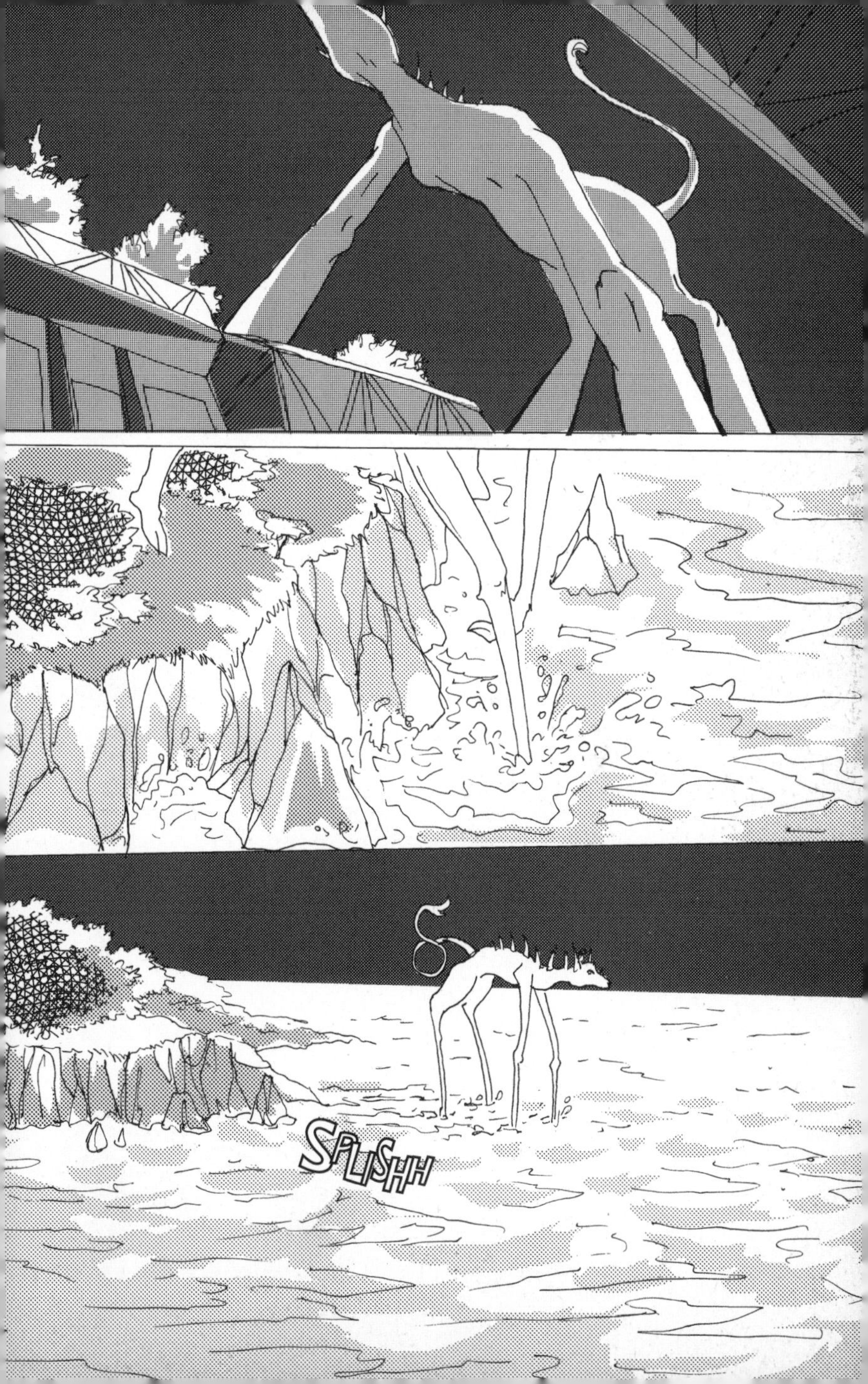
SPLISHH

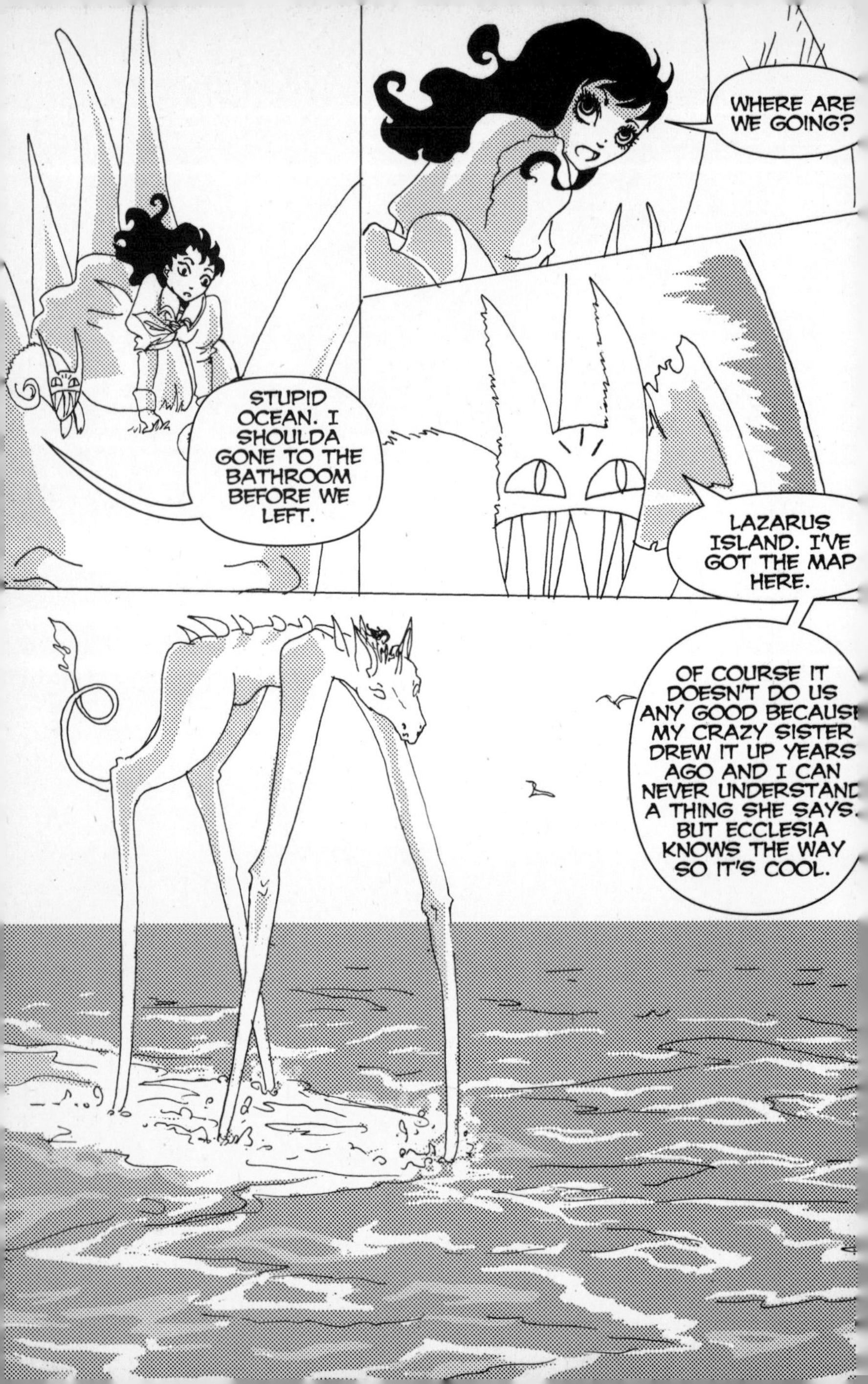
STUPID OCEAN. I SHOULDA GONE TO THE BATHROOM BEFORE WE LEFT.
WHERE ARE WE GOING?
LAZARUS ISLAND. I'VE GOT THE MAP HERE.
OF COURSE IT DOESN'T DO US ANY GOOD BECAUSE MY CRAZY SISTER DREW IT UP YEARS AGO AND I CAN NEVER UNDERSTAND A THING SHE SAYS. BUT ECCLESIA KNOWS THE WAY SO IT'S COOL.

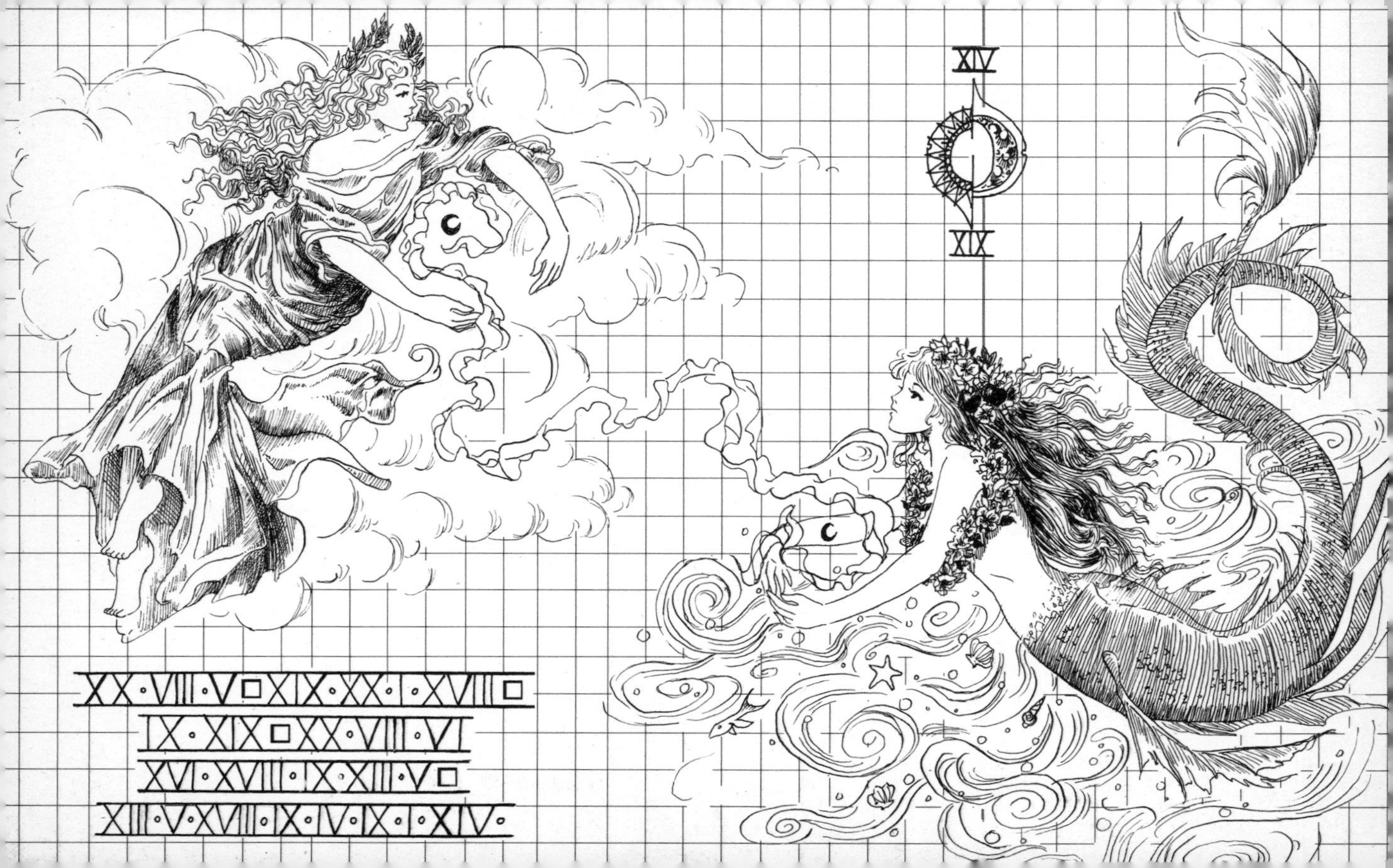
XIV
XIX
XX·VIII·V□XIX·XX·I·XVIII□
IX·XIX□XX·VIII·VI
XVI·XVIII·IX·XIII·V□
XIII·V·XVIII·IX·IV·IX·I·XIV·

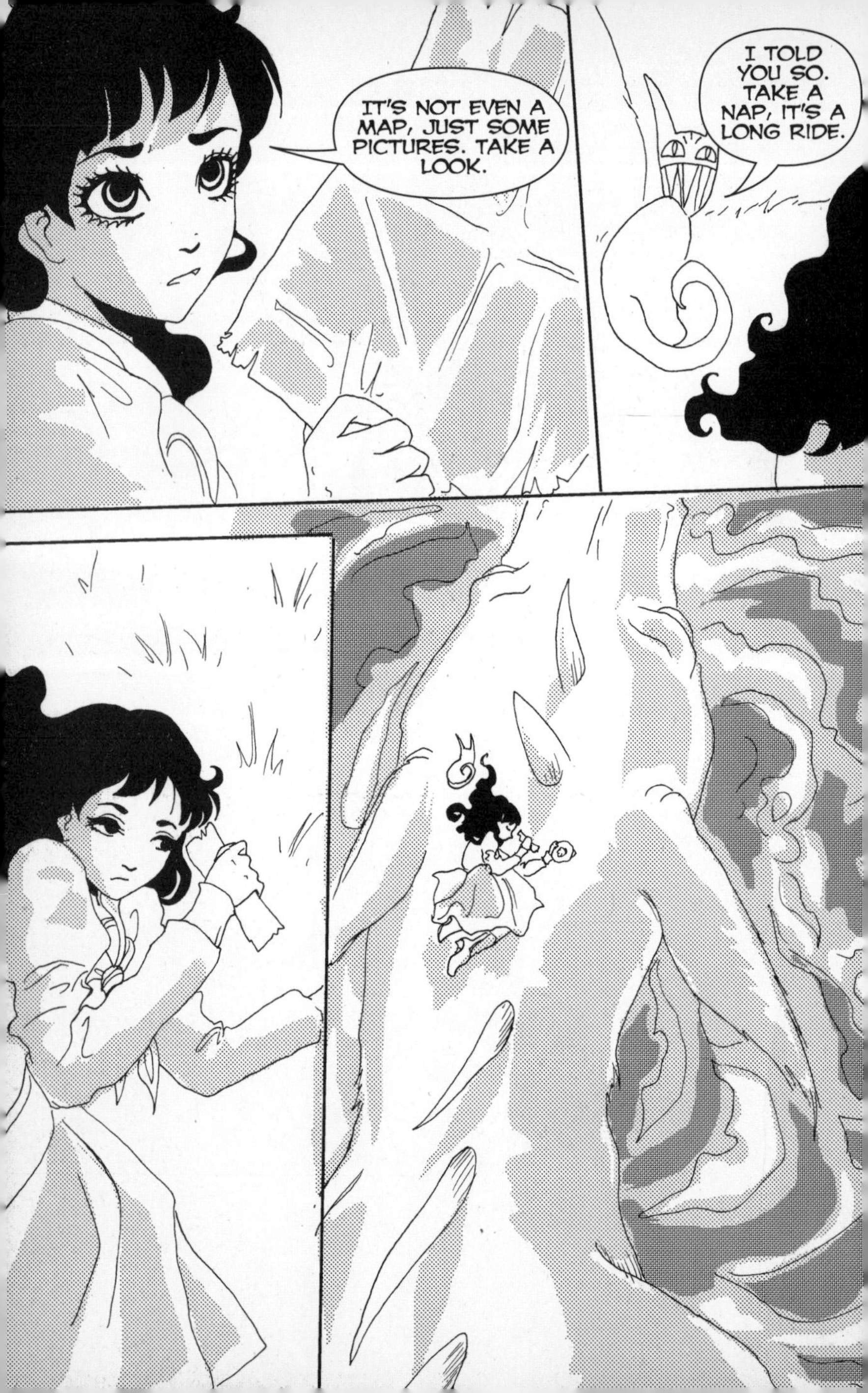
IT'S NOT EVEN A MAP, JUST SOME PICTURES. TAKE A LOOK.
I TOLD YOU SO. TAKE A NAP, IT'S A LONG RIDE.

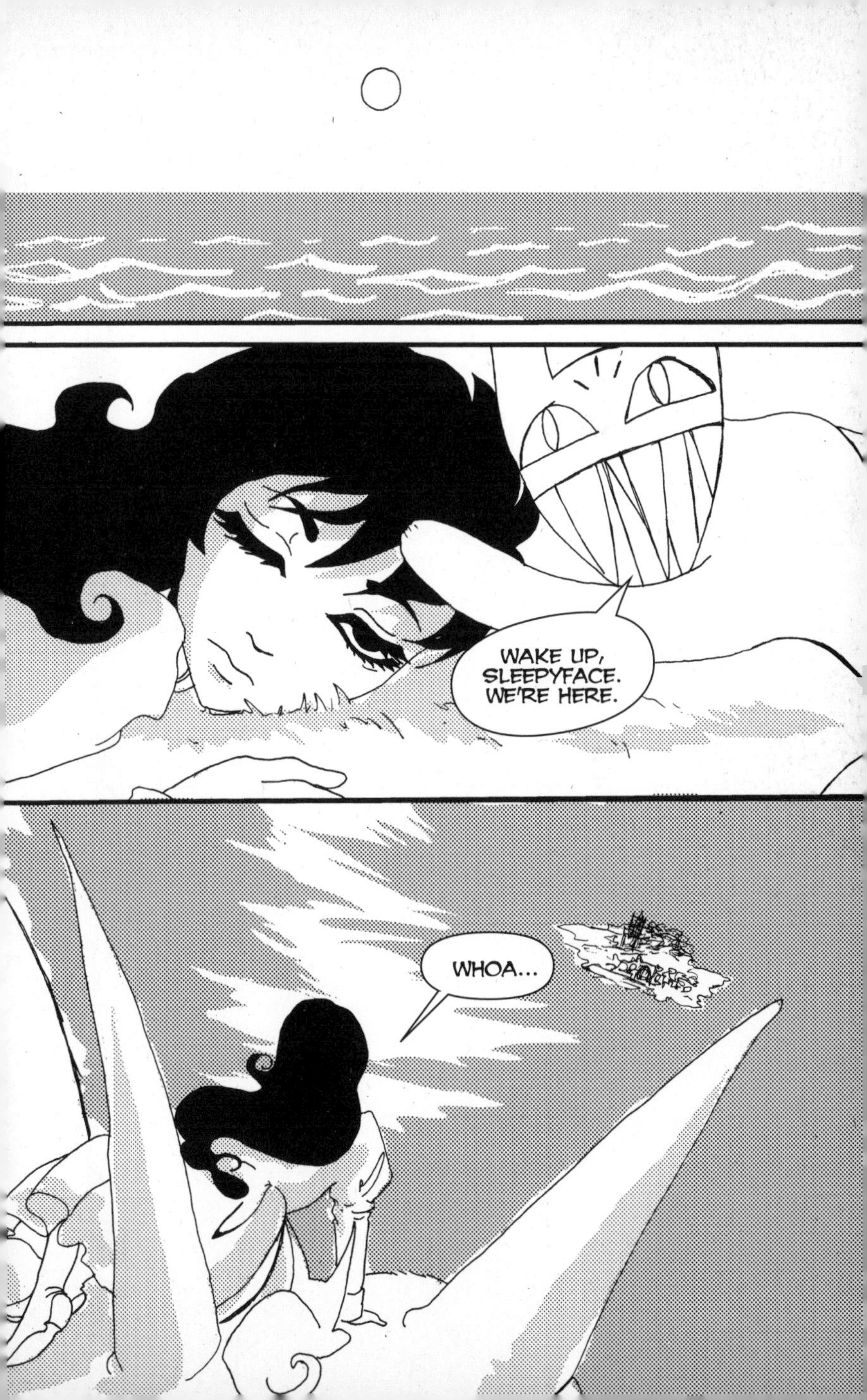
WAKE UP, SLEEPYFACE. WE'RE HERE.
WHOA...

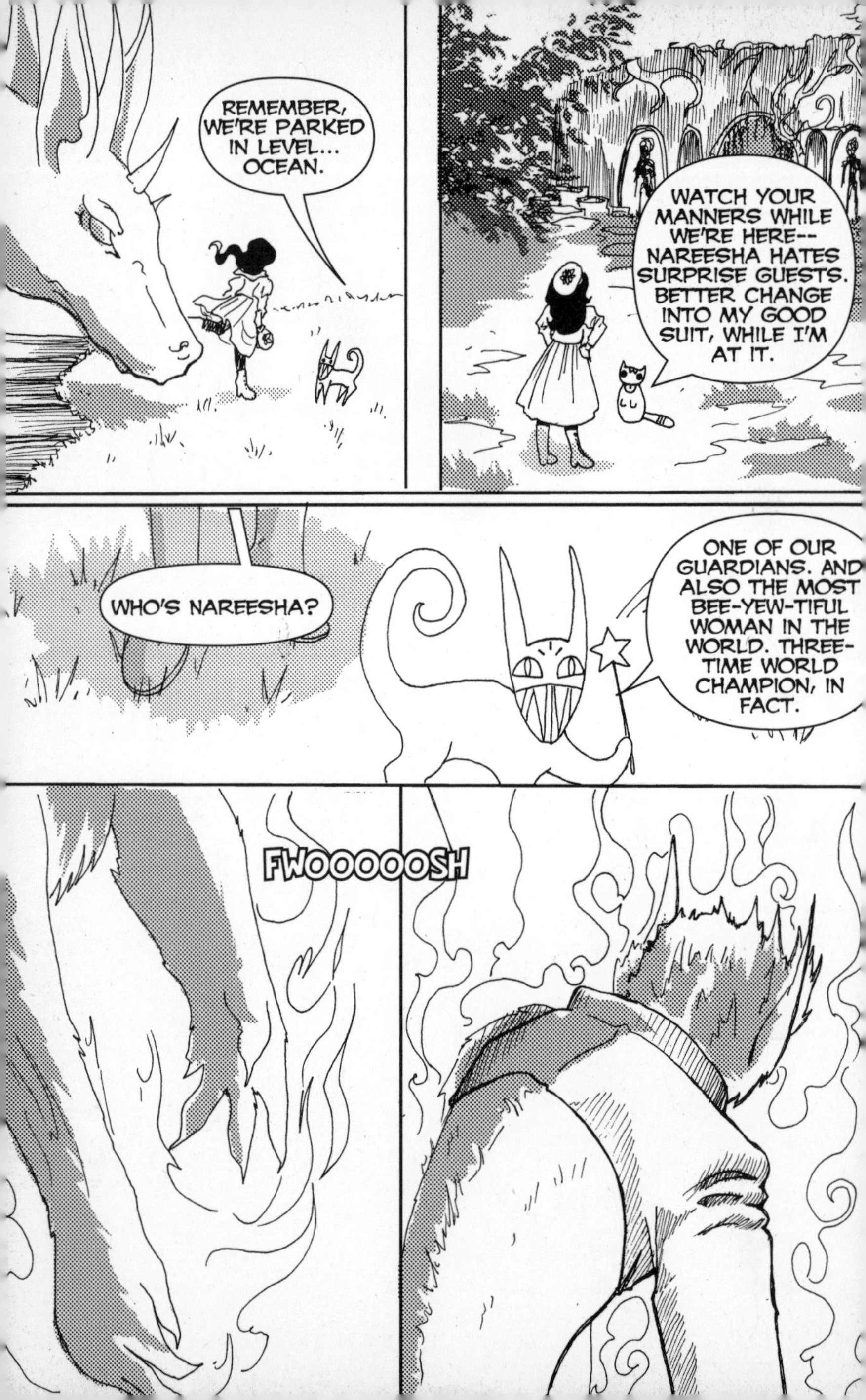
REMEMBER, WE'RE PARKED IN LEVEL... OCEAN.
WATCH YOUR MANNERS WHILE WE'RE HERE-- NAREESHA HATES SURPRISE GUESTS. BETTER CHANGE INTO MY GOOD SUIT, WHILE I'M AT IT.
WHO'S NAREESHA?
ONE OF OUR GUARDIANS. AND ALSO THE MOST BEE-YEW-TIFUL WOMAN IN THE WORLD. THREE-TIME WORLD CHAMPION, IN FACT.
FWOOOOOOSH

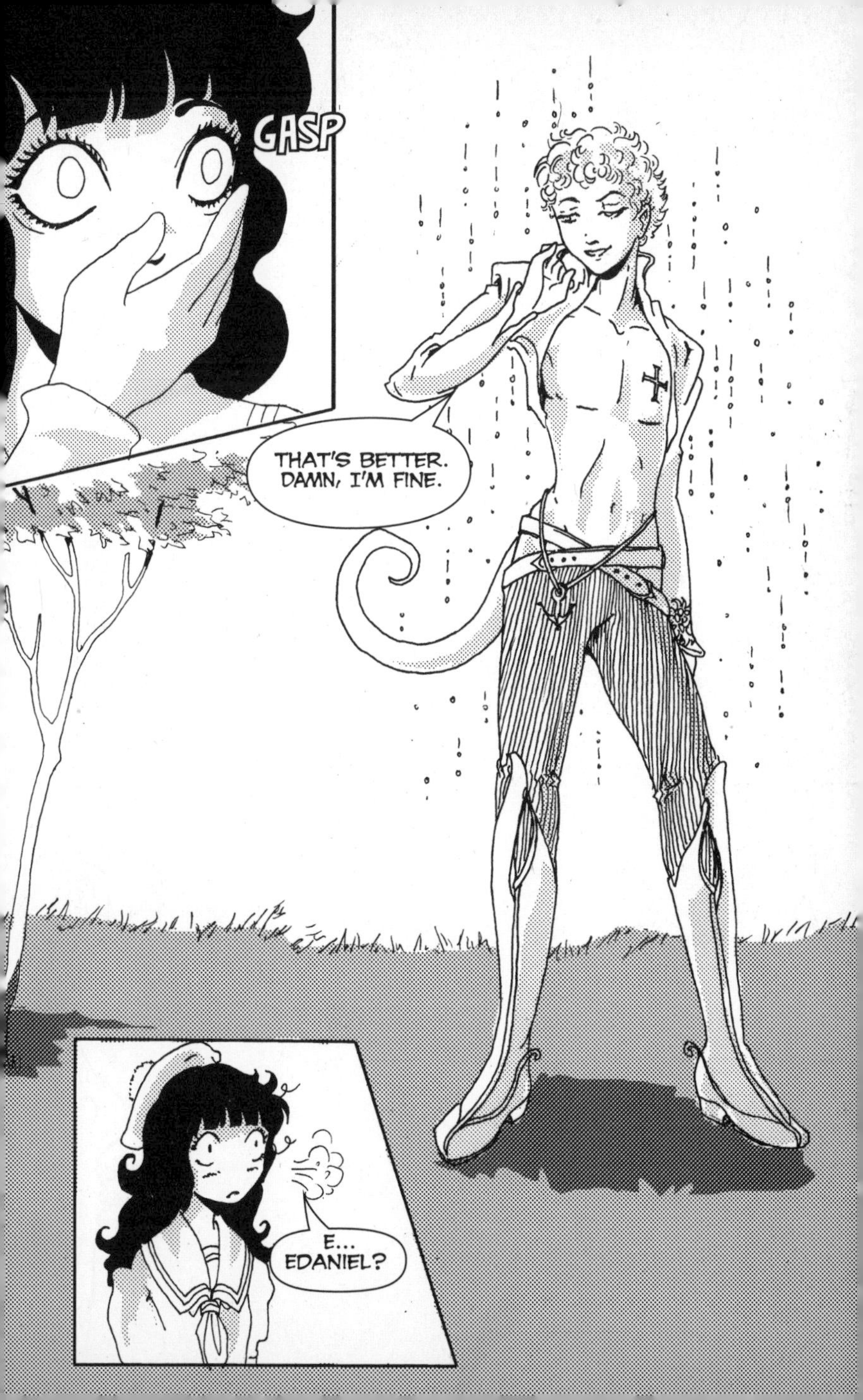
GASP
THAT'S BETTER. DAMN, I'M FINE.
E... EDANIEL?

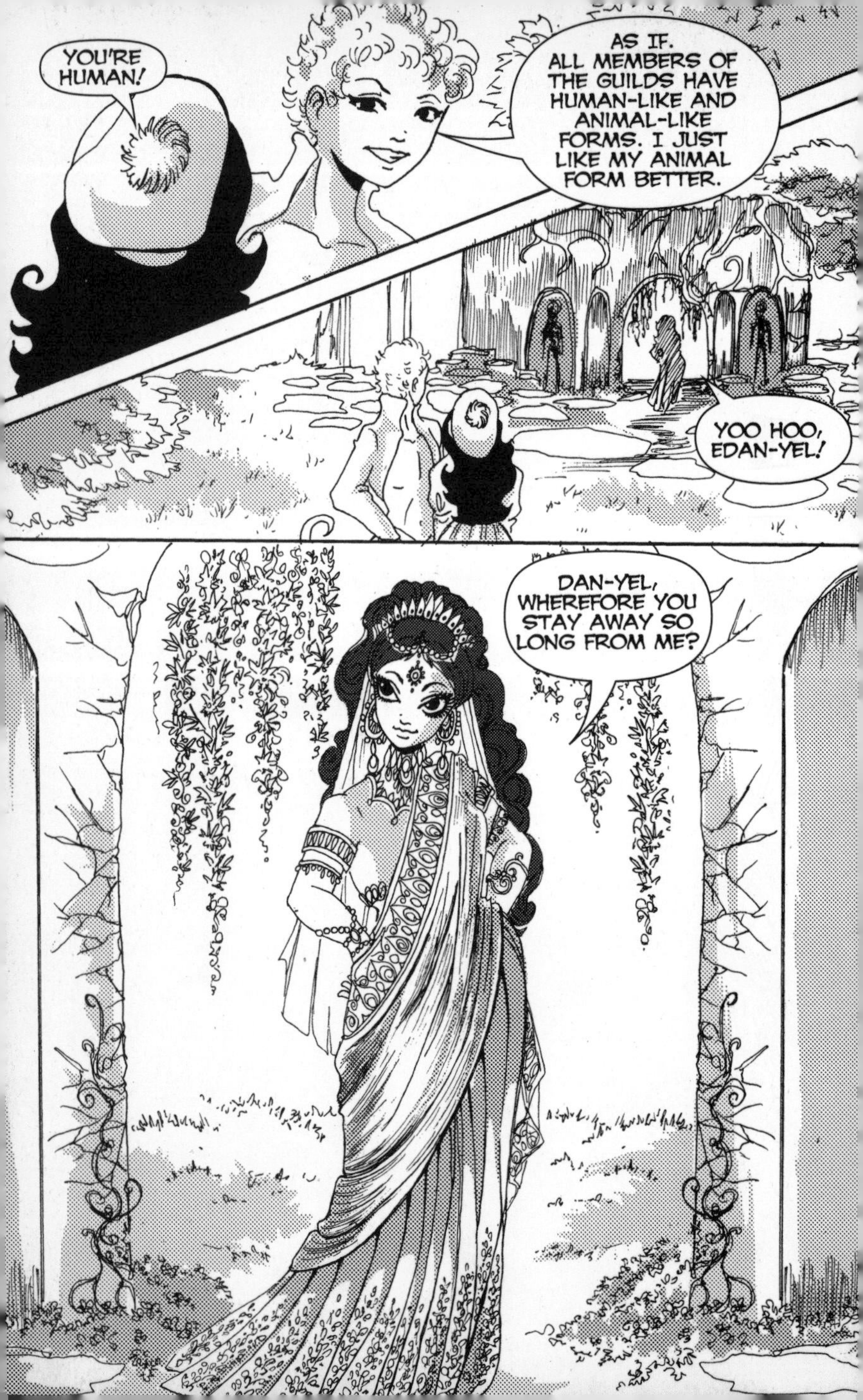
YOU'RE HUMAN!
AS IF. ALL MEMBERS OF THE GUILDS HAVE HUMAN-LIKE AND ANIMAL-LIKE FORMS. I JUST LIKE MY ANIMAL FORM BETTER.
YOO HOO, EDAN-YEL!
DAN-YEL, WHEREFORE YOU STAY AWAY SO LONG FROM ME?

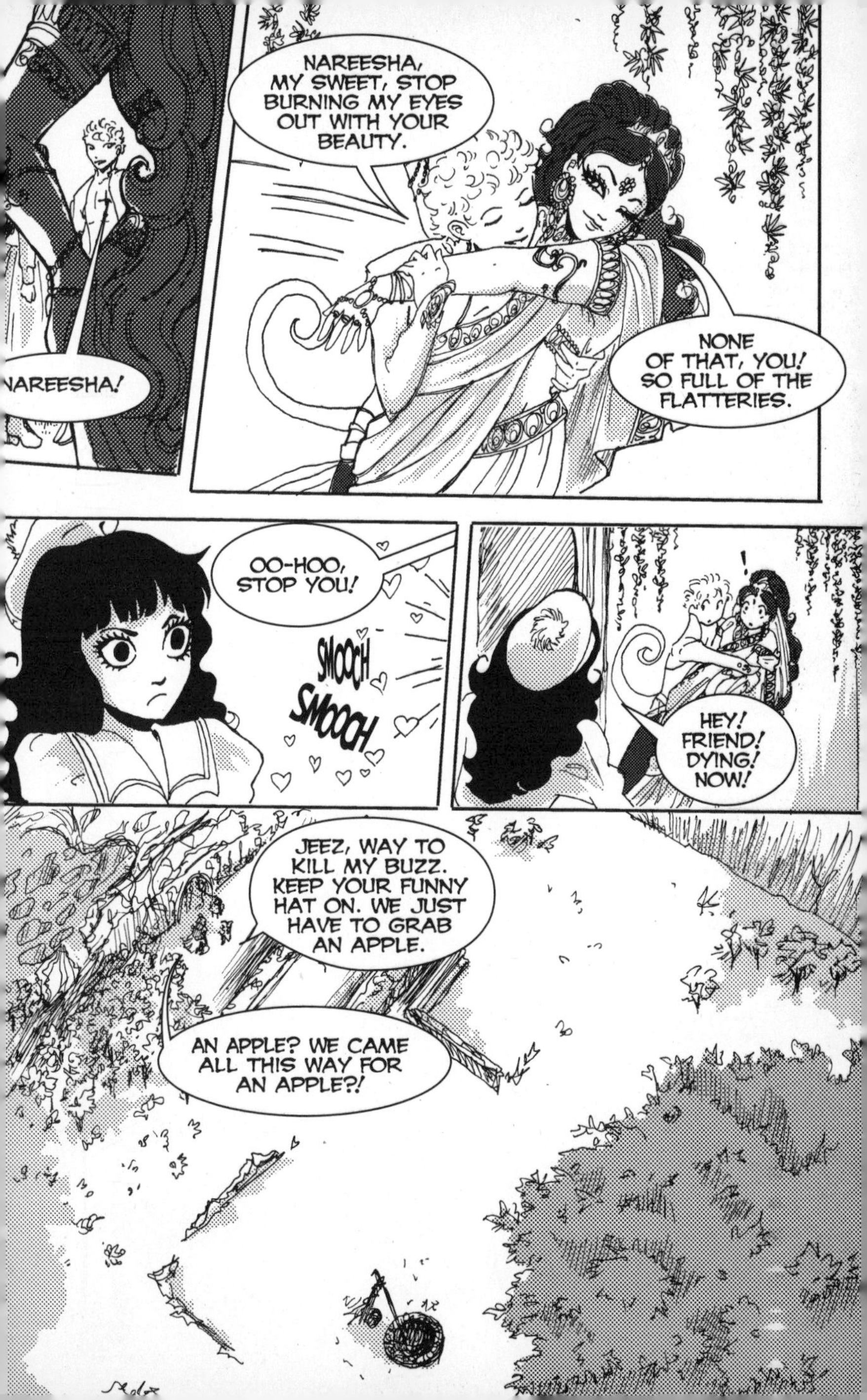
NAREESHA!
NAREESHA, MY SWEET, STOP BURNING MY EYES OUT WITH YOUR BEAUTY.
NONE OF THAT, YOU! SO FULL OF THE FLATTERIES.
OO-HOO, STOP YOU!
SMOOCH
SMOOCH
!
HEY! FRIEND! DYING! NOW!
JEEZ, WAY TO KILL MY BUZZ. KEEP YOUR FUNNY HAT ON. WE JUST HAVE TO GRAB AN APPLE.
AN APPLE? WE CAME ALL THIS WAY FOR AN APPLE?!

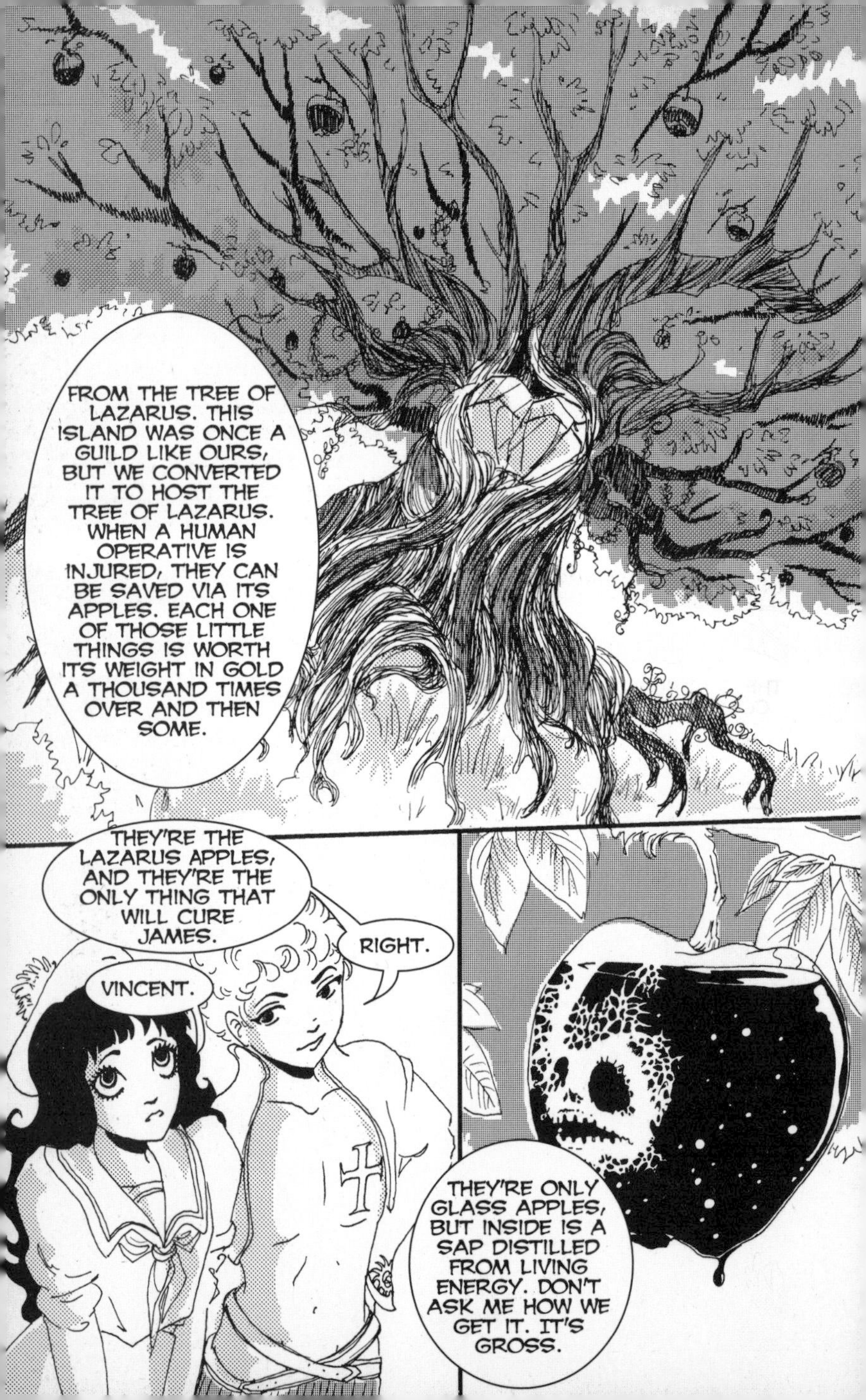
FROM THE TREE OF LAZARUS. THIS ISLAND WAS ONCE A GUILD LIKE OURS, BUT WE CONVERTED IT TO HOST THE TREE OF LAZARUS. WHEN A HUMAN OPERATIVE IS INJURED, THEY CAN BE SAVED VIA ITS APPLES. EACH ONE OF THOSE LITTLE THINGS IS WORTH ITS WEIGHT IN GOLD A THOUSAND TIMES OVER AND THEN SOME.
THEY'RE THE LAZARUS APPLES, AND THEY'RE THE ONLY THING THAT WILL CURE JAMES.
RIGHT.
VINCENT.
THEY'RE ONLY GLASS APPLES, BUT INSIDE IS A SAP DISTILLED FROM LIVING ENERGY. DON'T ASK ME HOW WE GET IT. IT'S GROSS.

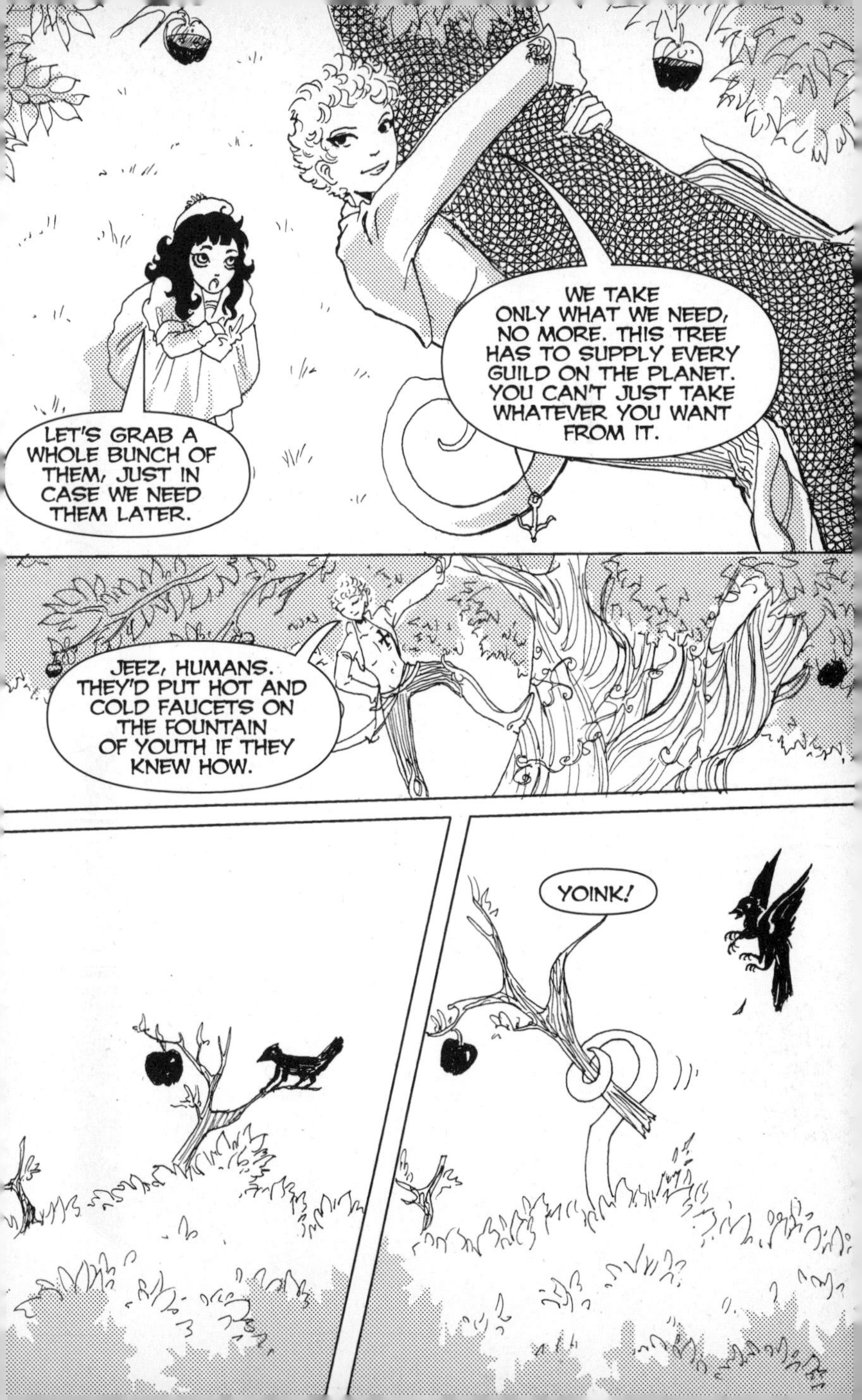
LET'S GRAB A WHOLE BUNCH OF THEM, JUST IN CASE WE NEED THEM LATER.
WE TAKE ONLY WHAT WE NEED, NO MORE. THIS TREE HAS TO SUPPLY EVERY GUILD ON THE PLANET. YOU CAN'T JUST TAKE WHATEVER YOU WANT FROM IT.
JEEZ, HUMANS. THEY'D PUT HOT AND COLD FAUCETS ON THE FOUNTAIN OF YOUTH IF THEY KNEW HOW.
YOINK!

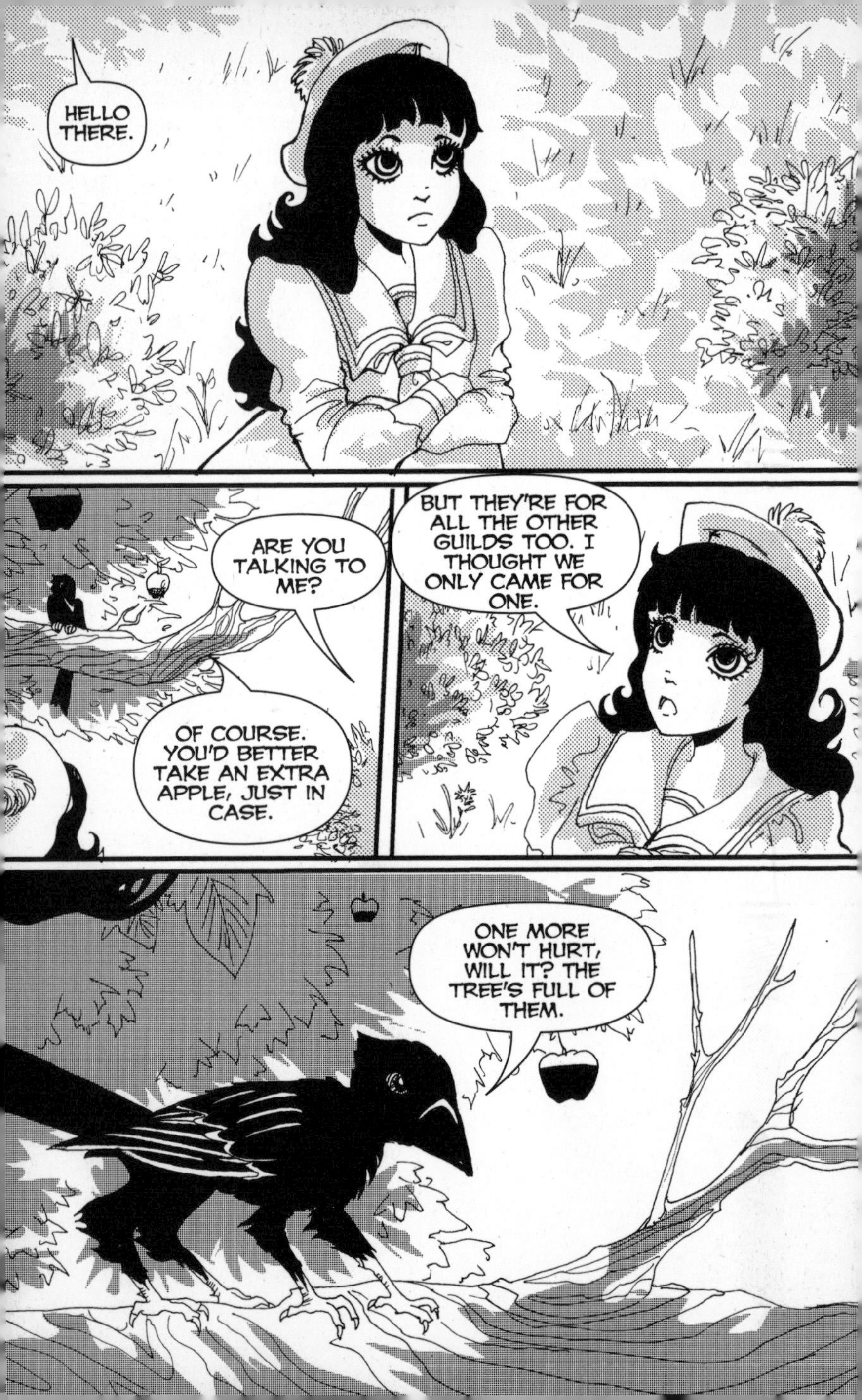
HELLO THERE.
ARE YOU TALKING TO ME?
OF COURSE. YOU'D BETTER TAKE AN EXTRA APPLE, JUST IN CASE.
BUT THEY'RE FOR ALL THE OTHER GUILDS TOO. I THOUGHT WE ONLY CAME FOR ONE.
ONE MORE WON'T HURT, WILL IT? THE TREE'S FULL OF THEM.

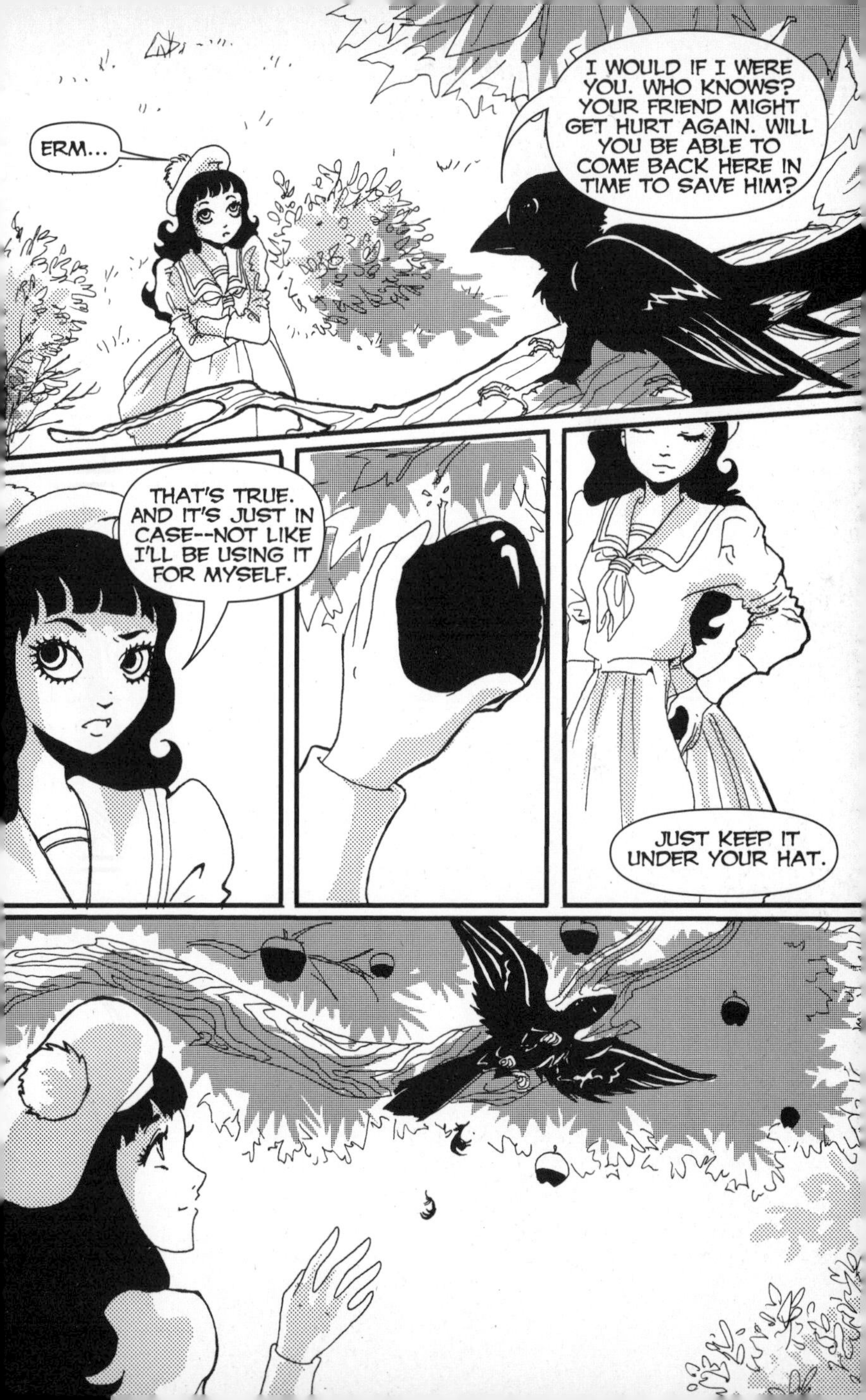
ERM...
I WOULD IF I WERE YOU. WHO KNOWS? YOUR FRIEND MIGHT GET HURT AGAIN. WILL YOU BE ABLE TO COME BACK HERE IN TIME TO SAVE HIM?
THAT'S TRUE. AND IT'S JUST IN CASE--NOT LIKE I'LL BE USING IT FOR MYSELF.
JUST KEEP IT UNDER YOUR HAT.

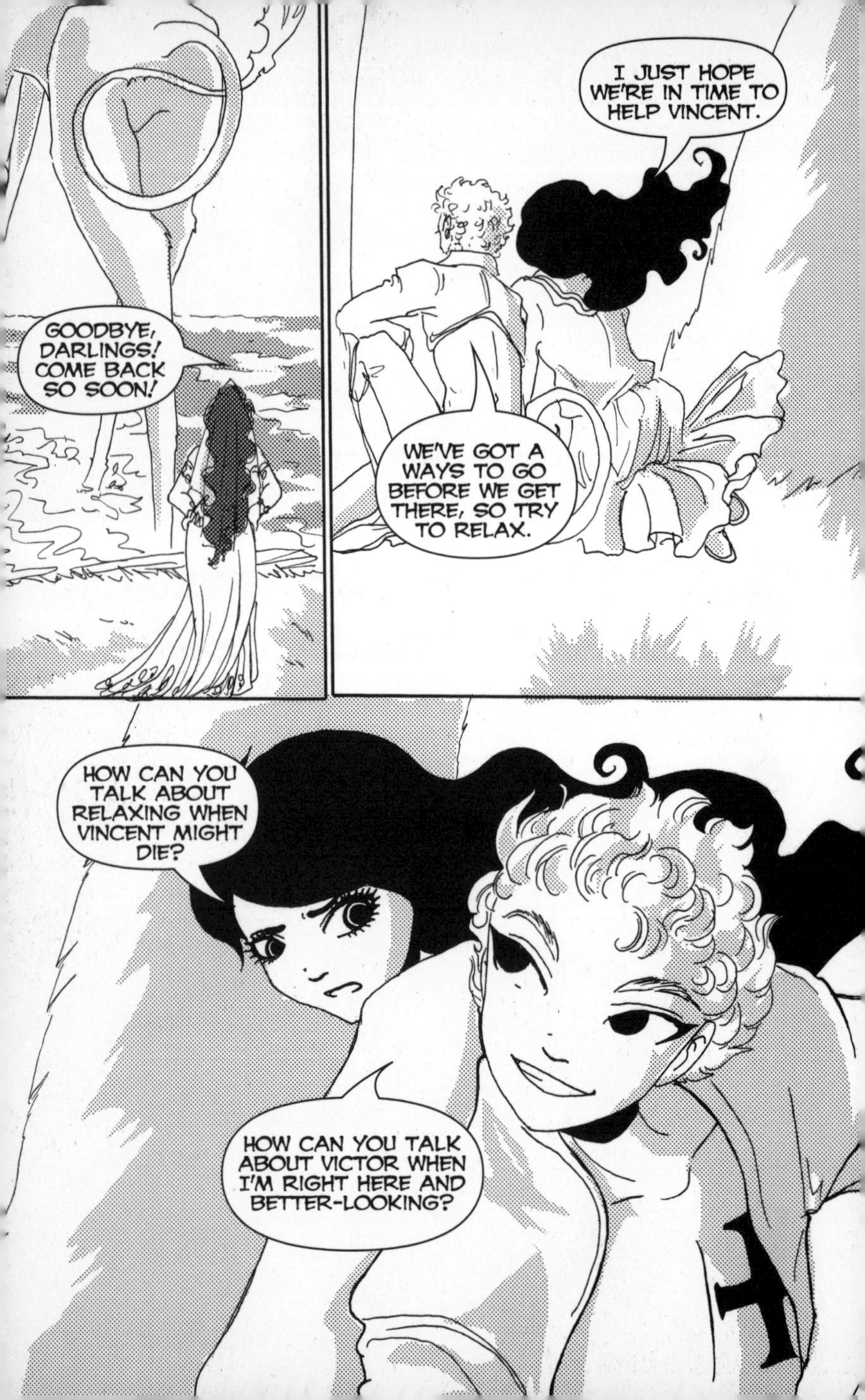
GOODBYE, DARLINGS! COME BACK SO SOON!
I JUST HOPE WE'RE IN TIME TO HELP VINCENT.
WE'VE GOT A WAYS TO GO BEFORE WE GET THERE, SO TRY TO RELAX.
HOW CAN YOU TALK ABOUT RELAXING WHEN VINCENT MIGHT DIE?
HOW CAN YOU TALK ABOUT VICTOR WHEN I'M RIGHT HERE AND BETTER-LOOKING?

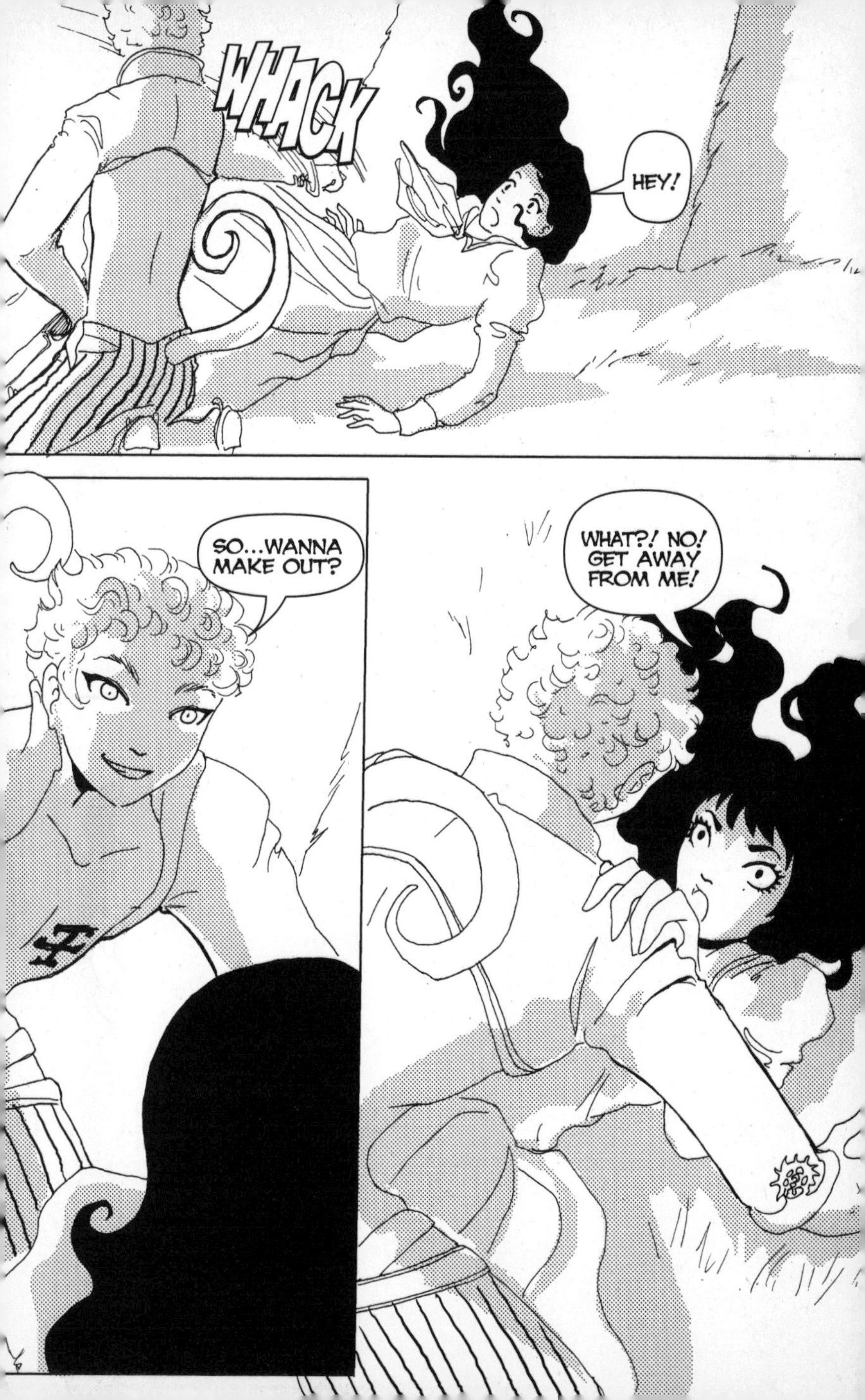
WHACK
HEY!
SO...WANNA MAKE OUT?
WHAT?! NO! GET AWAY FROM ME!

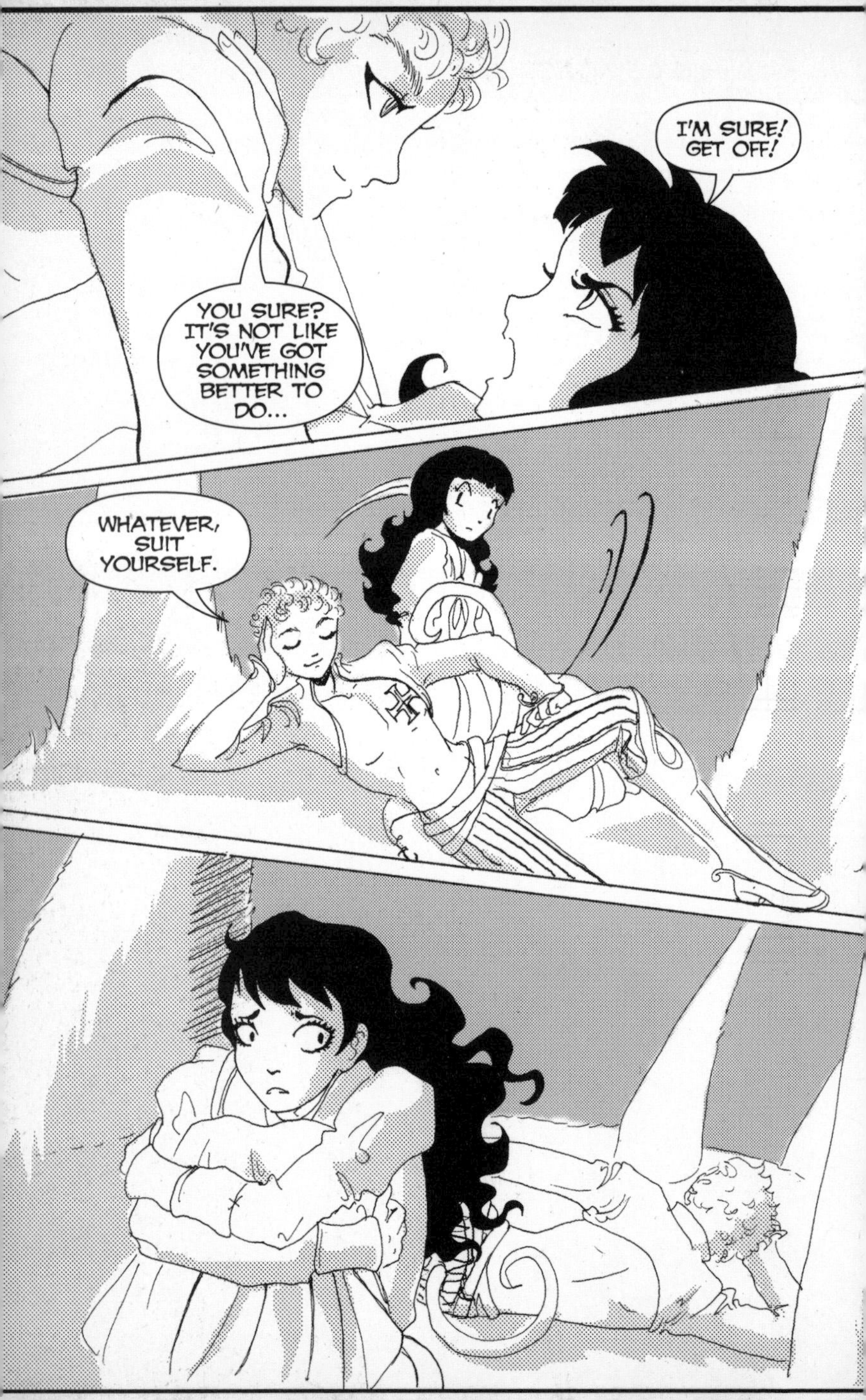
I'M SURE! GET OFF!
YOU SURE? IT'S NOT LIKE YOU'VE GOT SOMETHING BETTER TO DO...
WHATEVER, SUIT YOURSELF.

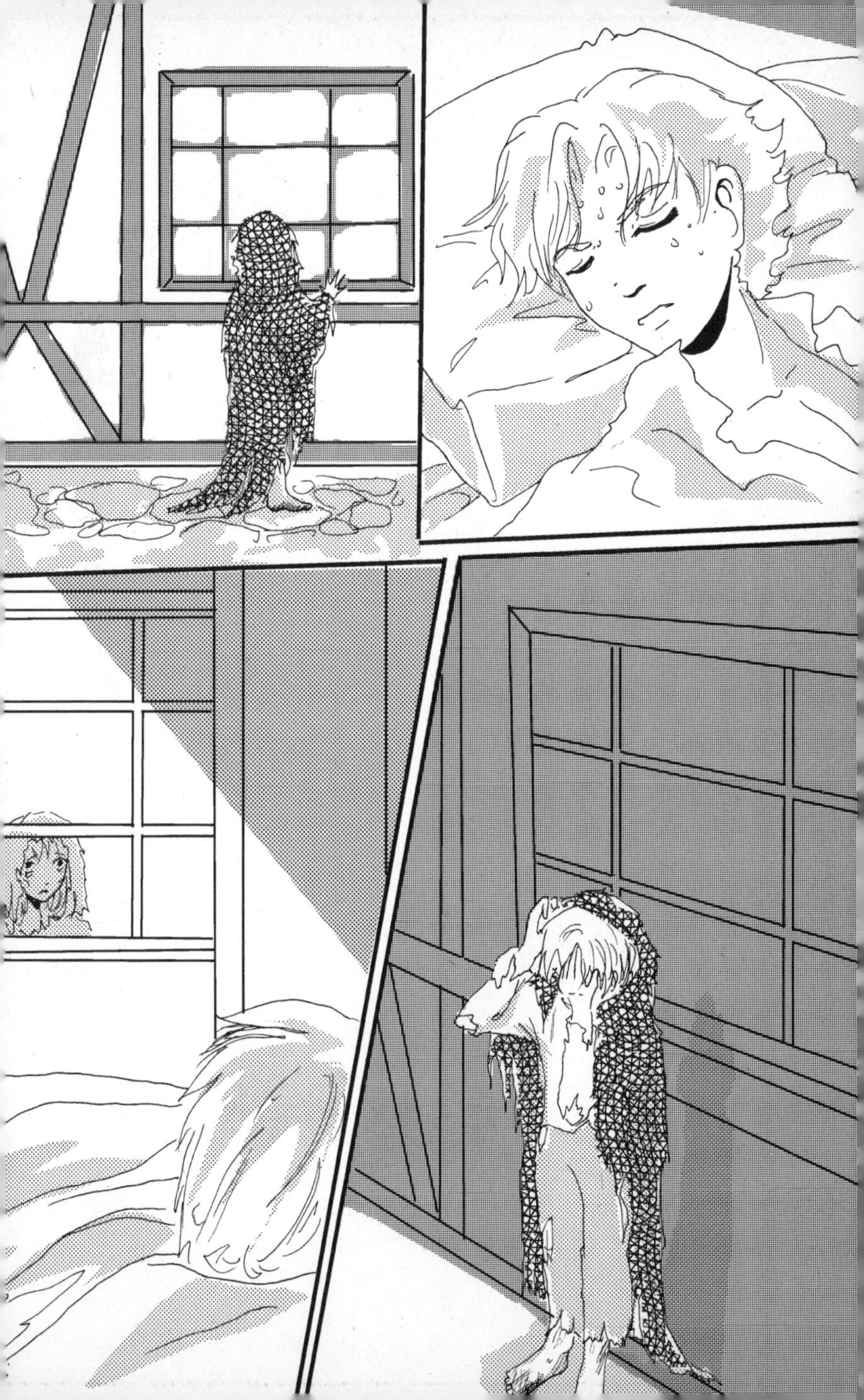

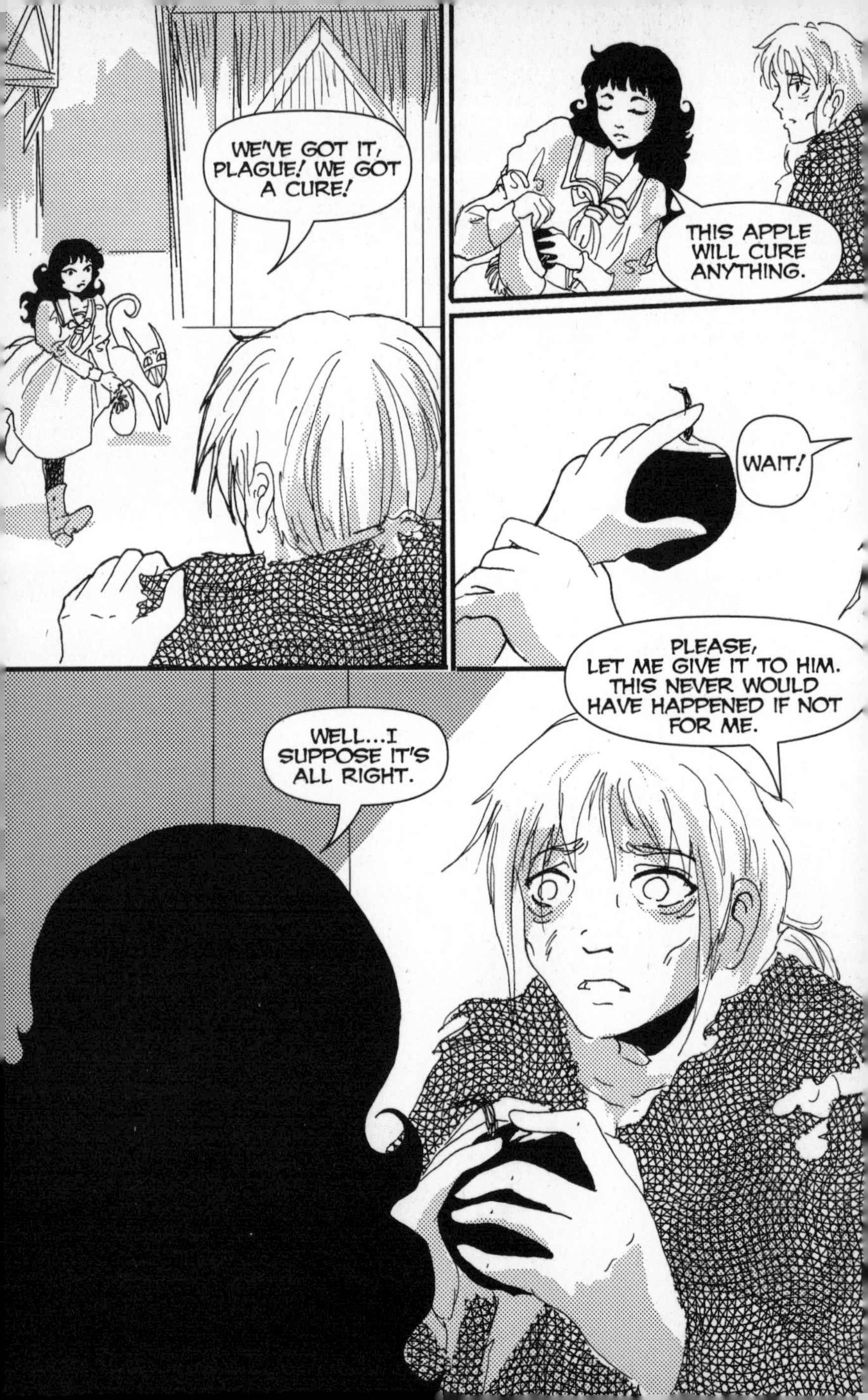
WE'VE GOT IT, PLAGUE! WE GOT A CURE!
THIS APPLE WILL CURE ANYTHING.
WAIT!
WELL...I SUPPOSE IT'S ALL RIGHT.
PLEASE, LET ME GIVE IT TO HIM. THIS NEVER WOULD HAVE HAPPENED IF NOT FOR ME.

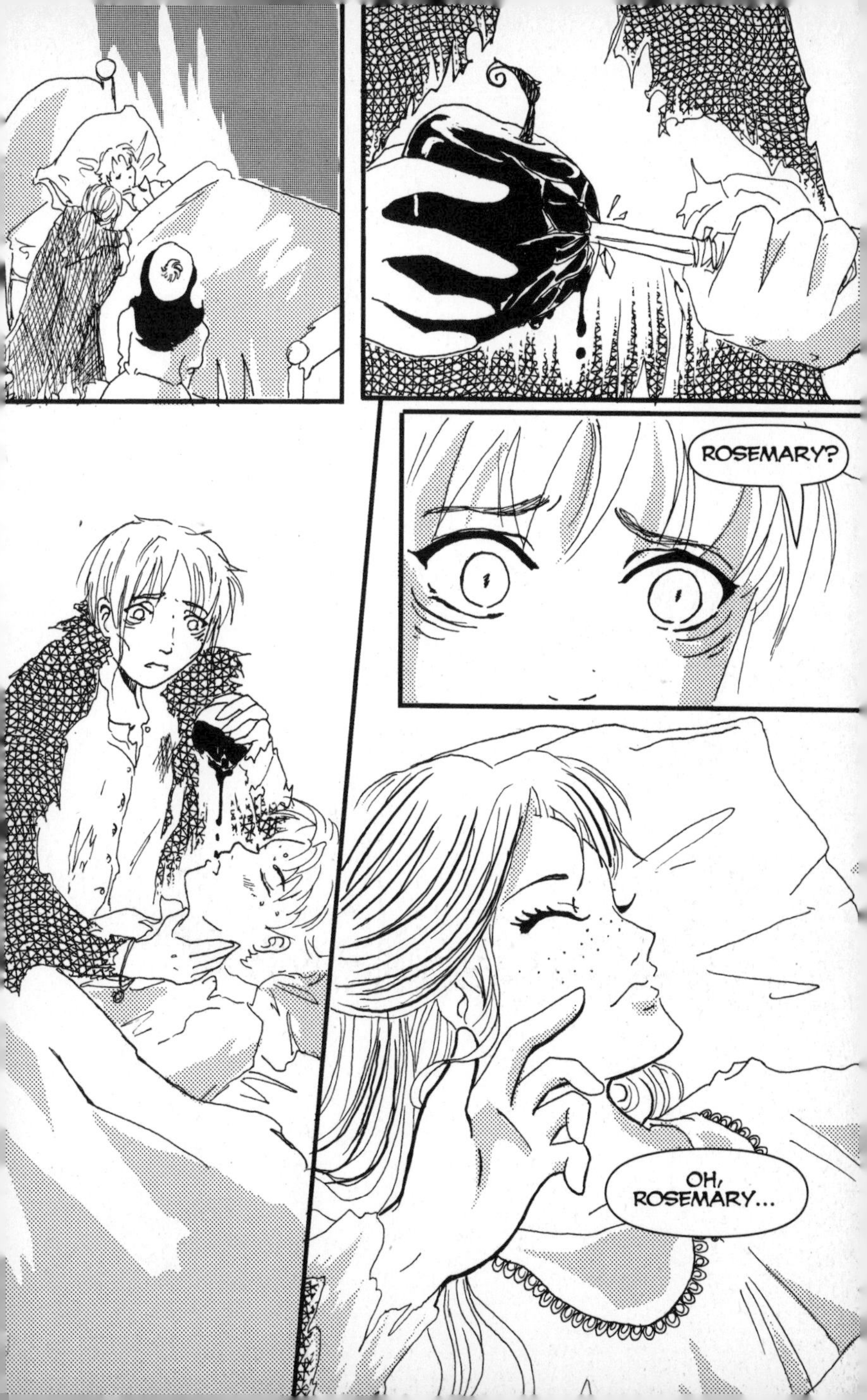
ROSEMARY?
OH, ROSEMARY...

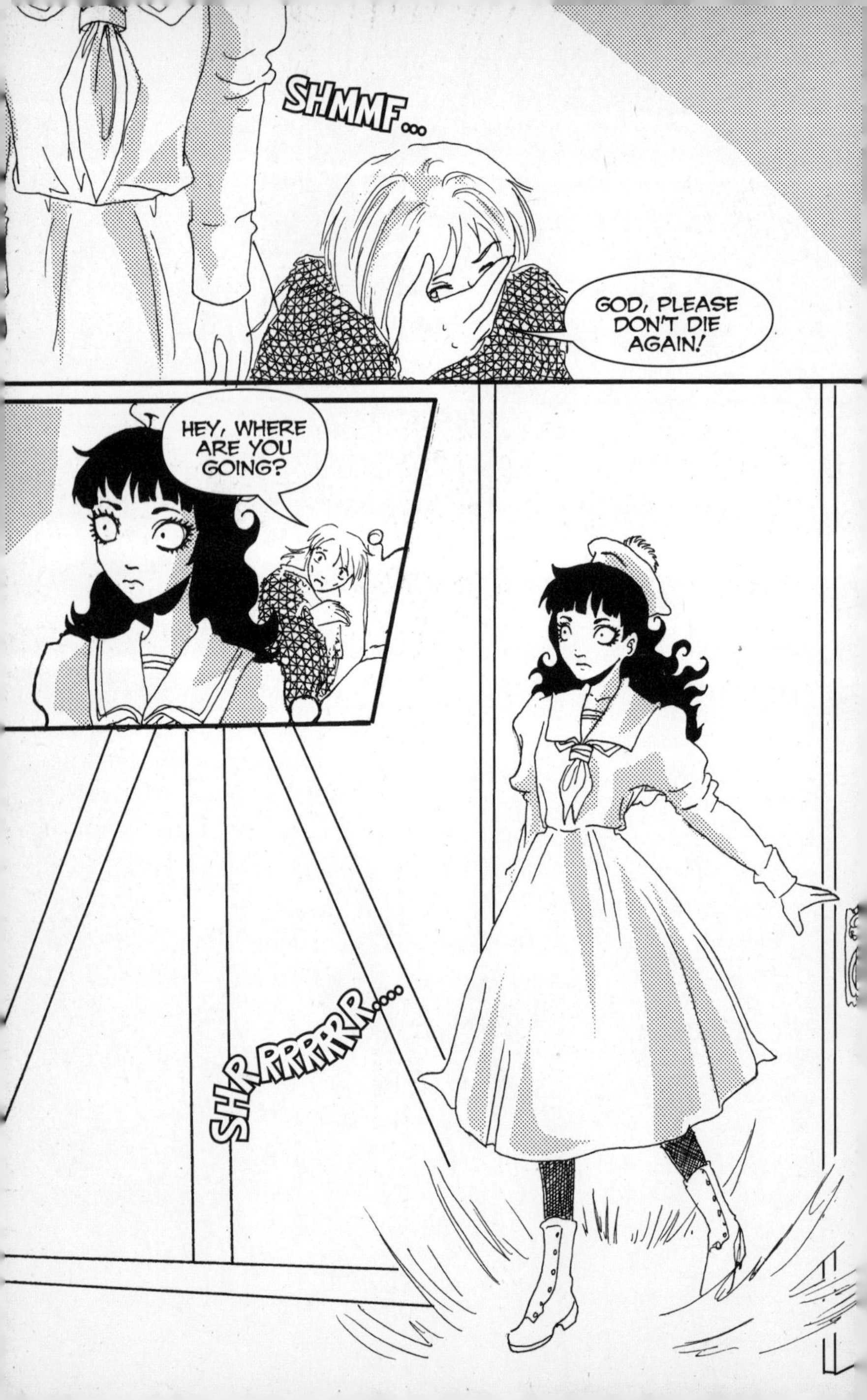
SHMMF...
GOD, PLEASE DON'T DIE AGAIN!
HEY, WHERE ARE YOU GOING?
SHRRRRRR....

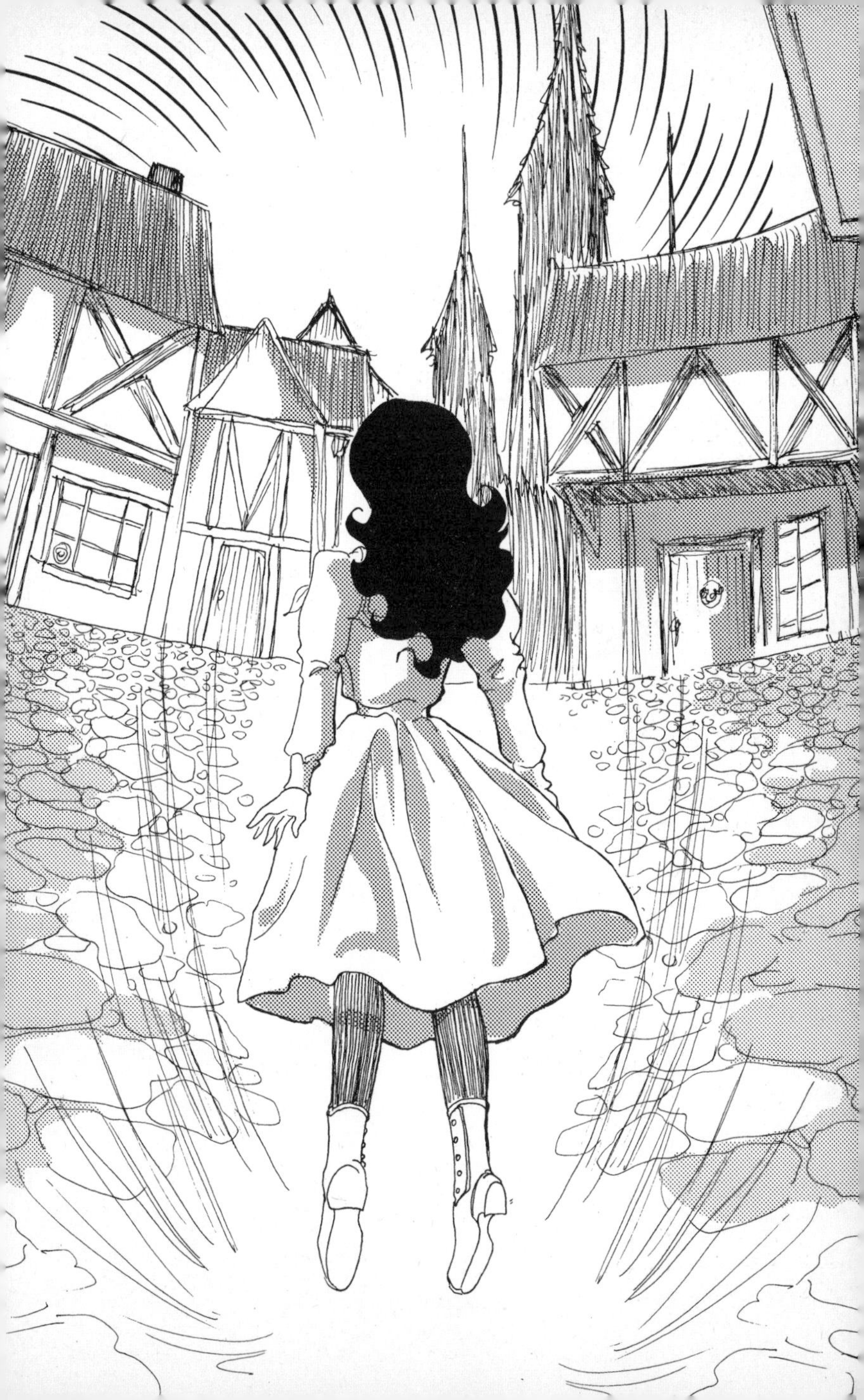

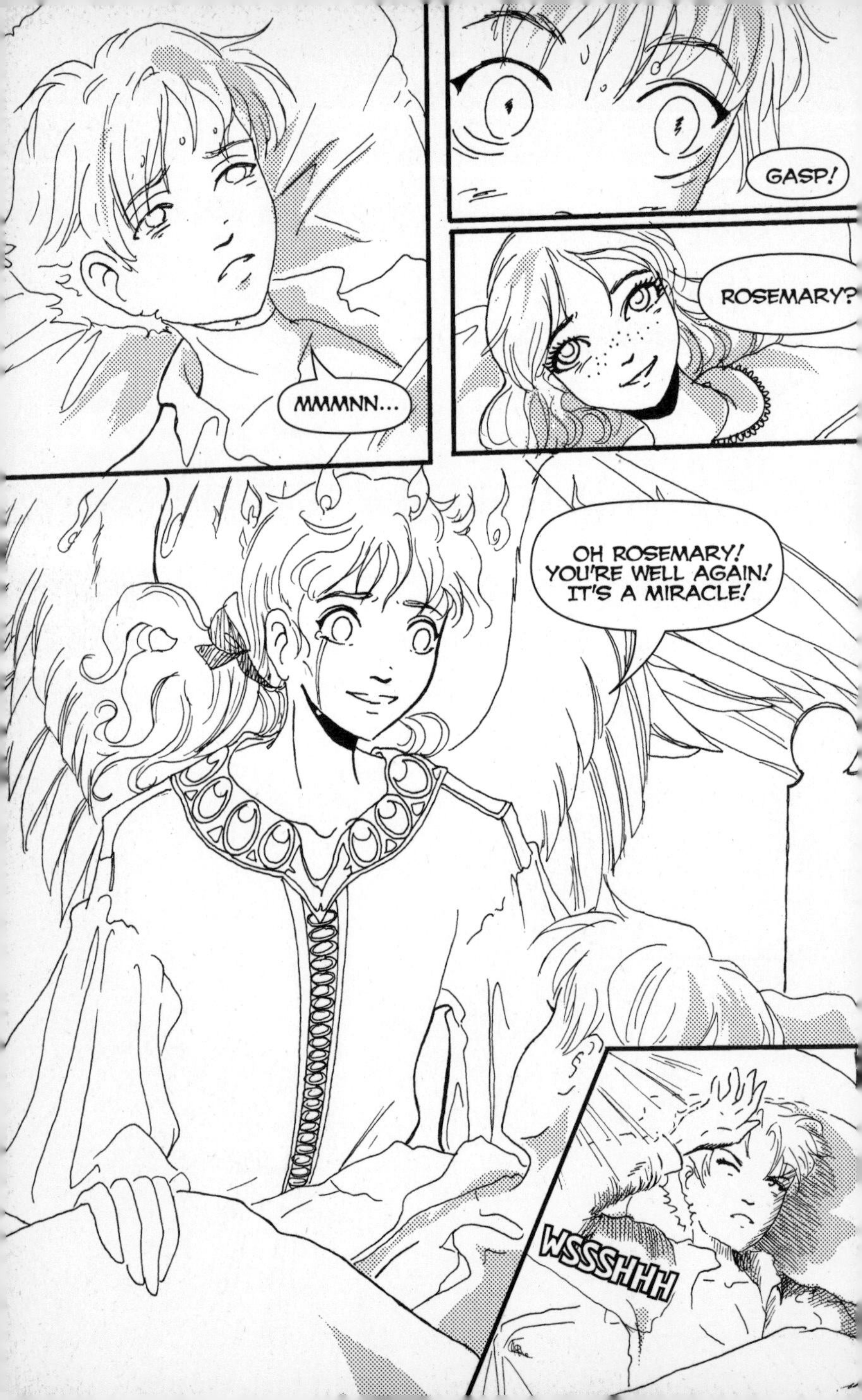
MMMNN...
GASP!
ROSEMARY?
OH ROSEMARY! YOU'RE WELL AGAIN! IT'S A MIRACLE!
WSSSHHH

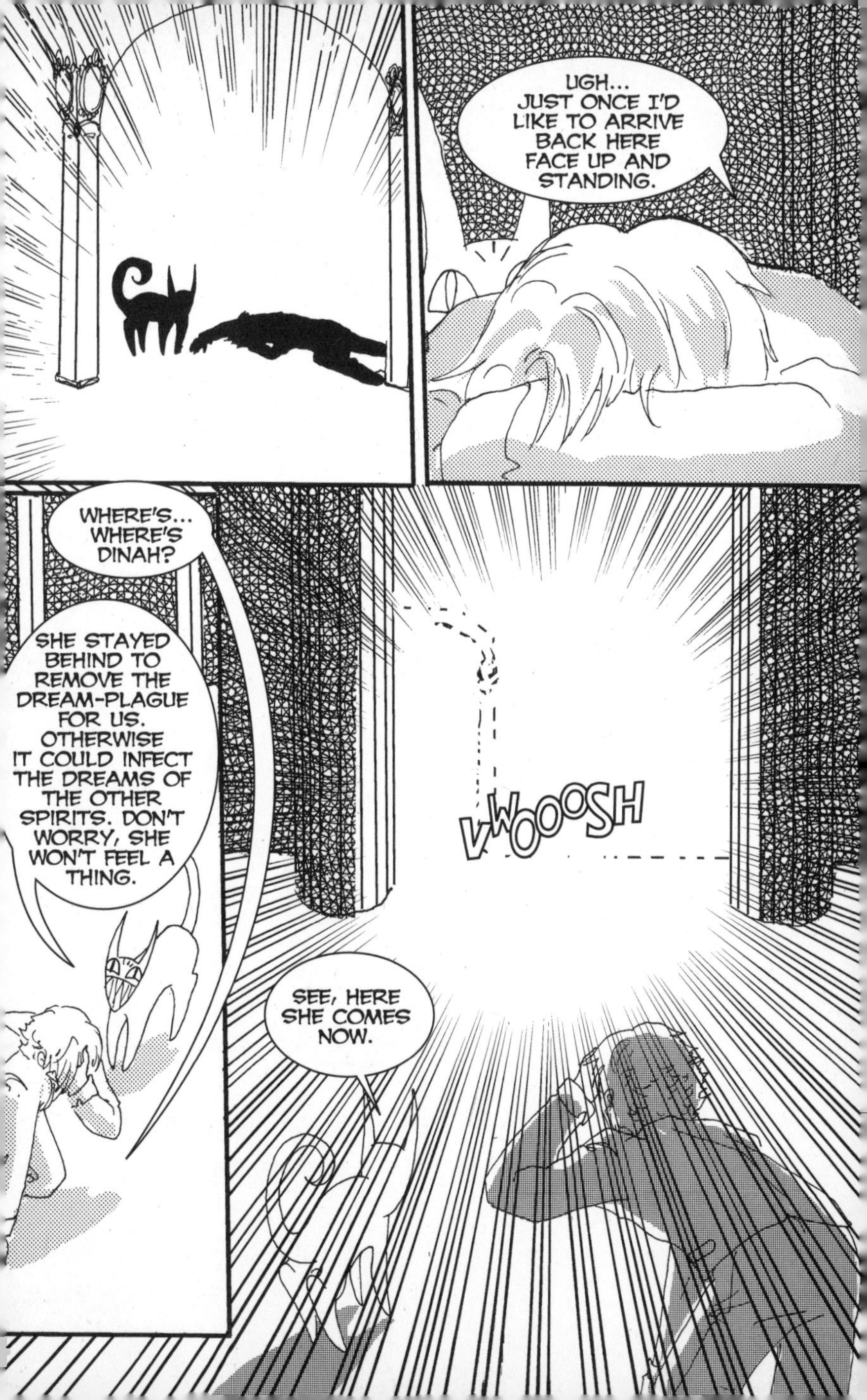
UGH... JUST ONCE I'D LIKE TO ARRIVE BACK HERE FACE UP AND STANDING.
WHERE'S... WHERE'S DINAH?
SHE STAYED BEHIND TO REMOVE THE DREAM-PLAGUE FOR US. OTHERWISE IT COULD INFECT THE DREAMS OF THE OTHER SPIRITS. DON'T WORRY, SHE WON'T FEEL A THING.
VWOOOOSH
SEE, HERE SHE COMES NOW.

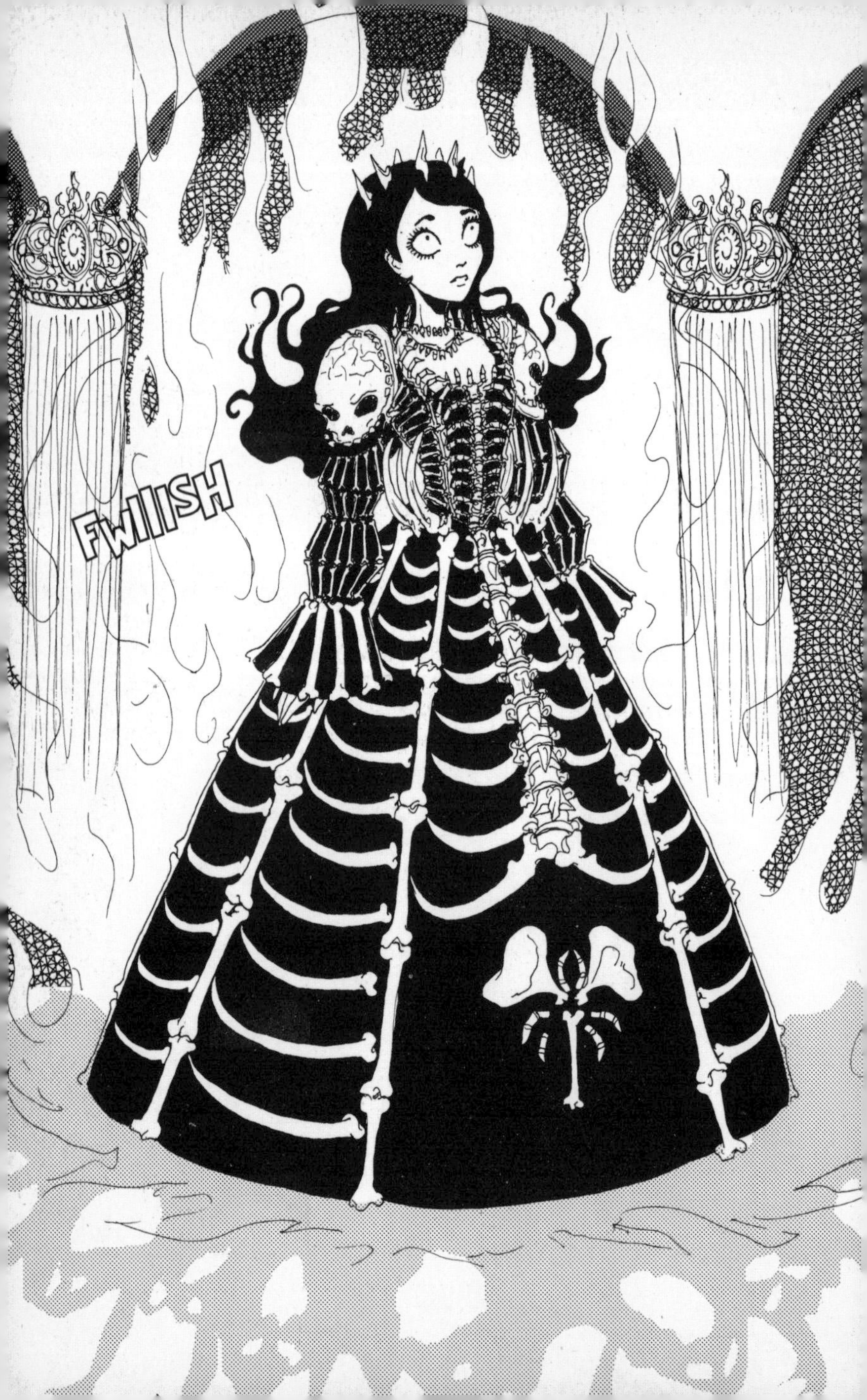
FWIIISH

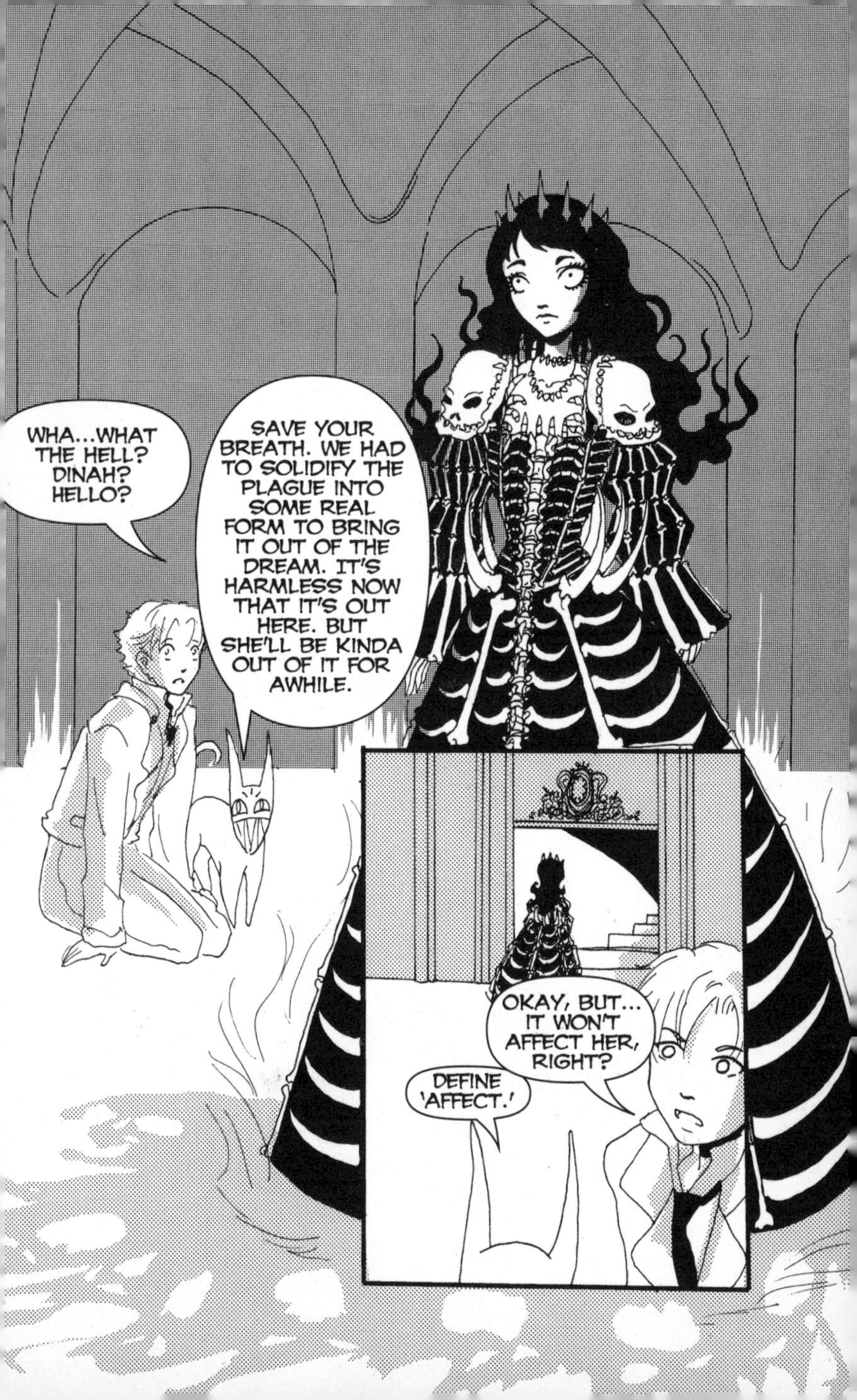
WHA...WHAT THE HELL? DINAH? HELLO?
SAVE YOUR BREATH. WE HAD TO SOLIDIFY THE PLAGUE INTO SOME REAL FORM TO BRING IT OUT OF THE DREAM. IT'S HARMLESS NOW THAT IT'S OUT HERE. BUT SHE'LL BE KINDA OUT OF IT FOR AWHILE.
OKAY, BUT... IT WON'T AFFECT HER, RIGHT?
DEFINE 'AFFECT.'

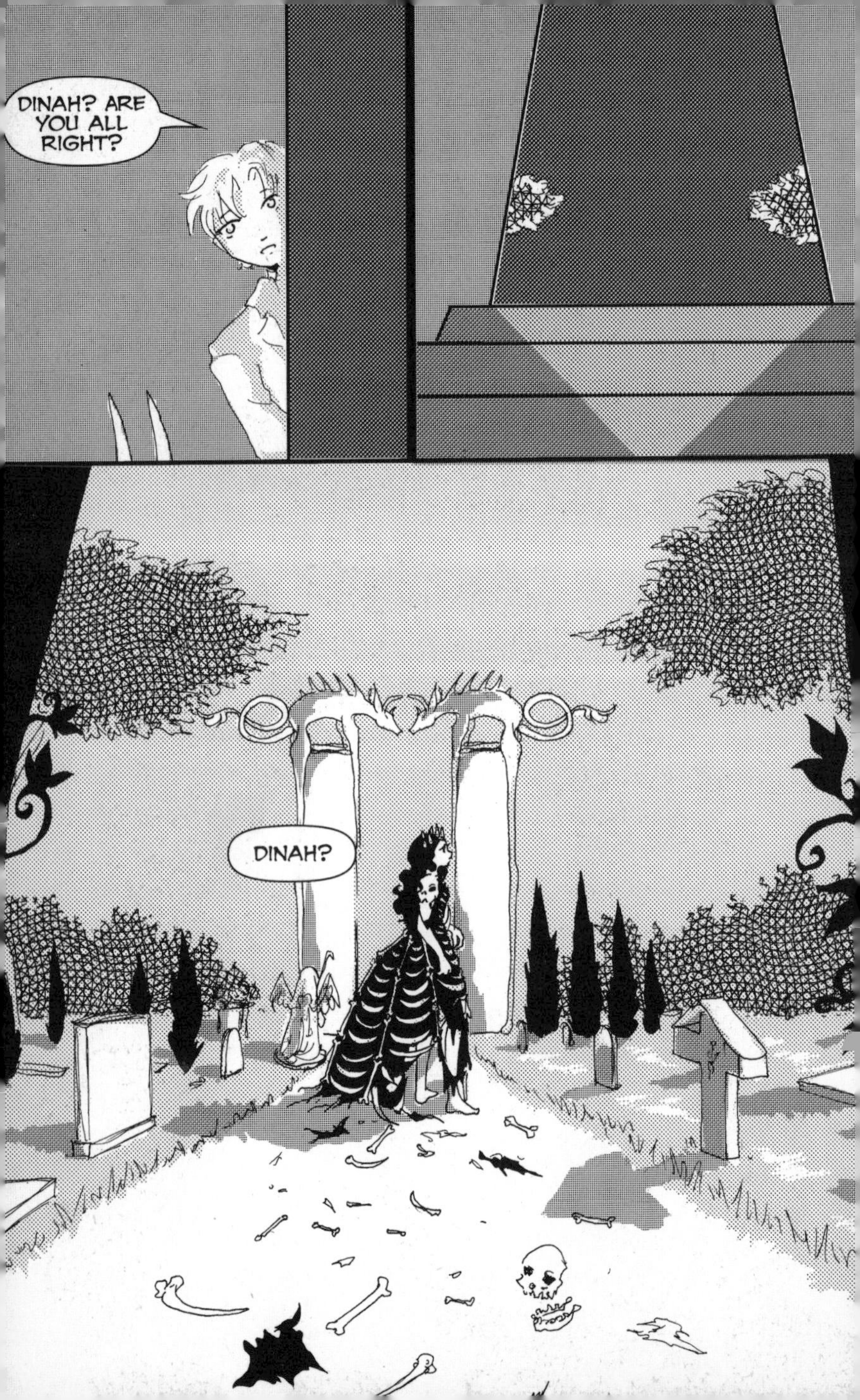
DINAH? ARE YOU ALL RIGHT?
DINAH?

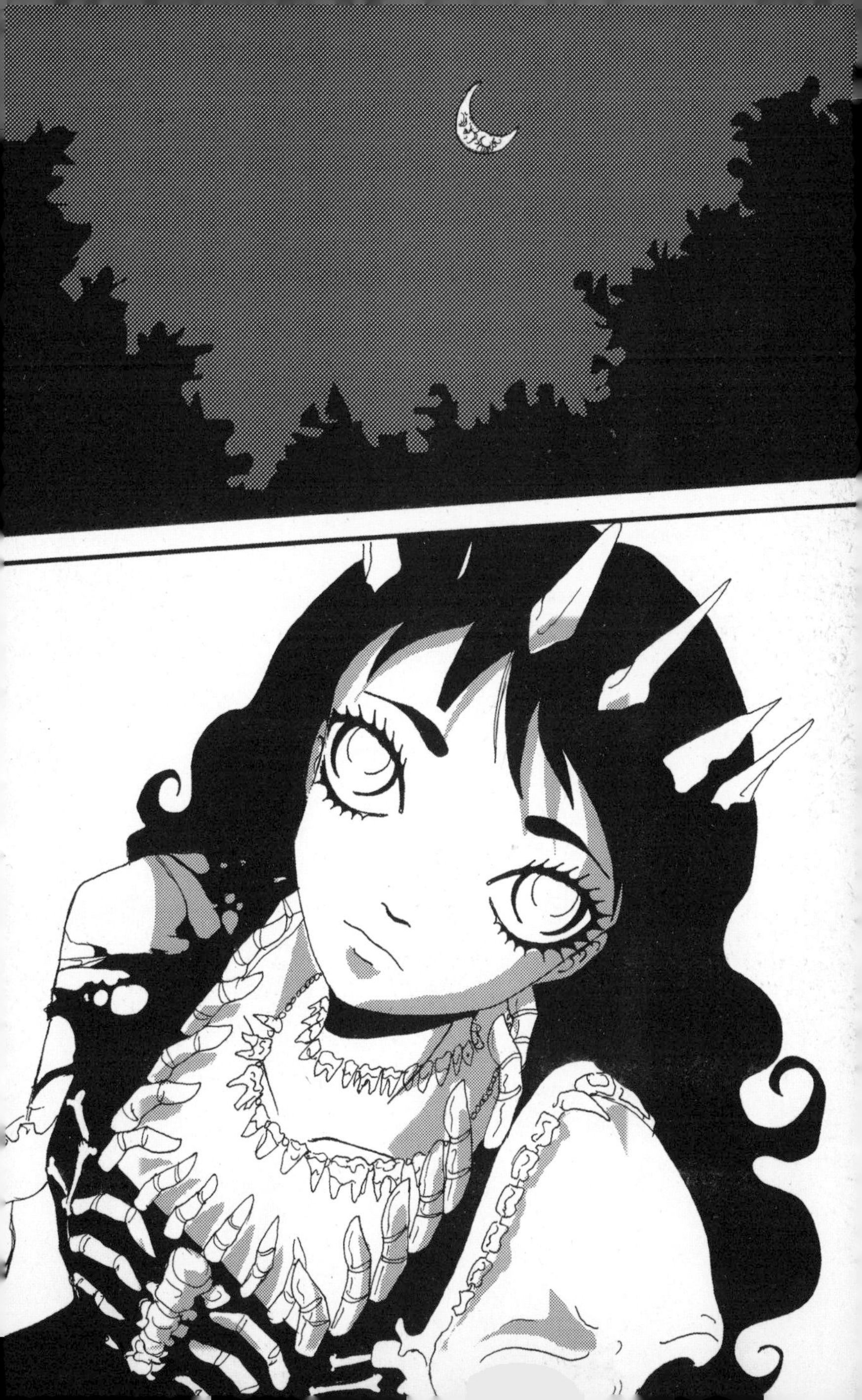

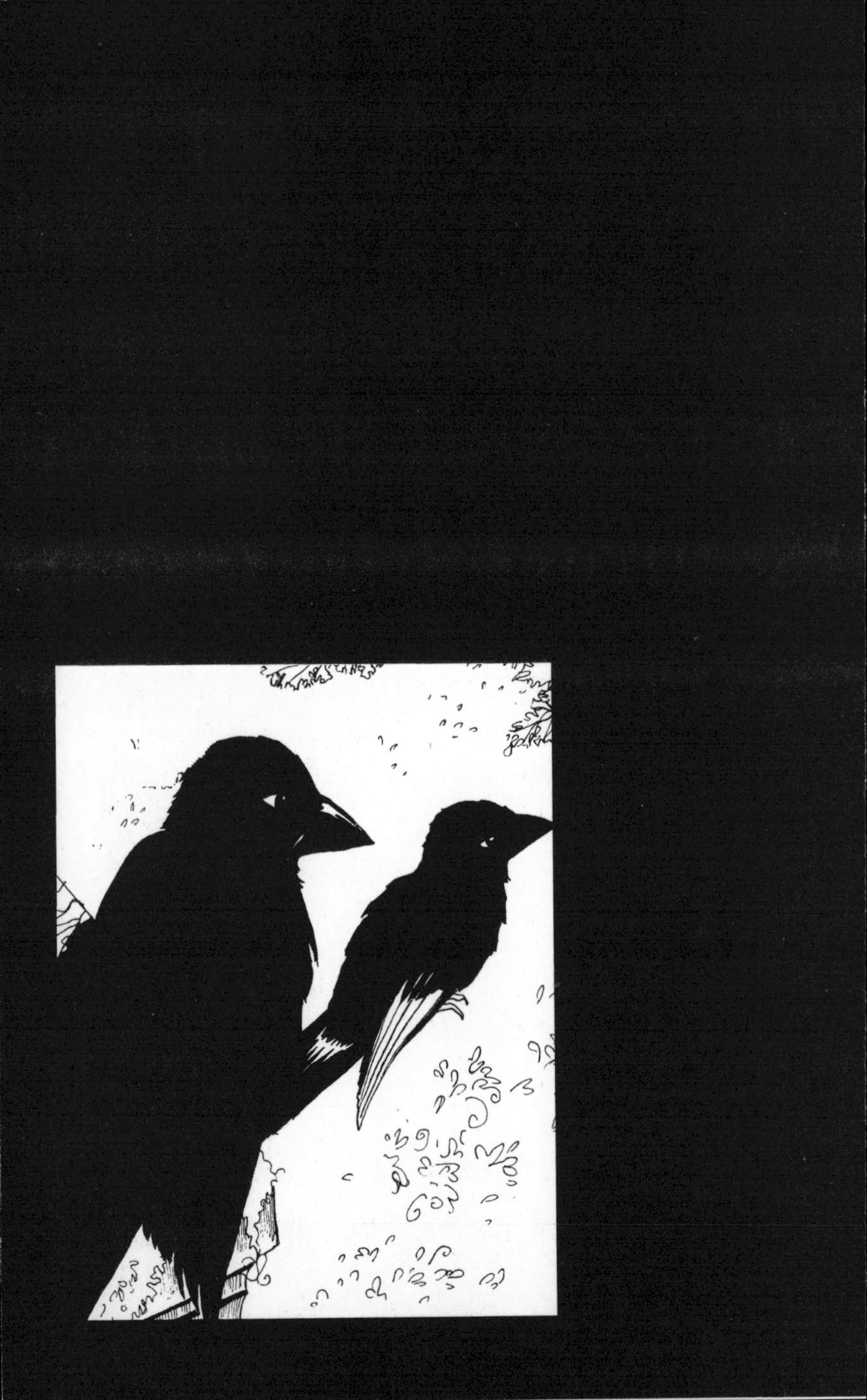

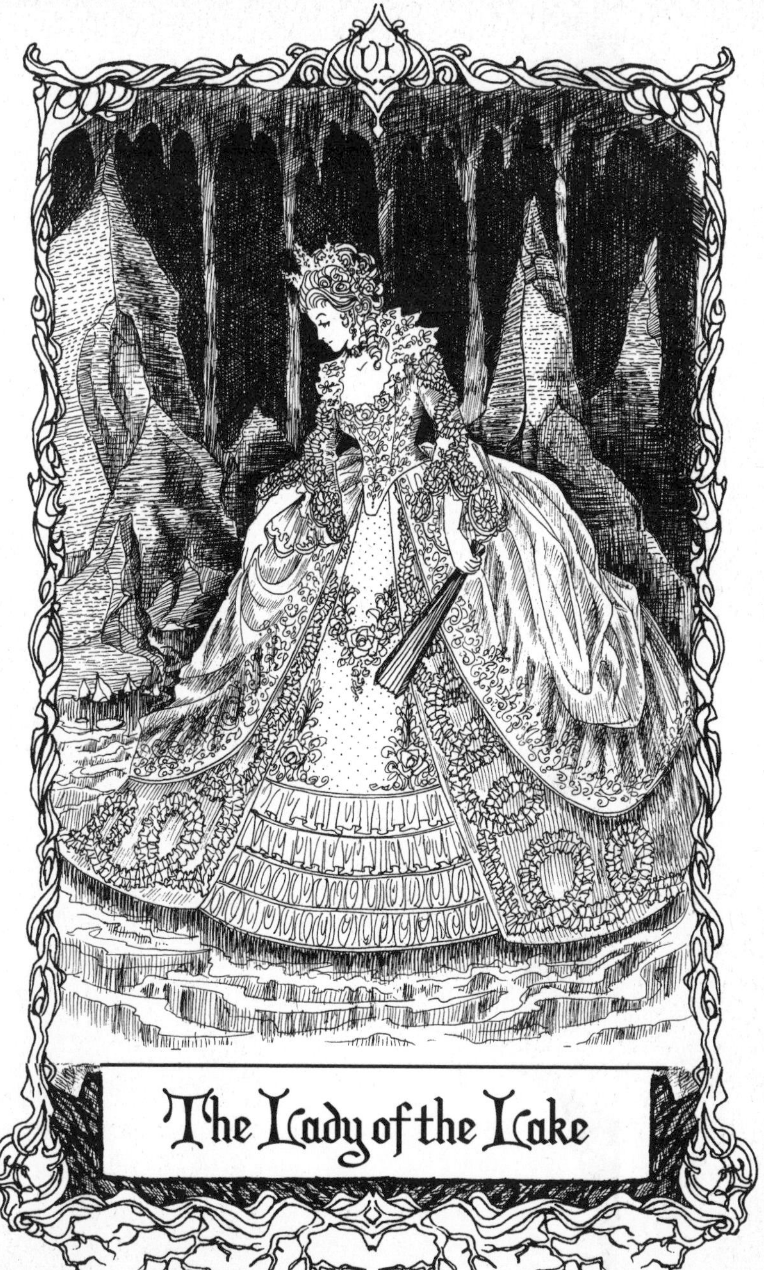
VI
The Lady of the Lake

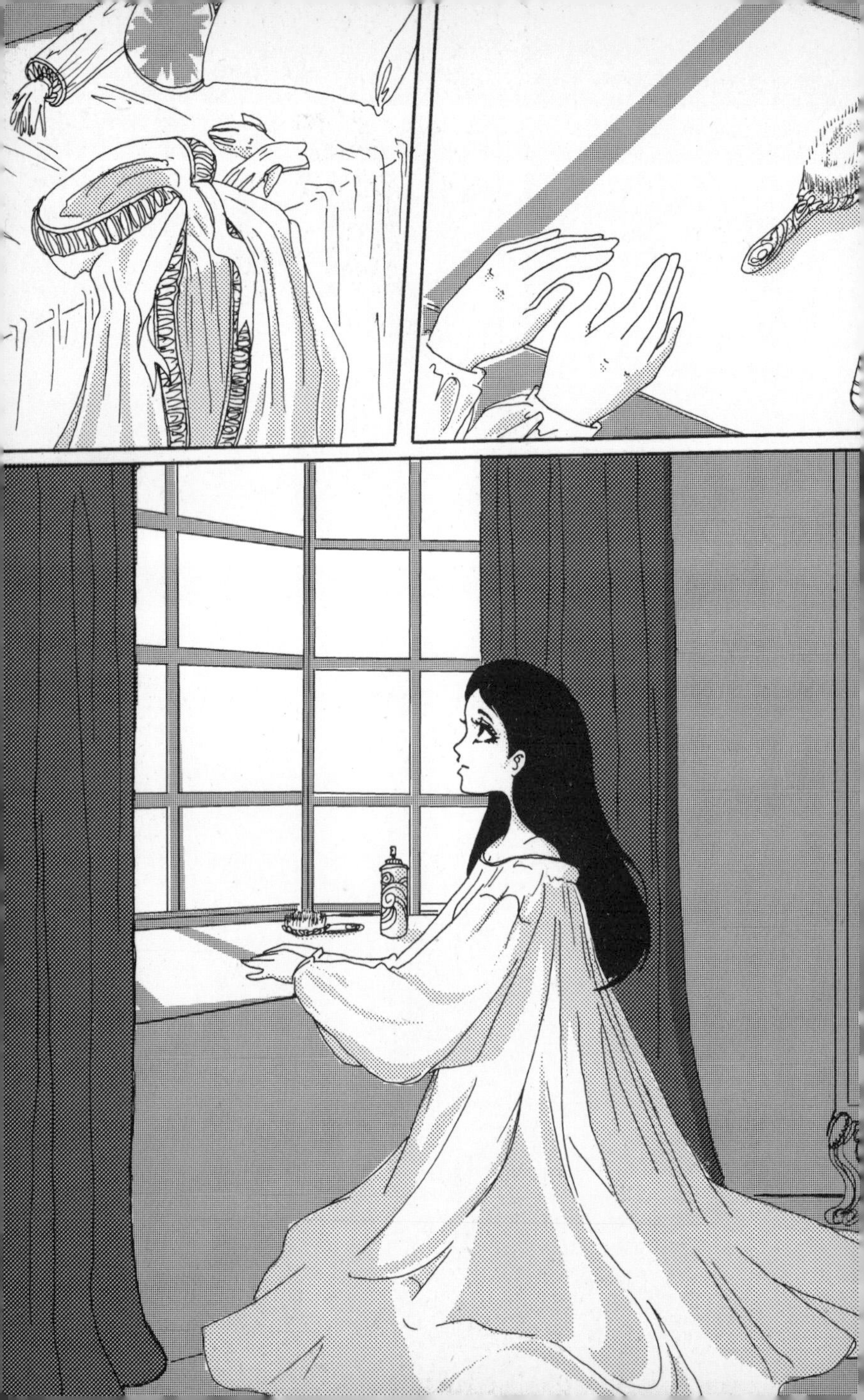

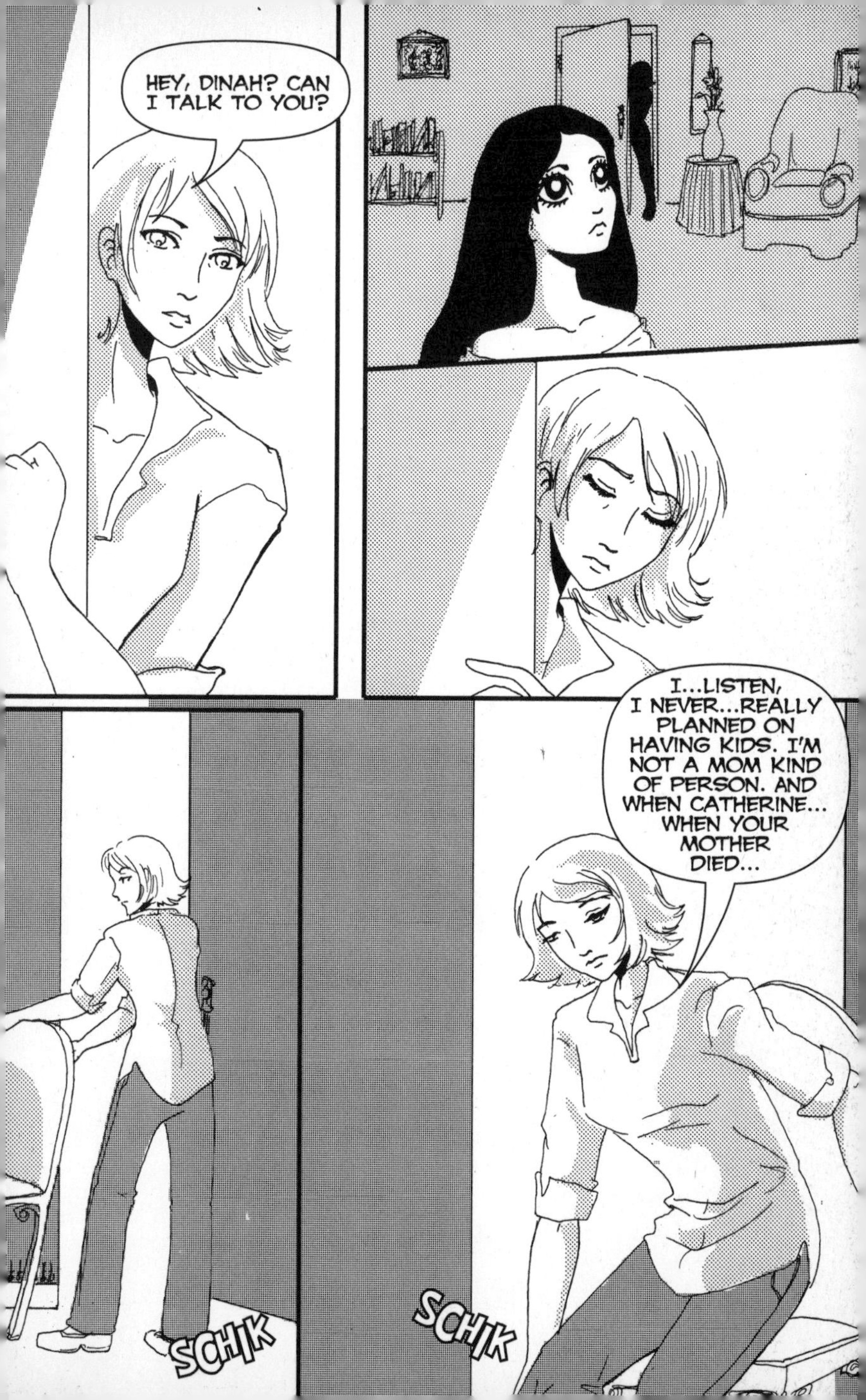
HEY, DINAH? CAN I TALK TO YOU?
SCHIK
SCHIK
I...LISTEN, I NEVER...REALLY PLANNED ON HAVING KIDS. I'M NOT A MOM KIND OF PERSON. AND WHEN CATHERINE... WHEN YOUR MOTHER DIED...

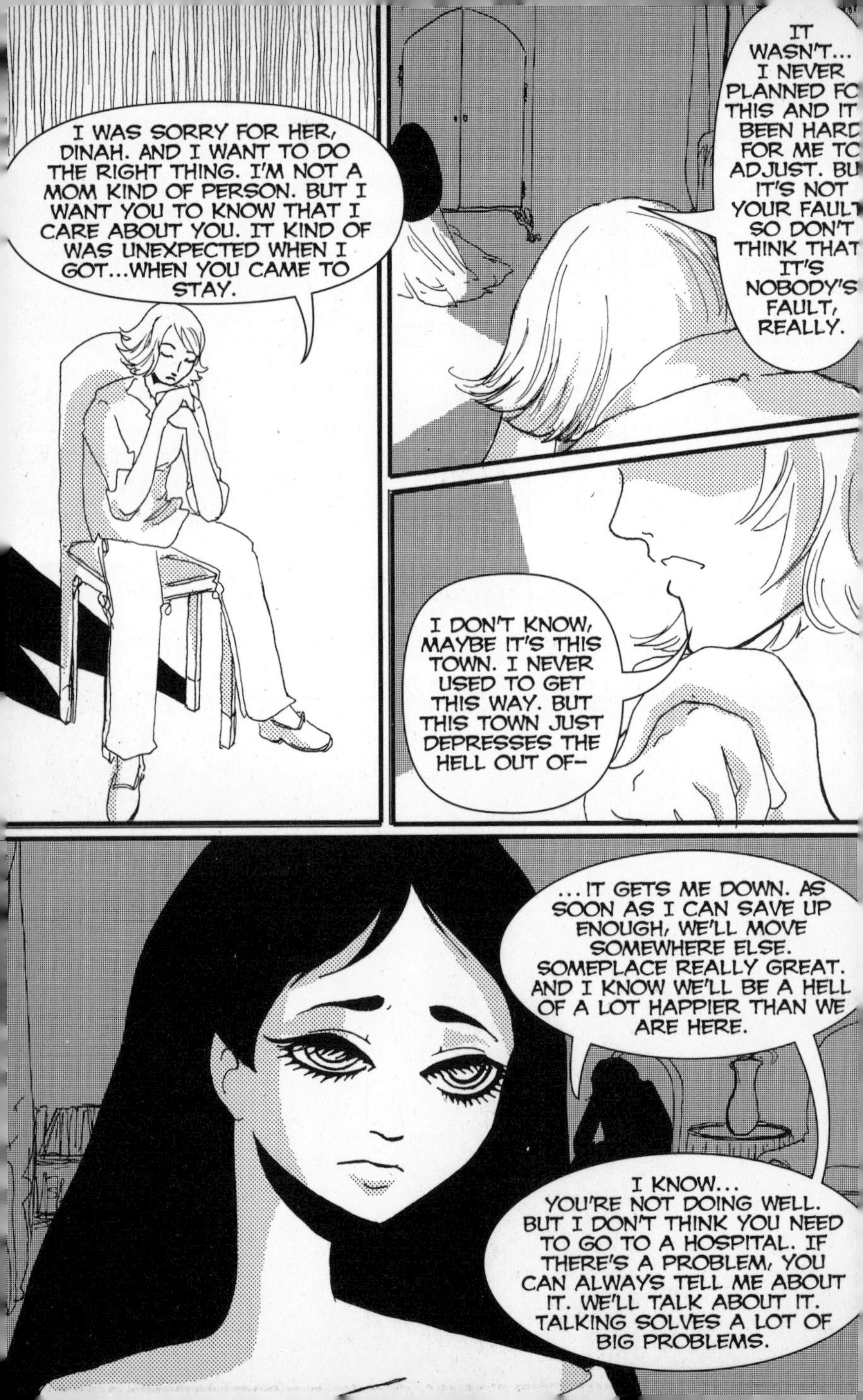
I WAS SORRY FOR HER, DINAH. AND I WANT TO DO THE RIGHT THING. I'M NOT A MOM KIND OF PERSON. BUT I WANT YOU TO KNOW THAT I CARE ABOUT YOU. IT KIND OF WAS UNEXPECTED WHEN I GOT...WHEN YOU CAME TO STAY.
IT WASN'T... I NEVER PLANNED FO THIS AND IT BEEN HARD FOR ME TO ADJUST. BU IT'S NOT YOUR FAULT SO DON'T THINK THAT IT'S NOBODY'S FAULT, REALLY.
I DON'T KNOW, MAYBE IT'S THIS TOWN. I NEVER USED TO GET THIS WAY. BUT THIS TOWN JUST DEPRESSES THE HELL OUT OF-
...IT GETS ME DOWN. AS SOON AS I CAN SAVE UP ENOUGH, WE'LL MOVE SOMEWHERE ELSE. SOMEPLACE REALLY GREAT. AND I KNOW WE'LL BE A HELL OF A LOT HAPPIER THAN WE ARE HERE.
I KNOW... YOU'RE NOT DOING WELL. BUT I DON'T THINK YOU NEED TO GO TO A HOSPITAL. IF THERE'S A PROBLEM, YOU CAN ALWAYS TELL ME ABOUT IT. WE'LL TALK ABOUT IT. TALKING SOLVES A LOT OF BIG PROBLEMS.

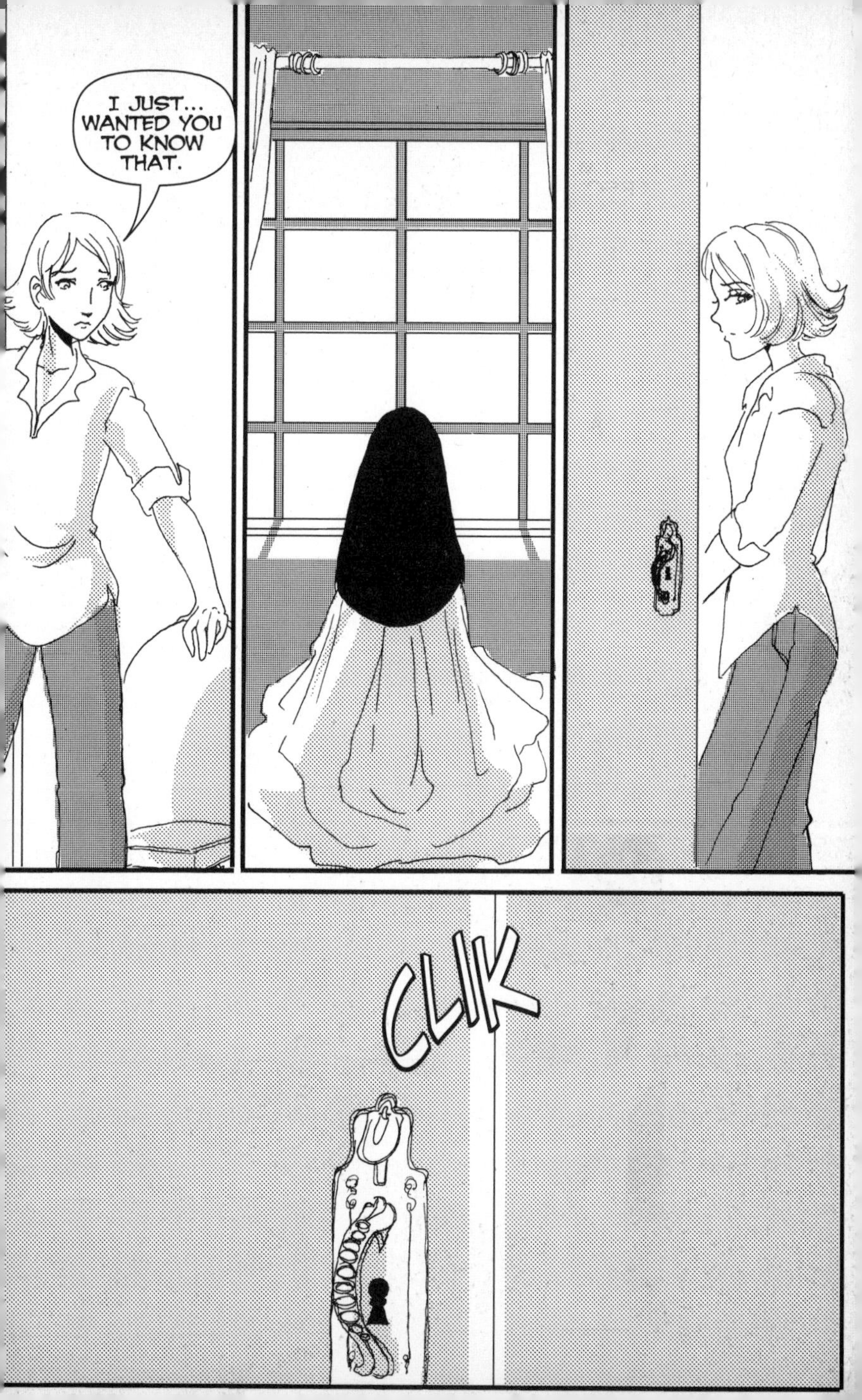
I JUST... WANTED YOU TO KNOW THAT.
CLIK

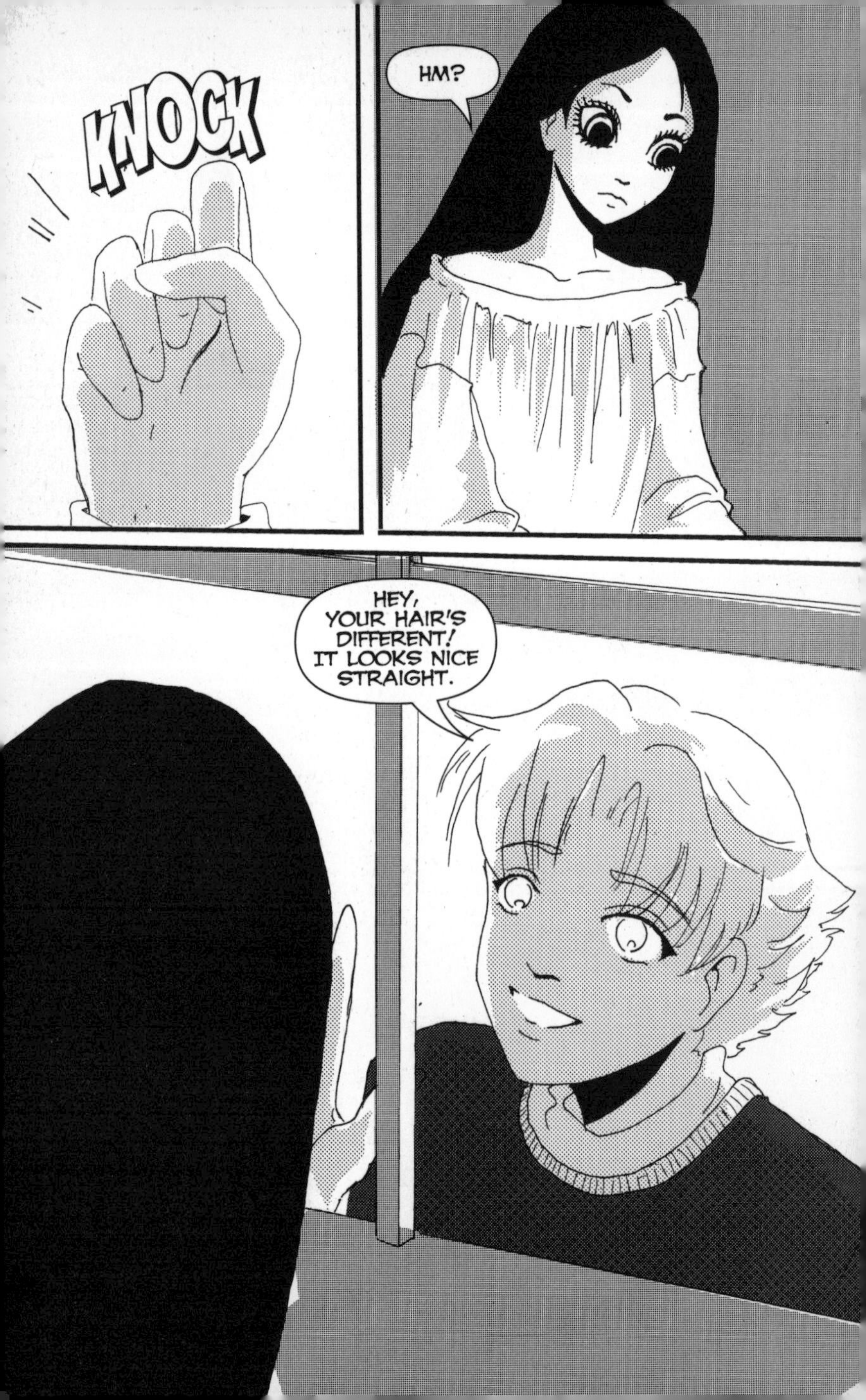
KNOCK
HM?
HEY, YOUR HAIR'S DIFFERENT! IT LOOKS NICE STRAIGHT.

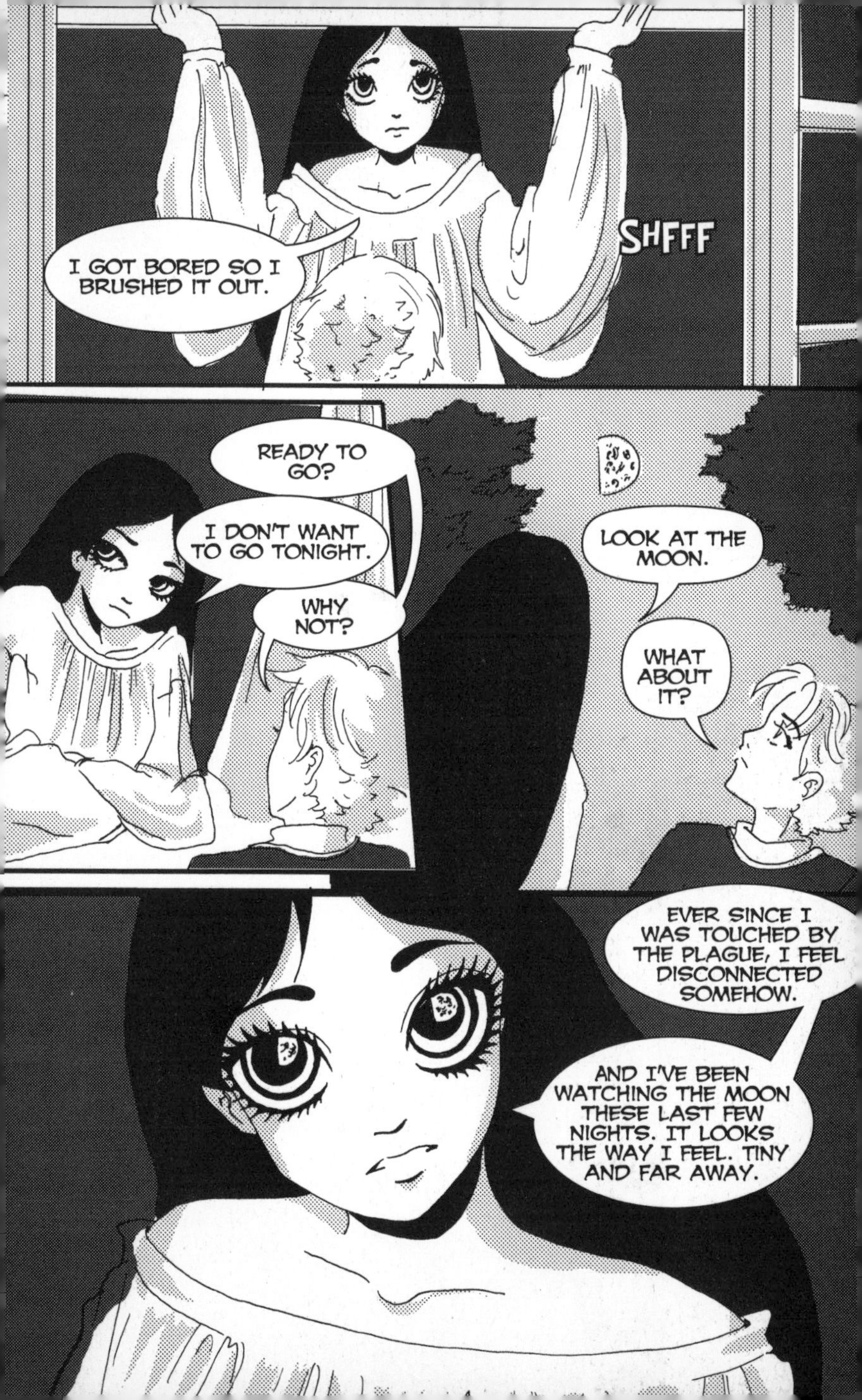
I GOT BORED SO I BRUSHED IT OUT.
SHFFF
READY TO GO?
I DON'T WANT TO GO TONIGHT.
WHY NOT?
LOOK AT THE MOON.
WHAT ABOUT IT?
EVER SINCE I WAS TOUCHED BY THE PLAGUE, I FEEL DISCONNECTED SOMEHOW.
AND I'VE BEEN WATCHING THE MOON THESE LAST FEW NIGHTS. IT LOOKS THE WAY I FEEL. TINY AND FAR AWAY.

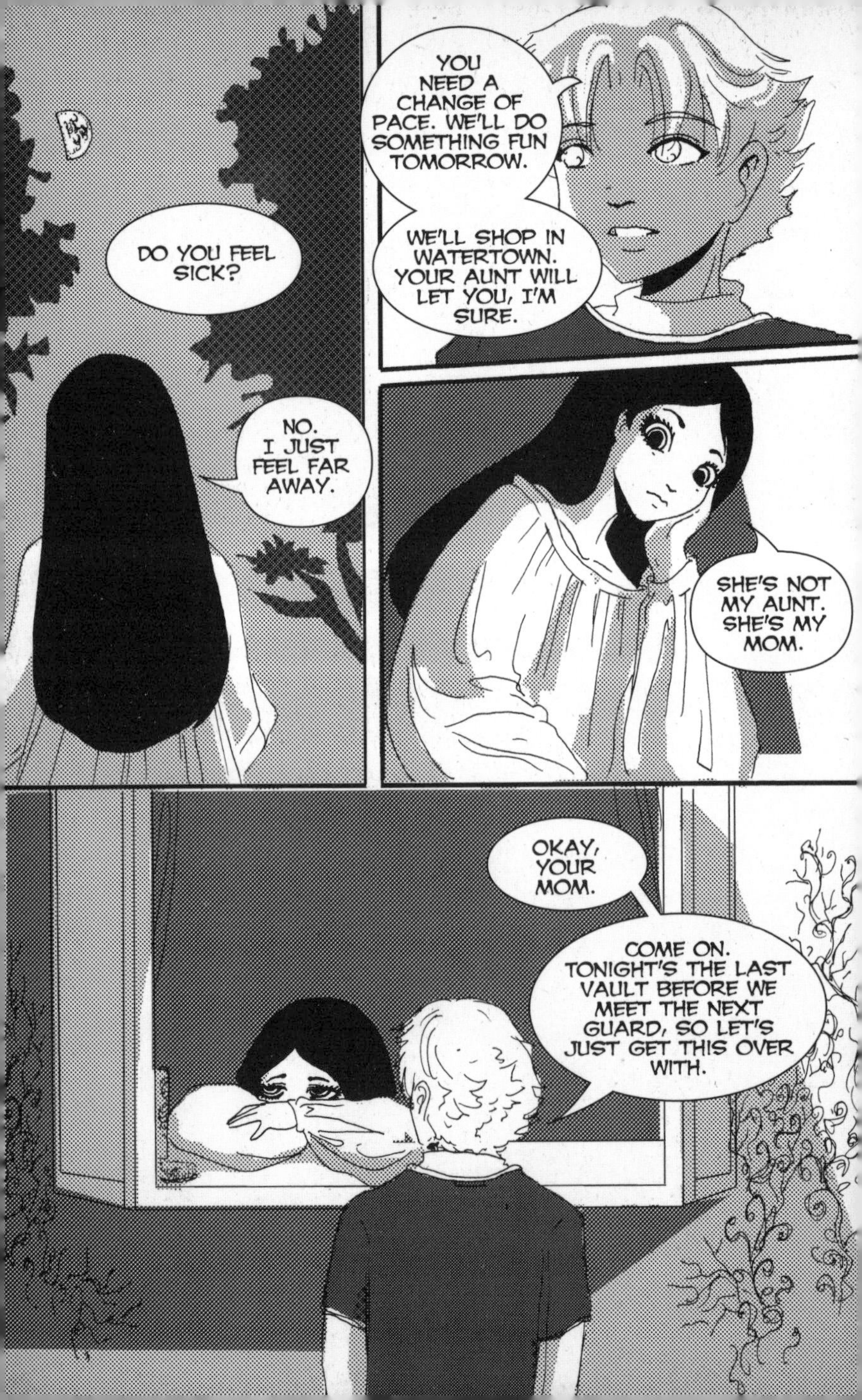
DO YOU FEEL SICK?
NO. I JUST FEEL FAR AWAY.
YOU NEED A CHANGE OF PACE. WE'LL DO SOMETHING FUN TOMORROW.
WE'LL SHOP IN WATERTOWN. YOUR AUNT WILL LET YOU, I'M SURE.
SHE'S NOT MY AUNT. SHE'S MY MOM.
OKAY, YOUR MOM.
COME ON. TONIGHT'S THE LAST VAULT BEFORE WE MEET THE NEXT GUARD, SO LET'S JUST GET THIS OVER WITH.

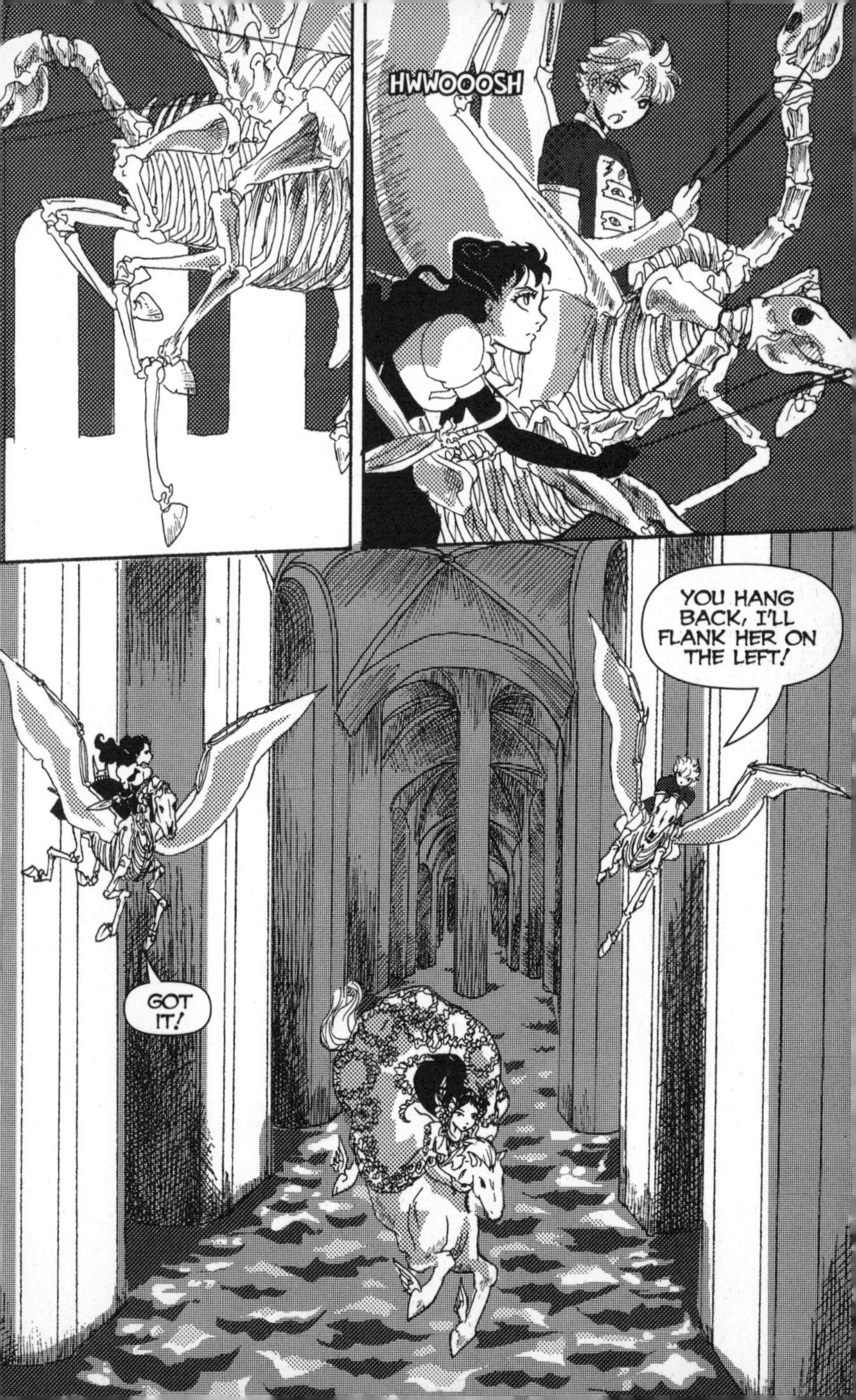
HWWOOOSH
YOU HANG BACK, I'LL FLANK HER ON THE LEFT!
GOT IT!

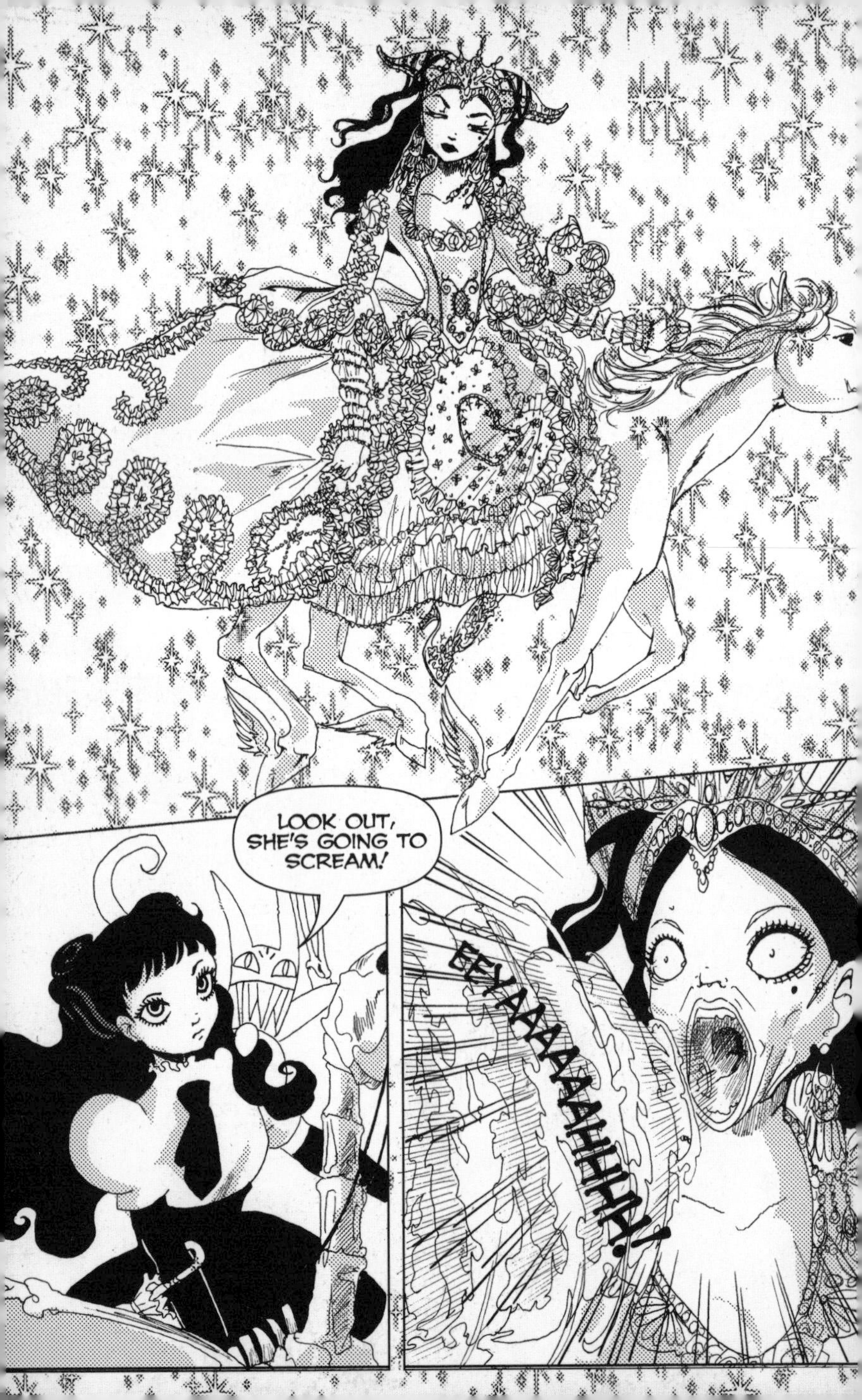
LOOK OUT, SHE'S GOING TO SCREAM!
EEYAAAAAAHHHH!

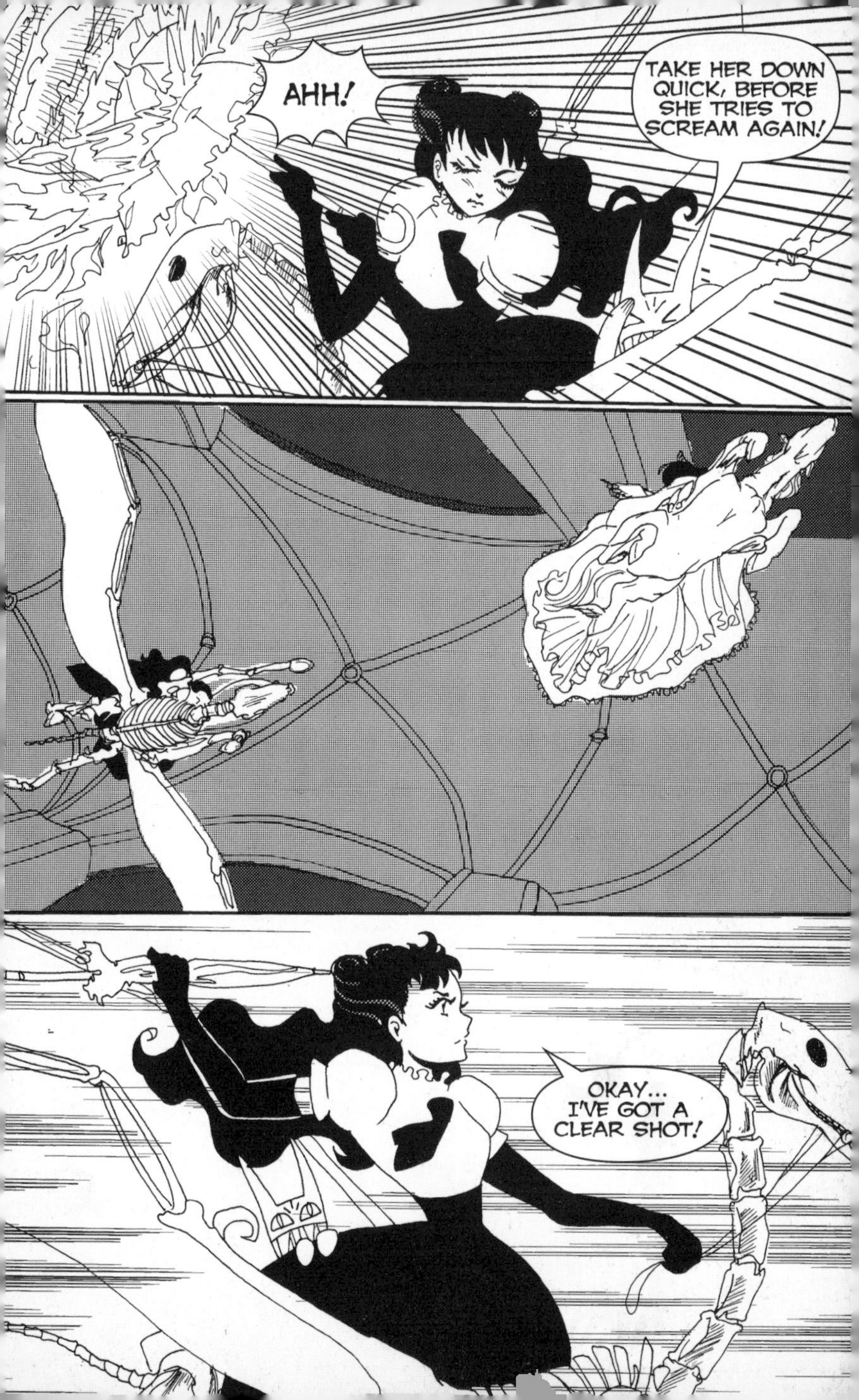
AHH!
TAKE HER DOWN QUICK, BEFORE SHE TRIES TO SCREAM AGAIN!
OKAY... I'VE GOT A CLEAR SHOT!

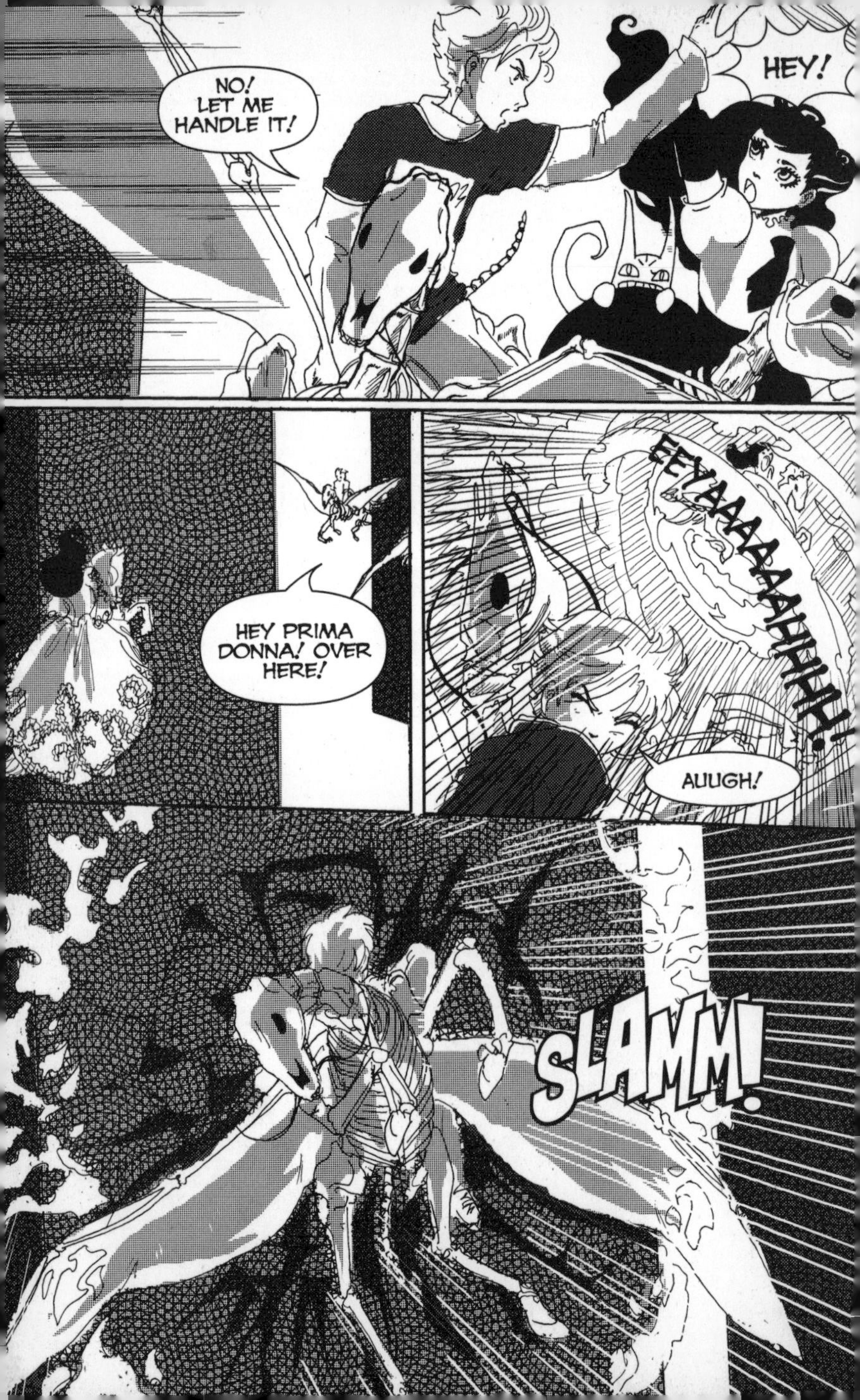
NO! LET ME HANDLE IT!
HEY!
HEY PRIMA DONNA! OVER HERE!
EEYAAAAAAAHHHHH!
AUUGH!
SLAMM!

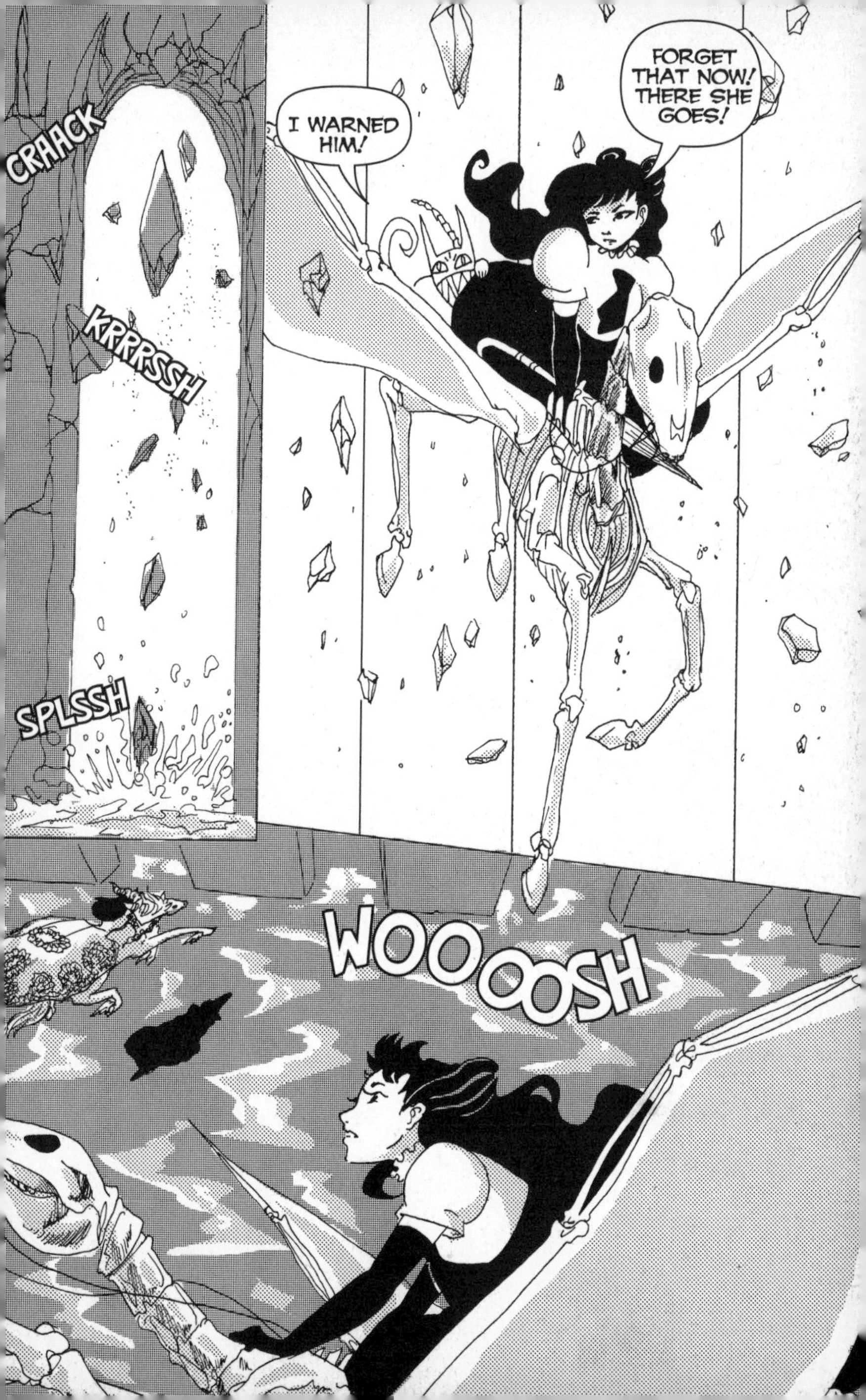

CRAACK
KRRRSSH
SPLSSH
I WARNED HIM!
FORGET THAT NOW! THERE SHE GOES!
WOOOOSH

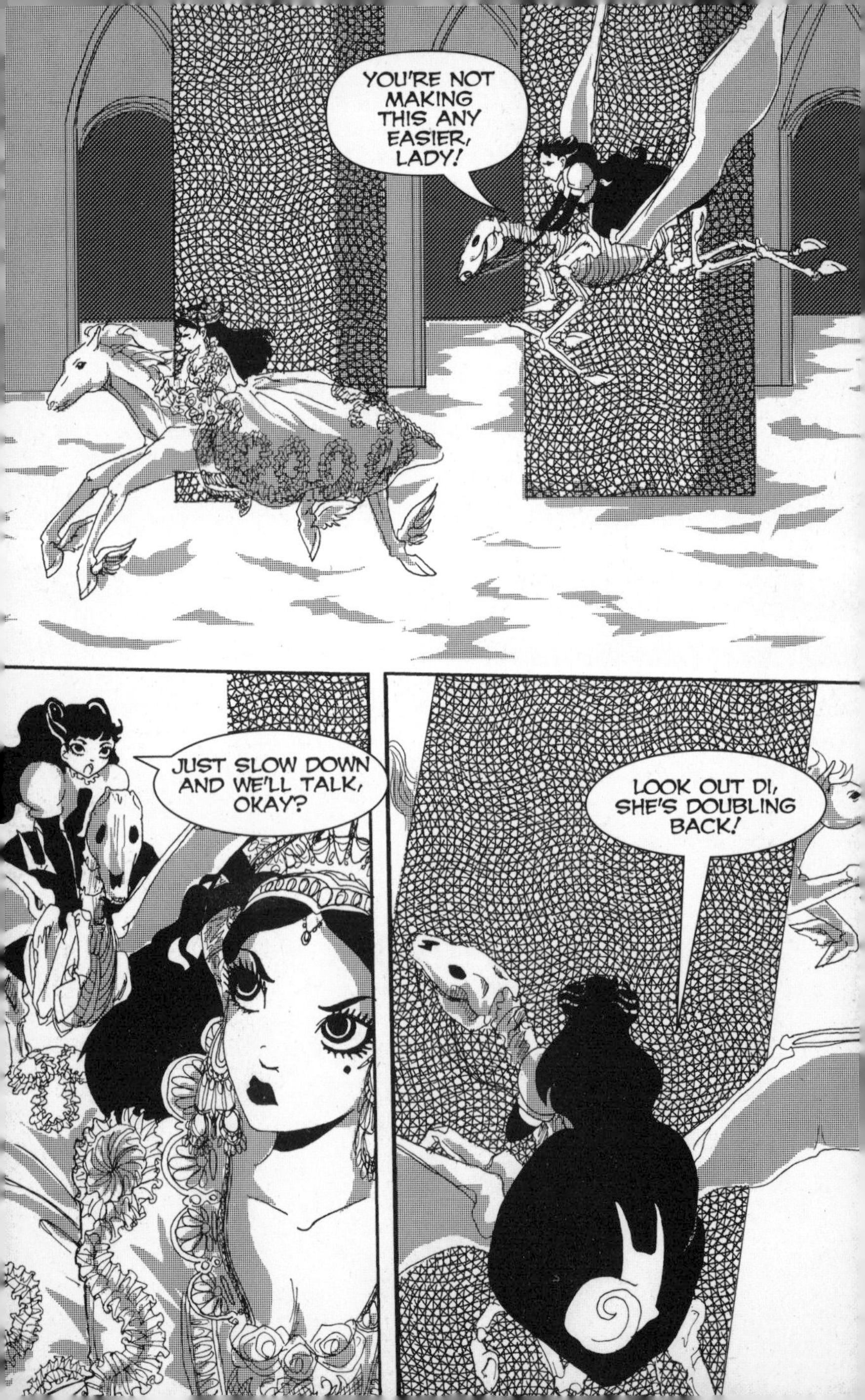
YOU'RE NOT MAKING THIS ANY EASIER, LADY!
JUST SLOW DOWN AND WE'LL TALK, OKAY?
LOOK OUT DI, SHE'S DOUBLING BACK!

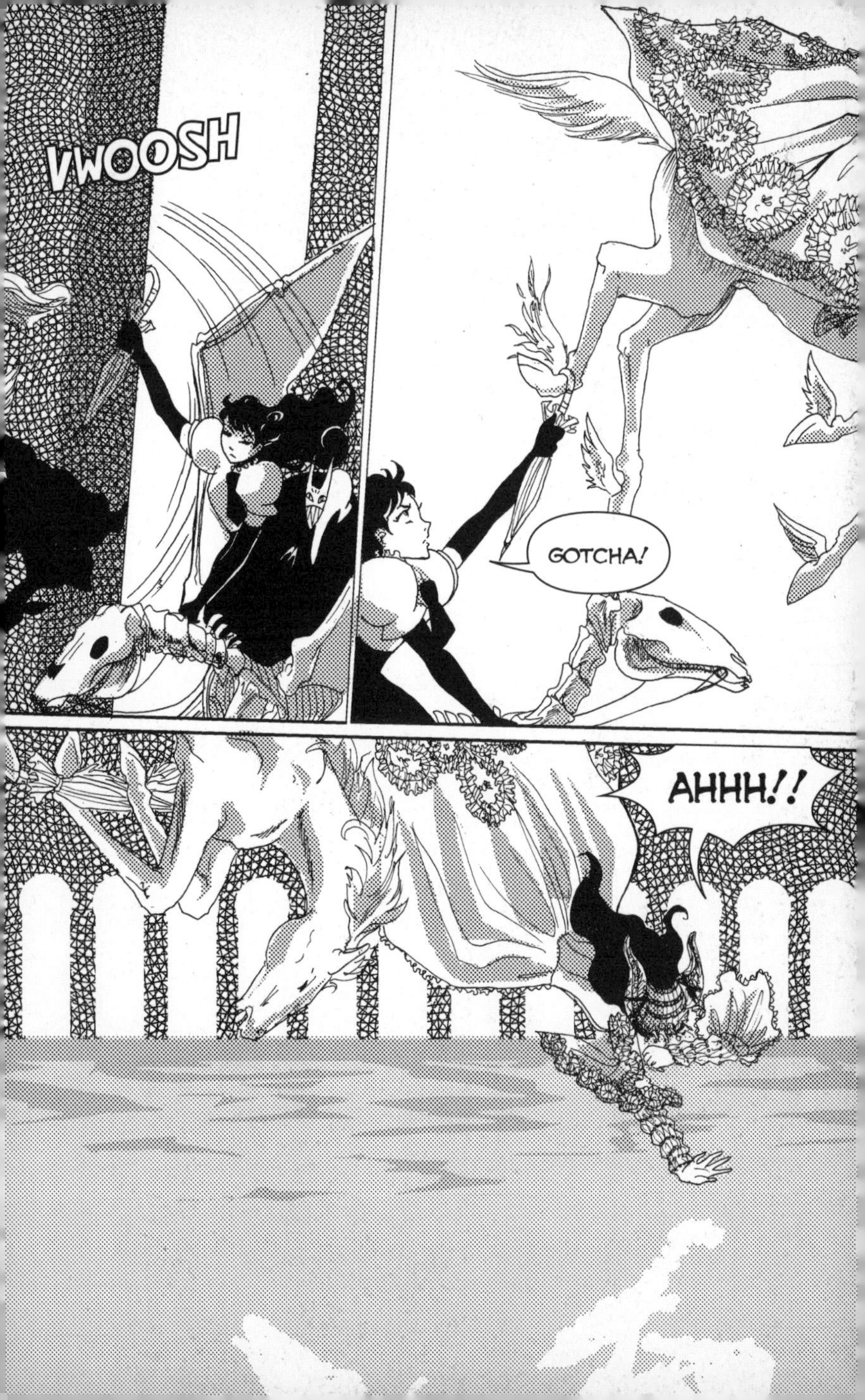
VWOOSH
GOTCHA!
AHHH!!

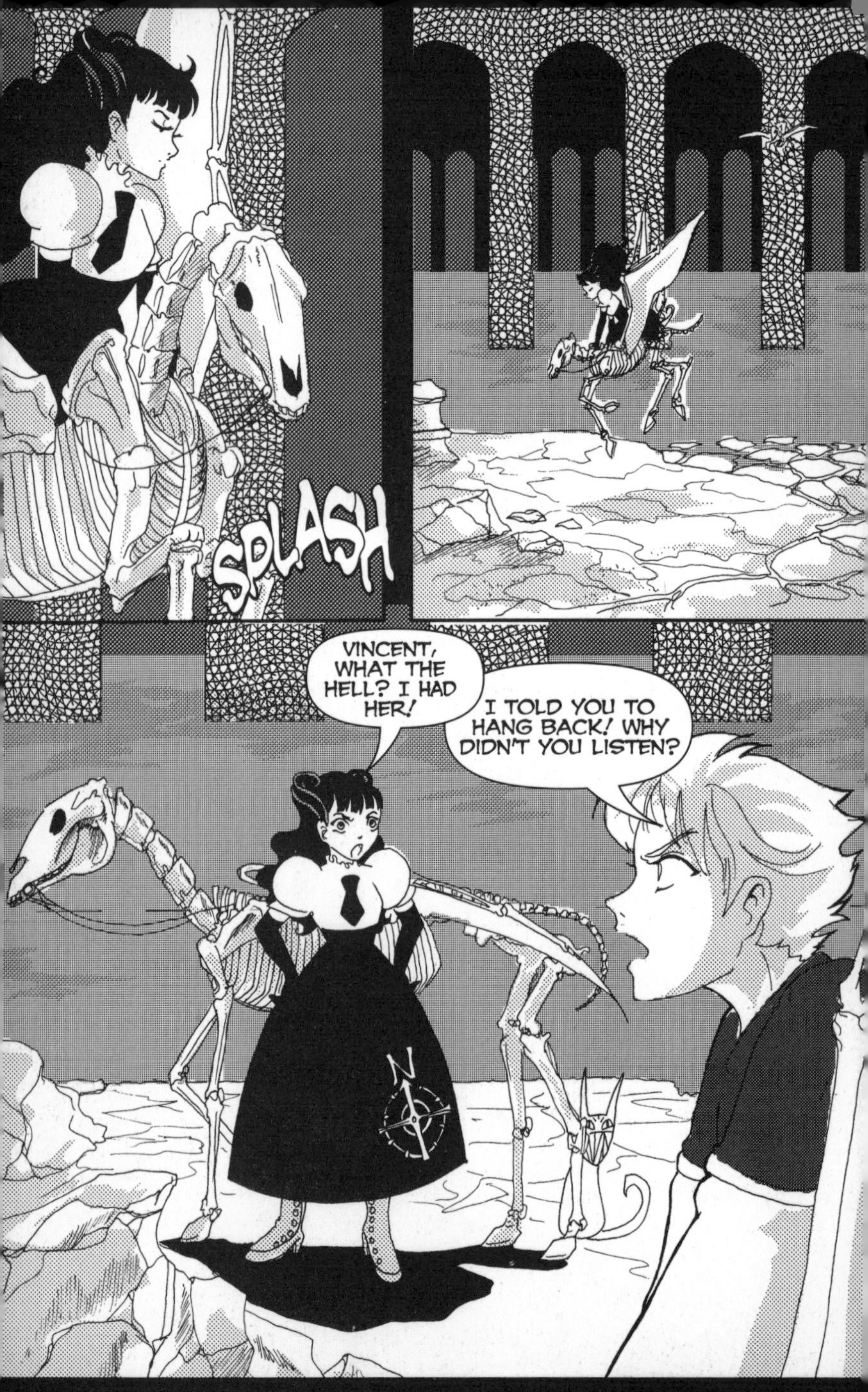
SPLASH
VINCENT, WHAT THE HELL? I HAD HER!
I TOLD YOU TO HANG BACK! WHY DIDN'T YOU LISTEN?

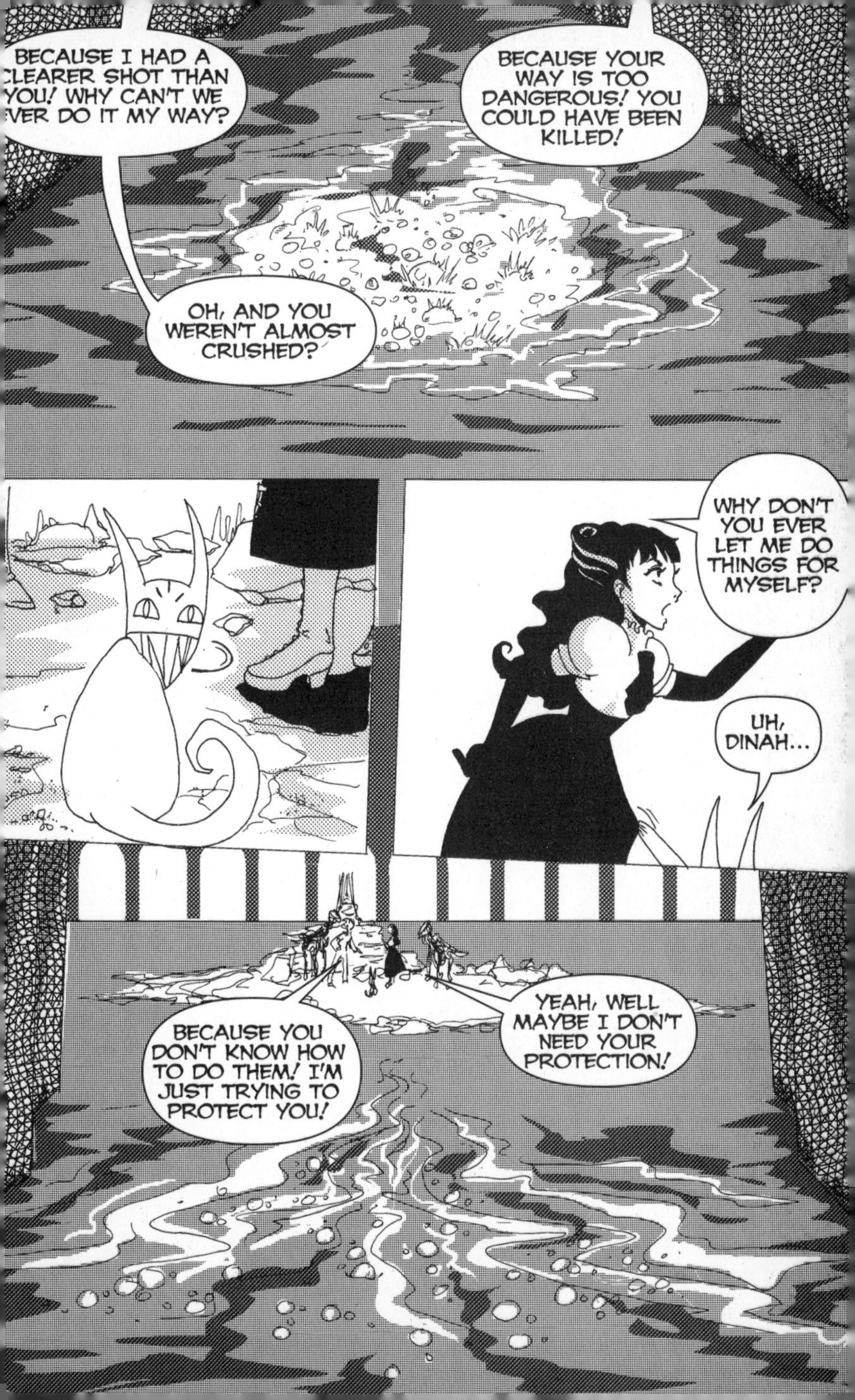
BECAUSE I HAD A CLEARER SHOT THAN YOU! WHY CAN'T WE EVER DO IT MY WAY?
BECAUSE YOUR WAY IS TOO DANGEROUS! YOU COULD HAVE BEEN KILLED!
OH, AND YOU WEREN'T ALMOST CRUSHED?
WHY DON'T YOU EVER LET ME DO THINGS FOR MYSELF?
UH, DINAH...
BECAUSE YOU DON'T KNOW HOW TO DO THEM! I'M JUST TRYING TO PROTECT YOU!
YEAH, WELL MAYBE I DON'T NEED YOUR PROTECTION!

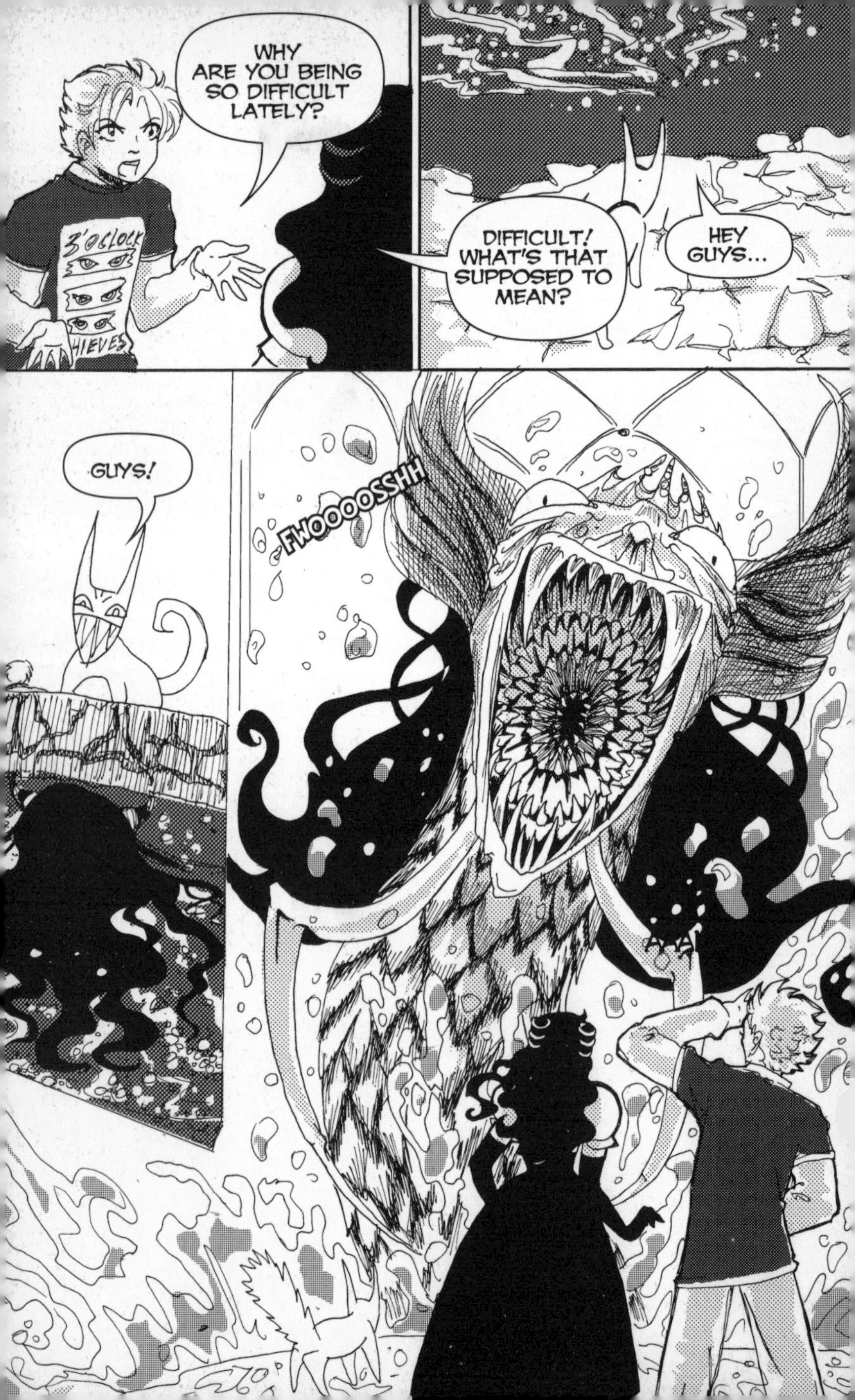
WHY ARE YOU BEING SO DIFFICULT LATELY?
DIFFICULT! WHAT'S THAT SUPPOSED TO MEAN?
HEY GUYS...
GUYS!
FWOOOOOSSHH
3 O'CLOCK THIEVES

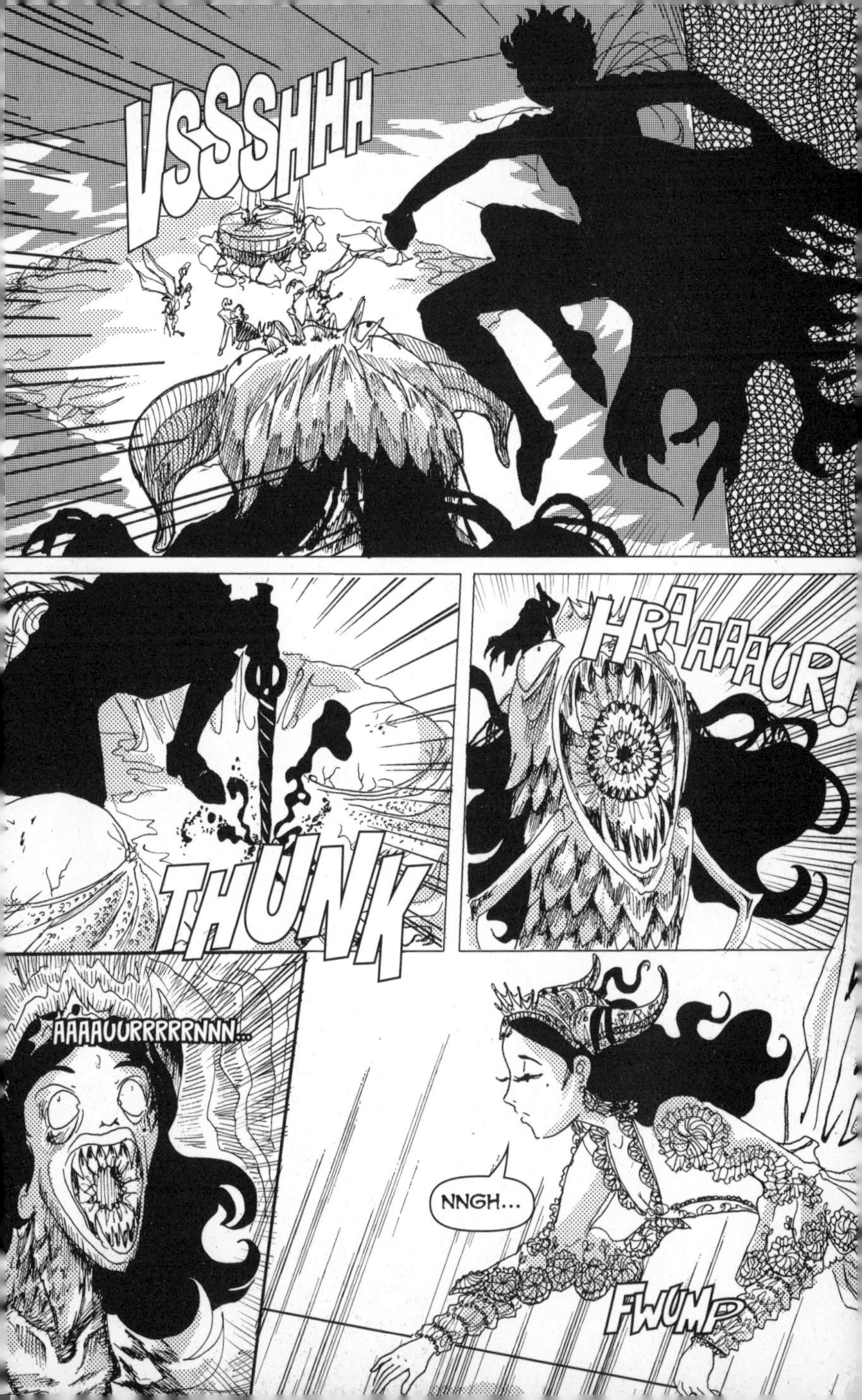
VSSSHHH
THUNK
HRAAAAAUR!
AAAAUURRRRRNNN...
NNGH...
FWUMP

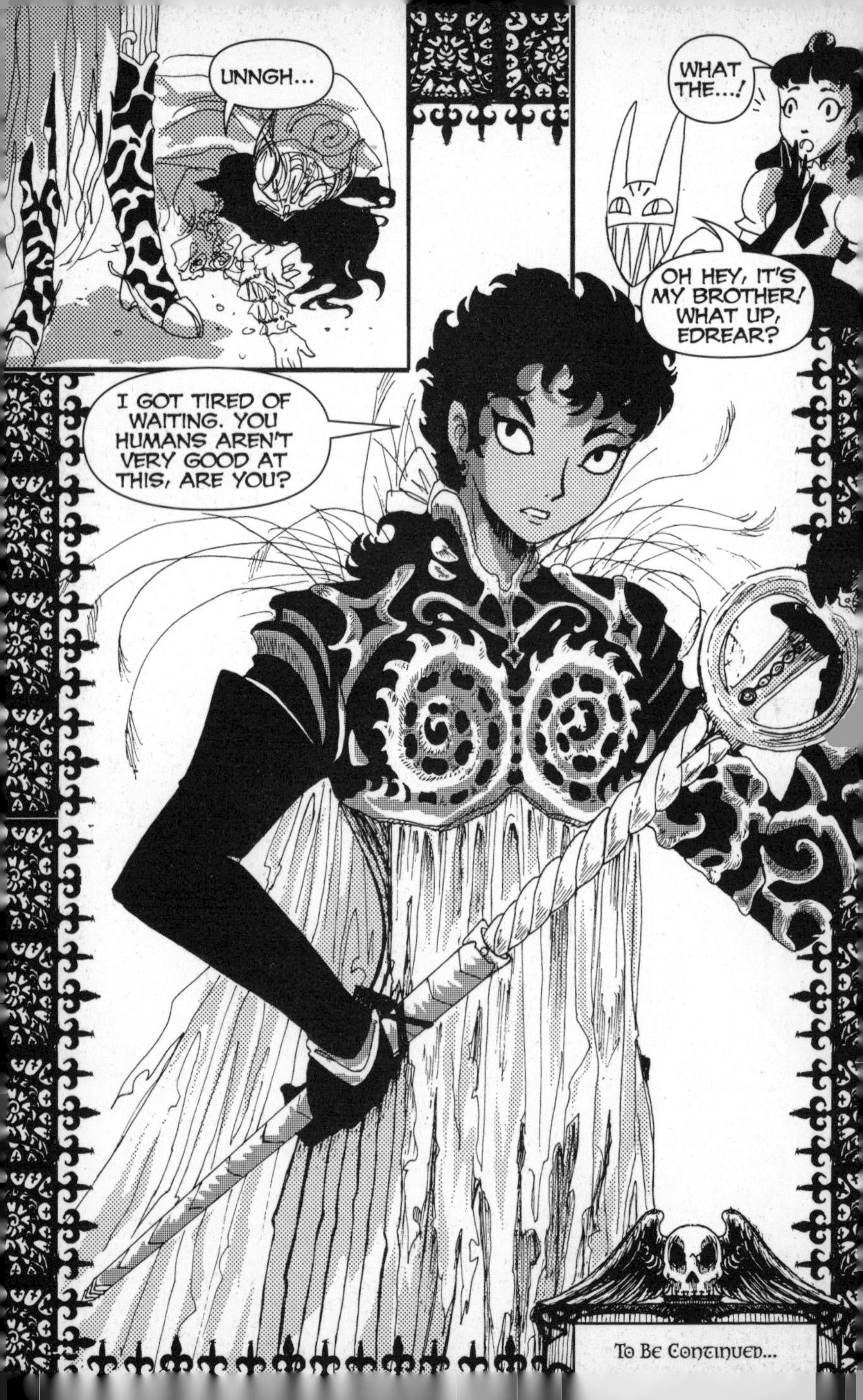
UNNGH...
WHAT THE....!
OH HEY, IT'S MY BROTHER! WHAT UP, EDREAR?
I GOT TIRED OF WAITING. YOU HUMANS AREN'T VERY GOOD AT THIS, ARE YOU?
To Be Continued...

In Volume Three of Bizenghast:

With two of the four tower guards to aid them, Dinah and Vincent are half-way to freedom from their nightly tasks. But a new set of vicious ghosts is only the first of many dangers for the pair. Something is hunting them down through the halls of the Mausoleum, and Dinah will soon discover that there are some creatures even the dead fear.

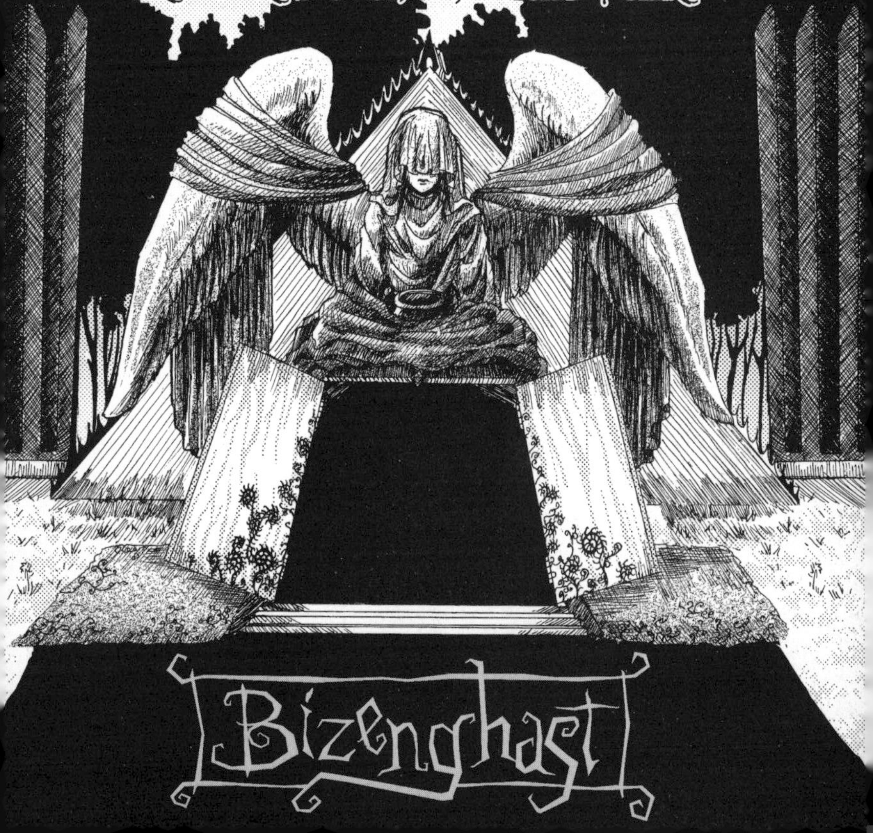
Bizenghast

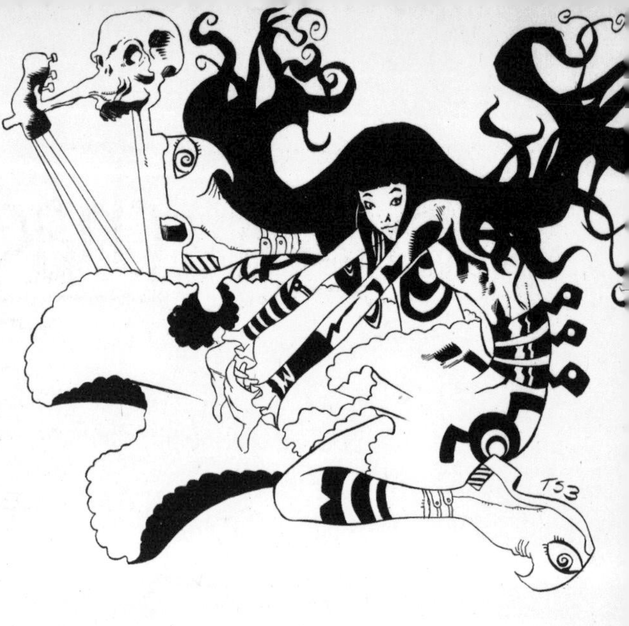
TS3

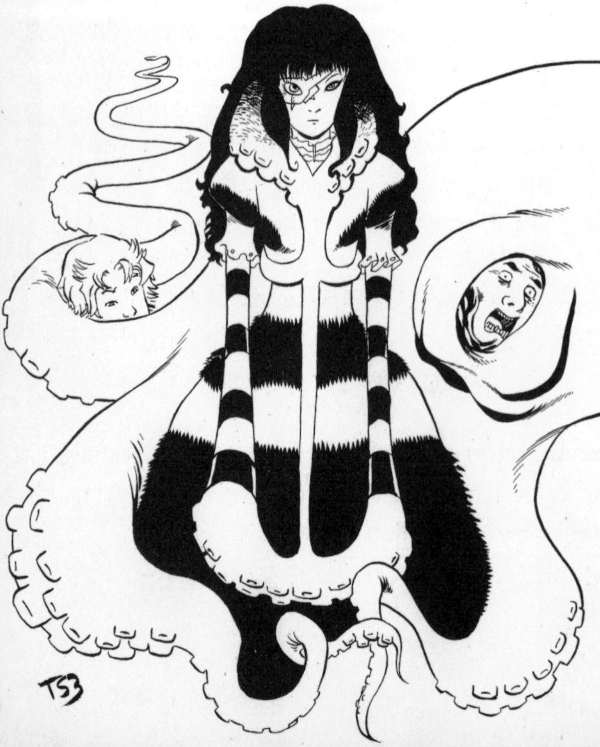
TS3

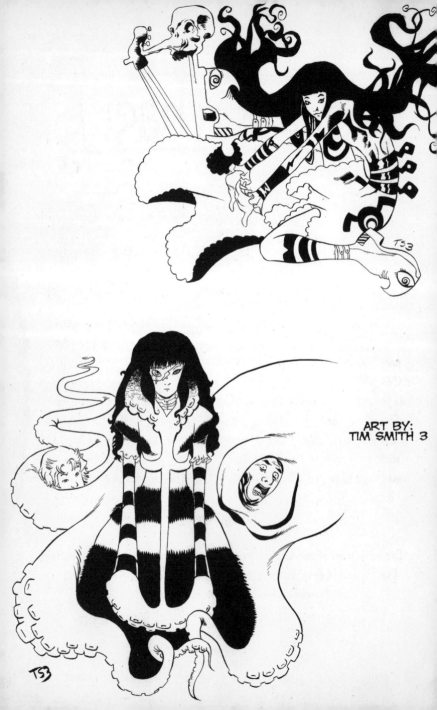

ART BY:
TIM SMITH 3

Special Bonus Section-
M. Alice LeGrow & Cosplay

The only thing I love more than drawing is sewing, and I'm an avid cosplayer. Cosplay is the hobby of making reproductions of outfits seen in anime, manga, Japanese musicals, and even non-Asian sources. Cosplayers convene all over the world at conventions year-round. We do photo shoots, trade costuming ideas, and host very tough competitions! Sometimes I compete and sometimes I'm a judge at these cons. I've even cosplayed in Japan! But for me, the best part about cosplay is being with my friends and making group costumes together. Cosplay lets me meet new people and stay in touch with my friends who live far away. If it wasn't for my friends, I never would have started cosplaying in the first place!

I've made a lot of cosplay outfits over the last six years, but more recently I've started to cosplay from my own art. The following are four of my favorite Bizenghast-related costumes. I hope you like them!

-M. Alice

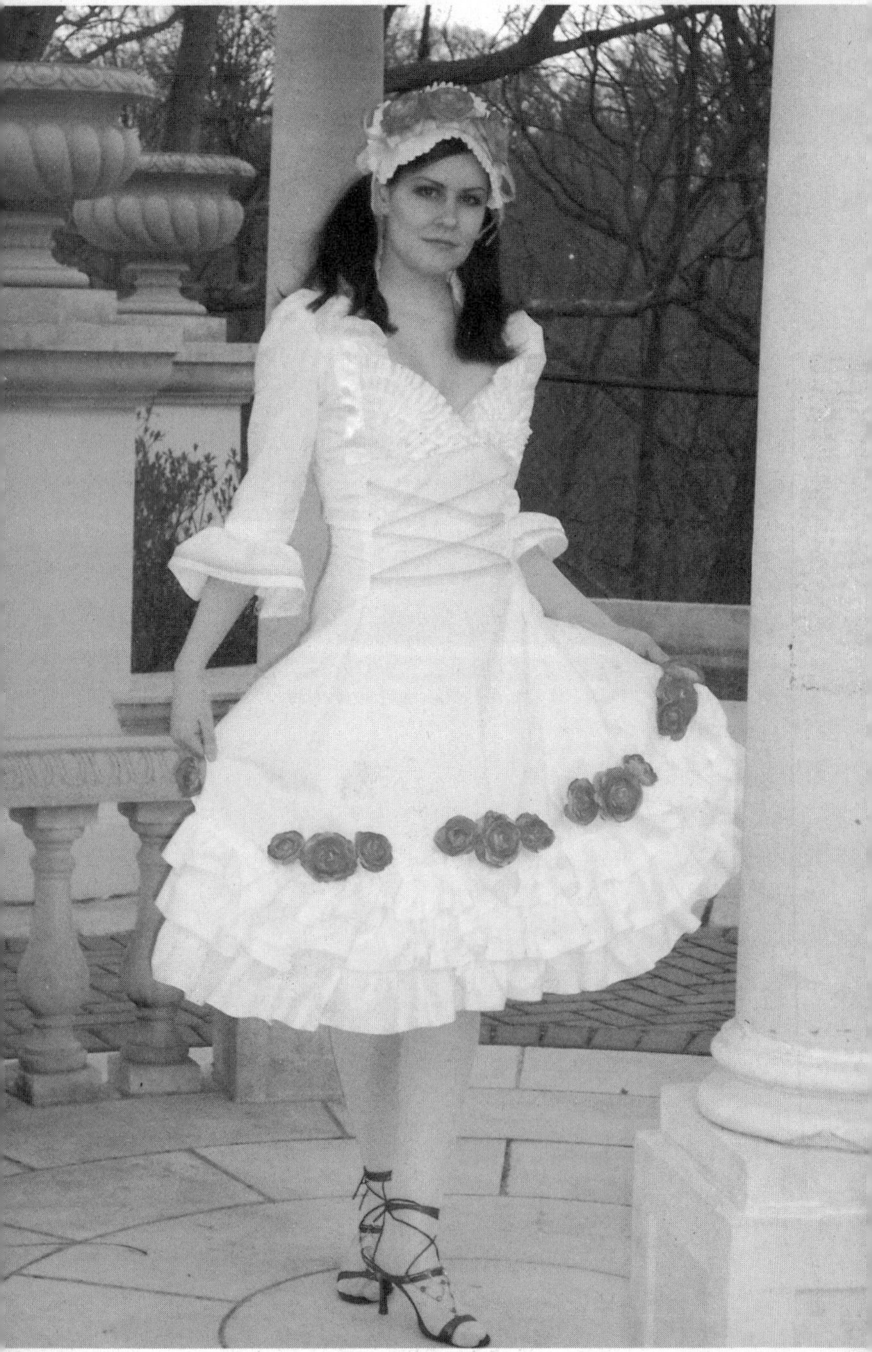

Costume name: Rosalind
Inspiration: Wedding cake
Time to make: 12 hours

I made this costume over the course of a day for a promotional model job in New York, then later took it to a convention. I didn't have any real design in mind for the dress, until I was inspired by a wedding cake I saw in a magazine that was pure white with three layers and orangey-red flowers. I wanted to make a dress that reminded me of that cake.

I think this might be a dress Dinah would wear if it wasn't white. Dinah's not very fond of wearing all white, whereas white is the dominant color in most things I personally wear. But the design is very Dinah-like and I can see her wearing this dress in shades of blue and navy.

My friends Paul, Kev and Ginny helped me take these pictures at Katsucon 2006. It was so cold out when we took these pictures, we were practically freezing! But it was worth it because the grounds behind the hotel were so beautiful.

Editor's Note:
Dinah in vol. 1—close, not quite the same!

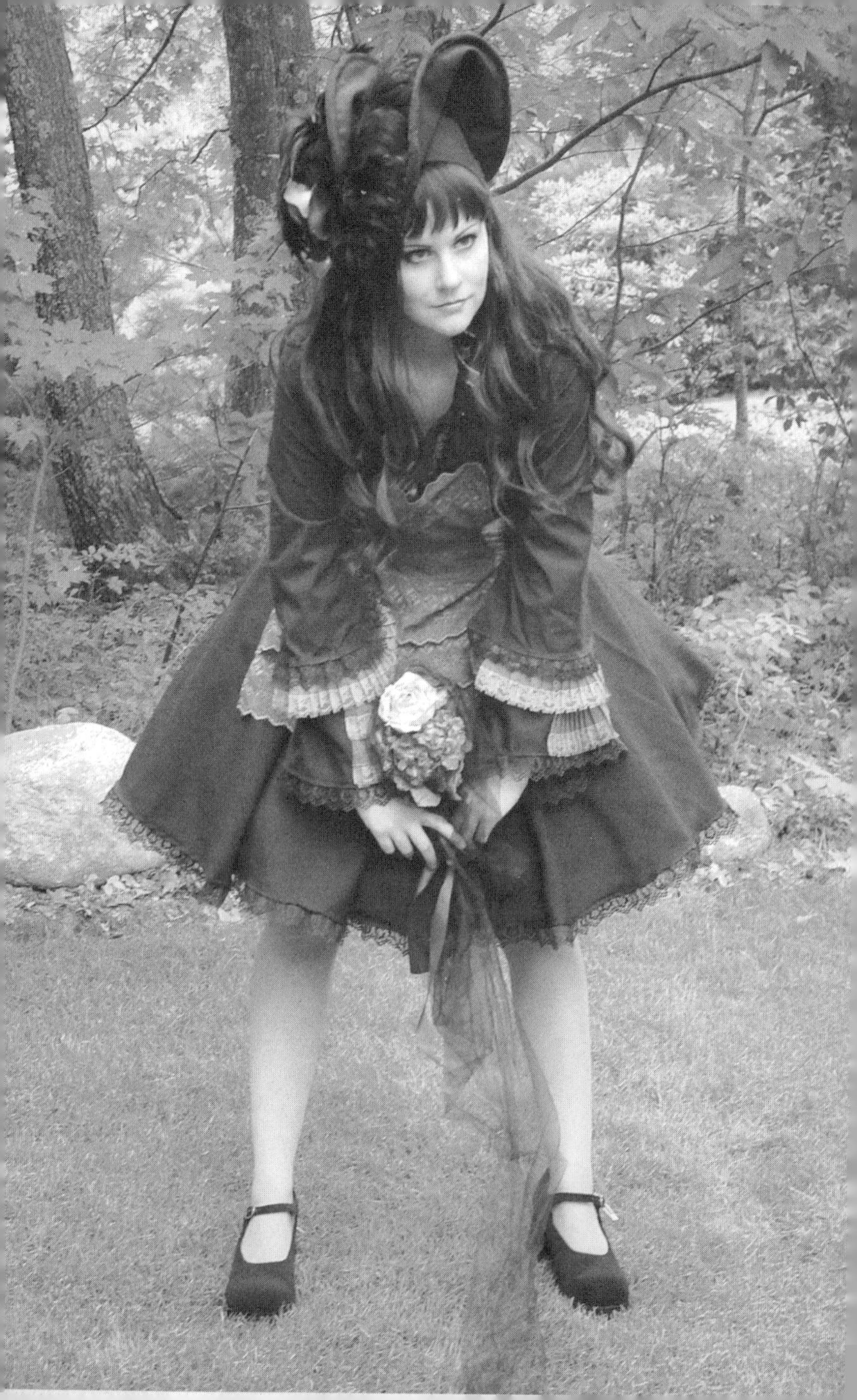

Costume name: Burgundy Lolita

Inspiration: My hat

Time to make: 2 days

I actually made the hat for this costume long before I made the rest of the outfit. I liked the burgundy flower and black feathers so much I decided to design a matching dress. Although I didn't design it specifically for Dinah, I think this ensemble is the most like something Dinah would want to wear.

The burgundy part of the costume is hand-dyed. I couldn't find a fabric to use that was the exact color I wanted, so I mixed up a pot of dye on the stove and spent an afternoon dyeing some off-white trim and eyelet fabric to the color I wished. It came out really nice!

The hat later had a small skull added to it for the last image in volume one of Bizenghast. This was the first hat I'd ever made, and I really like it a lot. It's made of black suiting, rigilene boning and black dyed rooster feathers. I wanted a nice big elaborate hat to go with multiple costumes and this was just such a fun design that I had to make it.

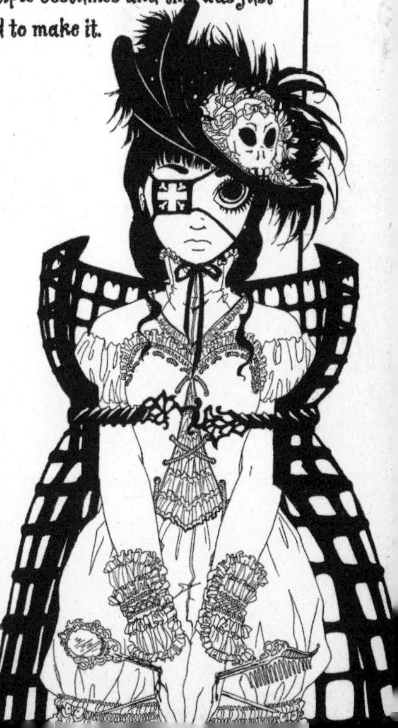

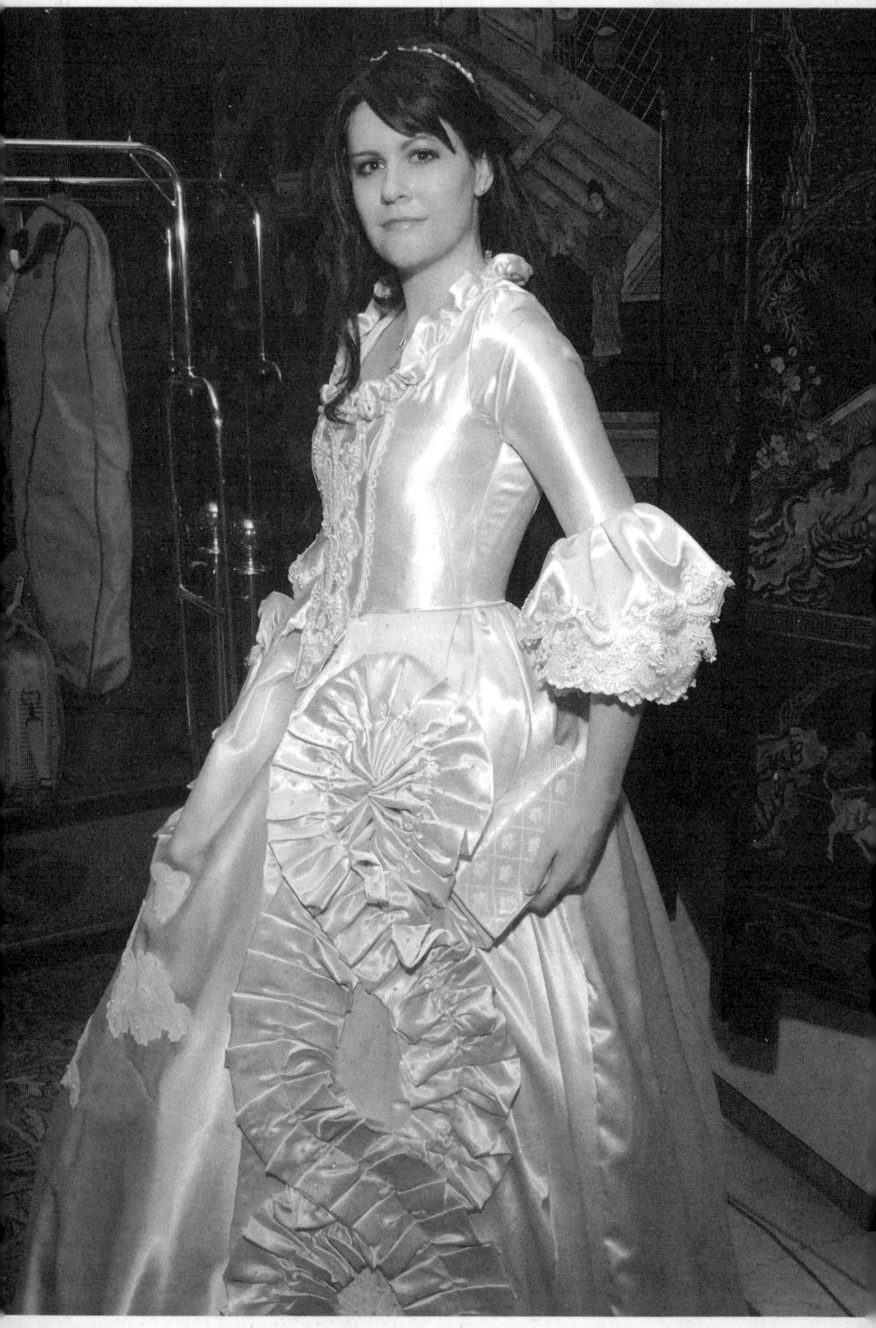

Costume name: Cinderella
Inspiration: Cinderella musical
Time to make: 2 weeks

This dress of Dinah's appeared on the very first page of the first volume of Bizenghast. I call it my Cinderella dress because it was inspired by the costumes in the 1976 musical film, "The Slipper and the Rose," which is a Cinderella adaptation. It's one of my favorite movies and I've always wanted a dress like the ones in the ballroom scene.

This was a very expensive dress to make, thanks to all the pink satin I had to use. Although it doesn't show in pictures, the dress also has over 300 hand-applied sequins on the front panels. The panels also have a large decoration of hand-ruffled satin that loops down the skirt.

This dress is pretty but extremely heavy to wear, and very hot! I recently lent it to a local school for their production of Beauty and the Beast.

Editor's Note: When M. Alice & I met up in 2005 at San Diego Comicon, she lent me this dress for an afternoon. I got to waltz around the TOKYOPOP booth feeling like a princess! I got tripped up on the skirt a lot, but it was still really neat.

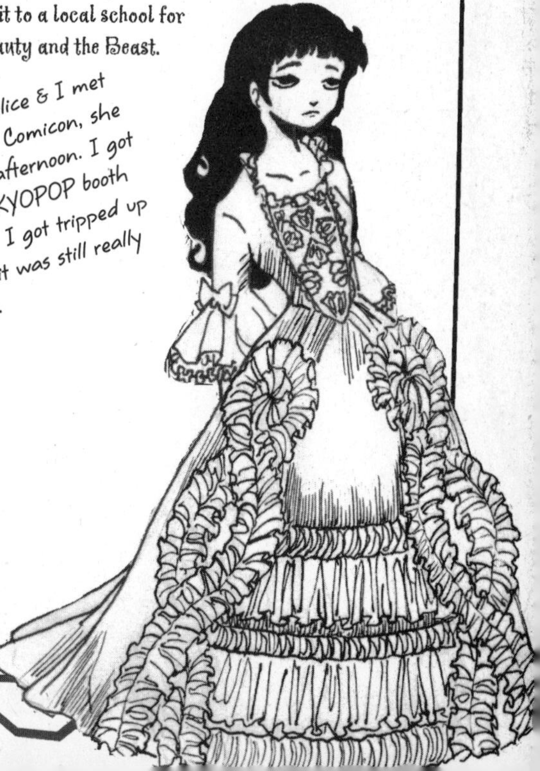

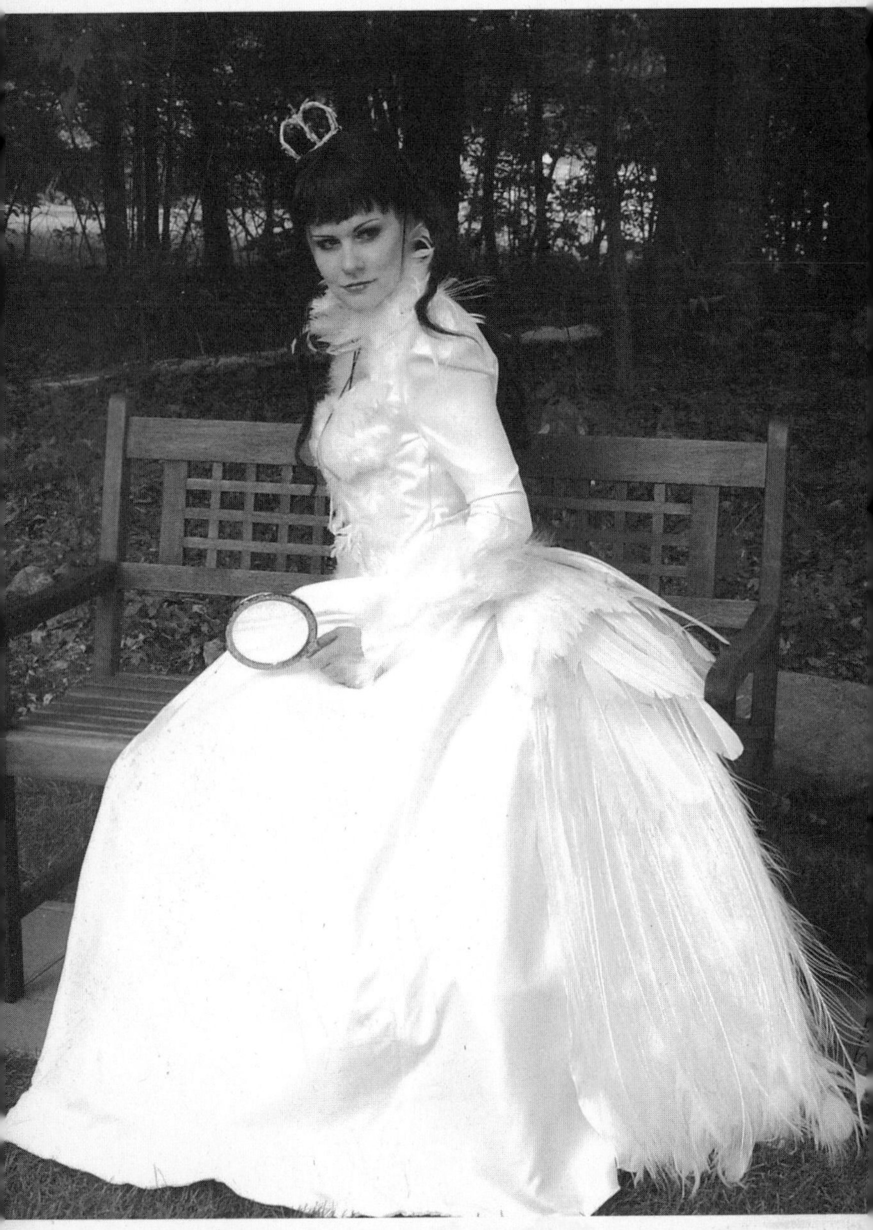

Name: Peacock Dress
Inspiration: White peacocks
Time to make: 1 week

This is Dinah's peacock dress from chapter two. I made this costume about the same time as I drew the chapter. I designed the costume to be made first, then drew Dinah's version of it by using the actual dress as reference.

I've always liked white peacocks better than regular ones. I found a white peacock pelt from a taxidermist online and used both the wing and tail feathers to make the feather train of the dress. I also filled out the bottom of the train with an extra bunch of tail feathers to give it extra fullness.
The collar is detachable and is made of bleached rooster feathers, as are the sleeve cuffs.

I really love this dress, but it's very difficult to transport, since the tail feathers are very long, and cannot be bent or folded. When I want to take it to conventions, the train of the dress must be packed all by itself in a garment box almost five feet tall.

This is probably my favorite costume that I've made in the last year!

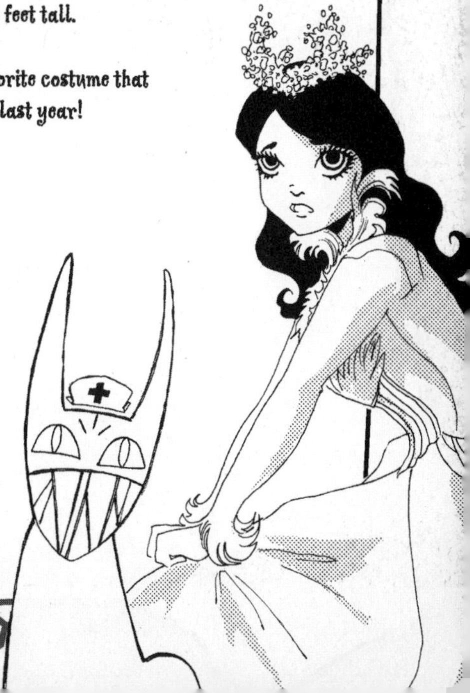

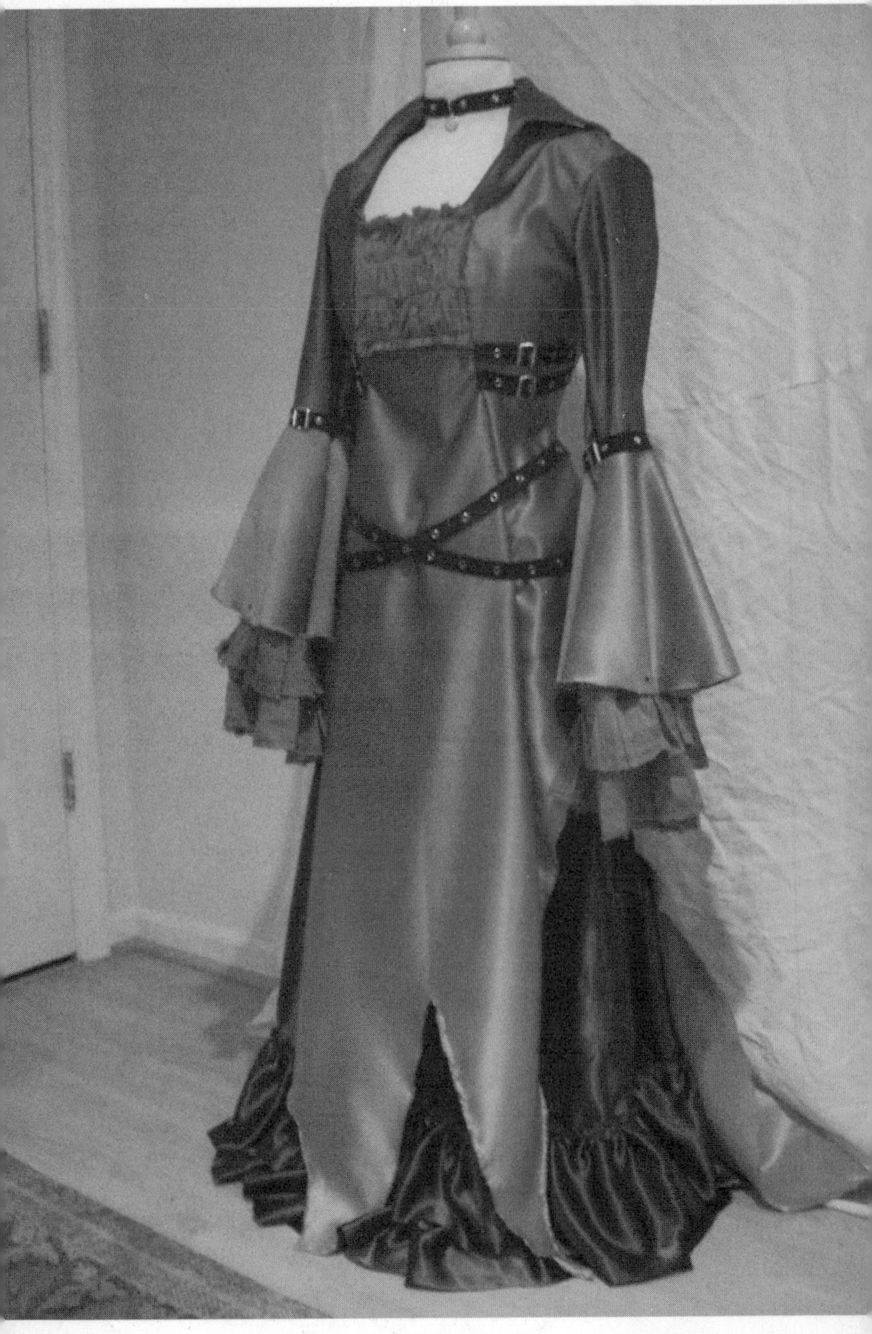

BONUS COSTUME
Costume name: Princess Ai
Inspiration: Punk
Time to make: 3 days

This costume was made especially for a TOKYOPOP
Princess Ai promotional project. I had to come up with a design
that would suit Ai and fit in with her other outfits, so I combined
three already existing outfits of hers into a new design. I used
some pretty pink and purple faded satin over a charcoal grey
satin ruffled skirt, with studded belts around the bodice and
sleeves.

The request was for an Ai design that was sharp and asymmet-
rical, and a little rough around the edges. To that end, I used
a bohemian pink skirt to be cut up and made into inner sleeves
and on the front of the bodice with unfinished edges. The over-
skirt was given a jagged, uneven hem. I also included a black
vinyl choker with silver studs and a gold filigree pendant.
I think the whole costume came out very well! I really enjoyed
making it!

DRAMACON™

Sometimes even two's a crowd.

When Christie settles in the Artist Alley of her first-ever anime convention, she only sees it as an opportunity to promote the comic she has started with her boyfriend. But conventions are never what you expect, and soon a whirlwind of events sweeps Christie off her feet and changes her life. Who is the mysterious cosplayer who won't even take off his sunglasses indoors? What do you do when you fall in love with a guy who is going to be miles away from you in just a couple of days?

CREATED BY SVETLANA CHMAKOVA!

"YOU CAN'T AVOID FALLING UNDER ITS CHARM." -IGN.COM

READ AN ENTIRE CHAPTER ONLINE FOR FREE:
WWW.TOKYOPOP.COM/MANGAONLINE

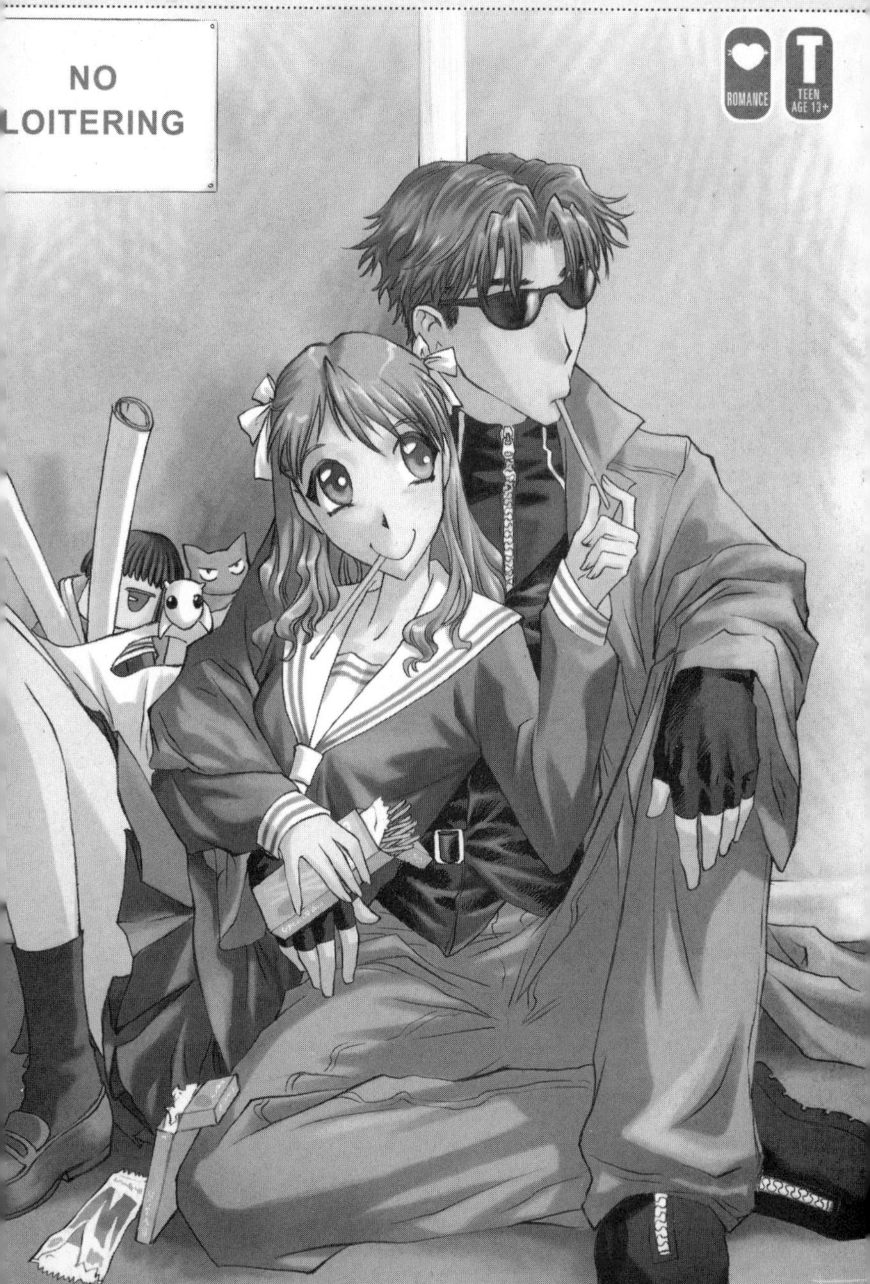
NO LOITERING
ROMANCE
T
TEEN AGE 13+